BIT MCA

Entrance Exam

Latest Edition
Practice Kit

10 Tests
10 Mock Test

Based On Real Exam Pattern

✓ Thoroughly Revised and Updated

✓ Detailed Analysis of all MCQs

Title	: BIT MCA Entrance Exam
Author Name	: Mr. Rohit Manglik
Published By	: EduGorilla Community Pvt. Ltd.
Publishers Address	: 12/651, First Floor Opp. Arvindo Park, Near Jama Masjid, Indira Nagar, Lucknow, Uttar Pradesh-226016, India

Copyright EduGorilla

ISBN : 978-93-90239-97-9

Second Edition

Disclaimer EduGorilla

Compiled and created by EduGorilla Community Pvt. Ltd

Printed By EduGorilla Community Pvt. Ltd.

ROHIT MANGLIK
CEO, EduGorilla

Dear Applicants,

People say *"Success comes to those who work hard."* But I've seen people working hard for their exams day in and day out for marginal success. While others succeed in their examinations by putting in just half the work. So are they God Gifted? No! I believe that it's because they work *smart* and not just *hard*. Similarly, for your exams, you should strategize your preparation so as to increase the likelihood of success. Well with EduGorilla get ready to increase your *chances of selection* in your exam by *16x*.

EduGorilla helps you in not only working *hard* but also working in a *smart and strategic* manner. With EduGorilla's preparation package, you get a chance to make your exam preparation easy, and a fun learning path towards selection. Finding the right path to your preparations can be difficult if you don't know in which direction to head. Don't worry, we have you covered! EduGorilla will be your guide to success in your journey. With our Preparation Package, you can prepare strategically and beat the exam in just one attempt.

EduGorilla's Preparation Package includes-

• **Test Series**   • **Books**

Our preparation package is handcrafted as per the latest changes, expert opinions, and students' discretion. Thus, enabling you to get through each stage of the selection process for your exam.

Our Books are designed by the teachers and experts of the respective exam with a combined 150+ years of experience; to provide you with easy, efficient, and effective learning. Our books are smart, in the sense that not only do they give you the answers to the questions but also provide similar questions for practice.

EduGorilla's competent Test Series gives you real-time experience and confidence through which you can clear your offline or online exam in just one attempt. We currently host 83,000+ mock tests for 1,440+ competitive and academic exams.

Thus, EduGorilla misses no chance to assist you in your preparation and covers all stages of the exam, so that you don't have to look anywhere else.

We provide complete preparation packages for defense, banking, teaching, and other National & State-Level exams. Hence, it doesn't matter which exam you aspire to because you will reach your success.

ALL THE BEST !
Let EduGorilla be your Guide to Success.

Rohit Manglik,
Founder and CEO, EduGorilla

INTRODUCTION

EduGorilla focuses on guiding students to succeed in their examinations. With that in mind, our book, titled "BIT MCA : Entrance Exam", has been drafted through the collective efforts of our distinguished experts with 150+ years of combined experience. This book consists of questions that are created following the latest changes in the syllabus and exam pattern. We compiled the book on the basis of questions that are most likely to appear in the BIT MCA. Through EduGorilla's "BIT MCA : Entrance Exam" your chances of success will increase 16x.

EduGorilla does this through our Complete Preparation Package. This package consists of well-conceptualized and structured content in the form of questions that are tailor-made according to your needs and will help you practice for exams in a smart way by pinpointing all the necessary information. It also provides hints and solutions, along with a smart answer sheet for your self-evaluation. You can assess your shortcomings and work accordingly on areas that may require more of your attention.

EduGorilla promises to help you succeed in your examination and accomplish your dream goals. We believe in our aspirants and see them at the top of the merit list. And the first step towards the top is to start preparing with us. EduGorilla's "BIT MCA : Entrance Exam" includes the following attributes.

➤ Well-Researched Content

➤ Top-Notch Quality

➤ Detailed Answers and Analysis

➤ Smart Answer Sheet

➤ Exam Relevant Questions

Therefore, EduGorilla fortifies your preparation and makes it durable enough to help you stand tall and beat the examination.

BIT MCA

Scan QR code for Eligibility, Exam Pattern, Syllabus and more.

Book ID: 0240

TABLE OF CONTENTS

Mathematics

Q.1 If R is a relation from a non – empty set A to a non – empty set B, then

A. R = A ∪ B

B. R = A ∩ B

C. R = A × B

D. R ⊂ A × B

Q.2 Let A = { 2 , 3 , 6 }. Which of the following relations on A are reflexive ?

A. None of these

B. R_2 = {(2,2) , (3,3) , (3,6) , (6,3)}

C. R_1 = {(2,2) , (3,3) , (6,6)}

D. R_3 = {(2,2) , (3,6) , (2,6)}

Q.3 Let R be the relation on N defined as xRy if x + 2 y = 8. The domain of R is

A. {2, 4, 6}

B. {1, 2, 3, 4}

C. {2, 4, 8}

D. {2, 4, 6, 8}

Q.4 Which of the following is not an equivalence relation on I, the set of integers: x, y

A. xRy, x – y is an even integer

B. xRy, x + y is an even integer

C. xRy, x ≤ y

D. xRy, x = y

Q.5 Let A = {a, b, c} and R = {(a, a), (b, b), (c, c), (b, c) } be a relation on A. Here, R is

A. reflexive

B. transitive

C. anti – symmetric

D. symmetric

Q.6 R = {(1, 1), (2, 2), (1, 2), (2, 1), (2, 3)} be a relation on A, then R is

A. symmetric

B. not anti symmetric

C. anti symmetric

D. Reflexive

Q.7 The number of all possible matrices of order 3×3 with each entry 0 or 1 is

A. 18

B. 512

C. 81

D. none of these

Q.8 The order of the given matrix is:

$$A = \begin{bmatrix} 2 & 4 \\ -1 & 0 \\ 6 & 5 \end{bmatrix}$$

A. 3 × 3

B. 3 × 2

C. 2 × 3

D. 2 × 2

Q.9 If A is a matrix of order 3 × 4 , then each row of A has

A. 3 elements

B. 4 elements

C. 7 elements.

D. 12 elements

Q.10 If matrices P is of order 2 × 3 and matrices Q is of order 3 × 2, then matrices PQ is of order

A. 2 × 2

B. 3 × 3

C. 2 × 3

D. 3 × 2

Q.11 The number of all the possible matrices of order 2 × 2 with each entry 0, 1 or 2 is

A. 12

B. 64

C. none of these

D. 81

Q.12 If A =

$$\begin{bmatrix} 0 & 0 & 0 \\ 0 & 0 & 0 \\ 0 & 1 & 0 \end{bmatrix}$$ then A is

A. none of these

B. an idempotent matrix

C. a nilpotent matrix

D. an invertible matrix

Q.13 Direction cosines of a line are

A. The sines of the angles made by the line with the positive directions of the coordinate axes.

B. The cosines of the angles made by the line with the positive directions of the coordinate axes.

C. The cotangents of the angles made by the line with the negative directions of the coordinate axes.

D. The tangents of the angles made by the line with the negative directions of the coordinate axes.

Q.14 If l, m, n are the direction cosines of a line, then

A. $l^2+ m^2+ n^2= 1.$

B. $2l^2+ m^2+ n^2= 1.$

C. $l^2+ m^2+ 2n^2= 1.l2$

D. $l^2+ 2m^2+ n^2= 1.$

Q.15 If l, m and n are the direction cosines of a line, Direction ratios of the line are the numbers which are

A. Inversely Proportional to the direction cosine l of the line

B. Proportional to the direction cosines of the line

C. Proportional to the direction cosine l of the line

D. Inversely Proportional to the direction cosines of the line

Q.16 Define Skew lines in a three dimensional space

A. parallel and intersecting parallel and intersecting

B. neither parallel nor intersecting

C. parallel

D. intersecting

Q.17 How do we measure the angle between skew lines ?

A. The angle between any two lines parallel to the given skew lines and passing through a common point in space

B. The angle between two non intersecting lines drawn from any point anti – parallel to each of the skew lines

C. The angle between two non intersecting lines drawn from any point parallel to each of the skew lines

D. The angle between two intersecting lines drawn from any point perpendicular to each of the skew lines

Q.18 If a_1, b_1, c_1 and a_2, b_2, c_2 are the direction ratios of two lines and θ is the angle between the two lines; write the formula for the angle between them.

A. $$\cos\theta = \left|\frac{a_1 a_2 + b_1 b_2 + c_1 c_2}{\sqrt{a_1^2 + b_1^2 + c_1^2}\sqrt{a_2^2 + b_2^2 + c_2^2}}\right|$$

B. $$\cos\theta = \left|\frac{a_1 a_2 + b_1 b_2 + c_1 a_2}{\sqrt{a_1^2 + b_1^2 + c_1^2}\sqrt{a_2^2 + b_2^2 + c_2^2}}\right|$$

C. $$\cos\theta = \left|\frac{a_1 a_2 + b_1 c_2 + c_1 c_2}{\sqrt{a_1^2 + b_1^2 + c_1^2}\sqrt{a_2^2 + b_2^2 + c_2^2}}\right|$$

D. $$\cos\theta = \left|\frac{a_1 b_2 + b_1 b_2 + c_1 c_2}{\sqrt{a_1^2 + b_1^2 + c_1^2}\sqrt{a_2^2 + b_2^2 + c_2^2}}\right|$$

Q.19 The instantaneous rate of change at t = 1 for the function f (t) $=te^{-t} + 9$ is

A. – 1   **B.** 0   **C.** 2   **D.** 9

Q.20 If the graph of a differentiable function y = f (x) meets the lines y = – 1 and y = 1, then the graph

A. meets the line y = 0 at least once
B. does not meet the line y = 0
C. meets the line y = 0 at least twice
D. meets the line y = 0 at least thrice

Q.21 $\int e^{-\log|x|}dx$ is equal to

A. $-xe^{-\log|x|}$ **B.** $\log|x|+C$
C. $-e^{-\log|x|}$ **D.** none of these

Q.22 If $\int f(x)\ dx = g(x) + C$ and also $\int f(x)\ dx = h(x) + D$, then

A. g(x)/h(x)=constant
B. g (x) - h (x) = constant
C. h (x) + g (x) = constant
D. g (x) . h (x) = constant

Q.23 The area of ellipse $x^2/a^2+y^2/b^2=1$ is

A. None of these   **B.** $\pi(a^2+b^2)/4$
C. Π(a + b)   **D.** πab

Q.24 The area of the loop between the curve y = a sin x and the x – axis and x= 0 , x=π. is

A. 2a square units   **B.** none of these
C. 3a   **D.** a

Q.25 Differential equations are equations containing functions y = f(x), g(x) and

A. derivatives of y   **B.** minima of y
C. tangent of y at zero   **D.** maxima of y

Q.26 Order of a differential equation is defined as

A. the number of derivative terms
B. the number of constant terms
C. the order of the lowest order derivative of the dependent variable
D. the order of the highest order derivative of the dependent variable

Q.27 Degree of a differential equation, when the equation is polynomial equation in y′ is

A. Highest power(positive integral index) of the highest order derivative in the given differential equation.
B. Lowest power(positive integral index) of the highest order derivative in the given differential equation.
C. Highest(positive integral index) of the lowest order derivative in the given differential equation.
D. Lowest power(positive integral index) of the lowest order derivative in the given differential equation.

Q.28 The order of the equation $d^2y/dx^2+y=0$ is

A. 2   **B.** 1   **C.** 4   **D.** 3

Q.29 The order of the equation $d^3y/dx^3+x^2(d^2y/dx^2)^3= 0$ is

A. 2   **B.** 1   **C.** 4   **D.** 3

Q.30 The degree of the equation $(dy/dx)^2+dy/dx- \sin^2y = 0$ is

A. 2   **B.** 0   **C.** 1   **D.** 3

Q.31 Vector has

A. direction
B. None of these
C. magnitude as well as direction
D. magnitude

Q.32 Position vectors of points A, B, C, etc., with respect to the origin O are generally denoted by

A. $\vec{a},\ \vec{b}, \vec{c}$ **B.** $\vec{A},\ \vec{B}, \vec{C}$

C. $\overrightarrow{AB}, \overrightarrow{BC}, \overrightarrow{CA}$ **D.** $\overrightarrow{OA},\ \overrightarrow{OB}, \overrightarrow{OC}$

Q.33 Direction angles are

A. The angles α,β,γ made by the position vector $\vec{r}$ with the positive directions of x, y and z-axes respectively
B. The angles denoted by $\vec{a},\ \vec{b}, \vec{c}$
C. The angles α,β,γ made by the perpendicular to position vector $\vec{r}$ with the negative directions of x, y and z-axes respectively
D. The angles that show the tip of the vector

Q.34 Direction cosines

A. are cosines of Direction angles
B. are cotangents of Direction angles
C. are tangents of Direction angles
D. are sines of Direction angles

Q.35 If l, m and n are direction cosines of the position vector OP the coordinates of P are

A. l, mr and nr   **B.** lr, mr and n
C. lr, mr and nr   **D.** lr, m and nr

Q.36 Zero Vector

A. A vector whose initial points are at origin
B. A vector whose terminal points are at origin
C. A vector whose initial and final points are different

D. A vector whose initial and terminal points coincide

Q.37 The value of $\cos^2 15° - \cos^2 30° + \cos^2 45° - \cos^2 60° + \cos^2 75°$ is

A. 1/2   **B.** 0   **C.** 2   **D.** 1/4

Q.38 The maximum value of sinx + cosx is

A. 2   **B.** √2   **C.** 1/√2   **D.** 1

Q.39 The minimum value of sinx - cosx is

A. 0   **B.** -1   **C.** -√2   **D.** 1

Q.40

$$\text{If } 5\sin\theta = 3 \text{ then, } \frac{\sec\theta + \tan\theta}{\sec\theta - \tan\theta} \text{ is equal to}$$

A. 4   **B.** 2
C. None of these   **D.** 1/4

Q.41

$$\text{If } \sec\theta = x + \frac{1}{4x}, x \in R, x \neq 0, \text{then the value of } \sec\theta + \tan\theta \text{ is}$$

A. 2x or 1/2x   **B.** None of these
C. only 2x   **D.** only 1/2x

Q.42 cos2θ is not equal to

A. $1+\tan^2\theta / 1-\tan^2\theta$ **B.** $2\cos^2\theta - 1$
C. $1-\tan^2\theta / 1+\tan^2\theta$ **D.** $1-2\sin^2\theta$

Q.43 The conditional probability of an event E, given the occurrence of the event F is given by

A. $P(E|F) = \dfrac{P(E \cup F)}{P(F)}, \ P(F) \neq 0$

B. $P(E|F) = \dfrac{P(E \cap F)}{P(F)}, \ P(F) \neq 0$

C. $P(E|F) = \dfrac{P(E \cap F)}{P(F)}, \ P(F) < 0$

D. $P(E|F) = \dfrac{P(E \cap F)}{P(E)}, \ P(F) \neq 0$

Q.44 The conditional probability of an event E, given the occurrence of the event F lies between

A. 0 ≤ P (E|F) < 1   **B.** 0 ≤ P (E|F) ≤ 1
C. 0 < P (E|F) ≤ 1   **D.** 0 < P (E|F) < 1

Q.45 The conditional probability of the event E', given that F has occurred is given by

A. P (E'|F) = – 1 + P (E|F)
B. P (E'|F) = 1 – P (E|F)
C. P (E'|F) = P (E|F)
D. P (E'|F) = 1

Q.46 If E, F and G are events with P(G) ≠ 0 then P ((E ∪ F)|G) given by

A. P (E|G) + P (F|G) – P ((E ∩ F)|F)
B. P (G|E) + P (F|G) – P ((E ∩ F)|E)
C. P (E|G) + P (G|F) – P ((E ∩ F)|G)

D. P (E|G) + P (F|G) – P ((E ∩ F)|G)

Q.47 If E and F are events then P (E ∩ F) =

A. P (E) P (E|F), P (E) ≠ 0
B. P (E∪F) P (F|E), P (E) ≠ 0
C. P (E ∩ F) P (F|E), P (E) ≠ 0
D. P (E) P (F|E), P (E) ≠ 0

Q.48 Two coins are tossed once ,where E : tail appears on one coin , F : one coin shows head. Find P(E/F)

A. 0.33   **B.** 0.24   **C.** 0.23   **D.** 1

Q.49 A linear programming problem is one that is concerned with

A. finding the optimal value (maximum or minimum) of a linear function of several variables
B. finding the upper limits of a linear function of several variables
C. finding the lower limit of a linear function of several variables
D. finding the limiting values of a linear function of several variables

Q.50 Which of the following types of problems cannot be solved by linear programming methods

A. Traffic signal control
B. Manufacturing problems
C. Transportation problems
D. Diet problems

Q.51 In linear programming feasible region (or solution region) for the problem is

A. The common region determined by all the x ⩾ 0, y ⩾ 0 and the objective function
B. The common region determined by all the x ⩾ 0 and the objective function
C. The common region determined by all the constraints including the non – negative constraints x ⩾ 0, y⩾ 0
D. The common region determined by all the objective functions including the non – negative constraints x ⩾ 0, y ⩾ 0

Q.52 In linear programming infeasible solutions

A. fall outside the feasible region
B. fall inside the feasible region
C. fall on the x = 0 plane
D. fall inside the a regular polygon

Q.53 In linear programming, optimal solution

A. satisfies all the constraints only
B. is not unique
C. maximizes the objective function only
D. satisfies all the constraints as well as the objective function

Q.54 Let R be the feasible region (convex polygon) for a linear programming problem and let Z = ax + by be the objective function. When Z has an optimal value (maximum or minimum), where the variables x and y are subject to constraints described by linear inequalities,

A. optimal value must occur at a corner point (vertex) of the feasible region.

B. optimal value must occur at the midpoints of the corner points (vertices) of the feasible region.

C. optimal value must occur at the centroid of the feasible region.

D. None of these

Ques (55-56):Direction: Study the bar graph and answer the following question.

In Bar Graph, shows the number of students who passed in XII class from 6 schools.

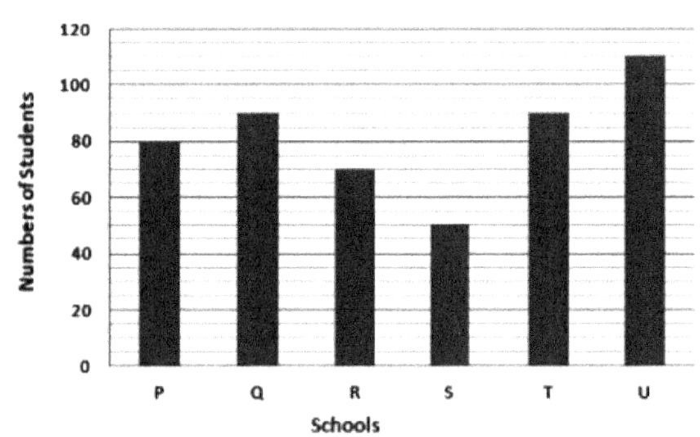

Q.55 If the fail percentage of school P is 60% then, find the number of students who failed from school P is what percentage of the number of students who passed from school T.

A. 80%　　**B.** 133.33%　　**C.** 90%　　**D.** 105%

Q.56 If the ratio between the total number of students who passed to the total number of students who failed from all schools is 7 : 3, then find the total number of failed students from all schools together.

A. 210　　**B.** 250　　**C.** 140　　**D.** 220

Q.57 A and **B** throws one dice for a stake of Rs 11, which is to be won by the player who first throws a six. The game ends when the stake is won by **A** or **B**. If **A** has the first throw, then what are their respective expectations?

A. 5 and 6　　　　**B.** 6 and 5
C. 11 and 10　　　**D.** 10 and 11

Q.58 On January 1, 2004 two new societies s_1 and s_2 are formed, each n numbers. On the first day of each subsequent month, s_1 adds b members while s_2 multiples its current numbers by a constant factor **r**. Both the societies have the same number of members on July 2, 2004. If **b=10.5n**, what is the value of **r**?

A. 2　　**B.** 1.9　　**C.** 1.8　　**D.** 1.7

Q.59 Abhishek had a certain number of Re 1 coins, Rs 2 coins and Rs 10 coins. If the number of Re 1 coins he had is six times the number of Rs 2 coins Abhishek had, and the total worth of his coins is Rs 160, find the maximum number of Rs 10 coins Abhishek could have had.

A. 12　　**B.** 10　　**C.** 8　　**D.** 6

Q.60 In a family of husband, wife and a daughter, the sum of the husband's age, twice the wife's age, and thrice the daughter's age is 85; while the sum of twice the husband's age, four times the wife's age, and six times the daughter's age is

170. It is also given that the sum of five times the husband's age, ten times the wife's age and fifteen times the daughter's age equals 450. The number of possible solutions, in terms of the ages of the husband, wife and the daughter, to this problem is:

A. 0　　　　　　　　**B.** 1
C. 2　　　　　　　　**D.** Infinitely many

Analytical Ability & Logical Reasoning

Q.61 1, 9, 25, 49, ?, 121. What will come at the place of question mark ?

A. 100　　**B.** 91　　**C.** 64　　**D.** 81

Q.62 4, 7, 12, 19, 28, ?

A. 49　　**B.** 36　　**C.** 30　　**D.** 39

Q.63 6, 11, 21, 36, 56, ?

A. 91　　**B.** 51　　**C.** 81　　**D.** 42

Q.64 10, 100, 200, 310, ?

A. 430　　**B.** 420　　**C.** 410　　**D.** 400

Q.65 Find the missing character?

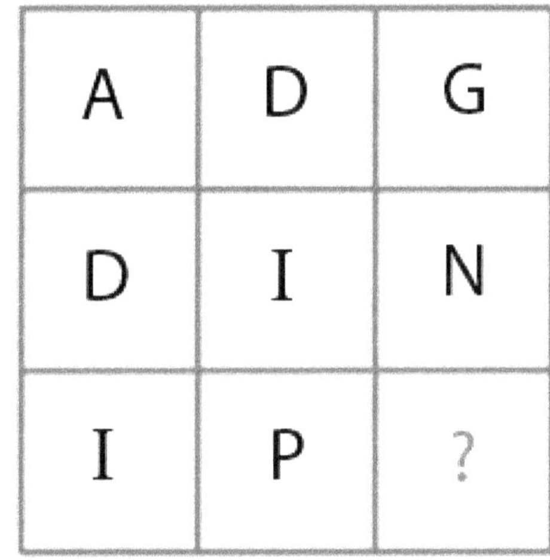

A. V　　**B.** X　　**C.** W　　**D.** Y

Q.66 Find the missing character?

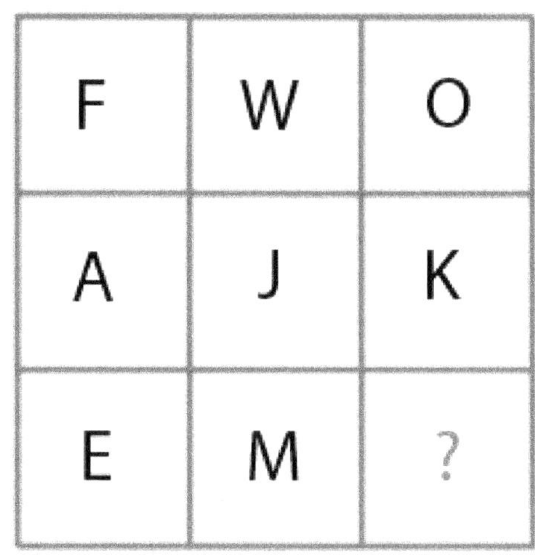

F	W	O
A	J	K
E	M	?

A. N   **B.** P   **C.** X   **D.** D

Q.67 Find the missing character?

4C	2B	3A
28A	?	45B
7C	5A	15B

A. 10C   **B.** 12C   **C.** 13C   **D.** 7C

Q.68 Find the missing character?

7B	5C	6B
3C	9B	19A
15A	17A	?

A. 14B   **B.** 12C   **C.** 16C   **D.** 10

Q.69 Find the odd number/letters from the given alternatives.
A. Swimming   **B.** Sailing
C. Diving   **D.** Driving

Q.70 Find the odd number / letters / word from the given alternative.
A. Discernment   **B.** Perception
C. Penetration   **D.** Insinuation

Q.71 Find the odd number / letters / word from the given alternative.
A. 5720   **B.** 6710   **C.** 2640   **D.** 4270

Q.72 Find the odd number/letters from the given alternatives.
A. 626   **B.** 841   **C.** 962   **D.** 1090

Q.73 A is son of C while C and Q are the sisters to one another. Z is the mother of Q. If P is the son of Z, Which one of the following statements is correct ?
A. Q is the grandfather of A
B. P is the maternal uncle of A
C. P is the cousin of A
D. Z is the brother of C

Q.74 Pointing at a photo, Dinesh said, "His father is only son of my mother." The photo belongs to- :
A. Dinesh   **B.** Dinesh's brother
C. Dinesh's father   **D.** Dinesh's son

Q.75 Looking at a portrait of a man, Sanjay said, "His mother is the wife of my father's son. Brothers and sisters I have none." At whose portrait was Sanjay Looking.
A. His son   **B.** His nephew
C. His cousin   **D.** His uncle

Q.76 A man said to a lady, "The son of your only brother is the brother of my wife." What is the lady to the man.
A. Mother
B. Sister
C. Sister of father-in-law
D. Grandfather

Q.77 Insect : Disease :: War : ?
A. Army   **B.** Defeat
C. Arsenal   **D.** Destruction

Q.78 Book : Cover :: Painting : ?
A. Example   **B.** Wall   **C.** Colour   **D.** Frame

Q.79 Float : Sink :: Boat : ?
A. Ship   **B.** War
C. Submarine   **D.** Missile

Q.80 Water : Dam :: Trade: ?
A. Commerce   **B.** Economy
C. Goods   **D.** Trade Policy

Computer Awareness

Q.81 A light sensitive device that converts drawing, printed text or other images into digital form is

A. Keyboard　　　　　**B.** Plotter
C. Scanner　　　　　　**D.** OMR

Q.82 Which protocol provides e-mail facility among different hosts?
A. FTP　　　　　　　**B.** SMTP
C. TELNET　　　　　**D.** SNMP

Q.83 The basic architecture of computer was developed by
A. John Von Neumann　　　**B.** Charles Babbage
C. Blaise Pascal　　　　　　**D.** Garden Moore

Q.84 In order to tell Excel that we are entering a formula in cell, we must begin with an operator such as
A. $　　　**B.** @　　　**C.** +　　　**D.** =

Q.85 If there are multiple recycle bin for a hard disk
A. You can set different size for each recycle bin
B. You can choose which recycle bin to use to store your deleted files
C. You can make any one of them default recycle bin
D. None of above

Q.86 Identify false statement
A. You can find deleted files in recycle bin
B. You can restore any files in recycle bin if you ever need
C. You can increase free space of disk by sending files in recycle bin
D. You can right click and choose Empty Recycle Bin to clean it at once

Q.87 If the displayed system time and date is wrong, you can reset it using
A. Write　　　　　　**B.** Calendar
C. Write file　　　　**D.** Control panel

Q.88 You should save your computer from?
A. Viruses　　　　　**B.** Time bombs
C. Worms　　　　　　**D.** All of the above

Q.89 The ability to combine name and addresses with a standard document is called ________
A. document formatting
B. database management
C. mail merge
D. form letters

Q.90 Which enables us to send the same letter to different persons?
A. macros　　　　　　**B.** template
C. mail merge　　　　**D.** none

Q.91 A word processor would most likely be used to do
A. keep an account of money spent
B. do a computer search in media center
C. maintain an inventory
D. type a biography

Q.92 What is gutter margin?
A. Margin that is added to the left margin when printing
B. Margin that is added to right margin when printing
C. Margin that is added to the binding side of page when printing
D. Margin that is added to the outside of the page when printing

Q.93 Which of the following format you can decide to apply or not in AutoFormat dialog box?
A. Number format　　　**B.** Border format
C. Font format　　　　**D.** All of above

Q.94 How can you remove borders applied in cells?
A. Choose None on Border tab of Format cells
B. Open the list on Border tool in Formatting toolbar then choose first tool (no border)
C. Both of above
D. None of above

Q.95 Where can you set the shading color for a range of cells in Excel?
A. Choose required color form Patterns tab of Format Cells dialog box
B. Choose required color on Fill Color tool in Formatting toolbar
C. Choose required color on Fill Color tool in Drawing toolbar
D. All of above

Q.96 You can set Page Border in Excel from
A. From Border tab in Format Cells dialog box
B. From Border tool in Formatting toolbar
C. From Line Style tool in Drawing toolbar
D. You can not set page border in Excel

Q.97 Which tab is not available on left panel when you open a presentation?
A. Outline
B. Slides
C. Notes
D. All of above are available

Q.98 Which of the following statements is not true?
A. You can type text directly into a PowerPoint slide but typing in text box is more convenient.
B. From Insert menu choose Picture and then File to insert your images into slides.
C. You can view a PowerPoint presentation in Normal, Slide Sorter or Slide Show view.
D. You can show or hide task pane from View >> Toolbars.

Q.99 To start Microsoft PowerPoint application
A. Click on Start >> Programs >> All Programs >> Microsoft PowerPoint
B. Hit Ctrl + R then type ppoint.exe and Enter
C. Click Start >> Run then type powerpnt then press Enter
D. All of above

Q.100 Which of the following section does not exist in a slide layout?
A. Titles　　　　　　**B.** Lists
C. Charts　　　　　　**D.** Animations

English

Q.101 Arrange the sentences in the correct order

A. Good writers use more verbs.

B. However, it is hard to write without verbs.

C. The reason is that if unnecessary words are reduced, the verb-percentage goes up as a mathematical necessity.

D. So "use verbs" is not really good advice; writers have to use verbs, and trying to add extra ones would not turn out well.

A. ABCD   **B.** ACBD   **C.** ABDC   **D.** DBCA

Q.102 Arrange the sentences in the correct order

A. The French Revolution created a vision for a new moral universe: that sovereignty resides in nations; that a constitution and the rule of law govern politics; that people are equal and enjoy inalienable rights; and that church and state should be separate.

B. The French Revolution invented modern revolution —the idea that humans can transform the world according to a plan—and so has a central place in the study of the social sciences.

C. It ushered in modernity by destroying the foundations of the "Old Regime"—absolutist politics, legal inequality, a "feudal" economy (characterized by guilds, manorialism, and even serfdom), and an alliance of church and state.

D. That vision is enshrined in the Declaration of the Rights of Man and Citizen of 1789, whose proclamation of "natural, imprescriptible, and inalienable" rights served as the model for the 1948 United Nations Universal Declaration of Human Rights.

A. ADBC   **B.** BADC   **C.** ACBD   **D.** BCAD

Q.103 Arrange the sentences in the correct order

A. During the 24-hour darkness of the austral autumn and winter, the South Pole Telescope operates nonstop under impeccable conditions for astronomy.

B. The atmosphere is thin (the pole is more than 9,300 feet above sea level, 9,000 of which are ice), stable (due to the absence of the heating and cooling effects of a rising and setting Sun) and the pole has some of the calmest winds on Earth, blowing almost always from the same direction.

C. "The South Pole has the harshest environment on Earth, but also the most benign," says William Holzapfel, a University of California at Berkeley astrophysicist, the on-site lead researcher at the South Pole Telescope.

D. From an astronomer's perspective, not until the Sun goes down and stays down—March through September— does the South Pole get "benign."

A. ABCD   **B.** CDBA   **C.** CDAB   **D.** ACBD

Q.104 Arrange the sentences in the correct order

A. As "operating systems", Latin and French outlived the strategic pre-eminence of Rome and France.

B. Nor will Chinese, Russian, or Indian culture soon shoulder aside the American version-high or low- whose draw is embodied by Harvard and Hollywood.

C. Once a standard exists, it tends to perpetuate itself-just like the dollar, for all its ups and downs will not soon yield to the Euro or the Renminbi.

D. By such measures, no other rival, not even China, comes close to America, whatever the country's many familiar failings and riches of the rising rest.

A. ACBD   **B.** BADC   **C.** CBAD   **D.** CABD

Q.105 Arrange the sentences in the correct order

A. The oldest fossil grasses are just 70 million years old, although grass may have evolved a bit earlier than that.

B. There have been land plants for 465 million years, yet there were no flowers for over two-thirds of that time.

C. The equally-familiar grasses appeared even more recently.

D. Flowering plants only appeared in the middle of the dinosaur era.

A. DCBA   **B.** BCAD   **C.** CADB   **D.** BDCA

Q.106 Choose the grammatically correct option

Though all competitive exams do not allow using a calculator, but where they are permitted, there are restrictions on the models allowed.

A. Though all competitive exams do not allow using calculators,

B. Not all competitive exams allow the use of a calculator,

C. Every competitive exam does not allow using of calculators,

D. No correction required

Q.107 Choose the grammatically correct option

Denouncing it as anti-democratic,the Lobbying Act was slammed by critics, imposing draconian limits on the activities of trade unions.

A. the Lobbying Act, which imposes draconian limits on the activities of trade unions, was slammed by critics.

B. critics slammed the Lobbying Act, imposing draconian limits on the activities of trade unions.

C. critics slammed the Lobbying Act, which imposes draconian limits on the activities of trade unions.

D. No correction required

Q.108 Choose the grammatically correct option

While people in the Middle East have good reason to feel gravely threatened by terrorism,but elsewhere in the world, its more that people are paying greater attention to the terrorist threat then they used to.

A. but, elsewhere in the world, it's more that people are paying greater attention to the terrorist threat then they used to.

B. elsewhere in the world, it's more that people are paying greater attention to the terrorist threat than they used to.

C. but elsewhere in the world, it's more that people are paying greater attention to the terrorist threat than they used to

D. elsewhere in the world, its more that people are paying greater attention to the terrorist threat than they used to.

Q.109 Choose the grammatically correct option

Long-term risk is rarely taken by air-quality indices into account, they also vary from place to place.

A. Air-quality indices rarely take long-term risk into account;

B. Rarely do air-quality indices take long-term risk into account,

C. Though long-term risk is rarely taken by air-quality indices into account,

D. No correction required

Q.110 Choose the grammatically correct option

The solution that he worked out was not only correct but complicated.

A. was not only correct but also complicated.

B. was correct but complicated.

C. was correct only but complicated.

D. No correction required

Q.111 Reading Comprehension

The first systems of writing developed and used by the Germanic peoples were runic alphabets. The runes functioned as letters, but they were much more than just letters in the sense in which we today understand the term. Each rune was an ideographic or pictographic symbol of some cosmological principle or power, and to write a rune was to invoke and direct the force for which it stood. Indeed, in every Germanic language, the word "rune" (from Proto-Germanic *runo) means both "letter" and "secret" or "mystery," and its original meaning, which likely predated the adoption of the runic alphabet, may have been simply "(hushed) message."

Each rune had a name that hinted at the philosophical and magical significance of its visual form and the sound for which it stands, which was almost always the first sound of the rune's name. For example, the T-rune, called *Tiwaz in the Proto-Germanic language, is named after the god Tiwaz (known as Tyr in the Viking Age). Tiwaz was perceived to dwell within the daytime sky, and, accordingly, the visual form of the T-rune is an arrow pointed upward (which surely also hints at the god's martial role). The T-rune was often carved as a standalone ideograph, apart from the writing of any particular word, as part of spells cast to ensure victory in battle.

The runic alphabets are called "futharks" after the first six runes (Fehu, Uruz, Thurisaz, Ansuz, Raidho, Kaunan), in much the same way that the word "alphabet" comes from the names of the first two Hebrew letters (Aleph, Beth). There are three principal futharks: the 24-character Elder Futhark, the first fully-formed runic alphabet, whose development had begun by the first century CE and had been completed before the year 400; the 16-character Younger Futhark, which began to diverge from the Elder Futhark around the beginning of the Viking Age (c. 750 CE) and eventually replaced that older alphabet in Scandinavia; and the 33-character Anglo-Saxon Futhorc, which gradually altered and added to the Elder Futhark in England. On some inscriptions, the twenty-four runes of the Elder Futhark were divided into three ættir (Old Norse, "families") of eight runes each, but the significance of this division is unfortunately unknown.

Runes were traditionally carved onto stone, wood, bone, metal, or some similarly hard surface rather than drawn with ink and pen on parchment. This explains their sharp, angular form, which was well-suited to the medium.

Much of our current knowledge of the meanings the ancient Germanic peoples attributed to the runes comes from the three "Rune Poems," documents from Iceland, Norway, and England that provide a short stanza about each rune in their respective futharks (the Younger Futhark is treated in the Icelandic and Norwegian Rune Poems, while the Anglo-Saxon Futhorc is discussed in the Old English Rune Poem).

While runologists argue over many of the details of the historical origins of runic writing, there is widespread agreement on a general outline. The runes are presumed to have been derived from one of the many Old Italic alphabets in use among the Mediterranean peoples of the first century CE, who lived to the south of the Germanic tribes. Earlier Germanic sacred symbols, such as those preserved in northern European petroglyphs, were also likely influential in the development of the script.

The earliest possibly runic inscription is found on the Meldorf brooch, which was manufactured in the north of modern-day Germany around 50 CE. The inscription is highly ambiguous, however, and scholars are divided over whether its letters are runic or Roman. The earliest unambiguous runic inscriptions are found on the Vimose comb from Vimose, Denmark and the Øvre Stabu spearhead from southern Norway, both of which date to approximately 160 CE. The earliest known carving of the entire futhark, in order, is that on the Kylver stone from Gotland, Sweden, which dates to roughly 400 CE.

The transmission of writing from southern Europe to northern Europe likely took place via Germanic warbands, the dominant northern European military institution of the period, who would have encountered Italic writing firsthand during campaigns amongst their southerly neighbors. This hypothesis is supported by the association that runes have always had with the god Odin, who, in the Proto-Germanic period, under his original name *Woðanaz, was the divine model of the human warband leader and the invisible patron of the warband's activities. The Roman historian Tacitus tells us that Odin ("Mercury" in the interpretatio romana) was already established as the dominant god in the pantheons of many of the Germanic tribes by the first century.

From the perspective of the ancient Germanic peoples themselves, however, the runes came from no source as mundane as an Old Italic alphabet. The runes were never "invented," but are instead eternal, pre-existent forces that Odin himself discovered by undergoing a tremendous ordeal.

The word "pantheon" in the passage refers to

A. A temple of all the gods

B. All the gods collectively of a religion

C. A monument or building commemorating a nation's dead heroes

D. A domed circular temple at Rome, erected a.d. 120–124 by Hadrian

Q.112 Reading Comprehension

The first systems of writing developed and used by the Germanic peoples were runic alphabets. The runes functioned as letters, but they were much more than just letters in the sense in which we today understand the term. Each rune was an ideographic or pictographic symbol of some cosmological principle or power, and to write a rune was to invoke and direct the force for which it stood. Indeed, in every Germanic language, the word "rune" (from Proto-Germanic *runo) means both "letter" and "secret" or "mystery," and its original meaning,

which likely predated the adoption of the runic alphabet, may have been simply "(hushed) message."

Each rune had a name that hinted at the philosophical and magical significance of its visual form and the sound for which it stands, which was almost always the first sound of the rune's name. For example, the T-rune, called *Tiwaz in the Proto-Germanic language, is named after the god Tiwaz (known as Tyr in the Viking Age). Tiwaz was perceived to dwell within the daytime sky, and, accordingly, the visual form of the T-rune is an arrow pointed upward (which surely also hints at the god's martial role). The T-rune was often carved as a standalone ideograph, apart from the writing of any particular word, as part of spells cast to ensure victory in battle.

The runic alphabets are called "futharks" after the first six runes (Fehu, Uruz, Thurisaz, Ansuz, Raidho, Kaunan), in much the same way that the word "alphabet" comes from the names of the first two Hebrew letters (Aleph, Beth). There are three principal futharks: the 24-character Elder Futhark, the first fully-formed runic alphabet, whose development had begun by the first century CE and had been completed before the year 400; the 16-character Younger Futhark, which began to diverge from the Elder Futhark around the beginning of the Viking Age (c. 750 CE) and eventually replaced that older alphabet in Scandinavia; and the 33-character Anglo-Saxon Futhorc, which gradually altered and added to the Elder Futhark in England. On some inscriptions, the twenty-four runes of the Elder Futhark were divided into three ættir (Old Norse, "families") of eight runes each, but the significance of this division is unfortunately unknown.

Runes were traditionally carved onto stone, wood, bone, metal, or some similarly hard surface rather than drawn with ink and pen on parchment. This explains their sharp, angular form, which was well-suited to the medium.

Much of our current knowledge of the meanings the ancient Germanic peoples attributed to the runes comes from the three "Rune Poems," documents from Iceland, Norway, and England that provide a short stanza about each rune in their respective futharks (the Younger Futhark is treated in the Icelandic and Norwegian Rune Poems, while the Anglo-Saxon Futhorc is discussed in the Old English Rune Poem).

While runologists argue over many of the details of the historical origins of runic writing, there is widespread agreement on a general outline. The runes are presumed to have been derived from one of the many Old Italic alphabets in use among the Mediterranean peoples of the first century CE, who lived to the south of the Germanic tribes. Earlier Germanic sacred symbols, such as those preserved in northern European petroglyphs, were also likely influential in the development of the script.

The earliest possibly runic inscription is found on the Meldorf brooch, which was manufactured in the north of modern-day Germany around 50 CE. The inscription is highly ambiguous, however, and scholars are divided over whether its letters are runic or Roman. The earliest unambiguous runic inscriptions are found on the Vimose comb from Vimose, Denmark and the Øvre Stabu spearhead from southern Norway, both of which date to approximately 160 CE. The earliest known carving of the entire futhark, in order, is that on the Kylver stone from Gotland, Sweden, which dates to roughly 400 CE.

The transmission of writing from southern Europe to northern Europe likely took place via Germanic warbands, the dominant northern European military institution of the period, who would have encountered Italic writing firsthand during campaigns amongst their southerly neighbors. This hypothesis is supported by the association that runes have always had with the god Odin, who, in the Proto-Germanic period, under his original name *Woðanaz, was the divine model of the human warband leader and the invisible patron of the warband's activities. The Roman historian Tacitus tells us that Odin ("Mercury" in the interpretatio romana) was already established as the dominant god in the pantheons of many of the Germanic tribes by the first century.

From the perspective of the ancient Germanic peoples themselves, however, the runes came from no source as mundane as an Old Italic alphabet. The runes were never "invented," but are instead eternal, pre-existent forces that Odin himself discovered by undergoing a tremendous ordeal.

Which of the following statements is incorrect?

A. Unlike the Latin alphabet, which is an essentially utilitarian script, the runes are symbols of some of the most powerful forces in the cosmos

B. Runic writing was probably first used in southern Europe and was carried north by Germanic tribes.

C. The word "rune" and its meaning was derived from the runic alphabet.

D. The first runic alphabets date back to the 1st century CE.

Q.113 Reading Comprehension

The first systems of writing developed and used by the Germanic peoples were runic alphabets. The runes functioned as letters, but they were much more than just letters in the sense in which we today understand the term. Each rune was an ideographic or pictographic symbol of some cosmological principle or power, and to write a rune was to invoke and direct the force for which it stood. Indeed, in every Germanic language, the word "rune" (from Proto-Germanic *runo) means both "letter" and "secret" or "mystery," and its original meaning, which likely predated the adoption of the runic alphabet, may have been simply "(hushed) message."

Each rune had a name that hinted at the philosophical and magical significance of its visual form and the sound for which it stands, which was almost always the first sound of the rune's name. For example, the T-rune, called *Tiwaz in the Proto-Germanic language, is named after the god Tiwaz (known as Tyr in the Viking Age). Tiwaz was perceived to dwell within the daytime sky, and, accordingly, the visual form of the T-rune is an arrow pointed upward (which surely also hints at the god's martial role). The T-rune was often carved as a standalone ideograph, apart from the writing of any particular word, as part of spells cast to ensure victory in battle.

The runic alphabets are called "futharks" after the first six runes (Fehu, Uruz, Thurisaz, Ansuz, Raidho, Kaunan), in much the same way that the word "alphabet" comes from the names of the first two Hebrew letters (Aleph, Beth). There are three principal futharks: the 24-character Elder Futhark, the first fully-formed runic alphabet, whose development had begun by the first century CE and had been completed before the year 400; the 16-character Younger Futhark, which began to diverge from the Elder Futhark around the beginning of the Viking Age (c.

750 CE) and eventually replaced that older alphabet in Scandinavia; and the 33-character Anglo-Saxon Futhorc, which gradually altered and added to the Elder Futhark in England. On some inscriptions, the twenty-four runes of the Elder Futhark were divided into three ættir (Old Norse, "families") of eight runes each, but the significance of this division is unfortunately unknown.

Runes were traditionally carved onto stone, wood, bone, metal, or some similarly hard surface rather than drawn with ink and pen on parchment. This explains their sharp, angular form, which was well-suited to the medium.

Much of our current knowledge of the meanings the ancient Germanic peoples attributed to the runes comes from the three "Rune Poems," documents from Iceland, Norway, and England that provide a short stanza about each rune in their respective futharks (the Younger Futhark is treated in the Icelandic and Norwegian Rune Poems, while the Anglo-Saxon Futhorc is discussed in the Old English Rune Poem).

While runologists argue over many of the details of the historical origins of runic writing, there is widespread agreement on a general outline. The runes are presumed to have been derived from one of the many Old Italic alphabets in use among the Mediterranean peoples of the first century CE, who lived to the south of the Germanic tribes. Earlier Germanic sacred symbols, such as those preserved in northern European petroglyphs, were also likely influential in the development of the script.

The earliest possibly runic inscription is found on the Meldorf brooch, which was manufactured in the north of modern-day Germany around 50 CE. The inscription is highly ambiguous, however, and scholars are divided over whether its letters are runic or Roman. The earliest unambiguous runic inscriptions are found on the Vimose comb from Vimose, Denmark and the Øvre Stabu spearhead from southern Norway, both of which date to approximately 160 CE. The earliest known carving of the entire futhark, in order, is that on the Kylver stone from Gotland, Sweden, which dates to roughly 400 CE.

The transmission of writing from southern Europe to northern Europe likely took place via Germanic warbands, the dominant northern European military institution of the period, who would have encountered Italic writing firsthand during campaigns amongst their southerly neighbors. This hypothesis is supported by the association that runes have always had with the god Odin, who, in the Proto-Germanic period, under his original name *Woðanaz, was the divine model of the human warband leader and the invisible patron of the warband's activities. The Roman historian Tacitus tells us that Odin ("Mercury" in the interpretatio romana) was already established as the dominant god in the pantheons of many of the Germanic tribes by the first century.

From the perspective of the ancient Germanic peoples themselves, however, the runes came from no source as mundane as an Old Italic alphabet. The runes were never "invented," but are instead eternal, pre-existent forces that Odin himself discovered by undergoing a tremendous ordeal.

Which of the following can be inferred from the passage?

a. Runic script was most likely derived from Old Italic script.

b. Runes were not used so much as a simple writing system, but rather as magical signs to be used for charms.

c. In the Proto-Germanic period, the god Tiwaz was associated with war, victory, marriage and the diurnal sky.

d. The knowledge of the meanings attributed to the runes of the Younger Futhark is derived from the three Rune poems.

A. All the above

B. ii and iv

C. i, ii and iv

D. i and iii

Q.114 Reading Comprehension

The first systems of writing developed and used by the Germanic peoples were runic alphabets. The runes functioned as letters, but they were much more than just letters in the sense in which we today understand the term. Each rune was an ideographic or pictographic symbol of some cosmological principle or power, and to write a rune was to invoke and direct the force for which it stood. Indeed, in every Germanic language, the word "rune" (from Proto-Germanic *runo) means both "letter" and "secret" or "mystery," and its original meaning, which likely predated the adoption of the runic alphabet, may have been simply "(hushed) message."

Each rune had a name that hinted at the philosophical and magical significance of its visual form and the sound for which it stands, which was almost always the first sound of the rune's name. For example, the T-rune, called *Tiwaz in the Proto-Germanic language, is named after the god Tiwaz (known as Tyr in the Viking Age). Tiwaz was perceived to dwell within the daytime sky, and, accordingly, the visual form of the T-rune is an arrow pointed upward (which surely also hints at the god's martial role). The T-rune was often carved as a standalone ideograph, apart from the writing of any particular word, as part of spells cast to ensure victory in battle.

The runic alphabets are called "futharks" after the first six runes (Fehu, Uruz, Thurisaz, Ansuz, Raidho, Kaunan), in much the same way that the word "alphabet" comes from the names of the first two Hebrew letters (Aleph, Beth). There are three principal futharks: the 24-character Elder Futhark, the first fully-formed runic alphabet, whose development had begun by the first century CE and had been completed before the year 400; the 16-character Younger Futhark, which began to diverge from the Elder Futhark around the beginning of the Viking Age (c. 750 CE) and eventually replaced that older alphabet in Scandinavia; and the 33-character Anglo-Saxon Futhorc, which gradually altered and added to the Elder Futhark in England. On some inscriptions, the twenty-four runes of the Elder Futhark were divided into three ættir (Old Norse, "families") of eight runes each, but the significance of this division is unfortunately unknown.

Runes were traditionally carved onto stone, wood, bone, metal, or some similarly hard surface rather than drawn with ink and pen on parchment. This explains their sharp, angular form, which was well-suited to the medium.

Much of our current knowledge of the meanings the ancient Germanic peoples attributed to the runes comes from the three "Rune Poems," documents from Iceland, Norway, and England that provide a short stanza about each rune in their respective futharks (the Younger Futhark is treated in the Icelandic and Norwegian Rune Poems, while the Anglo-Saxon Futhorc is discussed in the Old English Rune Poem).

While runologists argue over many of the details of the historical origins of runic writing, there is widespread

agreement on a general outline. The runes are presumed to have been derived from one of the many Old Italic alphabets in use among the Mediterranean peoples of the first century CE, who lived to the south of the Germanic tribes. Earlier Germanic sacred symbols, such as those preserved in northern European petroglyphs, were also likely influential in the development of the script.

The earliest possibly runic inscription is found on the Meldorf brooch, which was manufactured in the north of modern-day Germany around 50 CE. The inscription is highly ambiguous, however, and scholars are divided over whether its letters are runic or Roman. The earliest unambiguous runic inscriptions are found on the Vimose comb from Vimose, Denmark and the Øvre Stabu spearhead from southern Norway, both of which date to approximately 160 CE. The earliest known carving of the entire futhark, in order, is that on the Kylver stone from Gotland, Sweden, which dates to roughly 400 CE.

The transmission of writing from southern Europe to northern Europe likely took place via Germanic warbands, the dominant northern European military institution of the period, who would have encountered Italic writing firsthand during campaigns amongst their southerly neighbors. This hypothesis is supported by the association that runes have always had with the god Odin, who, in the Proto-Germanic period, under his original name *Woðanaz, was the divine model of the human warband leader and the invisible patron of the warband's activities. The Roman historian Tacitus tells us that Odin ("Mercury" in the interpretatio romana) was already established as the dominant god in the pantheons of many of the Germanic tribes by the first century.

From the perspective of the ancient Germanic peoples themselves, however, the runes came from no source as mundane as an Old Italic alphabet. The runes were never "invented," but are instead eternal, pre-existent forces that Odin himself discovered by undergoing a tremendous ordeal.

Which of the following cannot be reasonably inferred with regard to the beliefs of the Proto-Germanic people?

A. Odin came upon the runes after going through a lot of torment.

B. The name of a rune was almost always the first sound of a God's name

C. The cosmological power represented by a rune was invoked by writing it.

D. Proto-German Gods were modeled on humans.

Q.115 Reading Comprehension

Hard cases, it is said, make bad law. The adage is widely considered true for the Supreme Court of India which held in the height of the Emergency, in ADM Jabalpur v. Shivkant Shukla that detenus under the Maintenance of Internal Security Act (MISA) could not approach the judiciary if their fundamental rights were violated. Not only was the law laid down unconscionable, but it also smacked of a Court more "executive-minded than the executive", complicit in its own independence being shattered by an all-powerful government. So deep has been the impact of this judgment that the Supreme Court's current activist avatar is widely viewed as having its genesis in a continuing need to atone. Expressions of such atonement have created another Court made to measure

— this time not to the measure of the government but rather the aggrandised self-image of some of its judges.

Let us look back to the ADM Jabalpur case. As a court of law, the Supreme Court was called upon in the case to balance the interest of public order in an Emergency with the right to life and personal liberty guaranteed to every person. Nine High Courts called upon to perform the same function had found a nuanced answer by which they had held that the right to life cannot be absolutely subservient to public order merely because the government declared so — the legality of detentions could be judicially reviewed, though the intention of the government would not be second-guessed by the Court. This was a delicate balance. The Supreme Court however reversed this view and made the right to life and personal liberty literally a bounty of the government. Given that the consequences of their error were entirely to the government's advantage, it was widely viewed as the death of an independent judiciary. The excessively deferential, almost apologetic language used by the judges confirmed this impression.

Today, however, while public interest litigation has restored the independent image of the Supreme Court, it has achieved this at the cost of quality, discipline and the constitutional role judges are expected to perform. The Court monitors criminal trials, protects the environment, regulates political advertising, lays down norms for sexual harassment in the workplace, sets guidelines for adoption, supervises police reform among a range of other tasks of government. That all these tasks are crucial but tardily undertaken by government can scarcely be questioned. But for an unelected and largely unaccountable institution such as the Supreme Court to be at the forefront of matters relating to governance is equally dangerous — the choice of issues it takes up is arbitrary, their remit is not legal, their results often counterproductive, requiring a degree of technical competence and institutional capacity in ensuring compliance that the Court simply does not possess. This sets an unhealthy precedent for other courts and tribunals in the country, particularly the latter whose chairpersons are usually retired Supreme Court Justices. To take a particularly egregious example, the National Green Tribunal has banned diesel vehicles more than 10 years old in Delhi and if reports are to be believed, is considering imposing a congestion charge for cars as well. That neither of these are judicial functions and are being unjustly being usurped by a tribunal that has far exceeded its mandate, is evidence of the chain reaction that the Supreme Court's activist avatar has set off across the judicial spectrum.

Finally, the Court's activism adds to a massive backlog of regular cases that makes the Indian justice delivery mechanism, slow, unreliable and inefficient for the ordinary litigant. As on March 1, 2015, there were over 61,000 cases pending in the Supreme Court alone. It might be worthwhile for the Court to set its own house in order, concomitantly with telling other wings of government how to do so.

As we mark 40 years of the Emergency and the darkest period in the Supreme Court's history, it might be time to not single-mindedly harp on the significance of an independent judiciary. Judicial independence, is and must remain a cherished virtue. However, it would be blinkered to not confront newer challenges that damage the credibility of our independent judiciary today — unpardonable delays and overweening judges taking on the mantle of national government by proxy. The Supreme Court 40 years on is a different institution — it must be cognizant of its history but not at the cost of being blind to its present.

Which of the following is a suitable title for the passage?

A. An Atonement Gone Too Far

B. Sanctimony from a Ruined Pedestal

C. The ADM Jabalpur's Case: The Supreme Court's Darkest Hour

D. Overcompensating for Past Mistakes

Q.116 Choose the correct option to fill the blanks

More often than not, mothers are __________ for oddities of behavior in their offspring. __________, single mothers' children, raised even in the most difficult of times, do not display 'outrageous' patterns of behavior, as do those of nuclear families.

A. appreciated, consequently

B. berated, therefore

C. praised, in the same manner

D. blamed, interestingly enough

Q.117 Choose the correct option to fill the blanks

In measuring electrical activity in different parts of the brain, researchers found that people who describe themselves as generally happy have more activity in the left prefrontal lobe of their brains than do other people. Therefore, a medication for __________ the left prefrontal lobe of the brain would be an __________ treatment for clinical depression.

A. suppressing, ineffective

B. stimulating, effective

C. improving, impressive

D. challenging, practical

Q.118 Choose the correct option to fill the blanks

Researchers found that when people's hands were crossed to other side of their bodies, it confused the brain by __________ the processing of information incoming from multiple regions. Lead researcher says the confusion results from a __________ between the brain's external mapping of where it normally assumes the hands will be (on the appropriate side of the body) and its internal map of the physical source of the new pain information.

A. quickening, alignment

B. transmitting, connection

C. interrupting, misalignment

D. hindering, alignment

Q.119 Choose the correct option to fill the blanks

__________around race, gender and religion sometimes seems to have gone beyond __________ in academic circles. The world would do better if we could all speak with a lighter heart more often about these things.

A. insensitivity, the pale

B. sensitivity, parody

C. sensitivity, the pale

D. insensitivity, reality

Q.120 Choose the correct option to fill the blanks

Democracy is better __________through the ballot box than it is through the crowding of main squares, which is a __________ image, but a misleading representation of the "people's will"

A. focused, ineffective

B. affected, moving

C. effected, powerful

D. realized, fleeting

// Smart Answer Sheet //

Correct Percentage of students who answered correctly. **Skipped** Percentage of students who skipped.

Q.	Ans.	Correct / Skipped	Q.	Ans.	Correct / Skipped	Q.	Ans.	Correct / Skipped	Q.	Ans.	Correct / Skipped	Q.	Ans.	Correct / Skipped
1	D	22.56 % / 13.79 %	17	A	9.77 % / 44.54 %	33	A	13.36 % / 46.98 %	49	A	14.8 % / 51.15 %	65	C	28.88 % / 39.22 %
2	C	41.52 % / 20.26 %	18	A	31.32 % / 41.96 %	34	A	19.54 % / 47.56 %	50	A	15.09 % / 50.71 %	66	D	10.49 % / 42.38 %
3	A	18.53 % / 28.88 %	19	B	16.52 % / 41.81 %	35	C	17.96 % / 48.28 %	51	C	10.49 % / 52.3 %	67	A	26.44 % / 41.66 %
4	C	19.68 % / 32.76 %	20	A	15.66 % / 43.97 %	36	D	12.07 % / 47.41 %	52	A	10.34 % / 51.01 %	68	C	16.09 % / 44.4 %
5	A	27.3 % / 31.18 %	21	B	23.28 % / 42.67 %	37	A	17.53 % / 48.56 %	53	D	10.49 % / 51.44 %	69	D	28.45 % / 39.22 %
6	B	14.08 % / 32.18 %	22	B	18.25 % / 44.82 %	38	B	14.22 % / 45.98 %	54	A	11.06 % / 52.45 %	70	D	15.37 % / 41.24 %
7	B	17.39 % / 33.18 %	23	D	13.51 % / 43.96 %	39	C	12.21 % / 46.99 %	55	B	12.36 % / 51.29 %	71	D	14.51 % / 43.1 %
8	B	38.51 % / 32.32 %	24	A	15.8 % / 46.7 %	40	A	15.23 % / 47.7 %	56	A	11.06 % / 52.01 %	72	B	16.38 % / 42.96 %
9	B	24.86 % / 33.47 %	25	A	19.25 % / 45.84 %	41	A	10.78 % / 50.28 %	57	B	17.24 % / 51.73 %	73	B	31.9 % / 41.81 %
10	A	19.4 % / 34.77 %	26	D	16.67 % / 44.54 %	42	A	13.36 % / 47.27 %	58	A	11.06 % / 53.02 %	74	D	17.53 % / 42.53 %
11	D	9.05 % / 37.36 %	27	A	19.83 % / 46.41 %	43	B	19.54 % / 49.71 %	59	A	9.48 % / 52.01 %	75	A	22.56 % / 43.53 %
12	C	17.67 % / 37.07 %	28	A	24.71 % / 44.69 %	44	B	17.67 % / 49.72 %	60	A	6.18 % / 51.58 %	76	C	26.87 % / 44.68 %
13	B	22.56 % / 40.37 %	29	D	22.41 % / 45.69 %	45	B	16.95 % / 50.0 %	61	D	41.95 % / 36.5 %	77	D	22.27 % / 42.82 %
14	A	38.07 % / 39.09 %	30	A	21.98 % / 45.69 %	46	D	8.05 % / 51.0 %	62	D	43.53 % / 37.5 %	78	D	23.13 % / 42.53 %
15	B	18.97 % / 42.52 %	31	C	35.34 % / 44.26 %	47	D	6.61 % / 51.15 %	63	C	46.98 % / 38.08 %	79	C	23.99 % / 42.96 %
16	B	17.67 % / 41.09 %	32	D	26.29 % / 45.84 %	48	D	14.51 % / 50.58 %	64	A	23.28 % / 38.65 %	80	D	13.94 % / 43.24 %

Q.	Ans.	Correct		Q.	Ans.	Correct		Q.	Ans.	Correct		Q.	Ans.	Correct		Q.	Ans.	Correct
		Skipped				Skipped				Skipped				Skipped				Skipped
81	C	47.7 %		89	C	21.84 %		97	C	19.54 %		105	D	9.34 %		113	D	3.02 %
		24.14 %				27.01 %				30.6 %				45.69 %				49.28 %
82	B	31.9 %		90	C	37.93 %		98	A	16.38 %		106	B	12.21 %		114	B	10.78 %
		25.71 %				27.59 %				33.05 %				44.69 %				49.85 %
83	A	24.71 %		91	D	28.02 %		99	C	11.06 %		107	C	12.07 %		115	A	6.9 %
		25.0 %				29.88 %				30.46 %				46.12 %				48.99 %
84	D	34.34 %		92	C	24.86 %		100	D	22.7 %		108	B	11.78 %		116	D	9.48 %
		26.0 %				33.33 %				31.61 %				46.98 %				47.27 %
85	A	12.5 %		93	D	37.79 %		101	B	22.7 %		109	A	9.77 %		117	B	17.67 %
		28.02 %				29.88 %				34.91 %				46.12 %				46.99 %
86	C	32.9 %		94	C	37.93 %		102	D	5.89 %		110	B	12.64 %		118	C	11.21 %
		27.3 %				30.03 %				41.67 %				46.7 %				47.12 %
87	D	39.51 %		95	D	25.43 %		103	C	13.36 %		111	B	12.36 %		119	B	9.34 %
		26.58 %				32.47 %				43.68 %				48.27 %				47.13 %
88	D	34.2 %		96	D	21.55 %		104	C	10.49 %		112	C	7.9 %		120	C	20.69 %
		26.58 %				31.75 %				44.97 %				49.14 %				46.12 %

//Hints and Solutions//

1. Let A and B be two sets. Then a relation R from set A to set B is a subset of A×B.Thus, R is a relation from A to B $\Leftrightarrow$ R $\subseteq$ A × B

2. R_1 is a reflexive on A, because (a,a) $\in$ R1 for each a $\in$ A

3. As xRy if x + 2 y = 8 , therefore, domain of the relation R is given by x = 8 – 2y $\in$ N. When y = 1, $\Rightarrow$ x = 6, when y = 2, $\Rightarrow$ x =4 , when y =3 , $\Rightarrow$ x = 2. Therefore, domain is { 2, 4, 6 }.

4. If R is a relation defined by xRy: if x$\leqslant$y, then R is reflexive and transitive. But, it is not symmetric. Hence, R is not an equivalence relation.

5. Any relation R is reflexive if xRx for all x $\in$ R. Here, (a, a), (b, b), (c, c)$\in$ R. Therefore, R is reflexive.

6. A relation R on a non empty set A is said to be reflexive if xRx for all x $\in$ R , Therefore , R is not reflexive.

A relation R on a non empty set A is said to be symmetric if xRy $\Leftrightarrow$ yRx, for all x , y $\in$ R. Therefore, R is not symmetric.

A relation R on a non empty set A is said to be antisymmetric if xRy and yRx $\Rightarrow$ x = y , for all x , y $\in$ R. Therefore, R is not antisymmetric.

7. $2^{3\times3} = 2^9 = 512$.

The number of elements in a 3 × 3 matrix is the product 3 × 3 = 9.

Each element can either be a 0 or a 1.

Given this, the total possible matrices that can be selected is $2^9 = 512$

8. As we know,

A matrix having m rows and n columns is called a matrix of order $m \times n$ or simply $m \times n$ matrix.

Given,

$$A = \begin{bmatrix} 2 & 4 \\ -1 & 0 \\ 6 & 5 \end{bmatrix}$$

As we can see that the given matrix A has 3 rows and 2 columns.

$\therefore$ The order of the given matrix A is 3×2.

Hence, the correct option is (B).

9. A =

$$\begin{bmatrix} a_{11} & a_{12} & a_{13} & a_{14} \\ a_{21} & a_{22} & a_{23} & a_{24} \\ a_{31} & a_{32} & a_{33} & a_{34} \end{bmatrix}_{3\times4}$$

,therefore matrix Am has 4 elements in each row.

10. Here, matrix P is of order 2 × 3 and matrix Q is of order 3 × 2 ,

then, the product PQ is defined only when :

no. of columns in P = no. of rows in Q.
And the order of resulting matrix is given by : rows in P x columns in Q.
Matrices PQ is order of 2 × 2.

11. The number of elements in a 2 × 2 matrix is the product 2 × 2 =4

Each element can either be a 0,1 or 2.

Given this, the total possible matrices that can be selected is 3^4.

$3^{2\times2} = 3^4 = 81$

12. A square matrix A for which A^n = 0, where n is a positive integer, is called a Nilpotent matrix.

The determinant and trace of the matrix is always Zero for a Nilpotent Matrix.

For the given matrix "A", determinant (A)=0 and trace(A)=0.

13. A line when intersect another line or axis two kind of angle form ,as an assumption we take positive side of y axis, to define the direction of line we take angle made from all three axis.and we take cos not other trigonometric function like sin,tan because we can define Direction cosines of a line are coefficient of i, j ,k of a unit vector along that line.

14. we know that direction cosines is coefficient of i,j,k of unit vector along that line ,i.e those coefficient are l,m,n .the length of the line r is such that

$$\vec{r} = l\hat{i} + m\hat{j} + n\hat{k} \; ;$$ and magnitute of unit vector r is

1 and . $\sqrt{l^2 + m^2 + n^2} = 1$ on squaring both side we get $l^2 + m^2 + n^2 = 1$.

15. If l, m and n are the direction cosines of a line, Direction ratios of the line are the numbers which are Proportional to the direction cosines of the line.

16. Two lines are said to be skew lines if they are neither parallel nor intersecting.this implies two lines are skew if they are not coplanner.

17. Angle between skew lines is the angle between two lines which are parallel to the given skew lines and passing through a common point in space.

18. If a_1, b_1, c_1 and a_2, b_2, c_2 are the direction ratios of two lines and θ is the angle between the two lines; then , the cosine of the angle between these two lines is given by :

$$\cos \theta = \left| \frac{a_1 a_2 + b_1 b_2 + c_1 c_2}{\sqrt{a_1^2 + b_1^2 + c_1^2}\sqrt{a_2^2 + b_2^2 + c_2^2}} \right|$$

19. $f'(t)=te^{-t}(-1)+e^{-t}\Rightarrow f'(1)=-e^{-1}+e^{-1}=0$

20. Since the graph cuts the lines y = -1 and y = 1, therefore ,it must cut the line y = 0 atleast once as the graph is a continuous curve in this case.

21. $\int e^{-\log x}dx=\int e^{\log x^{-1}}dx=\int x^{-1}dx=\log|x|+C$

22. Since g(x) and h(x) are integrals of the same function , therefore ; g(x) – h(x) is constant. 'OR'

[g(x)+C] - [f(x)+D]=0 => g(x) - f(x) = D-C, Which is a constant of integration.

23. Area of standard ellipse is given by :πab.

24.

$$\text{Required area} = \int_0^{\pi} a \sin x \, dx$$
$$= a\left[-\cos x\right]_0^{\pi}$$
$$= a(-\cos \pi + \cos 0) = a(1 + 1) = 2a$$

25. Differential equations are equations containing functions y = f(x), g(x) and derivatives of y with respect to x.

26. Order of a differential equation is defined as the order of the highest order derivative of the dependent variable present in the differential equation.

27. The power or index of the highest ordered derivative in the polynomial is the degree of the differential equation provided equation is in the standard form.

28. Since the equation has 2nd derivative as the highest derivative term.Hence, the order is 2

29. Since the highest derivative term is d^3y/dx^3 hence the order is 3.

30. the power of the highest order derivative i.e .(dy dx)^2 is 2.hence the degree 2

31. A vector has both magnitude as well as direction.

32. Position vectors of any point in space are usually calculated from the origin, so we write

$$\overrightarrow{OA}, \ \overrightarrow{OB}, \ \overrightarrow{OC}$$ for three points A ,B,C in space to represent the origin as the initial point.

33. the angles α,β,γ are called direction angles, which the position vector $\vec{r}$ makes with the positive x-axis ,y-axis and z-axis respectively

34. Cosines of the angles α,β,γ are called direction cosines.

35. If l , m and n are the direction cosines of vector $\vec{r}$ denoted by $\overrightarrow{OP}$, then , the coordinates of point P are given by : lr ,mr and nr respectively.

36. A vector whose initial and terminal points coincides is called Zero Vector. The magnitude of Zero Vector is also Zero.

37.

$$\cos^2 15^o - \cos^2 30^o + \cos^2 45^o - \cos^2 60^o + \cos^2 75^o$$
$$= \sin^2 75^o + \cos^2 75^o + \cos^2 45^o - \cos^2 60^o + \cos^2 30^o$$
$$= 1 + \left(\tfrac{1}{\sqrt{2}}\right)^2 - \left(\tfrac{1}{2}\right)^2 - \left(\tfrac{\sqrt{3}}{2}\right)^2 = \tfrac{1}{2}$$

38. Since, range of sine and cosine function is [-1,1]. But, sine is increasing function and cosine is decreasing function the highest that both together attain is 45^0

$$\left(\tfrac{1}{\sqrt{2}}\right) + \left(\tfrac{1}{\sqrt{2}}\right) = \sqrt{2}$$

39. Since, range of sine function and cosine function is [-1,1]. But, sine is increasing function and cosine is decreasing function. Therefore, the lowest that both together can attain is -45°

$$\left(-\tfrac{1}{\sqrt{2}}\right) + \left(-\tfrac{1}{\sqrt{2}}\right) = -\sqrt{2}$$

40.

$$\frac{\sec\theta + \tan\theta}{\sec\theta - \tan\theta} = \frac{\frac{1}{\cos\theta} + \frac{\sin\theta}{\cos\theta}}{\frac{1}{\cos\theta} - \frac{\sin\theta}{\cos\theta}} = \frac{1 + \sin\theta}{1 - \sin\theta} = \frac{1 + \frac{3}{5}}{1 - \frac{3}{5}} = 4$$

41.

$$\sec\theta = x + \tfrac{1}{4x}, x \in R, x \neq 0,$$
$$\sec\theta = x + \tfrac{1}{4x}$$
$$\Rightarrow \tan\theta = \sqrt{\sec^2\theta - 1} = \sqrt{\left(x + \tfrac{1}{4x}\right)^2 - 1}$$
$$\Rightarrow \tan\theta = \sqrt{x^2 + \tfrac{1}{(4x)^2} + \tfrac{1}{2} - 1} = \sqrt{\left(x - \tfrac{1}{4x}\right)^2}$$
$$\tan\theta = \left(x - \tfrac{1}{4x}\right)$$
$$\Rightarrow \tan\theta = x - \tfrac{1}{4x}, x \in R, x \neq 0, \Rightarrow \sec\theta + \tan\theta = x + \tfrac{1}{4x} + x - \tfrac{1}{4x} = 2x$$

When we will take negative value with tan we will get answer as 1/2x

42.

$$\cos 2\theta \text{ is equals to } \cos(\theta + \theta) = \cos\theta.\cos\theta - \sin\theta.\sin\theta = \cos^2\theta - \sin^2\theta$$
$$\frac{\cos^2\theta - \sin^2\theta}{\cos^2\theta + \sin^2\theta} = \frac{1 - \tan^2\theta}{1 + \tan^2\theta}$$

43. The conditional probability of an event E, given the occurrence of the event F is given by :

$$P(E|F) = \frac{P(E \cap F)}{P(F)}, \ P(F) \neq 0$$

44. As the probability of any event always lies between 0 and 1. Therefore , 0 ≤ P (E|F) ≤ 1.

45. We know that, P(S/F) =1

⟹ P(E U E'|F)=1   Since, E U E' = S

⟹P(E/F) +P(E'/F) =1 (Since E and E' are disjoint events)

⟹P(E'/F) = 1 - P(E/F)

46.

$$P(EUF/G) = \frac{P((E \cup F) \cap G)}{P(G)} = \frac{P((E \cap G) \cup (F \cap G)}{P(G)} = \frac{P(E \cap G) + P(F \cap G) - P(E \cap G \cap F \cap G)}{P(G)}$$
$$= \frac{P(E \cap G)}{P(G)} + \frac{P(F \cap G)}{P(G)} - \frac{P(E \cap F \cap G)}{P(G)}$$
$$= P(E|G) + P(F|G) - P((E \cap F)|G)$$

47. If E and F are events then P (E ∩ F) = P (E) P (F|E), P (E) ≠ 0. By the definition of conditional probability of two events

48.

$S = \{HH, HT, TH, TT\}$

$E = \{HT, TH\}$

$F = \{HT, TH\}$

$\Rightarrow P(E) = \frac{2}{4} = \frac{1}{2}, P(F) = \frac{2}{4} = \frac{1}{2}, P(E \cap F) = \frac{1}{2}$

$\Rightarrow P(E/F) = \frac{P(E \cap F)}{P(F)} = \frac{1/2}{1/2} = 1$

49. A linear programming problem is one that is concerned with finding the optimal value (maximum or minimum) of a linear function of several variables .

50. Traffic signal control types of problems cannot be solved by linear programming methods, because there is no need for optimization in such problems.

51. In linear programming feasible region (or solution region) for the problem is given by the common region determined by all the constraints including the non – negative constraints x ⩾ 0, y ⩾ 0

52. In linear programming infeasible solutions fall outside the feasible region. In other words, it the region other than the feasible region is called the infeasible region.

53. In linear programming, any point in the feasible region which gives that gives the optimal value (maximum or minimum) of the objective function is called optimal solution. In other words, it satisfies all the constraints as well as the objective function.

54. Let R be the feasible region (convex polygon) for a linear programming problem and let Z = ax + by be the objective function. When Z has an optimal value (maximum or minimum), where the variables x and y are subject to constraints described by linear inequalities then , optimal value must occur at a corner point (vertex) of the feasible region.

55. Given that:

Fail percentage of school P is 60%. Then, the pass percentage of school P is 40%.

We know that,

$\text{Percentage} = \left(\frac{\text{Actual}}{\text{Total}}\right) \times 100$

From the given graph,

Students who passed in school P = 80

$40\% = 80$

$\Rightarrow 1\% = 2$

$\Rightarrow 60\% = 60 \times 2 = 120$ (Failed students of school P)

Now, the number of students passed from school T = 90

Then, the required percentage,

$= \left(\frac{120}{90}\right) \times 100$

$= \left(\frac{4}{3}\right) \times 100$

$= 133.33\%$

∴ The required percentage is 133.33%.

Hence, the correct option is (B).

56. Given:

The ratio between passed and failed students from all schools = 7 : 3

Total number of passed students $= 80 + 90 + 70 + 50 + 90 + 110 = 490$

7 units $= 490$

$\Rightarrow 1$ unit $= 70$

Failed students $= 3$ units $= 70 \times 3 = 210$

∴ The total number of failed student from all schools is 210.

Hence, the correct option is (A).

57. Expectation of winning **A:**

$$\left[\left(\frac{1}{6}\right) + \left(\frac{5}{6} \times \frac{5}{6} \times \frac{1}{6}\right) + \ldots\right] \times 11$$

$$\left[\frac{\frac{1}{6}}{1 - \frac{25}{36}}\right] \times 11 = 6$$

Similarly we get the expectation of **B** as 5

58. it is 6 months, from January 1, 2004 to July 2, 2004. So, increase will be 6 times.

No. of members s_1 will be in A.P.

On July 2nd , 2004, s_1 will have **n+6b** members

=n+6×10.5n

=64n

No. of members in s_2 will be in **G.P.**

On July 2nd, 2004 Number of members in $s_2 = nr^6$

$\Rightarrow 64n = nr^6$

⇒r=2

59. If the Abhishek had **x** Re 1, **y** Rs 2 coins and z Rs 10 coins, the total value of coins he had:

=x**(1)**+y**(2)**+z**(10)=x+2y+10z=160**

Since, 6y=x

Thus, 8y+10z=160 i.e 8y is a multiple of 10 i.e. y=5 or y=10

i.e. (x,y,z)=(30,5,12) or (60,10,8)

Thus, the maximum value of 'z' is **12**

60. Let the age of husband wife and daughter be denoted by h,w and d respectively.

h+2w+3d=85 -------- (i)

2h+4w+6d=170 -------- (ii)

5h+10w+15d=450 -------- (iii)

Multiplying the first equation by 5 we get

5h+10w+15d=425

but Eq (iii) gives **5h+10w+15d=450**

So No solution possible.

61. $1^2 = 1.$

$3^2 = 9.$

$5^2 = 25.$

$7^2 = 49.$

$9^2 = 81.$

$11^2 = 121.$

62. First term,

4

Second,

4+3 = 7.

Third,

7+5 = 12.

Fourth,

12+7 = 19.

Fifth,

19+9 = 28.

Therefore,

28+11 = 39 will be the required term.

63. 6 (+5)→ 11 (+10)→ 21 (+15)→ 36 (+20)→ 56 (+25) → 81.

64. 1st term : 10

2nd term : 100 = 10+90

3rd term : 200 = 100+100

4th term : 310 = 200+110

5th Term: 430 = 310+120

Therefore, the answer is 430.

65. First Row

A ----(+3)---> D ----(+3)---> G.

Second Row

D ----(+5)---> I ----(+5)---> N.

Third Row

I ----(+7)---> P ----(+7)---> W.

66. Coding, A = 1, B = 2, C = 3, ... M = 13,..... Y = 25, Z = 26.

First Column

F-A = 6-1 = 5 = E.

Second Column

W-J = 23-10 = 13 = M.

Third Column

O-K = 15-11 = 4 = D.

67. In each row, A, B and C, each of these must appear once.

First column ==> 4*7 = 28.

Third column ==> 3*15 = 45.

Second Column ==> 2*5 = 10. So,

Missing Character = 10C.

68. In each column, A, B and C must have appeared once.

Along the digonals, the sum of two numbers is equal to the third number.

Thus, the missing number will be (7 +9) = 16 and the letter will be C.

Missing Character = 16C

69. Swimming ,Sailing and,Diving are related with water. So, Driving is odd one.

70. Discernment ,Perception and Penetration are in meaning.

71. 5720 → 5+2+0 = 7 (Second digit from Right)

6710 → 6+1+0 = 7 (Second digit from Right)

2640 → 2+4+0 = 6 (Second digit from Right)

4270 → 4+7+0 = 11 (Not the second digit from Right)

72. 626-1 = 625 = 252.

962-1 = 961 = 312.

1090-1 = 1089 = 332.

But,

841-1 = 840 (not a perfect square).

Otherwise, 841 is a perfect square of 29, other are not a perfect square.

73. Since, C and Q are sisters to one another and A is the son of C. Hence, C is the mother of Q, therefore, Z is maternal grandfather of A. As P is the son of Z. Hence, P is the maternal uncle of A.

74. Since, the only son of the mother of Dinesh, is Dinesh, therefore, the photo belongs to Dinesh's son.

75. Since, Sanjay has neither a sister nor a brother, therefore, Sanjay is the only son of his father. Hence, the mother of the portrait is wife of Sanjay. Therefore, the portrait is the wife of the Sanjay. Therefore, portrait was of Sanjay's son.

76. Since, the son of the only brother of the lady is the nephew of the lady, therefore, the wife of the man is the niece of the lady. Hence, the lady is the sister of the father-in-law of the man.

77. Insect invites disease and War invites destruction.

78. Cover is used to protect book in same way and frame is use to protect painting.

79. Float means above water and sink means under water. In same way, Boat floats on water and submarine moves under water.

80. Dam is constructed for water and Trade policy is formulated for Trade policy.

81. Scanner

82. SMTP (Simple Mail Transfer Protocol) is a TCP/IP protocol used in sending and receiving e-mail. However, since it is limited in its ability to queue messages at the receiving end, it is usually used with one of two other protocols, POP3 or IMAP that let the user save messages in a server mailbox and download them periodically from the server. SMTP usually is implemented to operate over Internet port 25.

Many mail servers now support Extended Simple Mail Transfer Protocol (ESMTP), which allows multimedia files to be delivered as e-mail.

83. In 1945, Professor J. von Neumann, who was then working at the Moore School of Engineering in Philadelphia, where the E.N.I.A.C. had been built, issued on behalf of a group of his co-workers, a report on the logical design of digital computers.

84. In MS Excel, formulas are equations that perform various calculations in your worksheets. Though Microsoft has introduced a handful of new functions over the years, the concept of Excel spreadsheet formulas is the same in all versions of Excel 2016, Excel 2013, Excel 2010, Excel 2007 and lower.

All Excel formulas begin with an equal sign (=).

85. You can set different size for each recycle bin

86. You can increase free space of disk by sending files in recycle bin

87. Control panel

88. All of the above

89. The automatic addition of names and addresses from a database to letters and envelopes in order to facilitate sending mail, especially advertising, to many addresses.

90. mail merge

91. type a biography

92. The gutter margin is a typographical term used to designate an additional margin added to a page layout to compensate for the part of the paper made unusable by the binding process. In a facing pages layout (Word refers to this type of layout as "mirror margins"), the gutter margin is on the very inside of both pages.

93. All of above

94. Choose None on Border tab of Format cells

Open the list on Border tool in Formatting toolbar then choose first tool (no border)

95. All of above

96. You can not set page border in Excel

97. Notes

98. You can type text directly into a PowerPoint slide but typing in text box is more convenient.

99.

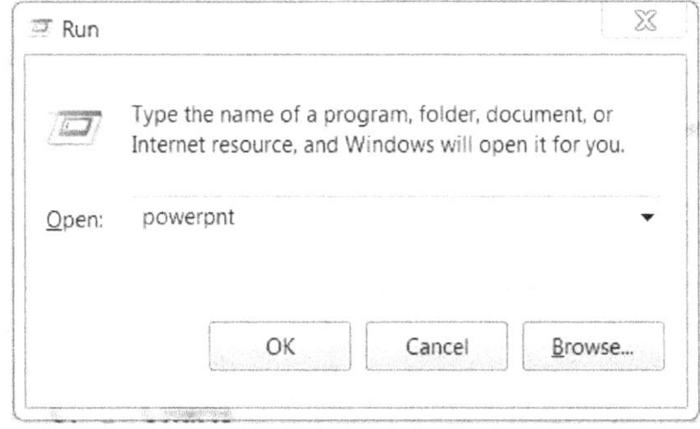

100. Animations

101. Sentence C talks of how verb usage goes up when unnecessary words are reduced. This ties in with sentence A which talks of how good writers use more verbs. It is also clear C follows A.

Sentence B says it is hard to write without verbs. Sentence D adds to this saying that "use verbs" is hence not good advice. Therefore D follows B.

By looking at the sentences we see that sentence A makes a good start to the paragraph.

Hence, the answer is **ACBD**

102. Sentences C and D start with "it" and "that" respectively and can be hence ruled out as starting sentences for the paragraph.

Sentence A talks of a vision. Sentence D starts with "That vision". So D should follow A. Only options (a) and (d) have this arrangement.

Sentence B is a general premise that the French Revolution invented modern revolution.

Sentence C talks of how the revolution brought in modernity by destroying the foundations of the Old Regime. We can see that there is a link between sentences B and C- both talk of "modernity". C follows B.

Sentence A talks of a "new moral universe" while Sentence C talks of the old regime. So again, A follows C.

Hence, the answer is **BCAD**

103. C talks of the South Pole being benign. D refers to the word benign in quotes. So, D should come after C, and quite possibly immediately after C.

The idea conveyed here is that the South Pole has the most benign weather and it is benign from March to September. So we can directly eliminate choice (d).

Sentence C makes a better choice for starting the paragraph than A.

Sentence A talks of impeccable conditions for astronomy and B explains what it is.

Hence, the answer is **CDAB**

104. This paragraph is focuses how set standards and "operating systems" tend to perpetuate, adding to the influence of the country that sets it.

Sentence B starts with a "nor", so we should ideally have an example preceding this. It is clear that only sentence C which talks of the dollar not being easily replaceable by other currencies fits the bill.

So we have the order CB_

Of the given answer options, only 1 and 3 have this pattern.

We can see D completes the paragraph.

Should the paragraph start with sentence A or C?

Sentence A is an example of how standards perpetuate. Sentence C starts off stating the premise of the paragraph, and continues the thought with an example. Hence C is a better sentence to start the paragraph than A.

Hence, the answer is **CBAD**

105. Sentences B and D talk of flowers and flowering plants. Sentence B talks of how land plants existed without flowers for several millions of years. Sentence D talks of when flowering plants appeared. It is clear D follows B.

Sentence C speaks of "equally familiar grasses". So obviously, some other example- in this case, flowering plants- precedes this.

Sentences A and C talk of the evolution of grasses. A follows C.

Hence, the answer is **BDCA**

106. Note that there is a 'but' in the sentence immediately following the clause given. So the option that starts with "though" isn't correct.

What do competitive exams allow/not allow? In answer to this question, "the use of a calculator" is the correct wording of the response. Both "using calculators" and "using of calculators" are incorrect.

The quantifier 'every' stresses all the members of the complete group. Here, we want to say that only some (not all) exams allow the use of a calculator. So option c is also incorrect.

The correct option is (b). Not all competitive exams allow the use of a calculator, but where they are permitted, there are restrictions on the models allowed.

Hence, the answer is option B

107. As the sentence starts off with "Denouncing it...", the clause that follows has to first refer to who denounced it- in this case, it is the critics.

Option B is not correct, as it implies critics impose draconian limits on the activities of trade unions.

The pronoun "which" after the "Lobbying Act" in option C clarifies that it is the Act that limits the activities of the trade unions.

Hence, the answer is option C

108. There are 3 errors to spot in the given sentence:

Firstly, as the sentence starts with "while...", any option that follows this clause with "but" is incorrect.

Secondly, "its" is a personal pronoun- not the correct word to use here. "It's" meaning "it is" is the right word to use in the given context.

Thirdly, the sentence says people are paying greater attention to the terrorist threat "then" they used to. This is incorrect. The correct word to use instead is "than".

The only option that corrects these errors is B.

Hence, the answer is option B

109. In the given sentence, 'they' in the second clause seems to refer to 'long-term risk', which is the subject of the first clause. So it is grammatically incorrect.

Now let us look at the answer options.

Option C does not make sense. So we rule this out.

Option B has two independent clauses- (1) Rarely do air-quality indices take long-term risk into account, and (2) they also vary from place to place. Each of these is a sentence in its own right. When joining two independent clauses without the use of a coordinating conjunction (and, but, or, or nor), a semicolon has to be used, not a comma. So option B is incorrect.

In option A, again, there are two independent clauses - (1) Air-quality indices rarely take long-term risk into account, and (2) they also vary from place to place. The clauses are joined by a semicolon. So option A is grammatically correct.

Hence, the answer is option A

110. "Correct" is a positive description of the solution, while "complicated" is not. So a parallel sentence construction (in this case, 'not only...but') is inappropriate.

Option C uses 'only' inappropriately.

Hence, the answer is option B

111. We find the word **"pantheon"** in the following line of the passage:

"The Roman historian Tacitus tells us that Odin ("Mercury" in the interpretatio romana) was already established as the dominant god in the pantheons of many of the Germanic tribes by the first century."

Here, clearly, it refers to Odin being the dominant god amongst all gods of the Germanic tribes.

Hence, the answer is B

112. Let us consider the statements in order.

Statement 1 - Unlike the Latin alphabet, which is an essentially utilitarian script, the runes are symbols of some of the most powerful forces in the cosmos.

From the passage, we know this to be true. Runes functioned as letters, but they were much more than just letters. Each rune was an ideographic or pictographic symbol of some cosmological power.

Statement 2 - Runic writing was probably first used in southern Europe and was carried north by Germanic tribes.

Again, this is stated in the passage and is correct.

Statement 3 - The word "rune" and its meaning was derived from the runic alphabet

The word "rune" means both "letter" and "secret" and its original meaning predated the adoption of the runic alphabet. Hence statement 3 is incorrect.

Statement 4 - The first runic alphabets date back to the 1st century CE.

Indeed, according to the passage, the development of the Elder Futhark had begun by the first century. So this statement is correct.

Hence, the answer is C

113. Statement i - Runic script was most likely derived from Italic script.

True. The runes are presumed to have been derived from one of the many Old Italic alphabets in use among the Mediterranean peoples of the first century CE, who lived to the south of the Germanic tribes.

Statement ii - Runes were not used so much as a simple writing system, but rather as magical signs to be used for charms.

False. Runes were used as a writing system. They were also used as magical signs. They were more than letters as we understand them today, not just magical signs.

Statement iii - In the Proto-Germanic period, the god Tiwaz was associated with war, victory, marriage and the diurnal sky.

True. We understand from the passage that Tiwaz was perceived to dwell within the daytime sky, had martial role and was associated with victory in battle.

Statement iv - The knowledge of the meanings attributed to the runes of the Younger Futhark is derived from the three Rune poems.

False. The Younger Futhark is treated in the Icelandic and Norwegian Rune Poems only, not all three rune poems as suggested in the statement above.

So, of the four statements above only i and iii can be inferred from the passage.

Hence, the answer is D

114. Let us consider the statements in order.

Statement a - Odin came upon the runes after going through a lot of torment.

True, stated in the last couple of paragraphs.

Statement b - The name of a rune was almost always the first sound of a God's name.

False. Each rune had a name which was almost always the first sound of the rune's name. Though the example of the T rune and Tiwaz is given in the passage, it is not stated as a general rule that the name of a rune is the first sound of a God's name. It is the first sound of the rune's name.

Statement c - The cosmological power represented by a rune was invoked by writing it.

True.

Statement d- Proto-German Gods were modeled on humans.

True. The passage gives the example of Woðanaz, the divine model of the human warband leader.

Hence, the answer is B

115. This passage starts off discussing the Emergency, considered as the "darkest hour" in India's judicial history and the impact the decision of the Supreme Court in the ADM Jabalpur case had on its subsequent rulings, leading to its current "activist avatar" in the continuing need to atone.

Let us consider the choices given.

a. An Atonement Gone Too Far

This title summarizes the main idea of the passage very well. The passage talks of the Supreme Court's unconscionable stance during the Emergency and its subsequent "activist avatar" to atone.

b. Sanctimony from a Ruined Pedestal

This title is too severe and condemnatory of the Supreme Court and does not fit the tone of the passage. While the author does talk of the Supreme Court damaging its credibility in the ADM, he believes that the independent image of the Supreme Court has since been restored.

c. The ADM Jabalpur's Case: The Supreme Court's Darkest Hour

This title deals with only one aspect of the passage. It does not capture the crux of the passage and can hence be ruled out as a choice for title.

d. Overcompensating for Past Mistakes

This title is similar in meaning to option a. However, the title talks of "past mistakes" whereas the passage discusses only one case- ADM Jabalpur- and the stand taken by the Supreme Court in the case. Option a wins over option d as a title for the paragraph.

Hence, the answer is A

116. Blank (1): We are talking of "oddities" in behavior of the offspring, which is not a positive thing. So we can directly eliminate options A and C, which give the words "appreciated" and "praised" respectively for the first blank.

Blank (2): The second sentence gives evidence that single mothers are better at managing kids, so they cannot be blamed for anything. We can hence eliminate the option that suggests 'therefore', since it doesn't logically fit.

So the correct answer is choice (D) blamed, interestingly enough.

Hence, the answer is D

117. Blank (1): If people are happy when there is more activity in a lobe, why should we suppress that lobe? 'Improving' doesn't make much sense here either. A medication to stimulate that lobe makes sense, not 'challenge' the lobe.

Blank (2): We are discussing some new insight; the discussion is towards finding something that will work. So the correct word here is effective.

Correct Answer: B. stimulating, effective

Hence, the answer is B

118. Blank (1): You cannot transmit the processing of information. Choice B is ruled out.

Blank (2): Confusion cannot arise out of alignment. So we can eliminate choices A and D.

The correct answer is (C) interrupting, misalignment

Hence, the answer is C

119. This is a slightly tricky one as more than one set of words seems to fits the blanks in sentence 1. We need to see what the second sentence says to understand the context.

It is clear from sentence 2 that talks of the need to speak with a "lighter heart" that the first sentence is not about the general lack of sensitivity around race, gender and religion in academic circles. So the correct word for blank (1) is sensitivity.

Blank (2): Going beyond the pale means going beyond limits of propriety. It doesn't make sense when used with the word 'sensitivity' in blank (1). The word parody makes sense when put in blank 2.

Hence, the correct answer is (b) sensitivity, parody

Hence, the answer is B

120. Blank (1): We can rule out focused and affected as choices, as they don't make sense in this blank. Effected and realized are possibilities here.

Blank (2): The part of the sentence that reads "but a misleading representation of people's will" tells us clearly that the appropriate word for this blank is powerful. A fleeting image does not make an impact and so does not make sense when used with "but..."

Hence, the answer is C

Mathematics

Q.1 Let A = {1, 2, 3}. Which of the following is not an equivalence relation on A ?

A. {(1, 1), (2, 2), (3, 3), (1, 2), (2, 1)}
B. None of these
C. {(1, 1), (2, 2), (3, 3)}
D. {(1, 1), (2, 2), (3, 3), (2, 3), (3, 2)}

Q.2 Let A = {1, 2, 3}, then the relation R = {(1, 1), (2, 2), (1, 3)} on A is

A. transitive
B. None of these
C. reflexive
D. symmetric

Q.3 Let A = {1, 2, 3}, then the relation R = {(1, 1), (1, 2), (2, 1)} on A is

A. None of these.
B. transitive
C. symmetric
D. reflexive

Q.4 If A is a finite set containing n distinct elements, then the number of relations on A is equal to

A. $2n^2$
B. $2n$
C. 2×2
D. n^2

Q.5 Let A = {1, 2, 3}, then the domain of the relation R = {(1, 1), (2, 3), (2, 1)} defined on A is

A. {1, 2, 3}
B. None of these.
C. {1, 3}
D. {1, 2}

Q.6 Let A = {a, b, c}, then the range of the relation R= {(a, b), (a, c), (b, c)} defined on A is

A. {a, b, c}
B. {b, c}
C. {a, b}
D. {c}

Q.7 Number of relations that can be defined on the set A = {a, b, c, d} is

A. 16
B. 4^4
C. 24
D. 2^{16}

Q.8 Let A = {1, 2, 3, 4, 5, 6}. Which of the following partitions of A correspond to an equivalence relation on A?

A. {1, 2, }, {3, 4}, {2, 3, 5, 6}
B. {1, 3}, {2, 4, 5}, {6}
C. {1, 2, 3}, {3, 4, 5, 6}.
D. {1, 2,3 }, {4, 5, 6}

Q.9 A relation R on a non – empty set A is an equivalence relation if it is

A. symmetric and transitive
B. Reflexive, antisymmetric, transitive
C. reflexive
D. reflexive, symmetric and transitive

Q.10 $\sin^2 25^0 + \sin^2 65^0$ is equal to

A. 1/2
B. 1
C. 0
D. None of these

Q.11 If $x+y=\pi/4$ then (1 + tanx)(1 + tany) is equal to

A. none of these
B. -1
C. 2
D. 1

Q.12 The period of the function f(x) = cos4x + tan3x is

A. $\pi/3$
B. $\pi/2$
C. None of these
D. π

Q.13

$$\frac{\cos 8^0 - \sin 8^0}{\cos 8^0 + \sin 8^0}$$

is equal to

A. $\tan 53^0$
B. None of these
C. $\tan 82^0$
D. $\tan 37^0$

Q.14 The general solution of the equation $\cot\theta - \tan\theta = \sec\theta$ is _____ where (n∈I).

A. $n\pi + \pi/6$
B. $n\pi + (-1)^n \pi/6$
C. $2n\pi + \pi/6$
D. $2n\pi \pm \pi/6$

Q.15 $\sin 265^0 - \cos 265^0$ is

A. Non-negative
B. Negative
C. Zero
D. Positive

Q.16 The order of

$$[x \ y \ z] \begin{bmatrix} a & h & g \\ h & b & f \\ g & f & c \end{bmatrix} \begin{bmatrix} x \\ y \\ z \end{bmatrix}$$

is

A. 3×1
B. 3×3
C. 1×1
D. 1×3

Q.17 If a matrix A is symmetric as well as skew symmetric, then A is a

A. unit matrix
B. null matrix
C. diagonal matrix
D. none of these

Q.18 A square matrix A is called idempotent if

A. $A^2 = O$
B. $2A = I$
C. $A^2 = A$
D. $A^2 = I$

Q.19 If A and B are invertible matrices of the same order, then $(AB)^{-1}$ is equal to

A. $B^{-1}A^{-1}$
B. AB^{-1}
C. $A^{-1}B^{-1}$
D. $A^{-1}B$

Q.20 A maximum or a minimum may not exist for a linear programming problem if

A. The feasible region is bounded
B. If the constraints are non-linear
C. The feasible region is unbounded
D. If the objective function is continuous

Q.21 Let R be the feasible region for a linear programming problem, and let Z = ax + by be the objective function. If R is bounded, then

A. the objective function Z has both a maximum and a minimum value on R

B. the objective function Z has only a maximum value on R

C. the objective function Z has no minimum value on R

D. the objective function Z has only a minimum value on R

Q.22 Let R be the feasible region for a linear programming problem,and let Z = ax + by be the objective function. If R is bounded, then the objective function Z has both a maximum and a minimum value on R and

A. each of these occurs at the midpoints of the edges of R

B. each of these occurs at the centre of R.

C. each of these occurs at some points except corner points of R.

D. each of these occurs at a corner point (vertex) of R.

Q.23 In Corner point method for solving a linear programming problem the first step is to

A. Find the infeasible region of the linear programming problem and determine its complement

B. Find the infeasible regions of the linear programming problem and determine theunion of the infeasible regions

C. Find the feasible region of the linear programming problem and determine its center points (vertices).

D. Find the feasible region of the linear programming problem and determine its corner points (vertices).

Q.24 In Corner point method for solving a linear programming problem the second step after finding the feasible region of the linear programming problem and determining its corner points is

A. Evaluate the objective function Z = ax + by at the center point

B. None of these

C. Evaluate the objective function Z = ax + by at each corner point.

D. Evaluate the objective function Z = ax + by at the mid points

Q.25 In Corner point method for solving a linear programming problem one finds the feasible region of the linear programming problem ,determines its corner points and evaluates the objective function Z = ax + by at each corner point. If M and m respectively be the largest and smallest values at corner points then

A. None of these

B. If the feasible region is bounded, M and m respectively are the maximum and minimum values of the objective function

C. If the feasible region is bounded, M and m respectively are the minimum and maximum values of the objective function

D. If the feasible region is unbounded, M and m respectively are the maximum and minimum values of the objective function

Q.26 In Corner point method for solving a linear programming problem one finds the feasible region of the linear

programming problem ,determines its corner points and evaluates the objective function Z = ax + by at each corner point. Let M and m respectively be the largest and smallest values at corner points. In case feasible region is unbounded, M is the maximum value of the objective function if

A. None of these

B. The open half plane determined by ax + by > M has no point in common with the feasible region

C. The open half plane determined by ax + by < M has no point in common with the feasible region

D. The open half plane determined by ax + by > M has points in common with the feasible region

Q.27 In Corner point method for solving a linear programming problem one finds the feasible region of the linear programming problem ,determines its corner points and evaluates the objective function Z = ax + by at each corner point. Let M and m respectively be the largest and smallest values at corner points. In case feasible region is unbounded, m is the minimum value of the objective function

A. if the open half plane determined by ax + by < m has no point in common with the feasible region

B. None of these

C. if the open half plane determined by ax + by > m has no point in common with the feasible region

D. if the open half plane determined by ax + by < m has points in common with the feasible region

Q.28 If two corner points of the feasible region are both optimal solutions of the same type, i.e., both produce the same maximum or minimum.

A. then any point on the line segment joining these two points is also an optimal solution of the same type

B. then any point on the line segment joining these two points is also an optimal solution of the opposite type

C. then no point on the line segment joining these two points is an optimal solution of the opposite type

D. then no point on the line segment joining these two points is an optimal solution of the same type

Q.29 Two coins are tossed once ,where E :no tail appears , F : no head appears. Find P(E/F).

A. 0.24 **B.** 0.25 **C.** 0.22 **D.** 0

Q.30 Given that E and F are events such that P(E) = 0.6, P(F) = 0.3 and P(E ∩ F) = 0.2, find P (E|F) and P(F|E)

A. P (E|F) =2/5,P(F|E) = 1/4

B. P (E|F) =2/3,P(F|E) = 1/3

C. P (E|F) =2/4,P(F|E) = 1/3

D. P (E|F) =2/3,P(F|E) = 1/4

Q.31 Compute P(A|B), if P(B) = 0.5 and P (A ∩ B) = 0.32

A. P(A|B) = 15/27 **B.** P(A|B) = 16/33

C. P(A|B) = 16/25 **D.** P(A|B) = 16/29

Q.32 If P (A) = 0.8, P (B) = 0.5 and P(B|A) = 0.4, find P(A ∩ B)

A. 0.35 **B.** 0.29 **C.** 0.37 **D.** 0.32

Q.33 If P (A) = 0.8, P (B) = 0.5 and P(B|A) = 0.4, find P(A|B)

A. 0.68 **B.** 0.66 **C.** 0.62 **D.** 0.64

Q.34 The digits of a three number are in AP. If the number is subtracted from the number formed by reversing its digits, the result is 396. What could be the original number?

A. 654   **B.** 135   **C.** 852   **D.** 753

Q.35 The total age of some 7 years old and some 5 years old children is 60 years. If I have to select a team from these children such that their total age is 48 years, In how many ways can it be done?

A. 3   **B.** 2   **C.** 1   **D.** 4

Q.36 In an A.P, the 12th term is 7 times the 2nd term and the 8th term is 3 more than 10 times the first term. What is the 5th term of the G.P whose first term is the first term of A.P and whose common ratio is equal to the common difference of the A.P.

A. 162   **B.** 144   **C.** 156   **D.** 136

Q.37 Find the share of the third son.

A. Rs 80,000   **B.** Rs 1,00,000
C. Rs 1,20,000   **D.** Rs 1,50,000

Q.38 If P (A) = 0.8, P (B) = 0.5 and P(B|A) = 0.4, find P(A ∪ B)

A. 0.25   **B.** 1.00   **C.** 0.98   **D.** 0.95

Q.39 Evaluate P(A∪B), if 2P(A) = P(B) =5/13 and P(A|B) =2/5

A. 11/29   **B.** 15/26   **C.** 11/26   **D.** 11/27

Q.40 If P(A) =6/11, P(B) =5/11 and P(A ∪ B) = 7/11. find P(A|B)

A. 4/5   **B.** 37   **C.** 45   **D.** 37

Q.41 If P(A) =6/11 , P(B) =5/11and P(A ∪ B) = 7/11.find P(B|A)

A. 2/3   **B.** 1/3   **C.** 3/5   **D.** 4/5

Q.42 The area bounded by the curve $y = x^3$, the x – axis and two ordinates x = 1 and x = 2 is

A. 15/2 sq. units   **B.** 17/4 sq. units
C. 17/2 sq. units   **D.** 15/4 sq. units

Q.43 If A is the area between the curve y = sin2x , x – axis and the lines x = π/4 and x = 3π/4 is :

A. none of these   **B.** 3
C. 1   **D.** 2

Q.44 The area bounded by y = 2cosx , x = 0 to x =2π and the axis of x in square units is -

A. 8   **B.** 6   **C.** 4   **D.** 7

Q.45 The area of the figure bounded by the curve y = logex , the x – axis and the straight line x = e is

A. 5 - e   **B.** 1
C. none of these   **D.** 3 + e

Q.46 The area enclosed by the curve $y=2\sqrt{(1-x^2)}$, x∈[0,1] is

A. π   **B.** none of these
C. π/4   **D.** π/2

Q.47 The area of the region between the curve $y = 4 -x^2$, 0⩽x⩽3 and the x –axis is equal to

A. 16/3   **B.** 7/3   **C.** 3   **D.** 23/3

Q.48 The area bounded by the curve |x|+ y =1 and the x –axis is

A. 2   **B.** 1   **C.** 4   **D.** 1/2

Q.49 Unit Vector is

A. A vector whose direction angle γ is unity
B. A vector whose direction angle β is unity
C. A vector whose magnitude is unity
D. A vector whose direction angle α is unity

Q.50 Coinitial Vectors are

A. Two or more vectors having the same initial point
B. Two or more vectors having the same final point
C. Two or more pseudo vectors having the same initial point
D. Two or more force vectors having the same initial point

Q.51 Vectors A and B are Collinear

A. if they are have equal magnitude
B. if they are parallel to the same line irrespective of their magnitudes and directions.
C. if they are in the same line
D. if the direction cosines of one are negatives of the other

Q.52 Vectors A and B are equal

A. if they have the same magnitude
B. if they have the same direction
C. if they have the same magnitude and direction
D. if they have the same magnitude and opposite direction

Q.53 Negative of a Vecto ra⃗ is a

A. A vector whose magnitude is the same as that a⃗ of but direction is opposite to that of a⃗
B. A scalar whose magnitude is the same as that a⃗
C. A vector whose magnitude is the same as that a⃗ of but direction is perpendicular to that of a⃗
D. A vector whose magnitude is the same as that a⃗ of but direction is 120°to that of a⃗

Q.54 If λ is a real number λa⃗ is a

A. vector   **B.** unit vector
C. inner product   **D.** scalar

Q.55 For vector addition which of the following is correct?

A. |a⃗ +b⃗ | = a⃗   **B.** |a⃗ +b⃗ | = a⃗ +b⃗
C. a⃗ +b⃗ =b⃗ +a⃗   **D.** a⃗ -b⃗ =b⃗ -a⃗

Q.56 How do we measure the angle between skew lines ?

A. The angle between two non intersecting lines drawn from any point parallel to each of the skew lines
B. The angle between two intersecting lines drawn from any point perpendicular to each of the skew lines
C. The angle between any two lines parallel to the given skew lines and passing through a common point in space
D. The angle between two non intersecting lines drawn from any point anti – parallel to each of the skew lines

Q.57 Write the vector equation of a line that passes through the given point whose position vector is a⃗ and parallel to a given vector b⃗ .

A. r⃗ =−a⃗ +λb⃗ ,λ∈R   **B.** r⃗ =−a⃗ −λb⃗ , λ∈R

C. $\vec{r} = \vec{a} - \lambda \vec{b}, \lambda \in R$ **D.** $\vec{r} = \vec{a} + \lambda \vec{b}, \lambda \in R$

Q.58

$$\underset{x \to \pi}{Lt} \frac{1 + \cos^3 x}{(x - \pi)^2}$$

is equal to

A. 3/2   **B.** 1/3
C. None of these   **D.** 1/2

Q.59

$$\underset{x \to 0}{Lt} \frac{\cos ec\ x - \cot x}{x}$$

is equal to

A. 1/2   **B.** None of these
C. 0   **D.** 1

Q.60

$$\underset{x \to 0}{Lt} \frac{1 - \cos 4x}{x^2}$$

is equal to

A. 8   **B.** None of these
C. 0   **D.** 1/2

Analytical Ability & Logical Reasoning

Q.61 Insect : Disease :: War : ?

A. Army   **B.** Defeat
C. Arsenal   **D.** Destruction

Q.62 Book : Cover :: Painting : ?
A. Example   **B.** Wall   **C.** Colour   **D.** Frame

Q.63 Float : Sink :: Boat : ?
A. Ship   **B.** War
C. Submarine   **D.** Missile

Q.64 Water : Dam :: Trade: ?
A. Commerce   **B.** Economy
C. Goods   **D.** Trade Policy

Q.65 A man walks 1 km to East and then he turns to South and walks 5 km. Again he turns to East and walks 2 km. After this he turns to North and walks 9 km. Now, how far is he from his starting point?
A. 3 km   **B.** 4 km   **C.** 5 km   **D.** 7 km

Q.66 I walk 30 metres in North-West direction from my house and then 30 metres in South-west direction. After this I walk 30 metres in South-East direction. Now, I turn to my house, in what direction am I going?
A. North-East   **B.** North-West
C. South-East   **D.** South-West

Q.67 A man faces towards north. Turning to his right, he walks 25 metes. He then turns to his left and walks 30 metres. Next, he moves 25 metres to his right. He then turns to his right again and walks 55 metres. Finally, he turns to the right and moves 40 metres. In which direction is he from his starting point ?
A. South-West   **B.** South
C. North-west   **D.** South-East

Q.68 If South-East becomes North and South becomes North-East and all the rest directions are changed in the same manner, the what will be the direction for West ?
A. North-East   **B.** North-West
C. South-East   **D.** South-West

Q.69 Direction : Two statements I and II are given. These statement may be either independent causes or may be effects of independent causes or a common cause. One of these statements may be the effect of the other statements. Read both the statements and decide which of the following answer choice correctly depicts the relationship between these two statements. Mark answer :

I. The Central Government has recently declared to finish the rebate on farming.

II. The Central Government faced financial loss on account of giving rebate on farming for the last few years.

A. If statement I is the cause and statement II is its effect.
B. If statement II is the cause and statement I is its effect.
C. If both the statements I and II are independent causes
D. If both the statements I and II are effects of independent causes.

Q.70 Direction : Two statements I and II are given. These statement may be either independent causes or may be effects of independent causes or a common cause. One of these statements may be the effect of the other statements. Read both the statements and decide which of the following answer choice correctly depicts the relationship between these two statements. Mark answer :

I. Many people visited the religious place during weekend.

II. Few people visited the religious place during the week days.

A. If statement I is the cause and statement II is its effect.
B. If both the statements I and II are independent causes
C. If both the statement I and II are effects of some common cause.
D. If both the statements I and II are effects of independent causes.

Q.71 Direction : Two statements I and II are given. These statement may be either independent causes or may be effects of independent causes or a common cause. One of these statements may be the effect of the other statements. Read both the statements and decide which of the following answer choice correctly depicts the relationship between these two statements.

I. Ram's father was ill.

II. Ram brought medicine after consulting the doctor.

A. If statement I is the cause and statement II is its effect.
B. If statement II is the cause and statement I is its effect.
C. If both the statements I and II are independent causes.
D. If both the statements I and II are effects of independent causes.

Q.72 Direction : Two statements I and II are given. These statement may be either independent causes or may be effects of independent causes or a common cause. One of these statements may be the effect of the other statements. Read both the statements and decide which of the following answer choice correctly depicts the relationship between these two statements.

I. The price of vegetables have been increased considerably during this summer.

II. There are tremendous increase in the temperature during this summer thereby damaging crops greatly

A. If statement I is the cause and statement II is its effect.

B. If statement II is the cause and statement I is its effect.

C. If both the statements I and II are independent causes.

D. If both the statements I and II are effects of independent causes.

Q.73 Find the missing number.

4	5	3	2	0
7	3	4	4	21
6	4	4	5	22
9	6	5	5	?

A. 34   **B.** 42   **C.** 44   **D.** 45

Q.74 Find the missing number.

56	65	78
12	?	30
44	14	48

A. 14   **B.** 44   **C.** 62   **D.** 51

Q.75 Find the missing number.

4	8	20
9	3	15
6	6	?

A. 22   **B.** 18   **C.** 16   **D.** 26

Q.76 Find the missing number.

13	54	?
7	45	32
27	144	68

A. 42   **B.** 4   **C.** 6   **D.** 36

Q.77 In a lake, there are 10 steps labelled using alphabets from A to J. Starting from step A, every minute a frog jumps to the 4th step from where it started - that is from the step A it would go to the step E and from E it would go to the step I and from I it would go to C etc. Where would the frog be at the 60th minute if it starts at the step A ?

A. B   **B.** A   **C.** H   **D.** D

Q.78 In a family there are several brothers and sisters. Every 2 boys have brothers as many as sisters and each girl has 2 brothers less than twice as many brothers as sisters. Now find the number of boys and girls.

A. 8 , 6   **B.** 6 , 4   **C.** 6 , 8   **D.** 12 , 10

Q.79 In a row of trees, a tree is 7th from left end and 14th from right end. How many tree are there in the row ?

A. 18   **B.** 19   **C.** 20   **D.** 21

Q.80 B is twice as old as A but twice younger than F. C is half the age of A but is twice older than d. Who is the second oldest ?

A. B   **B.** F   **C.** C   **D.** D

Computer Awareness

Q.81 A light sensitive device that converts drawing, printed text or other images into digital form is

A. Keyboard
B. Plotter
C. Scanner
D. OMR

Q.82 Which protocol provides e-mail facility among different hosts?

A. FTP
B. SMTP
C. TELNET
D. SNMP

Q.83 The basic architecture of computer was developed by

A. John Von Neumann
B. Charles Babbage
C. Blaise Pascal
D. Garden Moore

Q.84 In order to tell Excel that we are entering a formula in cell, we must begin with an operator such as

A. $
B. @
C. +
D. =

Q.85 If there are multiple recycle bin for a hard disk

A. You can set different size for each recycle bin
B. You can choose which recycle bin to use to store your deleted files
C. You can make any one of them default recycle bin
D. None of above

Q.86 Identify false statement

A. You can find deleted files in recycle bin
B. You can restore any files in recycle bin if you ever need
C. You can increase free space of disk by sending files in recycle bin
D. You can right click and choose Empty Recycle Bin to clean it at once

Q.87 If the displayed system time and date is wrong, you can reset it using

A. Write
B. Calendar
C. Write file
D. Control panel

Q.88 You should save your computer from?

A. Viruses
B. Time bombs
C. Worms
D. All of the above

Q.89 The ability to combine name and addresses with a standard document is called _______

A. document formatting
B. database management
C. mail merge
D. form letters

Q.90 Which enables us to send the same letter to different persons?

A. macros
B. template
C. mail merge
D. none

Q.91 A word processor would most likely be used to do

A. keep an account of money spent
B. do a computer search in media center
C. maintain an inventory
D. type a biography

Q.92 What is gutter margin?

A. Margin that is added to the left margin when printing
B. Margin that is added to right margin when printing
C. Margin that is added to the binding side of page when printing
D. Margin that is added to the outside of the page when printing

Q.93 Which of the following format you can decide to apply or not in AutoFormat dialog box?

A. Number format
B. Border format
C. Font format
D. All of above

Q.94 How can you remove borders applied in cells?

A. Choose None on Border tab of Format cells
B. Open the list on Border tool in Formatting toolbar then choose first tool (no border)
C. Both of above
D. None of above

Q.95 Where can you set the shading color for a range of cells in Excel?

A. Choose required color form Patterns tab of Format Cells dialog box
B. Choose required color on Fill Color tool in Formatting toolbar
C. Choose required color on Fill Color tool in Drawing toolbar
D. All of above

Q.96 You can set Page Border in Excel from

A. From Border tab in Format Cells dialog box
B. From Border tool in Formatting toolbar
C. From Line Style tool in Drawing toolbar
D. You can not set page border in Excel

Q.97 Which tab is not available on left panel when you open a presentation?

A. Outline
B. Slides
C. Notes
D. All of above are available

Q.98 Which of the following statements is not true?

A. You can type text directly into a PowerPoint slide but typing in text box is more convenient.
B. From Insert menu choose Picture and then File to insert your images into slides.
C. You can view a PowerPoint presentation in Normal, Slide Sorter or Slide Show view.
D. You can show or hide task pane from View >> Toolbars.

Q.99 To start Microsoft PowerPoint application

A. Click on Start >> Programs >> All Programs >> Microsoft PowerPoint
B. Hit Ctrl + R then type ppoint.exe and Enter
C. Click Start >> Run then type powerpnt then press Enter
D. All of above

Q.100 Which of the following section does not exist in a slide layout?

A. Titles　　　　　**B.** Lists
C. Charts　　　　　**D.** Animations

English

Q.101 Parajumbles: Good Writing

A. Good writers use more verbs.

B. However, it is hard to write without verbs.

C. The reason is that if unnecessary words are reduced, the verb-percentage goes up as a mathematical necessity.

D. So "use verbs" is not really good advice; writers have to use verbs, and trying to add extra ones would not turn out well.

A. ABCD　　**B.** ACBD　　**C.** ABDC　　**D.** DBCA

Q.102 The French Revolution

A. The French Revolution created a vision for a new moral universe: that sovereignty resides in nations; that a constitution and the rule of law govern politics; that people are equal and enjoy inalienable rights; and that church and state should be separate.

B. The French Revolution invented modern revolution —the idea that humans can transform the world according to a plan—and so has a central place in the study of the social sciences.

C. It ushered in modernity by destroying the foundations of the "Old Regime"—absolutist politics, legal inequality, a "feudal" economy (characterized by guilds, manorialism, and even serfdom), and an alliance of church and state.

D. That vision is enshrined in the Declaration of the Rights of Man and Citizen of 1789, whose proclamation of "natural, imprescriptible, and inalienable" rights served as the model for the 1948 United Nations Universal Declaration of Human Rights.

A. ADBC　　**B.** BADC　　**C.** ACBD　　**D.** BCAD

Q.103 The south pole telescope

A. During the 24-hour darkness of the austral autumn and winter, the South Pole Telescope operates nonstop under impeccable conditions for astronomy.

B. The atmosphere is thin (the pole is more than 9,300 feet above sea level, 9,000 of which are ice), stable (due to the absence of the heating and cooling effects of a rising and setting Sun) and the pole has some of the calmest winds on Earth, blowing almost always from the same direction.

C. "The South Pole has the harshest environment on Earth, but also the most benign," says William Holzapfel, a University of California at Berkeley astrophysicist, the on-site lead researcher at the South Pole Telescope.

D. From an astronomer's perspective, not until the Sun goes down and stays down—March through September— does the South Pole get "benign."

A. ABCD　　**B.** CDBA　　**C.** CDAB　　**D.** ACBD

Q.104 Perpetuating Strandards - Integers

A. As "operating systems", Latin and French outlived the strategic pre-eminence of Rome and France.

B. Nor will Chinese, Russian, or Indian culture soon shoulder aside the American version-high or low- whose draw is embodied by Harvard and Hollywood.

C. Once a standard exists, it tends to perpetuate itself-just like the dollar, for all its ups and downs will not soon yield to the Euro or the Renminbi.

D. By such measures, no other rival, not even China, comes close to America, whatever the country's many familiar failings and riches of the rising rest.

A. ACBD　　**B.** BADC　　**C.** CBAD　　**D.** CABD

Q.105 Plant Evolution

A. The oldest fossil grasses are just 70 million years old, although grass may have evolved a bit earlier than that.

B. There have been land plants for 465 million years, yet there were no flowers for over two-thirds of that time.

C. The equally-familiar grasses appeared even more recently.

D. Flowering plants only appeared in the middle of the dinosaur era.

A. DCBA　　**B.** BCAD　　**C.** CADB　　**D.** BDCA

Q.106 Though all competitive exams do not allow using a calculator, but where they are permitted, there are restrictions on the models allowed.

A. Though all competitive exams do not allow using calculators,

B. Not all competitive exams allow the use of a calculator

C. Every competitive exam does not allow using of calculators,

D. No correction required

Q.107 Denouncing it as anti-democratic,the Lobbying Act was slammed by critics, imposing draconian limits on the activities of trade unions.

A. the Lobbying Act, which imposes draconian limits on the activities of trade unions, was slammed by critics.

B. critics slammed the Lobbying Act, imposing draconian limits on the activities of trade unions

C. critics slammed the Lobbying Act, which imposes draconian limits on the activities of trade unions.

D. No correction required

Q.108 While people in the Middle East have good reason to feel gravely threatened by terrorism,but elsewhere in the world, its more that people are paying greater attention to the terrorist threat then they used to.

A. but, elsewhere in the world, it's more that people are paying greater attention to the terrorist threat then they used to.

B. elsewhere in the world, it's more that people are paying greater attention to the terrorist threat than they used to.

C. but elsewhere in the world, it's more that people are paying greater attention to the terrorist threat than they used to

D. elsewhere in the world, its more that people are paying greater attention to the terrorist threat than they used to.

Q.109 Long-term risk is rarely taken by air-quality indices into account, they also vary from place to place.

A. Air-quality indices rarely take long-term risk into account;

B. Rarely do air-quality indices take long-term risk into account

C. Though long-term risk is rarely taken by air-quality indices into account,

D. No correction required

Q.110 The solution that he worked out was not only correct but complicated.

A. was not only correct but also complicated.

B. was correct but complicated.

C. was correct only but complicated.

D. No correction required

Q.111 Upholding the Law

Hard cases, it is said, make bad law. The adage is widely considered true for the Supreme Court of India which held in the height of the Emergency, in ADM Jabalpur v. Shivkant Shukla that detenus under the Maintenance of Internal Security Act (MISA) could not approach the judiciary if their fundamental rights were violated. Not only was the law laid down unconscionable, but it also smacked of a Court more "executive-minded than the executive", complicit in its own independence being shattered by an all-powerful government. So deep has been the impact of this judgment that the Supreme Court's current activist avatar is widely viewed as having its genesis in a continuing need to atone. Expressions of such atonement have created another Court made to measure — this time not to the measure of the government but rather the aggrandised self-image of some of its judges.

Let us look back to the ADM Jabalpur case. As a court of law, the Supreme Court was called upon in the case to balance the interest of public order in an Emergency with the right to life and personal liberty guaranteed to every person. Nine High Courts called upon to perform the same function had found a nuanced answer by which they had held that the right to life cannot be absolutely subservient to public order merely because the government declared so — the legality of detentions could be judicially reviewed, though the intention of the government would not be second-guessed by the Court. This was a delicate balance. The Supreme Court however reversed this view and made the right to life and personal liberty literally a bounty of the government. Given that the consequences of their error were entirely to the government's advantage, it was widely viewed as the death of an independent judiciary. The excessively deferential, almost apologetic language used by the judges confirmed this impression.

Today, however, while public interest litigation has restored the independent image of the Supreme Court, it has achieved this at the cost of quality, discipline and the constitutional role judges are expected to perform. The Court monitors criminal trials, protects the environment, regulates political advertising, lays down norms for sexual harassment in the workplace, sets guidelines for adoption, supervises police reform among a range of other tasks of government. That all these tasks are crucial but tardily undertaken by government can scarcely be questioned. But for an unelected and largely unaccountable institution such as the Supreme Court to be at the forefront of matters relating to governance is equally dangerous — the choice of issues it takes up is arbitrary, their remit is not legal,

their results often counterproductive, requiring a degree of technical competence and institutional capacity in ensuring compliance that the Court simply does not possess. This sets an unhealthy precedent for other courts and tribunals in the country, particularly the latter whose chairpersons are usually retired Supreme Court Justices. To take a particularly egregious example, the National Green Tribunal has banned diesel vehicles more than 10 years old in Delhi and if reports are to be believed, is considering imposing a congestion charge for cars as well. That neither of these are judicial functions and are being unjustly being usurped by a tribunal that has far exceeded its mandate, is evidence of the chain reaction that the Supreme Court's activist avatar has set off across the judicial spectrum.

Finally, the Court's activism adds to a massive backlog of regular cases that makes the Indian justice delivery mechanism, slow, unreliable and inefficient for the ordinary litigant. As on March 1, 2015, there were over 61,000 cases pending in the Supreme Court alone. It might be worthwhile for the Court to set its own house in order, concomitantly with telling other wings of government how to do so.

As we mark 40 years of the Emergency and the darkest period in the Supreme Court's history, it might be time to not single-mindedly harp on the significance of an independent judiciary. Judicial independence, is and must remain a cherished virtue. However, it would be blinkered to not confront newer challenges that damage the credibility of our independent judiciary today — unpardonable delays and overweening judges taking on the mantle of national government by proxy. The Supreme Court 40 years on is a different institution — it must be cognizant of its history but not at the cost of being blind to its present.

Which of the following is a suitable title for the passage?

A. An Atonement Gone Too Far

B. Sanctimony from a Ruined Pedestal

C. The ADM Jabalpur's Case: The Supreme Court's Darkest Hour

D. Overcompensating for Past Mistakes

Q.112 Upholding the Law

Hard cases, it is said, make bad law. The adage is widely considered true for the Supreme Court of India which held in the height of the Emergency, in ADM Jabalpur v. Shivkant Shukla that detenus under the Maintenance of Internal Security Act (MISA) could not approach the judiciary if their fundamental rights were violated. Not only was the law laid down unconscionable, but it also smacked of a Court more "executive-minded than the executive", complicit in its own independence being shattered by an all-powerful government. So deep has been the impact of this judgment that the Supreme Court's current activist avatar is widely viewed as having its genesis in a continuing need to atone. Expressions of such atonement have created another Court made to measure — this time not to the measure of the government but rather the aggrandised self-image of some of its judges.

Let us look back to the ADM Jabalpur case. As a court of law, the Supreme Court was called upon in the case to balance the interest of public order in an Emergency with the right to life and personal liberty guaranteed to every person. Nine High

Courts called upon to perform the same function had found a nuanced answer by which they had held that the right to life cannot be absolutely subservient to public order merely because the government declared so — the legality of detentions could be judicially reviewed, though the intention of the government would not be second-guessed by the Court. This was a delicate balance. The Supreme Court however reversed this view and made the right to life and personal liberty literally a bounty of the government. Given that the consequences of their error were entirely to the government's advantage, it was widely viewed as the death of an independent judiciary. The excessively deferential, almost apologetic language used by the judges confirmed this impression.

Today, however, while public interest litigation has restored the independent image of the Supreme Court, it has achieved this at the cost of quality, discipline and the constitutional role judges are expected to perform. The Court monitors criminal trials, protects the environment, regulates political advertising, lays down norms for sexual harassment in the workplace, sets guidelines for adoption, supervises police reform among a range of other tasks of government. That all these tasks are crucial but tardily undertaken by government can scarcely be questioned. But for an unelected and largely unaccountable institution such as the Supreme Court to be at the forefront of matters relating to governance is equally dangerous — the choice of issues it takes up is arbitrary, their remit is not legal, their results often counterproductive, requiring a degree of technical competence and institutional capacity in ensuring compliance that the Court simply does not possess. This sets an unhealthy precedent for other courts and tribunals in the country, particularly the latter whose chairpersons are usually retired Supreme Court Justices. To take a particularly egregious example, the National Green Tribunal has banned diesel vehicles more than 10 years old in Delhi and if reports are to be believed, is considering imposing a congestion charge for cars as well. That neither of these are judicial functions and are being unjustly being usurped by a tribunal that has far exceeded its mandate, is evidence of the chain reaction that the Supreme Court's activist avatar has set off across the judicial spectrum.

Finally, the Court's activism adds to a massive backlog of regular cases that makes the Indian justice delivery mechanism, slow, unreliable and inefficient for the ordinary litigant. As on March 1, 2015, there were over 61,000 cases pending in the Supreme Court alone. It might be worthwhile for the Court to set its own house in order, concomitantly with telling other wings of government how to do so.

As we mark 40 years of the Emergency and the darkest period in the Supreme Court's history, it might be time to not single-mindedly harp on the significance of an independent judiciary. Judicial independence, is and must remain a cherished virtue. However, it would be blinkered to not confront newer challenges that damage the credibility of our independent judiciary today — unpardonable delays and overweening judges taking on the mantle of national government by proxy. The Supreme Court 40 years on is a different institution — it must be cognizant of its history but not at the cost of being blind to its present.

The author says that the Supreme Court was "more executive-minded than the executive" during the Emergency. Which of the following options captures the essence of what the writer means by the phrase: 'more "executive-minded than the executive"'?

A. The Supreme Court abdicated its independence to an authoritarian government by embracing its perspective

B. The Supreme Court was more emphatic than the Government about exercising executive power under the MISA.

C. The Supreme Court reflected the unconscionable actions taken by the government by upholding its laws.

D. The Supreme Court wanted to curry favor with the government through its deferential decisions during Emergency.

Q.113 Upholding the Law

Hard cases, it is said, make bad law. The adage is widely considered true for the Supreme Court of India which held in the height of the Emergency, in ADM Jabalpur v. Shivkant Shukla that detenus under the Maintenance of Internal Security Act (MISA) could not approach the judiciary if their fundamental rights were violated. Not only was the law laid down unconscionable, but it also smacked of a Court more "executive-minded than the executive", complicit in its own independence being shattered by an all-powerful government. So deep has been the impact of this judgment that the Supreme Court's current activist avatar is widely viewed as having its genesis in a continuing need to atone. Expressions of such atonement have created another Court made to measure — this time not to the measure of the government but rather the aggrandised self-image of some of its judges.

Let us look back to the ADM Jabalpur case. As a court of law, the Supreme Court was called upon in the case to balance the interest of public order in an Emergency with the right to life and personal liberty guaranteed to every person. Nine High Courts called upon to perform the same function had found a nuanced answer by which they had held that the right to life cannot be absolutely subservient to public order merely because the government declared so — the legality of detentions could be judicially reviewed, though the intention of the government would not be second-guessed by the Court. This was a delicate balance. The Supreme Court however reversed this view and made the right to life and personal liberty literally a bounty of the government. Given that the consequences of their error were entirely to the government's advantage, it was widely viewed as the death of an independent judiciary. The excessively deferential, almost apologetic language used by the judges confirmed this impression.

Today, however, while public interest litigation has restored the independent image of the Supreme Court, it has achieved this at the cost of quality, discipline and the constitutional role judges are expected to perform. The Court monitors criminal trials, protects the environment, regulates political advertising, lays down norms for sexual harassment in the workplace, sets guidelines for adoption, supervises police reform among a range of other tasks of government. That all these tasks are crucial but tardily undertaken by government can scarcely be questioned. But for an unelected and largely unaccountable institution such as the Supreme Court to be at the forefront of matters relating to governance is equally dangerous — the choice of issues it takes up is arbitrary, their remit is not legal, their results often counterproductive, requiring a degree of technical competence and institutional capacity in ensuring compliance that the Court simply does not possess. This sets an unhealthy precedent for other courts and tribunals in the country, particularly the latter whose chairpersons are usually retired Supreme Court Justices. To take a particularly egregious example, the National Green Tribunal has banned diesel vehicles more than 10 years old in Delhi and if reports are to be believed, is considering imposing a congestion charge for cars as well. That neither of these are judicial functions and are being unjustly being usurped by a tribunal that has far exceeded its mandate, is evidence of the chain reaction that the Supreme Court's activist avatar has set off across the judicial spectrum.

Finally, the Court's activism adds to a massive backlog of regular cases that makes the Indian justice delivery mechanism, slow, unreliable and inefficient for the ordinary litigant. As on March 1, 2015, there were over 61,000 cases pending in the Supreme Court alone. It might be worthwhile for the Court to set its own house in order, concomitantly with telling other wings of government how to do so.

As we mark 40 years of the Emergency and the darkest period in the Supreme Court's history, it might be time to not single-mindedly harp on the significance of an independent judiciary. Judicial independence, is and must remain a cherished virtue. However, it would be blinkered to not confront newer challenges that damage the credibility of our independent judiciary today — unpardonable delays and overweening judges taking on the mantle of national government by proxy. The Supreme Court 40 years on is a different institution — it must be cognizant of its history but not at the cost of being blind to its present.

Which of the following cannot be reasonably inferred from the passage?

A. The Supreme Court was complicit in curbing judicial independence during the Emergency.

B. Public interest litigations have, post-Emergency, led to the judiciary overreaching into the realm of legislature.

C. The Indian Judiciary ought not indulge in general supervisory jurisdiction to correct actions and policies of government.

D. The Indian judiciary must be equipped with technical competence and institutional capacity to ensure compliance to orders passed in relation to public interest litigations.

Q.114 Hard cases, it is said, make bad law. The adage is widely considered true for the Supreme Court of India which held in the height of the Emergency, in ADM Jabalpur v. Shivkant Shukla that detenus under the Maintenance of Internal Security Act (MISA) could not approach the judiciary if their fundamental rights were violated. Not only was the law laid down unconscionable, but it also smacked of a Court more "executive-minded than the executive", complicit in its own independence being shattered by an all-powerful government. So deep has been the impact of this judgment that the Supreme Court's current activist avatar is widely viewed as

having its genesis in a continuing need to atone. Expressions of such atonement have created another Court made to measure — this time not to the measure of the government but rather the aggrandised self-image of some of its judges.

Let us look back to the ADM Jabalpur case. As a court of law, the Supreme Court was called upon in the case to balance the interest of public order in an Emergency with the right to life and personal liberty guaranteed to every person. Nine High Courts called upon to perform the same function had found a nuanced answer by which they had held that the right to life cannot be absolutely subservient to public order merely because the government declared so — the legality of detentions could be judicially reviewed, though the intention of the government would not be second-guessed by the Court. This was a delicate balance. The Supreme Court however reversed this view and made the right to life and personal liberty literally a bounty of the government. Given that the consequences of their error were entirely to the government's advantage, it was widely viewed as the death of an independent judiciary. The excessively deferential, almost apologetic language used by the judges confirmed this impression.

Today, however, while public interest litigation has restored the independent image of the Supreme Court, it has achieved this at the cost of quality, discipline and the constitutional role judges are expected to perform. The Court monitors criminal trials, protects the environment, regulates political advertising, lays down norms for sexual harassment in the workplace, sets guidelines for adoption, supervises police reform among a range of other tasks of government. That all these tasks are crucial but tardily undertaken by government can scarcely be questioned. But for an unelected and largely unaccountable institution such as the Supreme Court to be at the forefront of matters relating to governance is equally dangerous — the choice of issues it takes up is arbitrary, their remit is not legal, their results often counterproductive, requiring a degree of technical competence and institutional capacity in ensuring compliance that the Court simply does not possess. This sets an unhealthy precedent for other courts and tribunals in the country, particularly the latter whose chairpersons are usually retired Supreme Court Justices. To take a particularly egregious example, the National Green Tribunal has banned diesel vehicles more than 10 years old in Delhi and if reports are to be believed, is considering imposing a congestion charge for cars as well. That neither of these are judicial functions and are being unjustly being usurped by a tribunal that has far exceeded its mandate, is evidence of the chain reaction that the Supreme Court's activist avatar has set off across the judicial spectrum.

Finally, the Court's activism adds to a massive backlog of regular cases that makes the Indian justice delivery mechanism, slow, unreliable and inefficient for the ordinary litigant. As on March 1, 2015, there were over 61,000 cases pending in the Supreme Court alone. It might be worthwhile for the Court to set its own house in order, concomitantly with telling other wings of government how to do so.

As we mark 40 years of the Emergency and the darkest period in the Supreme Court's history, it might be time to not single-mindedly harp on the significance of an independent judiciary. Judicial independence, is and must remain a cherished virtue.

However, it would be blinkered to not confront newer challenges that damage the credibility of our independent judiciary today — unpardonable delays and overweening judges taking on the mantle of national government by proxy. The Supreme Court 40 years on is a different institution — it must be cognizant of its history but not at the cost of being blind to its present.

The word "egregious" in the passage is farthest in meaning to :

A. outrageous   **B.** flagitious

C. distinguished   **D.** arrant

Q.115 Upholding the Law

Hard cases, it is said, make bad law. The adage is widely considered true for the Supreme Court of India which held in the height of the Emergency, in ADM Jabalpur v. Shivkant Shukla that detenus under the Maintenance of Internal Security Act (MISA) could not approach the judiciary if their fundamental rights were violated. Not only was the law laid down unconscionable, but it also smacked of a Court more "executive-minded than the executive", complicit in its own independence being shattered by an all-powerful government. So deep has been the impact of this judgment that the Supreme Court's current activist avatar is widely viewed as having its genesis in a continuing need to atone. Expressions of such atonement have created another Court made to measure — this time not to the measure of the government but rather the aggrandised self-image of some of its judges.

Let us look back to the ADM Jabalpur case. As a court of law, the Supreme Court was called upon in the case to balance the interest of public order in an Emergency with the right to life and personal liberty guaranteed to every person. Nine High Courts called upon to perform the same function had found a nuanced answer by which they had held that the right to life cannot be absolutely subservient to public order merely because the government declared so — the legality of detentions could be judicially reviewed, though the intention of the government would not be second-guessed by the Court. This was a delicate balance. The Supreme Court however reversed this view and made the right to life and personal liberty literally a bounty of the government. Given that the consequences of their error were entirely to the government's advantage, it was widely viewed as the death of an independent judiciary. The excessively deferential, almost apologetic language used by the judges confirmed this impression.

Today, however, while public interest litigation has restored the independent image of the Supreme Court, it has achieved this at the cost of quality, discipline and the constitutional role judges are expected to perform. The Court monitors criminal trials, protects the environment, regulates political advertising, lays down norms for sexual harassment in the workplace, sets guidelines for adoption, supervises police reform among a range of other tasks of government. That all these tasks are crucial but tardily undertaken by government can scarcely be questioned. But for an unelected and largely unaccountable institution such as the Supreme Court to be at the forefront of matters relating to governance is equally dangerous — the choice of issues it takes up is arbitrary, their remit is not legal, their results often counterproductive, requiring a degree of

technical competence and institutional capacity in ensuring compliance that the Court simply does not possess. This sets an unhealthy precedent for other courts and tribunals in the country, particularly the latter whose chairpersons are usually retired Supreme Court Justices. To take a particularly egregious example, the National Green Tribunal has banned diesel vehicles more than 10 years old in Delhi and if reports are to be believed, is considering imposing a congestion charge for cars as well. That neither of these are judicial functions and are being unjustly being usurped by a tribunal that has far exceeded its mandate, is evidence of the chain reaction that the Supreme Court's activist avatar has set off across the judicial spectrum.

Finally, the Court's activism adds to a massive backlog of regular cases that makes the Indian justice delivery mechanism, slow, unreliable and inefficient for the ordinary litigant. As on March 1, 2015, there were over 61,000 cases pending in the Supreme Court alone. It might be worthwhile for the Court to set its own house in order, concomitantly with telling other wings of government how to do so.

As we mark 40 years of the Emergency and the darkest period in the Supreme Court's history, it might be time to not single-mindedly harp on the significance of an independent judiciary. Judicial independence, is and must remain a cherished virtue. However, it would be blinkered to not confront newer challenges that damage the credibility of our independent judiciary today — unpardonable delays and overweening judges taking on the mantle of national government by proxy. The Supreme Court 40 years on is a different institution — it must be cognizant of its history but not at the cost of being blind to its present.

Which of the following is the author least likely to agree with?

A. The rise in judicial activism is in danger making the Supreme Court diffuse and ineffective, encroaching into the functions of government.

B. Where the Supreme Court is only moved for better governance and administration, which does not involve the exercise of any proper judicial function, it should refrain from acting.

C. Adoption, police reform and environment issues are the remit of the judiciary.

D. The Indian judicial system needs to focus on clearing the massive backlog of cases to re-establish its credibility.

Q.116 Child Rearing

More often than not, mothers are __________ for oddities of behavior in their offspring. __________, single mothers' children, raised even in the most difficult of times, do not display 'outrageous' patterns of behavior, as do those of nuclear families.

A. appreciated, consequently

B. berated, therefore

C. praised, in the same manner

D. blamed, interestingly enough

Q.117 Treating Depression

In measuring electrical activity in different parts of the brain, researchers found that people who describe themselves as generally happy have more activity in the left prefrontal lobe of their brains than do other people. Therefore, a medication for _________ the left prefrontal lobe of the brain would be an _________ treatment for clinical depression.

A. suppressing, ineffective
B. stimulating, effective
C. improving, impressive
D. challenging, practical

Q.118 Crossed Hands

Researchers found that when people's hands were crossed to other side of their bodies, it confused the brain by _________ the processing of information incoming from multiple regions. Lead researcher says the confusion results from a _________ between the brain's external mapping of where it normally assumes the hands will be (on the appropriate side of the body) and its internal map of the physical source of the new pain information.

A. quickening, alignment
B. transmitting, connection
C. interrupting, misalignment
D. hindering, alignment

Q.119 _______around race, gender and religion sometimes seems to have gone beyond _________ in academic circles. The world would do better if we could all speak with a lighter heart more often about these things.

A. insensitivity, the pale
B. sensitivity, parody
C. sensitivity, the pale
D. insensitivity, reality

Q.120 Democracy

Democracy is better _________through the ballot box than it is through the crowding of main squares, which is a __________ image, but a misleading representation of the "people's will"

A. focused, ineffective   B. affected, moving
C. effected, powerful   D. realized, fleeting

// Smart Answer Sheet //

Correct Percentage of students who answered correctly. **Skipped** | Percentage of students who skipped.

Q.	Ans.	Correct / Skipped	Q.	Ans.	Correct / Skipped	Q.	Ans.	Correct / Skipped	Q.	Ans.	Correct / Skipped	Q.	Ans.	Correct / Skipped
1	B	86.75 % / 11.07 %	17	B	85.91 % / 11.13 %	33	D	76.05 % / 13.25 %	49	C	83.0 % / 12.29 %	65	C	85.25 % / 12.27 %
2	A	77.26 % / 13.81 %	18	C	76.55 % / 13.36 %	34	B	88.09 % / 11.85 %	50	A	89.08 % / 10.2 %	66	A	79.79 % / 16.54 %
3	C	81.57 % / 14.26 %	19	A	81.72 % / 18.09 %	35	C	89.55 % / 10.28 %	51	B	83.07 % / 15.25 %	67	D	80.86 % / 15.57 %
4	A	84.3 % / 14.38 %	20	C	89.19 % / 10.44 %	36	A	81.83 % / 12.43 %	52	C	77.72 % / 12.48 %	68	C	77.27 % / 21.07 %
5	D	78.63 % / 13.14 %	21	A	88.61 % / 10.62 %	37	C	87.2 % / 10.84 %	53	A	82.22 % / 11.66 %	69	B	84.97 % / 12.23 %
6	B	86.0 % / 11.62 %	22	D	87.82 % / 10.65 %	38	C	81.52 % / 17.03 %	54	A	85.29 % / 12.3 %	70	C	87.48 % / 10.9 %
7	D	82.7 % / 13.05 %	23	D	82.71 % / 16.83 %	39	C	81.03 % / 15.14 %	55	C	79.22 % / 19.7 %	71	A	87.06 % / 11.6 %
8	B	83.99 % / 14.47 %	24	C	80.01 % / 16.24 %	40	C	86.34 % / 10.62 %	56	C	83.86 % / 15.31 %	72	B	76.26 % / 17.52 %
9	D	87.97 % / 11.56 %	25	B	84.18 % / 10.59 %	41	A	81.79 % / 10.19 %	57	D	81.97 % / 15.89 %	73	A	87.85 % / 10.77 %
10	B	89.26 % / 10.74 %	26	B	85.97 % / 12.72 %	42	D	79.96 % / 13.47 %	58	A	83.75 % / 10.86 %	74	D	81.35 % / 17.69 %
11	C	82.68 % / 14.1 %	27	A	77.07 % / 14.5 %	43	C	89.91 % / 10.05 %	59	A	83.46 % / 11.41 %	75	B	77.96 % / 20.38 %
12	D	89.52 % / 10.42 %	28	A	76.89 % / 14.27 %	44	A	77.05 % / 19.95 %	60	A	89.99 % / 10.01 %	76	B	82.06 % / 16.36 %
13	D	87.52 % / 10.26 %	29	D	79.95 % / 17.44 %	45	A	82.2 % / 10.45 %	61	D	83.92 % / 10.71 %	77	B	83.58 % / 13.99 %
14	B	78.42 % / 17.38 %	30	B	82.85 % / 16.26 %	46	D	76.16 % / 16.04 %	62	D	77.7 % / 19.06 %	78	A	79.55 % / 17.36 %
15	B	78.04 % / 10.6 %	31	C	84.16 % / 14.31 %	47	D	80.94 % / 11.17 %	63	C	79.26 % / 15.39 %	79	C	77.96 % / 13.2 %
16	C	82.62 % / 11.49 %	32	D	82.33 % / 10.47 %	48	B	77.01 % / 11.17 %	64	D	81.12 % / 16.2 %	80	A	76.53 % / 15.63 %

Q.	Ans.	Correct / Skipped	Q.	Ans.	Correct / Skipped	Q.	Ans.	Correct / Skipped	Q.	Ans.	Correct / Skipped	Q.	Ans.	Correct / Skipped
81	C	82.67 % / 12.28 %	89	C	88.2 % / 10.48 %	97	C	81.66 % / 17.97 %	105	D	78.37 % / 15.93 %	113	D	83.43 % / 16.52 %
82	B	83.18 % / 10.78 %	90	C	86.27 % / 13.33 %	98	A	88.37 % / 11.13 %	106	B	85.83 % / 12.03 %	114	C	84.58 % / 13.18 %
83	A	82.03 % / 14.98 %	91	C	86.39 % / 11.58 %	99	C	83.41 % / 15.3 %	107	C	79.15 % / 18.96 %	115	C	83.14 % / 10.42 %
84	D	85.88 % / 10.42 %	92	C	86.55 % / 12.38 %	100	D	76.92 % / 12.39 %	108	B	81.44 % / 14.79 %	116	D	89.34 % / 10.2 %
85	A	81.48 % / 13.98 %	93	D	78.54 % / 20.71 %	101	B	87.62 % / 12.22 %	109	A	89.01 % / 10.92 %	117	B	89.72 % / 10.03 %
86	C	88.28 % / 11.57 %	94	C	86.68 % / 12.71 %	102	D	88.62 % / 10.37 %	110	B	81.98 % / 10.02 %	118	C	85.77 % / 13.07 %
87	D	85.35 % / 11.4 %	95	D	85.4 % / 14.45 %	103	C	87.5 % / 11.8 %	111	A	86.02 % / 11.52 %	119	B	79.75 % / 18.39 %
88	D	89.31 % / 10.05 %	96	D	89.59 % / 10.09 %	104	C	81.64 % / 14.11 %	112	B	77.16 % / 13.71 %	120	C	85.51 % / 10.07 %

//Hints and Solutions//

1. A relation R on a non-empty set A is said to be reflexive iff xRx for all x ∈ R .

A relation R on a non-empty set A is said to be symmetric iff xRy⇔yRx, for all x , y ∈R .

A relation R on a non-empty set A is said to be transitive iff xRy and yRz ⇒ xRz, for all x ∈ R.

An equivalence relation satisfies all these three properties. .

None of the given relations satisfies all three properties of equivalence relation.

2. The given relation is not reflexive, as (3,3)∉R, The given relation is not symmetric, as (1,3)∈ R, but (3,1) ∉R, The given relation is transitive as (1,1))∈ R and (1,3))∈ R.

3. A relation R on a non empty set A is said to be symmetric iff xRy ⇔ yRx, for all x , y ∈ R Clearly, (1, 2), and (2, 1) both lies in R. Therefore, R is symmetric.

4. The number of elements in A x A is n x n = n^2. Hence ,the number of relations on A = number of subsets of A x A = $2^{n \times n}$ =$2n^2$

5. Since the domain is represented by the x- coordinate of the ordered pair (x , y).Therefore, domain of the given relation is { 1 , 2 }.

6. Since the range is represented by the y- coordinate of the ordered pair (x , y). Therefore, range of the given relation is { b , c }.

7. No. of elements in the set A = 4 . Therefore , the no. of elements in A × A = 4 × 4 = 16. As, the no. of relations in A × A = no. of subsets ofA × A = 2^{16} .

8. Conditions for the partition sub-sets to be an equivalence relation:

(i) The partition sub-sets must be disjoint i.e.there is no common elements between them

(ii) Their union must be equal to the main set (super-set)

Here, the set A={1,2,3,4,5,6},the partition sub-sets {1,3},{2,4,5},{6} are pairwise disjoint and their union i.e. {1,3} U {2,4,5} U {6} = {1,2,3,4,5,6} = A, which is the condition for the partition sub-sets to be an equivalence relation of the set A

9. By definition of Equivalence Relation, a relation is said to be equivalence if it is reflexive,symmetric and transitive.

10. $\sin^2 25^0 + \sin^2 65^0$ $= \sin^2(90^0 - 65^0) + \sin^2 65^0 = \cos^2 65^0 + \sin^2 65^0 = 1$

11. If x+y=π/4 then (1 + tanx)(1 + tany)

⇒(1+tanx)(1+tan(π/4−x))

⇒(1+tanx)(1+₁₋ₜₐₙₓ/₍₁₊ₜₐₙₓ

⇒(1+tanx)(2/(1+tanx))=2

12. f(π)=(cos4π+tan3π) gives the same value as f (0).Therefore,the period of the function is π

13.

$$\frac{\cos 8^0 - \sin 8^0}{\cos 8^0 + \sin 8^0}$$

$$= \frac{\dfrac{\cos 8^0}{\cos 8^0} - \dfrac{\sin 8^0}{\cos 8^0}}{\dfrac{\cos 8^0}{\cos 8^0} + \dfrac{\sin 8^0}{\cos 8^0}}$$

$$= \frac{1 - \tan 8^0}{1 + \tan 8^0} =$$

$$\tan(45^0 - 8^0) = \tan 37^0$$

14. $\cot\theta - \tan\theta = \sec\theta$

$$\Rightarrow \frac{\cos\theta}{\sin\theta} - \frac{\sin\theta}{\cos\theta} = \frac{1}{\cos\theta}$$

$$\Rightarrow \frac{\cos^2\theta - \sin^2\theta}{\sin\theta.\cos\theta} = \frac{1}{\cos\theta}$$

$$\Rightarrow \cos^2\theta - \sin^2\theta = \sin\theta$$

$$\Rightarrow \cos 2\theta = \sin\theta$$

$$\Rightarrow \sin\left(\frac{\pi}{2} - 2\theta\right) = \sin\theta$$

$$\Rightarrow \frac{\pi}{2} - 2\theta = \theta \quad \Rightarrow \theta = \frac{\pi}{6}$$

General solution is $\theta = n\pi + (-1)^n \dfrac{\pi}{6}$

15. $\sin 265^0 - \cos 265^0 = -\cos 5^0 + \sin 5^0$ between 0 to 90^0, $\cos\theta > \sin\theta$, therefore answer is negative.

16.

$$[xyz]_{1 \times 3} \begin{bmatrix} a & h & g \\ h & b & f \\ g & f & c \end{bmatrix}_{3 \times 3} \begin{bmatrix} x \\ y \\ z \end{bmatrix}_{3 \times 1} = [A]_{1 \times 1}$$

(

where ; matrix A denotes the product of three given matrices.)

17. Only a null matrix can be symmetric as well as skew symmetric.

In Symmetric Matrix A^T = A,

Skew Symmetric Matrix A^T = -A,

Given that the matrix is satisfying both the properties.Therefore, Equating the RHS we get A = -A i.e 2A = 0 .

Therefore A=0,which is a null matrix.

18. If the product of any square matrix with itself is the matrix itself, then the matrix is called Idempotent.

19. By the property of inverse $(AB)^{-1}$ is equal to $B^{-1}A^{-1}$.

20. A maximum or a minimum may or may not exist for a linear programming problem if the feasible region is unbounded. However if it exits it must occur at the corner points of R.

21. Let R be the feasible region for a linear programming problem, and let Z = ax + by be the objective function. If R is bounded, then the objective function Z has both a maximum and a minimum value on R and each of these occur at the corner point (vertex) of R.

22. Let R be the feasible region for a linear programming problem,and let Z = ax + by be the objective function. If R is bounded, then the objective function Z has both a maximum and a minimum value on R and each of these occurs at a corner point (vertex) of R.

23. In Corner point method for solving a linear programming problem the first step is : To find the feasible region of the linear programming problem and determine its corner points (vertices) either by inspection or by solving the two equations of the lines intersecting at that point.

24. In Corner point method for solving a linear programming problem the second step after finding the feasible region of the linear programming problem and determining its corner points is : To evaluate the objective function Z = ax + by at each corner point.

25. In Corner point method for solving a linear programming problem one finds the feasible region of the linear programming problem ,determines its corner points and evaluates the objective function Z = ax + by at each corner point. If Mand m respectively be the largest and smallest values at corner points then If the feasible region is bounded, M and m respectively are the maximum and minimum values of the objective function .

26. In Corner point method for solving a linear programming problem one finds the feasible region of the linear programming problem ,determines its corner points and evaluates the objective function Z = ax + by at each corner point. Let M and m respectively be the largest and smallest values at corner points. In case feasible region is unbounded, M is the maximum value of the objective function if the open half plane determined by ax + by > M has no point in common with the feasible region . Otherwise, Z has no maximum value.

27. In Corner point method for solving a linear programming problem one finds the feasible region of the linear programming problem ,determines its corner points and evaluates the objective function Z = ax + by at each corner point. Let M and m respectively be the largest and smallest values at corner points. In case feasible region is unbounded, m is the minimum value of the objective function if the open half plane determined by ax + by < m has no point in common with the feasible region . Otherwise, Z has no minimum point.

28. If two corner points of the feasible region are both optimal solutions of the same type, i.e., both produce the same maximum or minimum , then any point on the line segment joining these two points is also an optimal solution of the same type .

29. S= {HH, HT, TH , TT}

E ={HH}

F= {TT}

E∩F=φ

⇒P(E)=14,P(F)=14,P(E∩F)=0

⇒P(E/F)=P(E∩F)P(F)=01/4=0

30. We have ,

P(E) = 0.6, P(F) = 0.3 and P(E ∩ F) = 0.2, then ,

P(E/F)=P(E∩F)/P(F)=0.2/0.3=2/3

P(F/E)=P(E∩F)/P(E)=0.2/0.6=1/3

31. We have , P(B) = 0.5 and P (A ∩ B) = 0.32

P(A/B)=P(A∩B)/P(B)=0.32/0.5=16/25

32. We have ,

P (A) = 0.8, P (B) = 0.5 and P(B|A) = 0.4

P(B/A)=P(A∩B)/P(A)⇒P(A∩B)=P(A)×P(B/A)=0.8×0.4=0.32

33. We have ,

P (A) = 0.8, P (B) = 0.5 and P(B|A) = 0.4

P(B/A)=P(A∩B)/P(A)⇒P(A∩B)=P(A)×P(B/A)=0.8×0.4=0.32

P(A/B)=P(A∩B)/P(B)=0.32/0.5=0.64

34. The difference between 3-digit number and its reverse is 99 times the difference between its extreme (hundred and units) digits.

As the first difference is 396, the second is 4.

Further as the digits are in AP and the hundred's digits is less than the unit's digit, we have following possibilities:

135,246,357,468,579.....

35. Let a children of 7 years and b children of 5 years be taken.

Then, 7a+5b=48

This is possible only when x=4 and b=4

Hence, only one combination is possible.

36. Let the progression be a,a+d,a+2d ....

⇒a+11d=7a+7d

⇒6a=4d

⇒3a=2d

Also, a+7d=10a+3

⇒7d=9a+3

⇒7d=6d+3

⇒d=3,a=2

The GP is 2,2×3,2×32,2×33,2×34

So the 5th term is 162

37. All amounts are in thousands of rupees.

Let P's total property be (20+10p)

The donation is 20+p

The 4th son's share is 20+p

The 1st son's share is 120+p

The 2nd son's share is 100+p

The 3rd son's share is 60+p

As, 4th,3rd and 2nd are in AP

Thus, 300+4p=9p

$\Rightarrow$p=60

The 3rd son's share is 60+p=120,000

38. We have ,

P (A) = 0.8, P (B) = 0.5 and P(B|A) = 0.4

P(B/A)=P(A∩B)/P(A)⇒P(A∩B)=P(A)×P(B/A)=0.8×0.4=0.32

∴P(A∪B)=P(A)+P(B)−P(A∩B)=0.8+0.5−0.32=1.30−0.32=0.98

39. if 2P(A)=P(B)=5/13 , therefore P(A)=5/26P(A/B)=2/5⇒P(A∩B)P(B)=2/5

⇒P(A∩B)=2/5×P(B)=2/5×5/13=2/13

∴P(A∪B)=P(A)+P(B)−P(A∩B)

=5/26+5/13−2/13=11/26

40. ∴P(A∪B)=P(A)+P(B)−P(A∩B)

⇒7/11=6/11+5/11−P(A∩B)

⇒P(A∩B)=4/11

P(A/B)=P(A∩B)/P(B)=(4/11)/(5/11)=4/5

41. If P(A) =6/11, P(B) =5/11and P(A ∪ B) =7/11

∴P(A∪B)=P(A)+P(B)−P(A∩B)

⇒7/11=6/11+5/11−P(A∩B)

⇒P(A∩B)=4/11

P(B/A)=P(A∩B)P(A)=(4/11)/(6/11)=23

42.

$$\int_{1}^{2} |y|\, dx = \int_{1}^{2} |x|^3\, dx = \int_{1}^{2} x^3\, dx = \left[\frac{x^4}{4}\right]_{1}^{2} = \left[\frac{16}{4} - \frac{1}{4}\right] = \frac{15}{4}\ \text{sq.units.}$$

43.

Required area :

$$= \int y\,dx + \int y\,dx = \int \sin 2x\, dx - \int \sin 2x\, dx = \left[\frac{-\cos 2x}{2}\right] + \left[\frac{\cos 2x}{2}\right] =$$

$$\frac{1}{2} + \frac{1}{2} = 1$$

44.

Required area :

$$= \int_{0}^{\frac{\pi}{2}} y\,dx = \int_{0}^{\frac{\pi}{2}} 2\cos x\,dx = [2\sin x]_{0}^{\frac{\pi}{2}} = 2$$

Therefore , total area from x= 0 to x = 2π is 4 X 2= 8 sq. units.

45.

Required area :

$$\int_{1}^{e} \log_e x\,dx = [x\log x - x]_{1}^{e} = (e\log e - e) - (1\log 1 - 1) = 1$$

46.

Required area :

$$= \int_{0}^{1} y\,dx = \int_{0}^{1} 2\sqrt{1 - x^2}\,dx = 2\left[\frac{x\sqrt{1-x^2}}{2} + \frac{1}{2}\sin^{-1} x\right]_{0}^{1} = 2\left(\frac{1}{2}\sin^{-1} 1\right) = \frac{\pi}{2}$$

47. y = 4−x²>0⇒−2<x<2 And y=4−x²<0⇒x<−2 or x > 2

Required area:

$$= \int_{0}^{2} (4 - x^2)\,dx + \left|\int_{2}^{3} (4 - x^2)\,dx\right| = \frac{16}{3} + \left|-\frac{7}{3}\right| = \frac{23}{3}\ sq.\,units$$

48.

The given curve consists of two straight lines x + y = 1 (x ≥ 0)and -x + y = 1 (x ≤ 0)

$$\text{Required area} = 2\int_{0}^{1} y\,dx = 2\int_{0}^{1} (1 - x)\,dx = 2\int_{0}^{1} (1 - x)\,dx = 2\left[x - \frac{x^2}{2}\right]_{0}^{1} = 1\ \text{sq.unit}$$

49. The vector whose magnitude is always 1 or unity is called a Unit Vector.

50. Two vectors whose initial point is same are called co- initial vectors.

51. Two vectors A and B are said to be collinear , if they are parallel to the same line irrespective of their magnitudes and directions.

52. Two vectors having same magnitude as well as same direction are always equal.

53. Negative of $\vec{a}$ is equal to $-\vec{a}$, i.e. A vector whose magnitude is the same as that of $\vec{a}$,but direction is opposite to that of $\vec{a}$.

54. If a vector is multiplied by any scalar then , the result is always a vector.

55. Addition of two vectors i.e. vector addition is commutative. i.e.$\vec{a} + \vec{b} = \vec{b} + \vec{a}$.

56. Angle between skew lines is the angle between two lines which are parallel to the given skew lines and passing through a common point in space

57. The vector equation of a line that passes through the given point whose position vector is $\vec{a}$ and parallel to a given vector $\vec{b}$ is given by : $\vec{r} = \vec{a} + \lambda\vec{b}$.,

λ∈R

Where,$\vec{r}$ =xi+yj+zk

$\vec{a}$ =a₁i+b₁j+c₁k

$\vec{b}$ =a₁i+b₁j+c₁k

58.

$$\lim_{x \to \pi} \frac{1+\cos^3 x}{(x-\pi)^2} = \lim_{h \to 0} \frac{1+\cos^3(\pi+h)}{(h)^2}$$

$$= \lim_{h \to 0} \frac{1-\cos^3 h}{(h)^2}$$

$$= \lim_{h \to 0} \frac{1-\cos h}{h^2} \cdot \lim_{h \to 0} (1 + \cos h + \cos^2 h)$$

$$= \frac{1}{2}(1 + 1 + 1) = \frac{3}{2}$$

59.

$$\lim_{x\to 0} \frac{\cos x \cdot x - \cot x}{x} = \lim_{x\to 0} \frac{1-\cos x}{x \sin x} = \lim_{x\to 0} \frac{(1-\cos x)(1+\cos x)}{x \sin x(1-\cos x)} = \lim_{x\to 0} \frac{\sin x}{x} \cdot \frac{1}{1+\cos x} = \frac{1}{2}$$

60.

$$\lim_{x\to 0} \frac{1-\cos 4x}{x^2}$$
$$= \lim_{x\to 0} \frac{4\sin 4x}{2x}$$
$$= \lim_{x\to 0} \frac{16\cos 4x}{2} = 8$$

(using L'Hospital Rule)

61. Insect invites disease and War invites destruction.

62. Cover is used to protect book in same way and frame is use to protect painting.

63. Float means above water and sink means under water. In same way, Boat floats on water and submarine moves under water.

64. Dam is constructed for water and Trade policy is formulated for Trade policy.

65. Man's Movement :

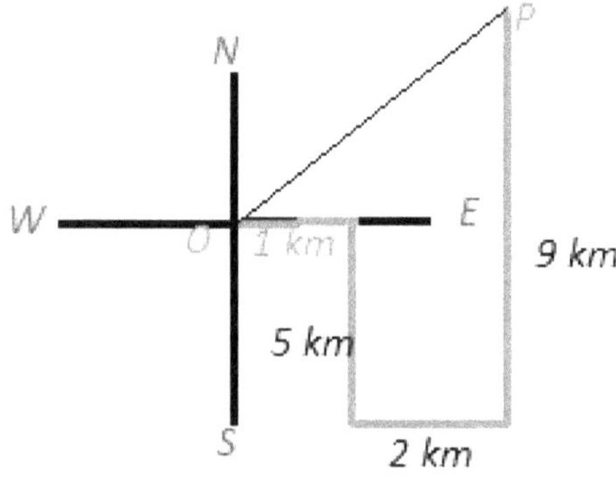

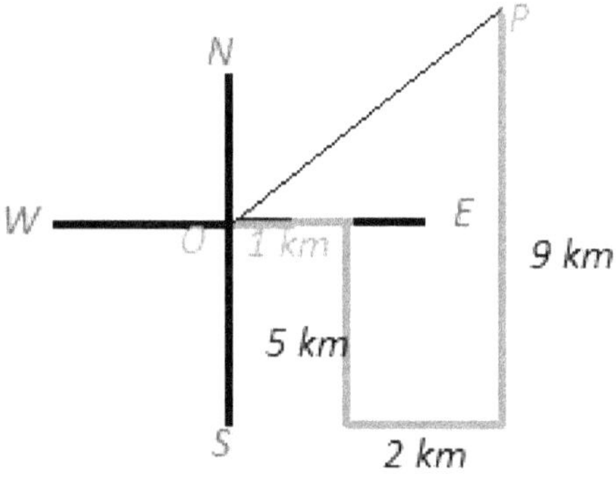

66. Movements are as follows:

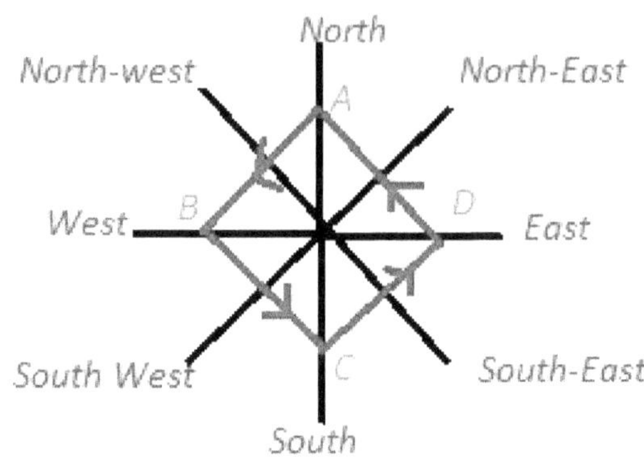

Now, I am going in North-East Direction.

67. Man\'s Movement :

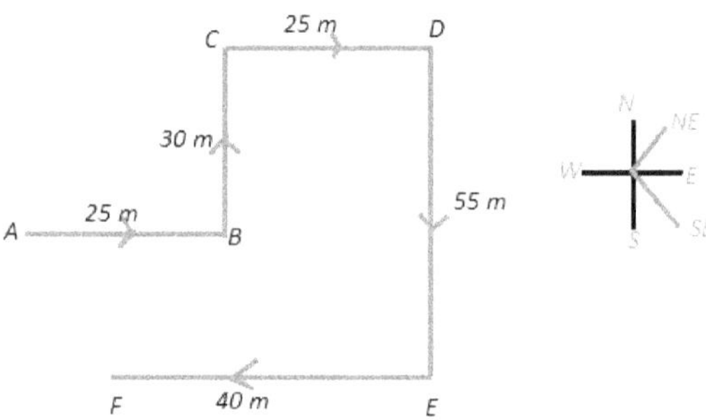

Finally he is towards the South-East from his starting Point.

68. If South-east becomes North and North East becomes West, therefore, the whole figure moves through 135 degree . Hence, West will be South-East.

See, Actual figure is rotating 135 degree anticlockwise. So, When West will be rotated by same degree anticlockwise. It will hold the place of south-East.

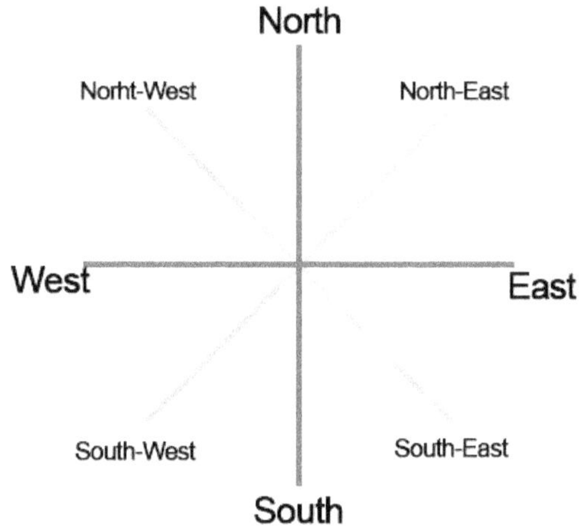

69. As the Central Government faced financial loss on accounts of giving rebate on farming for the last few years, therefore, they declared to finish the rebate on farming. Hence, II is the cause while I is the effect.

70. Clearly, lesser number of people is visiting a place during the week days and more people are visiting during the weekend, both imply events that go together, and must have happened due to a common cause such as, it being a holiday during the weekend.

71. As Ram's father was ill so he brought medicine on the advice of doctor. Therefore, Statement I is cause and II is the effect.

72. damage of crops due to high temperature may have resulted in a short supply of vegetables and hence an increase in their prices. Thus, statement II is cause and I is its effect.

73. Logic:

Column-Wise

(First Column Element * 4th Column element) - (2nd column element * 3rd Column element) = Last Column Element

(4*2)-(5+3) = 0

(7*4)-(3+4) = 21

(6*5)-(4+4) = 22

(9*5)-(6+5) = 34.

74. Logic:

First Row Element - Third Row Element = Second Row Element.

56 - 44 = 12

65 - 14 = 51

78 - 48 = 30.

Hence, in the missing number should be 51.

75. 20 = 8 x 2 + 4

15 = 3 x 2 + 9

Hence,

The number on the blank space,

6 x 2 + 6 = 18.

76. In the first column,

27- 7*2 = 13

In the second column,

144 - 45*2 = 54

So,

in the third column,

68 -32*2 = 4

77. The steps are labelled using alphabets from A to J.

TO MAKE IT EASY, WE HAVE ASSIGNED NUMBERS TO THE STEPS AS FOLLOWS:

Labelled with alphabets : A B C D E F G H I J

Labelled with numbers : 1 2 3 4 5 6 7 8 9 10

The frog takes total 60 minutes and takes 4 step length jumps every time.

Thus,

1st minute : 1 + 4 = 5th step (E)

2nd minute : 5 + 4 = 9th step (I)

3rd minute : 9 + 4 = 3rd step (C)

4th minute : 3 + 4 = 7th step (G)

5th minute : 7 + 4 = 11 = 10+1 = 1st step (A)

The same process is repeated 12 x 5 times.

Then, the jumping positions are

1 5 9 3 7

1 5 9 3 7

1 5 9 3 7 and so on.

After 15 cycles, frog will be in the 1st position i.e., at 5th minute, 10th minute,

15minutes....60th minute frog will be in the 1st position.

i.e., at 60t

78. Let B be the number of brothers and S be the number of sisters in the family.

Consider any two boys. They would be having (B - 2) brothers (excluding the two). But this number is equal to the number of sisters they have.

Therefore,

B - 2 = S

or , B - S = 2 ....(1) Each girl will have (S - 1) sisters. Twice the number of sisters = 2(S - 1).

Since, each girl has twice as many brothers as sisters, we have, 2(S-1)-2 = B

2S - 4 = B .... (2)

Substituting, eqn (2) in Eqn (1), we get

2S - 4 - S = 2

S = 6

On substituting S = 6 in eqn (1) , we get

B - 6 = 2

B = 8.

79. Total number of trees,

= 7+14-1

= 20

80. Let, A = x

Then, B = 2x

and, F = 4x

C = x/2

and D = x/4

Thus, The second oldest is B.

81. Scanner is right answer

82. SMTP (Simple Mail Transfer Protocol) is a TCP/IP protocol used in sending and receiving e-mail. However, since it is limited in its ability to queue messages at the receiving end, it is usually used with one of two other protocols, POP3 or IMAP that let the user save messages in a server mailbox and download them periodically from the server. SMTP usually is implemented to operate over Internet port 25.

Many mail servers now support Extended Simple Mail Transfer Protocol (ESMTP), which allows multimedia files to be delivered as e-mail.

83. In 1945, Professor J. von Neumann, who was then working at the Moore School of Engineering in Philadelphia, where the E.N.I.A.C. had been built, issued on behalf of a group of his co-workers, a report on the logical design of digital computers.

84. In MS Excel, formulas are equations that perform various calculations in your worksheets. Though Microsoft has introduced a handful of new functions over the years, the concept of Excel spreadsheet formulas is the same in all versions of Excel 2016, Excel 2013, Excel 2010, Excel 2007 and lower.

All Excel formulas begin with an equal sign (=).

85. You can set different size for each recycle bin is correct answer

86. You can increase free space of disk by sending files in recycle bin is right answer

87. Control panel is right answer

88. All of the above is right answer

89. The automatic addition of names and addresses from a database to letters and envelopes in order to facilitate sending mail, especially advertising, to many addresses.

90. mail merge is right answer

91. type a biography is right answer

92. The gutter margin is a typographical term used to designate an additional margin added to a page layout to compensate for the part of the paper made unusable by the binding process. In a facing pages layout (Word refers to this type of layout as "mirror margins"), the gutter margin is on the very inside of both pages.

93. All of above is right answer

94. Both of above is right answer

95. All of above is right answer

96. You can not set page border in Excel is right answer

97. Notes is right answer

98. You can type text directly into a PowerPoint slide but typing in text box is more convenient is right answer

99.

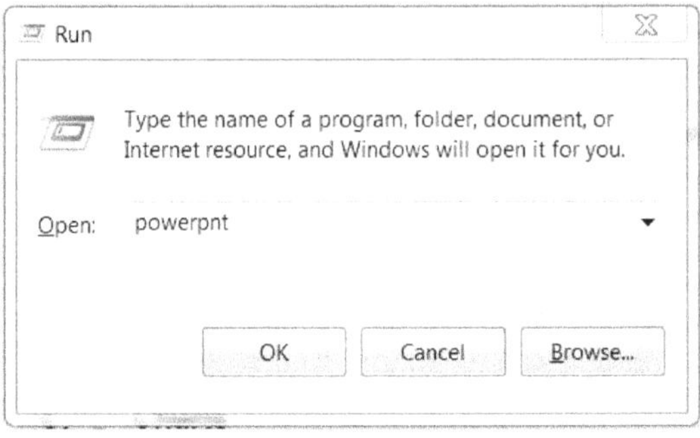

100. Animations is right answer

101. Sentence C talks of how verb usage goes up when unnecessary words are reduced. This ties in with sentence A which talks of how good writers use more verbs. It is also clear C follows A.

Sentence B says it is hard to write without verbs. Sentence D adds to this saying that "use verbs" is hence not good advice. Therefore D follows B.

By looking at the sentences we see that sentence A makes a good start to the paragraph.

Hence, the answer is ACBD

102. Sentences C and D start with "it" and "that" respectively and can be hence ruled out as starting sentences for the paragraph.

Sentence A talks of a vision. Sentence D starts with "That vision". So D should follow A. Only options (a) and (d) have this arrangement.

Sentence B is a general premise that the French Revolution invented modern revolution.

Sentence C talks of how the revolution brought in modernity by destroying the foundations of the Old Regime. We can see that there is a link between sentences B and C- both talk of "modernity". C follows B.

Sentence A talks of a "new moral universe" while Sentence C talks of the old regime. So again, A follows C.

Hence, the answer is BCAD

103. C talks of the South Pole being benign. D refers to the word benign in quotes. So, D should come after C, and quite possibly immediately after C.

The idea conveyed here is that the South Pole has the most benign weather and it is benign from March to September. So we can directly eliminate choice (d).

Sentence C makes a better choice for starting the paragraph than A.

Sentence A talks of impeccable conditions for astronomy and B explains what it is.

Hence, the answer is CDAB

104. This paragraph is focuses how set standards and "operating systems" tend to perpetuate, adding to the influence of the country that sets it.

Sentence B starts with a "nor", so we should ideally have an example preceding this. It is clear that only sentence C which talks of the dollar not being easily replaceable by other currencies fits the bill.

So we have the order CB_

Of the given answer options, only 1 and 3 have this pattern.

We can see D completes the paragraph.

Should the paragraph start with sentence A or C?

Sentence A is an example of how standards perpetuate. Sentence C starts off stating the premise of the paragraph, and continues the thought with an example. Hence C is a better sentence to start the paragraph than A.

Hence, the answer is CBAD

105. Sentences B and D talk of flowers and flowering plants. Sentence B talks of how land plants existed without flowers for several millions of years. Sentence D talks of when flowering plants appeared. It is clear D follows B.

Sentence C speaks of "equally familiar grasses". So obviously, some other example- in this case, flowering plants- precedes this.

Sentences A and C talk of the evolution of grasses. A follows C.

Hence, the answer is BDCA

106. Note that there is a 'but' in the sentence immediately following the clause given. So the option that starts with "though" isn't correct.

What do competitive exams allow/not allow? In answer to this question, "the use of a calculator" is the correct wording of the response. Both "using calculators" and "using of calculators" are incorrect.

The quantifier 'every' stresses all the members of the complete group. Here, we want to say that only some (not all) exams allow the use of a calculator. So option c is also incorrect.

The correct option is (b). Not all competitive exams allow the use of a calculator, but where they are permitted, there are restrictions on the models allowed.

Hence, the answer is option B

107. As the sentence starts off with "Denouncing it...", the clause that follows has to first refer to who denounced it- in this case, it is the critics.

Option B is not correct, as it implies critics impose draconian limits on the activities of trade unions.

The pronoun "which" after the "Lobbying Act" in option C clarifies that it is the Act that limits the activities of the trade unions.

Hence, the answer is option C

108. There are 3 errors to spot in the given sentence:

Firstly, as the sentence starts with "while...", any option that follows this clause with "but" is incorrect.

Secondly, "its" is a personal pronoun- not the correct word to use here. "It's" meaning "it is" is the right word to use in the given context.

Thirdly, the sentence says people are paying greater attention to the terrorist threat "then" they used to. This is incorrect. The correct word to use instead is "than".

The only option that corrects these errors is B.

Hence, the answer is option B

109. In the given sentence, 'they' in the second clause seems to refer to 'long-term risk', which is the subject of the first clause. So it is grammatically incorrect.

Now let us look at the answer options.

Option C does not make sense. So we rule this out.

Option B has two independent clauses- (1) Rarely do air-quality indices take long-term risk into account, and (2) they also vary from place to place. Each of these is a sentence in its own right. When joining two independent clauses without the use of a coordinating conjunction (and, but, or, or nor), a semicolon has to be used, not a comma. So option B is incorrect.

In option A, again, there are two independent clauses - (1) Air-quality indices rarely take long-term risk into account, and (2) they also vary from place to place. The clauses are joined by a semicolon. So option A is grammatically correct.

Hence, the answer is option A

110. "Correct" is a positive description of the solution, while "complicated" is not. So a parallel sentence construction (in this case, 'not only...but') is inappropriate.

Option C uses 'only' inappropriately.

Option B is the correct choice.

Hence, the answer is option B

111. This passage starts off discussing the Emergency, considered as the "darkest hour" in India's judicial history and the impact the decision of the Supreme Court in the ADM Jabalpur case had on its subsequent rulings, leading to its current "activist avatar" in the continuing need to atone.

Let us consider the choices given.

a. An Atonement Gone Too Far

This title summarizes the main idea of the passage very well. The passage talks of the Supreme Court's unconscionable stance during the Emergency and its subsequent "activist avatar" to atone.

b. Sanctimony from a Ruined Pedestal

This title is too severe and condemnatory of the Supreme Court and does not fit the tone of the passage. While the author does talk of the Supreme Court damaging its credibility in the ADM, he believes that the independent image of the Supreme Court has since been restored.

c. The ADM Jabalpur's Case: The Supreme Court's Darkest Hour

This title deals with only one aspect of the passage. It does not capture the crux of the passage and can hence be ruled out as a choice for title.

d. Overcompensating for Past Mistakes

This title is similar in meaning to option a. However, the title talks of "past mistakes" whereas the passage discusses only one case- ADM Jabalpur- and the stand taken by the Supreme Court in the case. Option a wins over option d as a title for the paragraph.

Hence, the answer is A

112. In saying that the Supreme Court was "more executive-minded than the executive" during the Emergency, the author implies that the Supreme Court was more extreme and illiberal than the Government in imposing the rules of the Emergency, an approach not justified by the law.

Let us consider the options.

a. The Supreme Court abdicated its independence to an authoritarian government by embracing its perspective.

The abdication of judicial independence by the Court to an authoritarian government does not explain the given phrase, 'more "executive –minded than the executive"'. It does not talk of the mindset or approach of the Court, which is what the author is discussing.

b. The Supreme Court was more emphatic than the Government about exercising executive power under the MISA.

This option is right on target in explaining why, according to the author, the Supreme Court was "more" executive-minded (unyielding) than the executive (the government) in enforcing the MISA and curbing fundamental rights.

c. The Supreme Court reflected the unconscionable actions taken by the government by upholding its laws.

The emphasis in the phrase "more executive-minded than the executive" is on the 'more'. The Supreme Court did not merely reflect the unjust actions of the government by upholding its laws: it went one step further, according to the author, by being more illiberal than the government in enforcing the law. Hence option c does not capture the essence of what the writer means when he says "more executive- minded than the executive".

d. The Supreme Court wanted to curry favor with the government through its deferential decisions during Emergency. The Supreme Court cannot be called "more executive-minded than the executive" for merely being deferential, i.e, submissive and complicit with the government during emergency. As discussed earlier, the key word here is "more". Statement d does not explain the phrase given satisfactorily.

Hence, the answer is B

113. Let us consider the statements in order and determine whether they are true or false.

Statement a - The Supreme Court was complicit in curbing judicial independence during the Emergency.

From the passage, we know this to be true.

Statement b - Public interest litigations have, post-Emergency, led to the judiciary overreaching into the realm of legislature.

Again, this is true, discussed at length in the passage.

Statement c - The Indian Judiciary ought not indulge in general supervisory jurisdiction to correct actions and policies of government.

True. The author opines in the passage that "an unelected and largely unaccountable institution such as the Supreme Court to be at the forefront of matters relating to governance is equally dangerous".

Statement d - The Indian judiciary must be equipped with technical competence and institutional capacity to ensure compliance to orders passed in relation to public interest litigations.

This is false. The author believes that the Supreme Court should focus on only judicial functions and not act in matters relating to governance where it does not have the competence or capacity to ensure compliance.

Hence, the answer is D

114. The word "egregious" is used in the passage to refer to the example of the National Green Tribunal, which the author believes has "unjustly usurped" functions that "far exceeded its mandate".

The words outrageous, flagitious and arrant all mean flagrant or extraordinary in a bad way and are similar in meaning to the word egregious used in the passage.

The word "distinguished" , which means extraordinary in a good way, is the word farthest in meaning to egregious.

Hence, the answer is distinguished

115. Statement a- The rise in judicial activism is in danger making the Supreme Court diffuse and ineffective, encroaching into the functions of government.

The author is likely to agree with this statement. The passage warns of the rising judicial activism of the Supreme Court and asserts that it should rein in its reach to legal matters and not involve itself in issues that the elected government should deal with.

Statement b- Where the Court is only moved for better governance and administration, which does not involve the exercise of any proper judicial function, it should refrain from acting.

Again, this is a clear point made by the author in the passage. He is likely to agree with this statement.

Statement c- Adoption, police reform and environment issues are the remit of the judiciary.

Adoption, police reform and environment issues are some topics the passage mentions are "crucial tasks" that are "tardily" dealt with by the government, but outside the remit of the Supreme Court. The author is unlikely to agree with statement c.

Statement d- The Indian judicial system needs to focus on clearing the massive backlog of cases to reestablish its credibility.

The author mentions this in the passage as the biggest challenge faced by the judiciary. He is likely to agree with statement d.

Hence, the answer is distinguished

116. Blank (1): We are talking of "oddities" in behavior of the offspring, which is not a positive thing. So we can directly eliminate options A and C, which give the words "appreciated" and "praised" respectively for the first blank.

Blank (2): The second sentence gives evidence that single mothers are better at managing kids, so they cannot be blamed for anything. We can hence eliminate the option that suggests 'therefore', since it doesn't logically fit.

So the correct answer is choice (D) blamed, interestingly enough.

Hence, the answer is D

117. Blank (1): If people are happy when there is more activity in a lobe, why should we suppress that lobe? 'Improving' doesn't make much sense here either. A medication to stimulate that lobe makes sense, not 'challenge' the lobe.

Blank (2): We are discussing some new insight; the discussion is towards finding something that will work. So the correct word here is effective.

Correct Answer: B. stimulating, effective

Hence, the answer is B

118. Blank (1): You cannot transmit the processing of information. Choice B is ruled out.

Blank (2): Confusion cannot arise out of alignment. So we can eliminate choices A and D.

The correct answer is (C) interrupting, misalignment

Hence, the answer is C

119. This is a slightly tricky one as more than one set of words seems to fits the blanks in sentence 1. We need to see what the second sentence says to understand the context.

It is clear from sentence 2 that talks of the need to speak with a "lighter heart" that the first sentence is not about the general lack of sensitivity around race, gender and religion in academic circles. So the correct word for blank (1) is sensitivity.

Blank (2): Going beyond the pale means going beyond limits of propriety. It doesn't make sense when used with the word 'sensitivity' in blank (1). The word parody makes sense when put in blank 2.

Hence, the correct answer is (b) sensitivity, parody.

Hence, the answer is B

120. Blank (1): We can rule out focused and affected as choices, as they don't make sense in this blank. Effected and realized are possibilities here.

Blank (2): The part of the sentence that reads "but a misleading representation of people's will" tells us clearly that the appropriate word for this blank is powerful. A fleeting image does not make an impact and so does not make sense when used with "but..."

So the correct answer choice is (c) effected, powerful

Hence, the answer is C

Mathematics

Q.1 If $x - y = 1$, then $x^3 - y^3 - 3xy$ equals

A. 0   **B.** 1   **C.** 2   **D.** $x^2 - y^2$

Q.2 If $6 \geq x \geq -2$ and $4 \geq y \geq -4$, then limits for y/x where x and y are non zero integers, is

A. $\dfrac{y}{x} \geq 2, \dfrac{y}{x} \leq \dfrac{2}{3}$ **B.** $\dfrac{y}{x} \geq \dfrac{-2}{3}, \dfrac{y}{x} \leq 2$

C. $\dfrac{y}{x} \geq \dfrac{-2}{3}, \dfrac{y}{x} \leq \dfrac{1}{4}$ **D.** $\dfrac{y}{x} \geq -4, \dfrac{y}{x} \leq 4$

Q.3 If (a, n)! is defined as product of n consecutive numbers starting from a, where a and n are both natural numbers, and if H is the HCF of (a, n)! and n!, then what can be said about H?

A. $h = a!$ **B.** $h = n!$ **C.** $h \geq n!$ **D.** $h \geq a * n$

Q.4 If a and b are prime numbers, which of the following is true?

I. a^2 has three positive integer factors.

II. ab has four positive integer factors.

III. a^3 has four positive integer factors.

Codes

A. I and II only   **B.** II and III only

C. All of these   **D.** None of these

Q.5 If $x = b + c$, $y = c a$, $z = a b$, then $x^2 + y^2 + z^2 - 2xy - 2xz + 2yz$ is equal to

A. $a + b + c$ **B.** $4b^2$ **C.** abc   **D.** $a^2 + b^2$

Q.6 An Egyptian fraction has a numerator equal to 1, and its denominator is a positive integer. What is the maximum number of different Egyptian fraction such that their sum is equal to 1, and their denominators are equal to 10 or less?

A. 3   **B.** 5   **C.** 7   **D.** 9

Q.7 Let R be a non-empty relation on a collection of sets defined by ARB if and only if $A \cap B = \emptyset$

Then (pick the TRUE statement)

A. R is relexive and transitive

B. R is symmetric and not transitive

C. R is an equivalence relation

D. R is not relexive and not symmetric

Q.8 The binary relation $S = \Phi$ (empty set) on set $A = \{1, 2, 3\}$ is

A. neither reflexive nor symmetric

B. symmetric and relexive

C. transitive and relexive

D. transitive and symmetric

Q.9 Which of the following sets are null sets ?

A. {0}   **B.** ø

C. { }   **D.** Both (b) & (c)

Q.10 Number of subsets of a set of order three is

A. 3   **B.** 6   **C.** 8   **D.** 9

Q.11 "n/m" means that n is a factor of m, then the relation T is

A. relexive and symmetric

B. transitive and symmetric

C. relexive, transitive and symmetric

D. relexive, transitive and not symmetric

Q.12 The set of all real numbers under the usual multiplication operation is not a group since

A. multiplication is not a binary operation

B. multiplication is not associative

C. identity element does not exist

D. zero has no inverse

Q.13 Rank of the matrix A =

$$\begin{bmatrix} 0 & 0 & 0 & 0 \\ 4 & 2 & 3 & 0 \\ 1 & 0 & 0 & 0 \\ 4 & 0 & 3 & 0 \end{bmatrix}$$

A. 0   **B.** 1   **C.** 2   **D.** 3

Q.14 A set of linear equations is represented by the matrix equation $Ax = b$. The necessary condition for the existence of a solution for this system is

A. A must be invertible

B. b must be linearly depended on the columns of A

C. b must be linearly independent of the columns of A

D. None of these

Q.15 Consider the following two statements:

I. The maximum number of linearly independent column vectors of a matrix A is called the rank of A.

II. If A is an n x n square matrix, it will be nonsingular is rank A = n.

With reference to the above statements, which of the following applies?

A. Both the statements are false

B. Both the statements are true

C. I is true but II is false.

D. I is false but II is true.

Q.16 The system of linear equations

$(4d - 1)x + y + z = 0$

$- y + z = 0$

$(4d - 1) z = 0$

has a non-trivial solution, if d equals

A. 1/2   **B.** 1/4   **C.** 3/4   **D.** 1

Q.17 The rank of a 3 x 3 matrix C (= AB), found by multiplying a non-zero column matrix A of size 3 x 1 and a non-zero row matrix B of size 1 x 3, is

A. 0   **B.** 1   **C.** 2   **D.** 3

Q.18 If A and B are square matrices of size n x n, then which of the following statement is not true?

A. det. (AB) = det (A) det (B)
B. det (kA) = k^n det (A)
C. det (A + B) = det (A) + det (B)
D. det (A^T) = 1/det (A^{-1})

Q.19 If

$$\phi(x) = \int_{x^2}^{0} \sqrt{t}\,dt, \quad then \frac{d\phi}{dx}$$

A. $2x^2$ **B.** $\sqrt{x}$ **C.** 0   **D.** 1

Q.20 The function f(x) = x3 - 6x2 + 9x + 25 has

A. a maxima at x= 1 and a minima at x = 3
B. a maxima at x = 3 and a minima at x = 1
C. no maxima, but a minima at x = 1
D. a maxima at x = 1, but no minima

Q.21 The value of a =

$$\int_{0}^{5p} (2 - sinx)dx$$

is

A. >0
B. 2
C. 0 - 1 + 100 - 10 + 1
D. undefined

Q.22 The interval in which the Lagrange's theorem is applicable for the function f(x) = 1/x is

A. [-3, 3]   **B.** [-2, 2]   **C.** [2, 3]   **D.** [-1, 1]

Q.23 If f(x) = | x |, then for interval [-1, 1] ,f(x)

A. satisied all the conditions of Rolle's Theorem
B. satisfied all the conditions of Mean Value Theorem
C. does not satisied the -conditions of Mean Value Theorem
D. None of these

Q.24 The minimum value of | x2 _ 5x + 21 | is

A. -5   **B.** 0   **C.** -1   **D.** -2

Q.25 If the two pairs of lines $x^2 - 2mxy - y^2 = 0$ and $x^2 - 2nxy - y^2 = 0$ are such that one of them represents the bisector of the angles between the other, then

A. mn + 1 = 0
B. mn – 1 = 0
C. 1/m + 1/n = 0
D. 1/m - 1/n = 0

Q.26

For any positive integer n, $\int \frac{dx}{x^{n+1} + x}$ is equal to

A. $\frac{1}{n} \log_e |x^n + 1| + c$

B. $\frac{1}{n} \log_e \left(\frac{1}{x^n + 1} \right) + c$

C. $\frac{1}{n} \log_e \left(\frac{x^n}{x^n + 1} \right) + c$

D. $\frac{1}{n + 1} \log_e \left(\frac{x^n}{x^n + 1} \right) + c$

Q.27

If $\vec{a}$ is perpendicular to $\vec{b}$ and $\vec{c}$, $|\vec{a}| = 2$, $|\vec{b}| = 3$, $|\vec{c}| = 4$ and the angle between $\vec{b}$ and $\vec{c}$ is $\frac{2\pi}{3}$, then $[\vec{a}\ \vec{b}\ \vec{c}]$ is equal to

A. $4\sqrt{3}$ **B.** $6\sqrt{3}$ **C.** $12\sqrt{3}$ **D.** $18\sqrt{3}$

Q.28 If f(x) = (x – 2)(x – 4)(x – 6)....(x – 2n), then f'(2) is equal to

A. $(-1)^n\, 2^{n-1}(n - 1)!$ **B.** $(-2)^{n-1}(n - 1)!$
C. $(-2)^n\, n!$ **D.** $(-1)^{n-1} 2^n\, (n - 1)!$

Q.29

The solution of the differential equation $x\frac{dy}{dx} + 2y = x^2$ is

A. $y = \frac{x^2 + c}{4x^2}$ **B.** $y = \frac{x^2}{4} + c$

C. $y = \frac{x^4 + c}{x^2}$ **D.** $y = \frac{x^4 + c}{4x^2}$

Q.30 The differential equation of all non - horizontal lines in a plane is

A. $d^2y/dx^2 = 0$ **B.** dx/dy = 0
C. dy/dx = 0   **D.** $d^2x/dy^2 = 0$

Q.31 The equation of the sphere concentric with the sphere $2x^2 + 2y^2 + 2z^2 - 6x + 2y - 4z = 1$ and double its radius is

A. $x^2 + y^2 + z^2 - x + y - z = 1$
B. $x^2 + y^2 + z^2 - 6x + 2y - 4z = 1$
C. $2x^2 + y^2 + z^2 - 6x + 2y - 4z - 15 = 0$
D. $2x^2 + 2y^2 + 2z^2 - 6x + 2y - 4z - 25 = 0$

Q.32 In how many ways can 8 students be arranged in a row?

A. 8!   **B.** 7!   **C.** 8   **D.** 7

Q.33 Let f : R be a differentiable function and f(1) = 4. Find the value of

$$\lim_{x \to 1} \int_{4}^{f(x)} \frac{2t}{x - 1}\,dt, \text{ if } f'(1) = 2$$

A. 16   **B.** 8   **C.** 4   **D.** 2

Q.34 If three natural numbers between 1 and 100 are selected randomly, then the probability that all are divisible by both 2 and 3 is

A. 4/105 **B.** 4/33 **C.** 4/35 **D.** 4/1155

Q.35

The sum to n terms of the series $\frac{4}{3} + \frac{10}{9} + \frac{28}{27} + \ldots$ is

A. $\dfrac{3^n (2n + 1) + 1}{2 \cdot 3^n}$ **B.** $\dfrac{3^n (2n + 1) - 1}{2 \cdot 3^n}$

C. $\dfrac{3^n n - 1}{2 \cdot 3^n}$ **D.** $\dfrac{3^n - 1}{2 \cdot 3^n}$

Q.36 A man of 2 m height walks at a uniform speed of 6 km/h away from a lamp post of 6 m height. The rate at which the length of his shadow increases is

A. 2 km/h **B.** 1 km/h **C.** 3 km/h **D.** 6 km/h

Q.37

The solution of $\dfrac{dy}{dx} = \dfrac{ax + h}{by + k}$ represents a parabola, when

A. $a = 0, b = 0$ **B.** $a = 1, b = 2$
C. $a = 0, b \neq 0$ **D.** $a = 2, b = 1$

Q.38

If $y = a^x \cdot b^{2x-1}$, then $\dfrac{d^2 y}{dx^2}$ is equal to

A. $y^2 . \log ab^2$ **B.** $y . \log ab^2$
C. $y . (\log ab^2)^2$ **D.** $y . (\log a^2 b)^2$

Q.39 A missile fired from the ground level rises x meters vertically upwards in t seconds, where $x = 100t - \frac{25}{2} t^2$. The maximum height reached is

A. 200 m **B.** 125 m **C.** 160 m **D.** 190 m

Q.40

A vector perpendicular to $2\hat{i} + \hat{j} + \hat{k}$ and coplanar with $\hat{i} + 2\hat{j} + \hat{k}$ and $\hat{i} + \hat{j} + 2\hat{k}$ is

A. $5(\hat{j} - \hat{k})$

B. $\hat{i} + 7\hat{j} - \hat{k}$

C. $5(\hat{j} + \hat{k})$

D. $2\hat{i} - 7\hat{j} - \hat{k}$

Q.41 If n(U) = 20, n(A) = 12, n(B) = 9, n(AB) = 4, where U is the universal set, A and B are subsets of U, then n | (A U B)o| is equal to

A. 17 **B.** 9 **C.** 11 **D.** 3

Q.42 The derivative of y = (1 - x)(2 - x)....(n - x) at x = 1 is equal to

A. 0 **B.** (-1) (n - 1)!
C. n! - 1 **D.** (-1)n - 1 (n - 1)!

Q.43 The circumradius of the triangle whose sides are 13, 12 and 5, is

A. 15 **B.** 13/2 **C.** 15/2 **D.** 6

Q.44 If $^nC_{12} = {^nC_6}$, then $^nC_2$ is equal to

A. 72 **B.** 153 **C.** 306 **D.** 2556

Q.45 The sum of 24 terms of the series $\sqrt{2} + \sqrt{8} + \sqrt{18} + \sqrt{32} + \ldots$ is

A. 300 **B.** 200 $\sqrt{2}$ **C.** 300 $\sqrt{2}$ **D.** 250 $\sqrt{2}$

Q.46 The equation of the circle with centre (2, 1) and touching the line 3x + 4y = 5 is

A. $x^2 + y^2 - 4x - 2y + 5 = 0$
B. $x^2 + y^2 - 4x - 2y - 5 = 0$
C. $x^2 + y^2 - 4x - 2y + 4 = 0$
D. $x^2 + y^2 - 4x - 2y - 4 = 0$

Q.47

If $\dfrac{x}{\alpha} + \dfrac{y}{\beta} = 1$ touches the circle $x^2 + y^2 = a^2$, then the point $(1/\alpha, 1/\beta)$ lies on a/an

A. straight line **B.** circle
C. parabola **D.** ellipse

Q.48 The horizontal distance between two towers is 60 m and the angles of depression of the top of the first tower as seen from the top of the second is 30°. If the height of the second tower is 150 m, then the height of the first tower is

A. 90 m **B.** (150 - 60√3)m
C. (150 + 20√3)m **D.** None of these

Q.49 If sin A + cos B = a and sin B + cos A = b, then sin (A + B) is equal to

A. $\dfrac{a^2 + b^2}{2}$ **B.** $\dfrac{a^2 - b^2 + 2}{2}$

C. $\dfrac{a^2 + b^2 - 2}{2}$ **D.** None of these

Q.50 If f(x) = ax² + bx + c and g(x) = px² + qx with g(1) = f(1), g(2) - f(2) = 1 and g(3) - f(3) = 4, then g(4) - f(4) is equal to

A. 0 **B.** 5
C. 6 **D.** None of these

Q.51

$\int \dfrac{e^x (1 + \sin x)}{1 + \cos x} dx$ is equal to

A. $e^x \tan\left(\dfrac{x}{2}\right) + c$

B. $e^x \tan x + c$

C. $e^x\left(\dfrac{1 + \sin x}{1 - \cos}\right) + c$

D. $c - e^x \cot\left(\dfrac{x}{2}\right)$

Q.52

For hyperbola $\dfrac{x^2}{\cos^2 \alpha} - \dfrac{y^2}{\sin^2 \alpha} = 1$, which of the following remains constant with change in α?

A. Abscissae of vertices
B. Abscissae of foci
C. Eccentricity
D. Directrix

Q.53 The number of common tangents to the circles $x^2 + y^2 + 2x + 8y - 23 = 0$ and $x^2 + y^2 - 4x - 10y + 9 = 0$, is

A. 1   **B.** 3
C. 2   **D.** None of these

Q.54

The modulus and the amplitude of $\dfrac{1 + 2i}{1 - (1 - i)^2}$ respectively are

A. $\sqrt{2}$ and $\pi/6$ **B.** 1 and 0
C. 1 and $\pi/3$ **D.** 1 and $\pi/4$

Q.55 The function

$f : R \to [-1, 1]$ defined by $f(x) = \dfrac{|x|}{1 + |x|}$, $x \in R$

is

A. Invertible
B. Injective but not surjective.
C. Surjective but not injective
D. Neither injective nor surjective.

Q.56 The distance of the point (3, 8, 2) from the line

$$\dfrac{x - 1}{2} = \dfrac{y - 3}{4} = \dfrac{z - 2}{3}$$

, measured parallel to the plane $3x + 2y - 2z + 15 = 0$ is-

A. 1   **B.** 2   **C.** 5   **D.** 7

Q.57 Find the differential equation of the family of ellipse such that its centre is on the origin

A. $-\dfrac{y}{x}\cdot\dfrac{dy}{dx} + y\dfrac{d^2 y}{dx^2} + \left(\dfrac{dy}{dx}\right)^2 = 0$

B. $\dfrac{1}{x}\cdot\dfrac{dy}{dx} + y\dfrac{d^2 y}{dx^2} + \left(\dfrac{dy}{dx}\right)^2 = 0$

C. $\dfrac{dy}{dx} - xy\dfrac{d^2 y}{dx^2} - \left(\dfrac{dy}{dx}\right)^2 = 0$

D. $\dfrac{y}{x}\cdot\dfrac{dy}{dx} + y\dfrac{d^2 y}{dx^2} + \left(\dfrac{dy}{dx}\right)^2 = 0$

Q.58

If $0 < x < 1$, then

$$\sqrt{1 + x^2}\left[\left\{x\cos\left(\cot^{-1}(x)\right) + \sin\left(\cot^{-1}(x)\right)\right\}^2 - 1\right]^{\frac{1}{2}}$$

is equal to

A. $\dfrac{x}{\sqrt{1 + x^2}}$ **B.** x

C. $x\sqrt{1 + x^2}$ **D.** $\sqrt{1 + x^2}$

Q.59 If Area occupied by the curves with equation given below is A then Value of A/2 is-

Equation 1: $(x - 5)^2 + y^2 = 25$
Equation 2: $y^2 = 9x$

A. $\dfrac{25}{2}\cos^{-1}\left(\dfrac{4}{5}\right) - 8 - \dfrac{25\pi}{4}$

B. $\dfrac{25}{2}\sin^{-1}\left(\dfrac{3}{5}\right) - 8 - \dfrac{25\pi}{4}$

C. $\dfrac{25}{2}\sin^{-1}\left(\dfrac{4}{5}\right) - 8 - \dfrac{25\pi}{2}$

D. $\dfrac{25\pi}{4} - 8 - \dfrac{25}{2}\sin^{-1}\left(\dfrac{4}{5}\right)$

Q.60

If the sum of odd coefficients of $(1 + z)^5$ is x, find the number of solutions of $a + b + c + d = x$ where $-x < a < x$.

A. $^{34}C_3$ **B.** $^{33}C_3$ **C.** $^{35}C_3$ **D.** $^{36}C_4$

Analytical Ability & Logical Reasoning

Q.61 224 : 817 :: 163 : ?
A. 497   **B.** 563   **C.** 572   **D.** 593

Q.62 REMEMBER : 79 :: ACOUSTIC : ?
A. 91   **B.** 99   **C.** 105   **D.** 109

Q.63 ARSENAL : GUNS :: INDEX : ?
A. Name of Author   **B.** Glossary

C. Contents   **D.** Summary

Q.64 EI : G :: GK :?
A. H   **B.** J   **C.** I   **D.** K

Q.65 14 : 225 : : 21 : ?
A. 441   **B.** 529   **C.** 400   **D.** 484

Q.66 Find the odd word/letter/ number from the given alternatives.
A. 64   **B.** 125   **C.** 225   **D.** 216

Q.67 In the following question, choose the number which is different from others in the group.
A. 903   **B.** 729   **C.** 552   **D.** 381

Q.68 For the following questions Find the odd word / letters / number from the given alternatives.
A. JF   **B.** UQ   **C.** PL   **D.** XS

Q.69 Select the odd pair of numbers from the given alternatives.
A. (126, 21)   **B.** (162, 27)   **C.** (165, 33)   **D.** (108, 18)

Q.70 Select the odd word/letters/number/word pair from the given alternatives.
A. 2367   **B.** 4374   **C.** 5319   **D.** 6182

Q.71 Each of the questions below contains three elements. These three elements may or may not have some linkage. Each group of the elements may fit into one of the diagrams at (A), (B), (C) and (D). You have to indicate groups of elements in each of the questions fit into which of the diagrams given below. The letter indicating the diagram is the answer.

 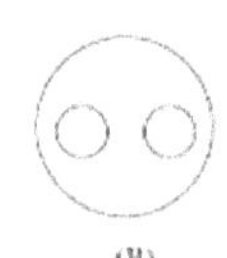 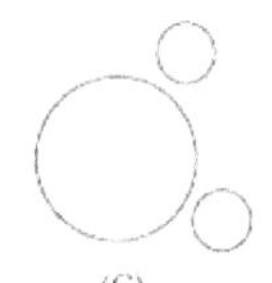 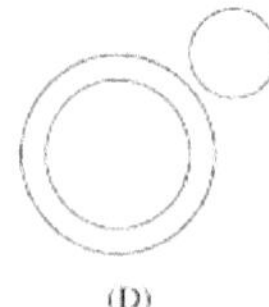
(A)   (B)   (C)   (D)

Elephants, Herbivores, Tigers
A. A   **B.** B   **C.** C   **D.** D

Q.72 Find the correct relation of police, doctors and lawyers-

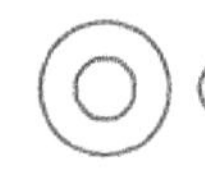    
(A)   (B)   (C)   (D)

A. A   **B.** B   **C.** C   **D.** D

Q.73 In Question identify the diagram that best represents the relationship among classes given below:

Ornaments, Gold, Silver.

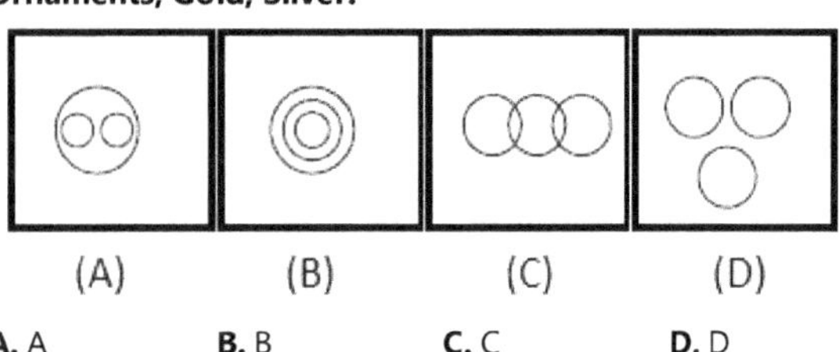
(A)   (B)   (C)   (D)

A. A   **B.** B   **C.** C   **D.** D

Q.74 In each of the following questions, which of the following Venn diagram best represents relation between given classes ?

Fruits, Apples, Oranges

 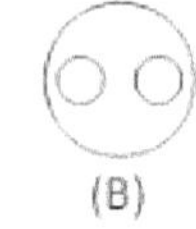 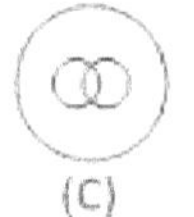 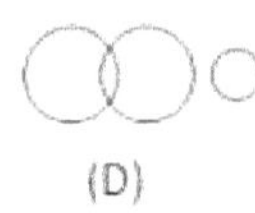
(A)   (B)   (C)   (D)

A. A   **B.** B   **C.** C   **D.** D

Q.75 In the given diagram, select the one which is not part of X?

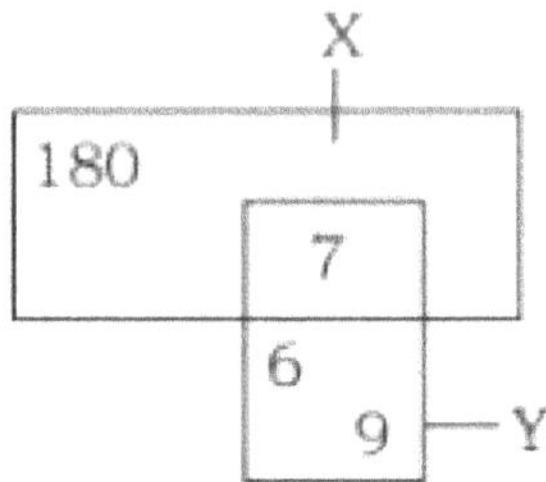

A. 7   **B.** 180   **C.** 6, 7 & 9   **D.** 6 & 9

Q.76 A piece of paper is folded and punched as shown below in the question figures. From the given answer figures, indicate how it will appear when opened?

Question figure

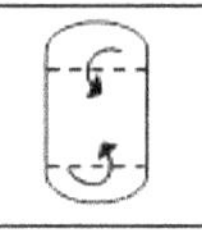 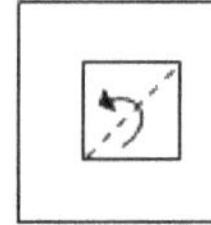 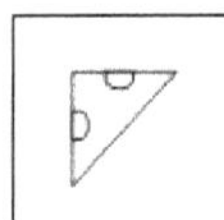

Answer figure

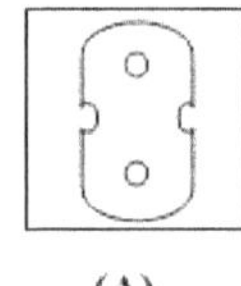  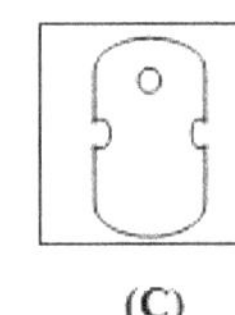 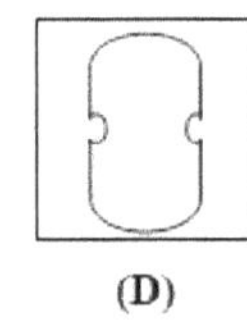
(A)   (B)   (C)   (D)

A. A   **B.** B   **C.** C   **D.** D

Q.77 Out of the four alternatives select the option which represents the unfolded form of figure (Z).

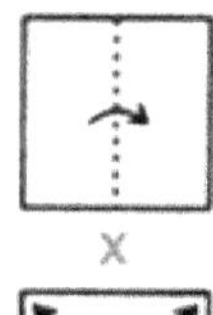 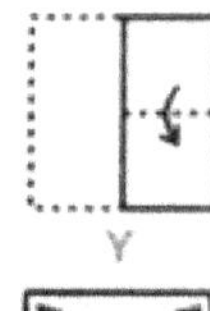 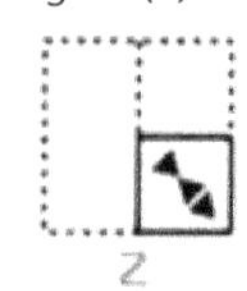
X   Y   Z

 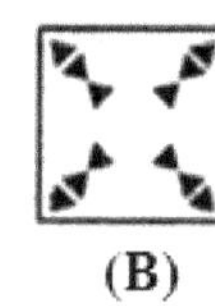 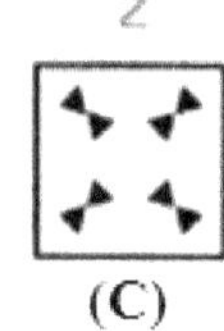 
(A)   (B)   (C)   (D)

A. A   **B.** B   **C.** C   **D.** D

Q.78 Choose the correct water image of the given figure (X) from among the four alternatives.

Question figure

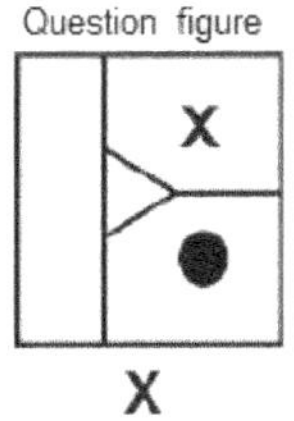

X

Answer figure

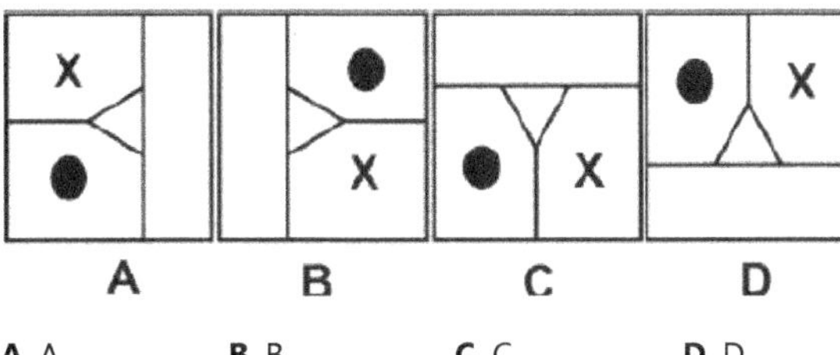

A. A **B.** B **C.** C **D.** D

Q.79 If a mirror is placed on the line MN, then which of the answer figures is the right image of the given figure?

Question figure:

Answer figures:

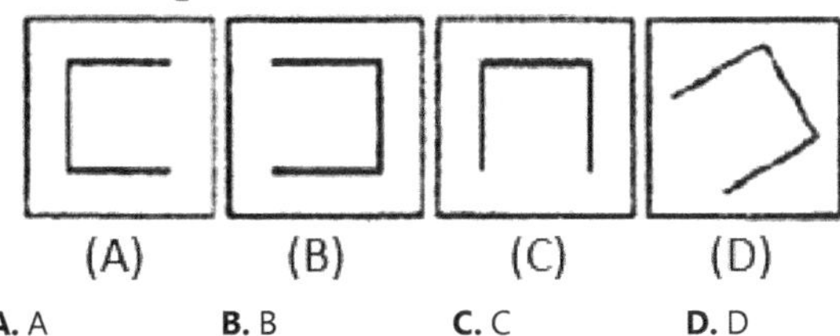

(A) (B) (C) (D)

A. A **B.** B **C.** C **D.** D

Q.80 In each of the following questions, choose the correct mirror image from the alternatives (a), (b), (c) and (d), when mirror is placed on the line AB.

Question figure

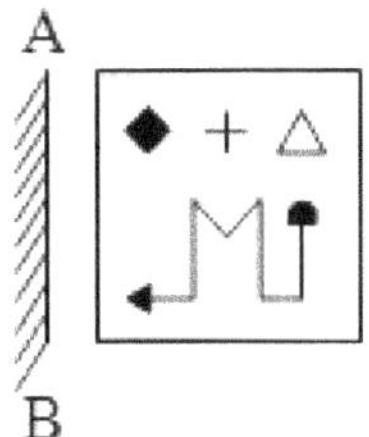

Answer figure

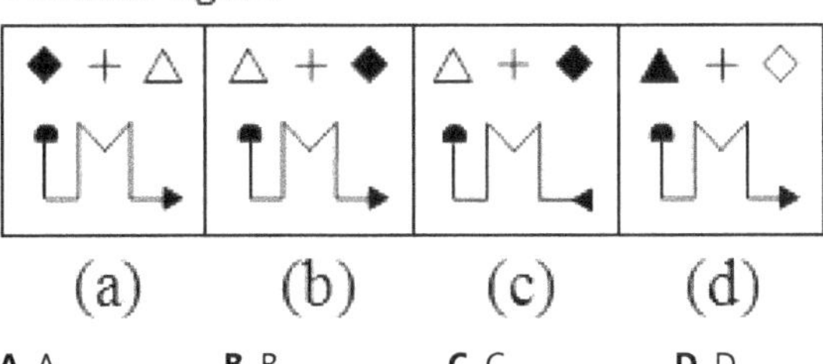

(a) (b) (c) (d)

A. A **B.** B **C.** C **D.** D

Computer Awareness

Q.81 GUI stands for
A. Graph Use Interface
B. Graphical Universal Interface
C. Graphical User Interface
D. Graphical Unique Interface

Q.82 Any data or instruction entered into the memory of a computer is considered as
A. Storage **B.** Output
C. Input **D.** Information

Q.83 Time during which a job is processed by the computer is:
A. Execution Time **B.** Delay Time
C. Real Time **D.** Waiting Time

Q.84 Which of the following circuit is used as a 'Memory device' in computers?
A. Rectifier **B.** Flip Flop
C. Comparator **D.** Attenuator

Q.85 Which of the following is an example of a real time operating system?
A. Lynx **B.** MS DOS
C. Windows XP **D.** Process Control

Q.86 Which of the following operating system does not implement the multitasking truly?
A. Windows 98 **B.** Windows NT
C. Windows XP **D.** MS DOS

Q.87 Which of the following windows version support 64 bit processor?
A. Windows 98 **B.** Windows 2000
C. Windows XP **D.** Windows 95

Q.88 What program runs first after computer is booted and loading GUI?
A. Desktop Manager **B.** File Manager
C. Windows Explorer **D.** Authentication

Q.89 End Key is used to
A. Moves the cursor end of the line
B. Moves the cursor end of the document
C. Moves the cursor end of the paragraph
D. Moves the cursor end of the screen

Q.90 "Ctrl + PageDown" is used to
A. Moves the cursor one Paragraph Down
B. Moves the cursor one Page Down
C. Moves the cursor one Line Down
D. Moves the cursor one Screen Down

Q.91 "Ctrl + Down Arrow" is used to
A. Moves the cursor one paragraph down
B. Moves the cursor one line down
C. Moves the cursor one page down
D. Moves the cursor one screen down

Q.92 Page Up Key uses for

A. Moves the cursor one line up

B. Moves the cursor one screen up

C. Moves the cursor one page up

D. Moves the cursor one paragraph up

Q.93 Which tool you will use to join some cells and place the content at the middle of joined cell?

A. From Format Cells dialog box click on Merge Cells check box

B. From Format Cells dialog box select the Centered alignment

C. From Format Cells dialog box choose Merge and Center check box

D. Click on Merge and Center tool on formatting toolbar

Q.94 Tab scroll buttons are place on Excel screen

A. towards the bottom right corner

B. towards the bottom left corner

C. towards the top right corner

D. towards the top left corner

Q.95 The Name box on to the left of formula bar

A. shows the name of workbook currently working on

B. shows the name of worksheet currently working on

C. shows the name of cell or range currently working on

D. None of above

Q.96 Each excel file is a workbook that contains different sheets. Which of the following can not be a sheet in workbook?

A. work sheet   **B.** chart sheet

C. module sheet   **D.** data sheet

Q.97 In slide layout panel how many layouts are available for text layout by default?

A. 4   **B.** 7

C. 12   **D.** None of above

Q.98 Which of the following statement is false?

A. If you choose to select from one of the pre-made slide layouts, you can change the positioning

B. If you choose to select from the pre-made slide layouts, you cannot delete the objects in the layout

C. Blank Slide is at the top of the 'Content Layouts' area in the Slide Layout panel

D. All of above are false statements

Q.99 What lets you to create new presentation by selecting ready-made font color and graphics effects?

A. Presentation Template

B. Master Slide

C. Design Template

D. Animation Scheme

Q.100 Which command will you use in PowerPoint if you need to change the color of different objects without changing content?

A. Design Template   **B.** Color Scheme

C. Font Color   **D.** Object Color

English

Q.101 Arrange the sentences in the correct order

A. Elite American colleges are now widely suspected of admitting male applicants with lower grades, to even up the numbers.

B. At least in the rich world, that wasteful truth has been triumphantly overcome.

C. Stendhal once wrote that all geniuses who were born women were lost to the public good.

D. Yet, despite this monumental advance, much ability, both male and female, is wasted because of tenacious stereotypes.

A. ABDC   **B.** ADCB   **C.** CBAD   **D.** CDBA

Q.102 Arrange the sentences in the correct order

A. Hate speech is characterized by a deliberate targeting of communities rather than beliefs.

B. What the management must seek to do is to not let political discussions and debates to descend into vituperative attacks and hate speech.

C. But such an association will be spurious, as questioning orthodoxy and conservatism is not tantamount to hate speech.

D. The student body's activism has been criticized by detractors and it has been sought to be associated with hate speech.

A. BACD   **B.** ACDB   **C.** DBCA   **D.** DCAB

Q.103 Arrange the sentences in the correct order

A. The main driving force of the British Empire's global expansion was the pursuit of commercial interests.

B. That entailed helping the weaker side in order to promote a regional balance of power and preventing the rise of a regional power, or at least reducing its impact on British security and interests.

C. Creating a balance of power and fostering regional stability could help to realize commercial goals; hence these became the core of the British Empire's strategy.

D. Britain put these practices to use in its continental policy for hundreds of years.

A. ADBC   **B.** CBDA   **C.** ACBD   **D.** CABD

Q.104 Arrange the sentences in the correct order

A. The crash in the Alps has launched a search for a solution to the problem of accessing the cockpit from outside if the plane has been commandeered from within.

B. Flight safety has so far focused on threats from the passenger side, and the 9/11 terror episode led to fortification of the cockpit.

C. But if they are in a position to act, pilots can override this mechanism.

D. In exceptional circumstances, such as an emergency affecting the pilot and the cockpit area, the crew can use a code that opens the cockpit door briefly, or it even opens automatically if the pilots are immobilized due to depressurization.

A. ABCD   **B.** ADCB   **C.** BADC   **D.** BDCA

Q.105 Arrange the sentences in the correct order

A. Indeed, Indian policy-planners find themselves in a predicament thanks to the continued monetary easing by some nations and the shrinkage in world trade..

B. In this context, a fund-starved country like India will do well to focus on foreign direct investment rather than get unduly worried about foreign institutional investment, which will have its ebb and flow depending on the environment outside..

C. With everyone waiting for the other to act first, the onus is definitely on the political bosses to devise quick solutions to accelerate the economy..

D. Given this 'new normal' kind of an environment, they will have to look at ways to protect the Indian economy from external vicissitudes.

A. ADBC   **B.** CDBA   **C.** BDCA   **D.** CABD

Q.106 Actual evidence of misconduct may not be the most important criteria to determine whether a President gets impeached.

A. the most important criteria to determining the impeachment of a President.

B. the most important criterion in determining whether a President gets impeached.

C. the most important criterion to determine if a President gets impeached.

D. the most important criteria for determining the impeachment of a President.

Q.107 The decision to pull the US out from the Paris agreement by the president drew heavy criticism within the US and internationally, including China, which swiftly recommitted itself to the agreement forged with the previous administration.

A. The decision to pull the US out of the Paris agreement by the president drew heavy criticism within the US and internationally, including China,

B. The decision by the president to pull the US out off the Paris agreement drew heavy criticism within the US and internationally, including China,

C. The president's decision to pull the US out of the Paris agreement drew heavy criticism within the US and internationally, including China,

D. The president's decision to pull the US out of the Paris agreement drew heavy criticism within the US and internationally, including in China,

Q.108 One of the problems that occur as a result of coal mining is the increasing incidences of lung cancer.

A. that occurs as a result of coal mining are the increasing incidences

B. that occurs as a result of coal mining is the increasing incidence

C. that occur as a result of coal mining are the increasing incidences

D. that occur as a result of coal mining is the increasing incidence

Q.109 Germany's NATO Framework Nation Concept is a ground-breaking project that serves both to increase European military capacity within NATO and create an European defence force that could eventually stand on its own.

A. both serves to increase European military capacity within NATO and create a European defence force that could eventually stand on its own.

B. both serves to increase European military capacity within NATO and to create an European defence force that could eventually stand on its own.

C. serves to both increase European military capacity within NATO and create an European defence force that could eventually stand on its own.

D. serves both to increase European military capacity within NATO and to create a European defence force that could eventually stand on its own.

Q.110 The sheer number of cars on the roads has all but paralyzed the traffic in the city.

A. The sheer number of cars on the roads have

B. The shear number of cars on the roads have

C. The shear number of cars on the roads has

D. No correction required

Q.111 Reading Comprehension

Sound the alarm! The kingdom of letters has admitted Trojan horses: James Frey, JT Leroy, Misha Defonseca, Margaret B. Jones, Herman Rosenblat, and now Matt McCarthy, portions of whose baseball memoir, the New York Times reports, are "incorrect, embellished or impossible." The watchmen have let down their guards.

I write: Hold your horses. In the rush to diagnose these fake memoirs as symptoms of a diseased culture, we have failed to consider an equally plausible alternative. What if the exposure of fake memoirists is not due to an increased frequency of lying, but rather to our increased ability to root out liars and hold them accountable for their verisimilitudes? Perhaps the outings of these hoaxes mark not a blurring of the line between fact and fiction, but a further demarcation.

Indeed, it may be helpful to remember that the novel was born from exactly such confusion. One of the standards by which the earliest novels were judged was their ability to convince readers that their narratives were, in fact, real. Authors deployed several tricks to scaffold the illusion. 'Robinson Crusoe' was "written by himself," according to the novel's title page, which omitted Daniel Defoe's name. Samuel Richardson's novel 'Pamela', an attempt to instruct in good conduct through entertainment, was written as a series of letters penned by the heroine. In his preface to the novel, which excluded his name altogether, Richardson included several real letters from friends to whom he had shown the manuscript, but he changed the salutation from "Dear Author" to "Dear Editor" and even, writing under the guise of "editor," praised "Pamela's" letters. However, this was a lie, but not a hoax. Richardson wanted his novels to be read with "Historical Faith", since they contained, he believed, "the truth of the possible- the truth of human nature". Richardson's authorship was revealed shortly after Pamela's publication, but rather than serving time on Oprah's couch, he was hailed as an innovator of the novelistic form.

Whereas novels were unashamedly fake memoirs at their conception, our recent hoaxes suggest that the line between the genres, once drawn, cannot easily be erased. This is in no small part due to the Internet's surveillance. All along, historians had raised questions about Misha Defonseca, who claimed to have survived the Holocaust by living with a pack of wolves, but the engine of her downfall was her former publisher Jane Daniel's blog. James Frey's sine qua non of the fudged-memoir genre, A Million Little Pieces, was debunked by the website The Smoking Gun, which posted his actual arrest records and compared them to Frey's embellished retellings. Deborah Lipstadt used her blog to gather evidence against Herman Rosenblat's memoir.

If anything, you could argue that the fact-checkers are doing too good a job. There seems to be some risk that, in attempting to hold memoirs to journalistic standards of factuality, the watchdogs miss the forest for the trees, fixating on minor details in books whose general pictures are correct. The New York Times includes in its dossier against Matt McCarthy disputations by teammates who McCarthy alleges threatened children and made fun of Hispanics, as though their denials of having said such self-incriminating things were more trustworthy than McCarthy's accusations. When Jose Canseco published his baseball memoirs Juiced and Vindicated, reviewers caviled over minor details and unsubstantiated claims, including that Alex Rodriguez had used steroids. Recent events have proven the gist of Canseco's memoirs largely correct.

Indeed, it seems unlikely that, say, every claim in Casanova's The Story of My Life would hold up to such scrutiny. And yet, if we knew this were the case, would we excise it from the canon? Writers' enormous talents can sometimes render moot questions of their works' factuality; our fraudsters, meanwhile, attempted to compensate for their meager talents by actually inhabiting their bloated fictions. They suffer not an excess of imagination, which can illuminate even the most mundane experiences, but a retreat from it. And yet simply because they lost their handles on the truth does not mean that the culture also has. Maybe the symptom of our age is not the fake memoirists themselves, but the catching of fake memoirists. In which case: Sound the church bells! The traitors are routed! The watchmen won!

Which of the following is the author unlikely to agree with?

A. There isn't more literary fraud in our age. More fraud is coming to light due to the Internet's surveillance.

B. The line dividing novels and fake memoirs was never clear.

C. As long as the main or essential part of a memoir is correct, it does not matter if lesser details do not stand up to verification.

D. There exists now a widespread, diseased culture of literary fraud.

Q.112 Reading Comprehension

Sound the alarm! The kingdom of letters has admitted Trojan horses: James Frey, JT Leroy, Misha Defonseca, Margaret B. Jones, Herman Rosenblat, and now Matt McCarthy, portions of whose baseball memoir, the New York Times reports, are "incorrect, embellished or impossible." The watchmen have let down their guards.

I write: Hold your horses. In the rush to diagnose these fake memoirs as symptoms of a diseased culture, we have failed to consider an equally plausible alternative. What if the exposure of fake memoirists is not due to an increased frequency of lying, but rather to our increased ability to root out liars and hold them accountable for their verisimilitudes? Perhaps the outings of these hoaxes mark not a blurring of the line between fact and fiction, but a further demarcation.

Indeed, it may be helpful to remember that the novel was born from exactly such confusion. One of the standards by which the earliest novels were judged was their ability to convince readers that their narratives were, in fact, real. Authors deployed several tricks to scaffold the illusion. 'Robinson Crusoe' was "written by himself," according to the novel's title page, which omitted Daniel Defoe's name. Samuel Richardson's novel 'Pamela', an attempt to instruct in good conduct through entertainment, was written as a series of letters penned by the heroine. In his preface to the novel, which excluded his name altogether, Richardson included several real letters from friends to whom he had shown the manuscript, but he changed the salutation from "Dear Author" to "Dear Editor" and even, writing under the guise of "editor," praised "Pamela's" letters. However, this was a lie, but not a hoax. Richardson wanted his novels to be read with "Historical Faith", since they contained, he believed, "the truth of the possible- the truth of human nature". Richardson's authorship was revealed shortly after Pamela's publication, but rather than serving time on Oprah's couch, he was hailed as an innovator of the novelistic form.

Whereas novels were unashamedly fake memoirs at their conception, our recent hoaxes suggest that the line between the genres, once drawn, cannot easily be erased. This is in no small part due to the Internet's surveillance. All along, historians had raised questions about Misha Defonseca, who claimed to have survived the Holocaust by living with a pack of wolves, but the engine of her downfall was her former publisher Jane Daniel's blog. James Frey's sine qua non of the fudged-memoir genre, A Million Little Pieces, was debunked by the website The Smoking Gun, which posted his actual arrest records and compared them to Frey's embellished retellings. Deborah Lipstadt used her blog to gather evidence against Herman Rosenblat's memoir.

If anything, you could argue that the fact-checkers are doing too good a job. There seems to be some risk that, in attempting to hold memoirs to journalistic standards of factuality, the watchdogs miss the forest for the trees, fixating on minor details in books whose general pictures are correct. The New York Times includes in its dossier against Matt McCarthy disputations by teammates who McCarthy alleges threatened children and made fun of Hispanics, as though their denials of having said such self-incriminating things were more trustworthy than McCarthy's accusations. When Jose Canseco published his baseball memoirs Juiced and Vindicated, reviewers caviled over minor details and unsubstantiated claims, including that Alex Rodriguez had used steroids. Recent events have proven the gist of Canseco's memoirs largely correct.

Indeed, it seems unlikely that, say, every claim in Casanova's The Story of My Life would hold up to such scrutiny. And yet, if we knew this were the case, would we excise it from the canon? Writers' enormous talents can sometimes render moot questions of their works' factuality; our fraudsters, meanwhile, attempted to compensate for their meager talents by actually inhabiting their bloated fictions. They suffer not an excess of imagination, which can illuminate even the most mundane experiences, but a retreat from it. And yet simply because they lost their handles on the truth does not mean that the culture also has. Maybe the symptom of our age is not the fake memoirists themselves, but the catching of fake memoirists. In

which case: Sound the church bells! The traitors are routed! The watchmen won!

With regard to the novel 'Pamela', the author states that Richardson's artifice " was a lie, but not a hoax". What does he mean?

A. It was an unintentional deception that contained the truth of human nature and was hence acceptable to readers.

B. It was just a ploy to capture the imagination of the readers with the truth of the possible.

C. It was a deception perpetrated simply to make money.

D. It was a mere prank, and did not generate public interest.

Q.113 Reading Comprehension

Sound the alarm! The kingdom of letters has admitted Trojan horses: James Frey, JT Leroy, Misha Defonseca, Margaret B. Jones, Herman Rosenblat, and now Matt McCarthy, portions of whose baseball memoir, the New York Times reports, are "incorrect, embellished or impossible." The watchmen have let down their guards.

I write: Hold your horses. In the rush to diagnose these fake memoirs as symptoms of a diseased culture, we have failed to consider an equally plausible alternative. What if the exposure of fake memoirists is not due to an increased frequency of lying, but rather to our increased ability to root out liars and hold them accountable for their verisimilitudes? Perhaps the outings of these hoaxes mark not a blurring of the line between fact and fiction, but a further demarcation.

Indeed, it may be helpful to remember that the novel was born from exactly such confusion. One of the standards by which the earliest novels were judged was their ability to convince readers that their narratives were, in fact, real. Authors deployed several tricks to scaffold the illusion. 'Robinson Crusoe' was "written by himself," according to the novel's title page, which omitted Daniel Defoe's name. Samuel Richardson's novel 'Pamela', an attempt to instruct in good conduct through entertainment, was written as a series of letters penned by the heroine. In his preface to the novel, which excluded his name altogether, Richardson included several real letters from friends to whom he had shown the manuscript, but he changed the salutation from "Dear Author" to "Dear Editor" and even, writing under the guise of "editor," praised "Pamela's" letters. However, this was a lie, but not a hoax. Richardson wanted his novels to be read with "Historical Faith", since they contained, he believed, "the truth of the possible- the truth of human nature". Richardson's authorship was revealed shortly after Pamela's publication, but rather than serving time on Oprah's couch, he was hailed as an innovator of the novelistic form.

Whereas novels were unashamedly fake memoirs at their conception, our recent hoaxes suggest that the line between the genres, once drawn, cannot easily be erased. This is in no small part due to the Internet's surveillance. All along, historians had raised questions about Misha Defonseca, who claimed to have survived the Holocaust by living with a pack of wolves, but the engine of her downfall was her former publisher Jane Daniel's blog. James Frey's sine qua non of the fudged-memoir genre, A Million Little Pieces, was debunked by the website The Smoking Gun, which posted his actual arrest records and compared them to Frey's embellished retellings.

Deborah Lipstadt used her blog to gather evidence against Herman Rosenblat's memoir.

If anything, you could argue that the fact-checkers are doing too good a job. There seems to be some risk that, in attempting to hold memoirs to journalistic standards of factuality, the watchdogs miss the forest for the trees, fixating on minor details in books whose general pictures are correct. The New York Times includes in its dossier against Matt McCarthy disputations by teammates who McCarthy alleges threatened children and made fun of Hispanics, as though their denials of having said such self-incriminating things were more trustworthy than McCarthy's accusations. When Jose Canseco published his baseball memoirs Juiced and Vindicated, reviewers caviled over minor details and unsubstantiated claims, including that Alex Rodriguez had used steroids. Recent events have proven the gist of Canseco's memoirs largely correct.

Indeed, it seems unlikely that, say, every claim in Casanova's The Story of My Life would hold up to such scrutiny. And yet, if we knew this were the case, would we excise it from the canon? Writers' enormous talents can sometimes render moot questions of their works' factuality; our fraudsters, meanwhile, attempted to compensate for their meager talents by actually inhabiting their bloated fictions. They suffer not an excess of imagination, which can illuminate even the most mundane experiences, but a retreat from it. And yet simply because they lost their handles on the truth does not mean that the culture also has. Maybe the symptom of our age is not the fake memoirists themselves, but the catching of fake memoirists. In which case: Sound the church bells! The traitors are routed! The watchmen won!

The word 'verisimilitude' in the passage is farthest in meaning to

A. absurdity   **B.** plausibility

C. authenticity   **D.** credibleness

Q.114 Reading Comprehension

Considered amongst the greatest works of Western literature, the Iliad, paired with its sequel, the Odyssey, is attributed to Homer.

However, that the author of the Iliad was not the same as the compiler of the fantastic tales in the Odyssey is arguable on several scores. The two epics belong to different literary types; the Iliad is essentially dramatic in its confrontation of opposing warriors who converse like the actors in Attic tragedy, while the Odyssey is cast as a novel narrated in more everyday human speech. In their physical structure, also, the two epics display an equally pronounced difference. The Odyssey is composed in six distinct cantos of four chapters ("books") each, whereas the Iliad moves unbrokenly forward with only one irrelevant episode in its tightly woven plot. Readers who examine psychological nuances see in the two works some distinctly different human responses and behavioral attitudes. For example, the Iliad voices admiration for the beauty and speed of horses, while the Odyssey shows no interest in these animals. The Iliad dismisses dogs as mere scavengers, while the poet of the Odyssey reveals a modern sentimental sympathy for Odysseus's faithful old hound, Argos.

But the most cogent argument for separating the two poems by assigning them to different authors is the archeological criterion of implied chronology. In the Iliad the Phoenicians are praised as skilled craftsmen working in metal and weavers of elaborate, much-prized garments. The shield which the metalworking god Hephaistos forges for Achilles in the Iliad seems inspired by the metal bowls with inlaid figures in action made by the Phoenicians and introduced by them into Greek and Etruscan commerce in the 8th century B.C. In contrast, in the Odyssey Greek sentiment toward the Phoenicians has undergone a drastic change. Although they are still regarded as clever craftsmen, in place of the Iliad's laudatory polydaidaloi ("of manifold skills") the epithet is parodied into polypaipaloi ("of manifold scurvy tricksters"), reflecting the competitive penetration into Greek commerce by traders from Phoenician Carthage in the 7th century B.C.

One thing, however, is certain: both epics were created without recourse to writing. Between the decline of Mycenaean and the emergence of classical Greek civilization—which is to say, from the late 12th to the mid-8th century B.C.—the inhabitants of the Greek lands had lost all knowledge of the syllabic script of their Mycenaean fore-bears and had not yet acquired from the easternmost shore of the Mediterranean that familiarity with Phoenician alphabetic writing from which classical Greek literacy (and in turn, Etruscan, Roman, and modern European literacy) derived. The same conclusion of illiterate composition may be reached from a critical inspection of the poems themselves. Among many races and in many different periods there has existed (and still exists sporadically) a form of purely oral and unwritten poetic speech, distinguishable from normal and printed literature by special traits that are readily recognizable and specifically distinctive. To this class the Homeric epics conform. Hence it would seem an inevitable inference that they must have been created either before the end of the 8th century B.C. or so shortly after that date that the use of alphabetic writing had not yet been developed sufficiently to record lengthy compositions. It is this illiterate environment that explains the absence of all contemporary historical record of the authors of the two great epics.

It is probable that Homer's name was applied to two distinct individuals differing in temperament and artistic accomplishment, born perhaps as much as a century apart, but practicing the same traditional craft of oral composition and recitation. Although each became known as "Homer, " it may be (as one ancient source asserts) that "homros "was a dialectal word for a blind man and so came to be used generically of the old and often sightless wandering reciters of heroic legends in the traditional meter of unrhymed dactylic hexameters. Thus there could have been many Homers. The two epics ascribed to Homer, however, have been as highly prized in modern as in ancient times for their marvelous vividness of expression, their keenness of personal characterization, their unflagging interest, whether in narration of action or in animated dramatic dialogue.

Which of the following cannot be reasonably inferred from the passage?

A. Before the 12th century BC , the use of syllabic writing existed in Ancient Greece.

B. Phoenician traders flourished in Greece at the time the Homeric epics were composed.

C. Greek, Roman and modern European literacy can be traced back to the Phoenicians.

D. Iliad and Odyssey are purely oral poetic speech, set to rhyme.

Q.115 Reading Comprehension

Considered amongst the greatest works of Western literature, the Iliad, paired with its sequel, the Odyssey, is attributed to Homer.

However, that the author of the Iliad was not the same as the compiler of the fantastic tales in the Odyssey is arguable on several scores. The two epics belong to different literary types; the Iliad is essentially dramatic in its confrontation of opposing warriors who converse like the actors in Attic tragedy, while the Odyssey is cast as a novel narrated in more everyday human speech. In their physical structure, also, the two epics display an equally pronounced difference. The Odyssey is composed in six distinct cantos of four chapters ("books") each, whereas the Iliad moves unbrokenly forward with only one irrelevant episode in its tightly woven plot. Readers who examine psychological nuances see in the two works some distinctly different human responses and behavioral attitudes. For example, the Iliad voices admiration for the beauty and speed of horses, while the Odyssey shows no interest in these animals. The Iliad dismisses dogs as mere scavengers, while the poet of the Odyssey reveals a modern sentimental sympathy for Odysseus's faithful old hound, Argos.

But the most cogent argument for separating the two poems by assigning them to different authors is the archeological criterion of implied chronology. In the Iliad the Phoenicians are praised as skilled craftsmen working in metal and weavers of elaborate, much-prized garments. The shield which the metalworking god Hephaistos forges for Achilles in the Iliad seems inspired by the metal bowls with inlaid figures in action made by the Phoenicians and introduced by them into Greek and Etruscan commerce in the 8th century B.C. In contrast, in the Odyssey Greek sentiment toward the Phoenicians has undergone a drastic change. Although they are still regarded as clever craftsmen, in place of the Iliad's laudatory polydaidaloi ("of manifold skills") the epithet is parodied into polypaipaloi ("of manifold scurvy tricksters"), reflecting the competitive penetration into Greek commerce by traders from Phoenician Carthage in the 7th century B.C.

One thing, however, is certain: both epics were created without recourse to writing. Between the decline of Mycenaean and the emergence of classical Greek civilization—which is to say, from the late 12th to the mid-8th century B.C.—the inhabitants of the Greek lands had lost all knowledge of the syllabic script of their Mycenaean fore-bears and had not yet acquired from the easternmost shore of the Mediterranean that familiarity with Phoenician alphabetic writing from which classical Greek literacy (and in turn, Etruscan, Roman, and modern European literacy) derived. The same conclusion of illiterate composition may be reached from a critical inspection of the poems themselves. Among many races and in many different periods there has existed (and still exists sporadically) a form of purely oral and unwritten poetic speech, distinguishable from normal and printed literature by special traits that are readily recognizable and specifically distinctive. To this class the Homeric epics conform. Hence it would seem an inevitable

inference that they must have been created either before the end of the 8th century B.C. or so shortly after that date that the use of alphabetic writing had not yet been developed sufficiently to record lengthy compositions. It is this illiterate environment that explains the absence of all contemporary historical record of the authors of the two great epics.

It is probable that Homer's name was applied to two distinct individuals differing in temperament and artistic accomplishment, born perhaps as much as a century apart, but practicing the same traditional craft of oral composition and recitation. Although each became known as "Homer, " it may be (as one ancient source asserts) that "homros "was a dialectal word for a blind man and so came to be used generically of the old and often sightless wandering reciters of heroic legends in the traditional meter of unrhymed dactylic hexameters. Thus there could have been many Homers. The two epics ascribed to Homer, however, have been as highly prized in modern as in ancient times for their marvelous vividness of expression, their keenness of personal characterization, their unflagging interest, whether in narration of action or in animated dramatic dialogue.

Which of the following can be characterized as the main idea of the passage?

A. There could have been many Homers, old and often sightless wandering reciters of heroic legends.

B. Attributing the composition of the Iliad and Odyssey to one Homer is erroneous.

C. Both Iliad and Odyssey were created without recourse to writing.

D. The Iliad and the Odyssey are of distinct literary types, physical structure and style.

Q.116 It had long been presumed that stone tool-making was a hallmark of our ____________, Homo. ____________,the recent discovery, in northwestern Kenya, of 3.3-million-year-old stone tools that are 7,00,000 years older than any other such stone tools ever found suggests it was the more ancient human ancestors who made the cognitive leap needed for crafting such implements.

A. genius, per contra   B. genius, additionally

C. genus, after all   D. genus, however

Q.117 Even in the__________ Nordic countries, household chores are still not evenly distributed, but at least the language is changing. When a reporter asked a young Swedish father whether he helped with the child care, she was ______________ for asking the wrong question. He did not "help": he did his share.

A. elitist, reprimanded

B. egalitarian, rebuked

C. prejudiced, admonished

D. non partisan, condemned

Q.118 __________ they gained control of Italy and defeated the Carthaginians, the Romans became the strongest power in the Mediterranean. They greatly benefited from the ___________ nature of Mediterranean politics, oftentimes getting help from local allies to defeat a far-off enemy.

A. though, fractious   B. after, facetious

C. once, factious   D. since, factitious

Q.119 It is ______________ rhetoric that the government "shutdown" was devastating. In actuality only seventeen percent of the federal government was actually shutdown as a result of partisan ____________.

A. efficacious, discord

B. specious, disagreement

C. spurious, comity

D. facile, agreement

Q.120 Connoisseurs ____ sport know an uber moment when they have witnessed one. ________ greatness does not require a quorum, as the stands erupted that Friday on the Centre Court, Wimbledon welcomed with open arms Roger Federer, a player who can turn prose into poetry.

A. into, since   B. of, while

C. in, though   D. on, now

// Smart Answer Sheet //

Correct — Percentage of students who answered correctly.   **Skipped** — Percentage of students who skipped.

Q.	Ans.	Correct / Skipped	Q.	Ans.	Correct / Skipped	Q.	Ans.	Correct / Skipped	Q.	Ans.	Correct / Skipped	Q.	Ans.	Correct / Skipped
1	B	88.04 % / 11.09 %	17	B	78.04 % / 10.06 %	33	A	85.2 % / 12.94 %	49	C	82.84 % / 11.06 %	65	D	85.46 % / 13.39 %
2	D	76.94 % / 12.21 %	18	C	81.15 % / 13.47 %	34	D	83.32 % / 15.11 %	50	D	80.49 % / 17.83 %	66	C	89.14 % / 10.3 %
3	D	84.47 % / 11.25 %	19	A	82.52 % / 14.96 %	35	B	87.31 % / 11.01 %	51	A	83.3 % / 16.43 %	67	B	79.41 % / 15.39 %
4	C	85.2 % / 13.89 %	20	A	84.84 % / 10.43 %	36	C	76.99 % / 13.31 %	52	B	82.88 % / 10.2 %	68	D	83.53 % / 14.31 %
5	B	86.16 % / 10.55 %	21	A	80.69 % / 10.73 %	37	C	84.27 % / 14.62 %	53	C	80.62 % / 12.23 %	69	C	77.04 % / 17.63 %
6	A	82.81 % / 15.97 %	22	C	86.68 % / 10.18 %	38	C	89.22 % / 10.2 %	54	B	85.68 % / 11.16 %	70	D	85.93 % / 10.73 %
7	B	79.19 % / 12.04 %	23	C	83.56 % / 13.03 %	39	A	79.77 % / 11.47 %	55	D	85.4 % / 10.99 %	71	D	86.97 % / 11.74 %
8	D	88.56 % / 11.27 %	24	B	78.96 % / 20.4 %	40	A	89.33 % / 10.28 %	56	D	76.53 % / 15.1 %	72	D	89.01 % / 10.16 %
9	D	87.37 % / 12.4 %	25	A	78.97 % / 14.6 %	41	D	78.04 % / 11.4 %	57	A	88.94 % / 10.14 %	73	A	84.87 % / 12.45 %
10	C	79.84 % / 18.45 %	26	C	78.19 % / 21.71 %	42	B	88.79 % / 11.18 %	58	C	81.2 % / 11.62 %	74	B	83.43 % / 11.38 %
11	D	87.7 % / 10.03 %	27	C	79.88 % / 18.13 %	43	B	87.17 % / 10.27 %	59	D	89.26 % / 10.19 %	75	D	89.43 % / 10.12 %
12	D	85.84 % / 13.78 %	28	B	82.43 % / 10.07 %	44	B	79.11 % / 20.68 %	60	C	86.21 % / 11.7 %	76	A	85.43 % / 11.67 %
13	D	78.13 % / 19.72 %	29	D	81.31 % / 15.45 %	45	C	79.72 % / 18.61 %	61	A	79.14 % / 14.85 %	77	B	85.47 % / 11.65 %
14	A	86.84 % / 11.55 %	30	A	83.76 % / 12.19 %	46	C	88.54 % / 10.31 %	62	A	78.03 % / 19.01 %	78	B	82.45 % / 13.95 %
15	B	89.8 % / 10.1 %	31	D	86.84 % / 11.97 %	47	B	81.78 % / 13.48 %	63	C	80.16 % / 10.73 %	79	C	83.21 % / 16.11 %
16	B	83.9 % / 10.88 %	32	A	89.29 % / 10.0 %	48	C	80.02 % / 12.23 %	64	C	86.67 % / 12.06 %	80	B	79.83 % / 14.8 %

Q.	Ans.	Correct	Q.	Ans.	Correct	Q.	Ans.	Correct	Q.	Ans.	Correct	Q.	Ans.	Correct
		Skipped			Skipped			Skipped			Skipped			Skipped
81	C	79.99 %	89	A	79.91 %	97	A	86.19 %	105	A	88.81 %	113	A	89.47 %
		17.97 %			18.85 %			12.33 %			10.09 %			10.02 %
82	C	80.11 %	90	B	80.21 %	98	B	79.21 %	106	B	77.9 %	114	D	81.94 %
		12.69 %			12.32 %			18.96 %			16.23 %			11.49 %
83	A	82.65 %	91	A	79.91 %	99	C	78.02 %	107	D	86.15 %	115	B	85.93 %
		11.85 %			14.94 %			14.06 %			10.58 %			13.83 %
84	B	86.04 %	92	B	76.95 %	100	B	88.28 %	108	D	78.52 %	116	D	77.09 %
		11.34 %			17.11 %			10.48 %			18.36 %			20.35 %
85	D	87.65 %	93	D	79.58 %	101	C	80.42 %	109	D	81.73 %	117	B	85.72 %
		10.33 %			11.05 %			12.9 %			12.46 %			12.16 %
86	D	80.08 %	94	B	87.93 %	102	D	79.16 %	110	D	76.45 %	118	C	89.51 %
		17.67 %			11.63 %			20.57 %			12.78 %			10.14 %
87	C	88.59 %	95	C	80.24 %	103	C	81.06 %	111	D	81.3 %	119	B	76.81 %
		10.99 %			11.55 %			18.82 %			11.48 %			18.35 %
88	D	85.68 %	96	D	79.27 %	104	D	85.86 %	112	B	89.97 %	120	B	83.44 %
		13.25 %			15.44 %			14.11 %			10.02 %			16.39 %

//Hints and Solutions//

1. $x^3 - y^3 - 3xy = x^3 - y^3 - 3xy(x y)$....as $(x - y) = 1$

$= (x - y)^3 = 1.$

2. y 4 3 2 1 -1 -3 -4

x 6 5 4 3 1 -1 -2

Hence, minimun value of

y/x = 4/-1 = 4

And maximum value of

$$\frac{y}{x} = \frac{4}{1} = 4$$
$$\therefore \frac{y}{x} \geq -4 \, and \, \frac{y}{x} \leq 4$$

3. (a. n)! = product of n consecutive natural numbers starting from 'a' which is atleast divisible by n!. (n)! = product of n consecutive natural numbers. For n = 2 : (a. n)! = a(a + 1) and n! = 2 a(a + 1) is divisible by 2!. For n = 3 : (a n)! = a(a + 1)(a + 2) and n! = 6. One of the factors of a(a + 1)(a + 2) is divisible by 3 and other by 2. Thus, proceeding in this manner, (a. n)! and n! have HCF = n! ∴ H = n!.

4. Factors of a^2 are 1. a and a^2.

Factors of ab are 1, a, b and ab.

Factors of a^3 are 1. a. a^2 and a^3.

5. $x^2 + y^2 + z^2 - 2xy - 2xz + 2yz$

$= (x - y - z)^2$

$= (b+c-c+a-a+b)^2 = 4b^2$

6. We ignore 1/7 and 1/9 because no sum of other denominator.numbers is going to give 7ths or 9ths in the denominator

Also, 1/5 and 1/10 are not enough to add up to anything (1/10, 2/10 and 3/10 are going to leave tenths left over no matter what else you add)

What's left is 1/2, 1/3, 1/4, 1/6, 1/8.

Sum total of these is 11/8. So we need all of them except 3/8, which means 1/2+1/3+1/6.

Which is the only way to do this with egyptian fractions whose denominators are 10 or less.

Hence maximum number of Egyptian fractions needed is 3

7. R is symmetric and not transitive

8. transitive and symmetric

9. Both (b) & (c)

10. 8

11. relexive, transitive and not symmetric

12. zero has no inverse

13. Determinant A = 0

⇒

$$\begin{vmatrix} 4 & 2 & 3 \\ 1 & 0 & 0 \\ 4 & 0 & 3 \end{vmatrix}$$

Hence rank of A=3

14. $x = A^{-1}b$

15. Both the statements are true

16. The system of homogeneous linear equations has a non-trivial solution if

$$\begin{bmatrix} 4d-1 & 1 & 1 \\ 0 & -1 & 1 \\ 0 & 0 & 4d-1 \end{bmatrix} = 0$$

=> $-(4d-1)^2 = 0$

=> $d = 1/4$

17.

$$Let \ A = \begin{bmatrix} a1 \\ b1 \\ c1 \end{bmatrix}; \quad B = \begin{bmatrix} a2 b2 c2 \end{bmatrix};$$

$$\therefore \quad C = \begin{bmatrix} a1a2 & a1b2 & a1c2 \\ b1a2 & b1b2 & b1c2 \\ c1a1 & c1b2 & c1c2 \end{bmatrix}$$

18. det (A + B) = det (A) + det (B)

19.

$$\phi(x) = \int_{x^2}^{0} \sqrt{t}\, dt = \frac{2}{3} t^{3/2} \Big|_{0}^{x^2} = \frac{2}{3} x^3$$

$$\frac{d\phi}{dx} = \frac{2}{3} \times 3x^2 = 2x^2$$

20. f '(x) = 3(x²-4x+3)   f ''(x)=6(x)-12

at x=1, f ''(1)

at x=3, f ''(3) = +ve

21.

$$\int_{0}^{5\pi} (2 - sinx)dx = [2x + cosx]_{0}^{5\pi}$$
$$= 10\pi - 1 - 1 = 10\pi - 2 > 0$$

22. Since f(x) = (1/x) is not continuous in [- 3, 3] [- 4, 2] or [- 1, 1], The point of discontinuity is '0'. Only in [2, 3] the function is continuous, and differentiable hence mean value theorem is applicable in [2, 3].

23. Since $f(x) = |x|$ is continuous in $[-1, 1]$ but it is not differentiable at $x = 0 \, \epsilon \, (-1, 1)$

24. Since value of a mod function cannot be less than zero, therefore

$f(x) = |x2 - 5x + 21|$ is zero.

25.

Equation of the bisectors of the angle between the lines $x^2 - 2mxy - y^2 = 0$ are given by

$$\frac{x^2 - y^2}{1 - (-1)} = \frac{xy}{-m} \quad \Rightarrow \quad x^2 + \frac{2}{m} xy - y^2 = 0 \quad \dots \text{(i)}$$

Since, (i) and $x^2 - 2nxy - y^2 = 0$ represents the same pair of lines.

$$\therefore \quad \frac{1}{1} = \frac{\frac{2}{m}}{-2n}$$

$$\Rightarrow \quad mn = -1 \quad \Rightarrow \quad mn + 1 = 0$$

26.

$$\text{Let } I = \int \frac{dx}{x \, (x^n + 1)}$$

$$\Rightarrow \quad I = \int \frac{x^{n-1}}{x^n \, (x^n + 1)} \, dx$$

$$\text{Put} \quad x^n = t$$

$$\Rightarrow \quad nx^{n-1} dx = dt$$

$$\Rightarrow \quad x^{n-1} \, dx = \frac{1}{n} \, dt$$

$$\therefore \quad I = \frac{1}{n} \int \left(\frac{1}{t} - \frac{1}{t + 1} \right) dt$$

$$= \frac{1}{n} \log \left(\frac{t}{t + 1} \right) = \frac{1}{n} \log \left(\frac{x^n}{x^n + 1} \right) + c$$

27.

$$\because \, [\vec{a} \ \vec{b} \ \vec{c}] = \vec{a} \cdot (\vec{b} \times \vec{c})$$

$$= \vec{a} \cdot \left(|\vec{b}| \, \vec{c} | \sin \frac{2\pi}{3} \, \hat{n} \right)$$

$$= |\vec{a}| \cdot |\vec{b}| |\vec{c}| \left(\sin \frac{2\pi}{3} \right) = 2 \times 3 \times 4 \times \frac{\sqrt{3}}{2}$$

$$= 12\sqrt{3}$$

28.

$$\because f(x) = (x - 2)(x - 4)(x - 6)\dots(x - 2n)$$

Taking log on both sides, we get

$$\log f(x) = \log(x - 2) + \log(x - 4)$$
$$+ \dots + \log(x - 2n)$$

On differentiating w.r.t. x, we get

$$\frac{1}{f(x)} f'(x) = \frac{1}{(x - 2)} + \frac{1}{(x - 4)}$$
$$+ \dots + \frac{1}{(x - 2n)}$$

$$f'(x) = (x - 4)(x - 6)\dots(x - 2n)$$
$$+ (x - 2)(x - 6)\dots(x - 2n)$$
$$+ \dots + (x - 2)(x - 6)\dots(x - 2(n - 1))$$

$$\therefore \quad f'(2) = (-2)(-4)\dots(2 - 2n)$$
$$= (-2)^{n-1}(1 \cdot 2 \dots (n - 1)) = (-2)^{n-1}(n - 1)!$$

29.

$$x \frac{dy}{dx} + 2y = x^2$$

$$\therefore \quad \frac{dy}{dx} + \frac{2}{x} y = x$$

$$\text{Integrating factor} = e^{\int \frac{2}{x} dx} = x^2$$

$$\therefore \text{Required solution is}$$

$$y \cdot x^2 = \int x^3 \, dx = \frac{x^4}{4} + c' = \frac{x^4 + c}{4}$$

$$\therefore \quad y = \frac{x^4 + c}{4x^2}$$

30.

Let $y = mx + c$ represents all non horizontal lines in a plane.

$$\therefore \quad \frac{dy}{dx} = m \text{ and } \frac{d^2y}{dx^2} = 0$$

31.

Equation of sphere is

$$2x^2 + 2y^2 + 2z^2 - 6x + 2y - 4z - 1 = 0$$

Radius of sphere is

$$\sqrt{\frac{9}{4} + \frac{1}{4} + \frac{4}{4} + \frac{1}{2}} = 2$$

Equation of family of concentric sphere is

$$x^2 + y^2 + z^2 - 3x + y - 2z + \lambda = 0 \quad \ldots(i)$$

$\therefore$ According to question,

$$\sqrt{\frac{9}{4} + \frac{1}{4} + 1 - \lambda} = 4$$

$$\Rightarrow \qquad \frac{14}{4} - \lambda = 16$$

$$\Rightarrow \qquad \lambda = \frac{14}{4} - 16 = -\frac{25}{2}$$

$\therefore$ From Eq. (i)

$$x^2 + y^2 + z^2 - 3x + y - 2z - \frac{25}{2} = 0$$

$$\Rightarrow 2x^2 + 2y^2 + 2z^2 - 6x + 2y - 4z - 25 = 0$$

32. Required number of ways = 8!

33.

$$\lim_{x \to 1} \frac{\displaystyle\int_{4}^{f(x)} 2t \, dt}{x - 1}$$

$$= \lim_{x \to 1} \frac{2f(x) \cdot f'(x)}{1}$$

$$= 2 f(1) \cdot f'(1) = 2 \cdot 4 \cdot 2 = 16$$

34.

Let E = Events of numbers divisible by 2 and 3

$$(i.e., \text{ divisible by } 6)$$

$$= (6, 12, \ldots, 96)$$

$$n(E) = 16$$

$\therefore$ Required probability $= \dfrac{^{16}C_3}{^{100}C_3}$

$$= \frac{\dfrac{16 \times 15 \times 14}{3 \times 2 \times 1}}{\dfrac{100 \times 99 \times 98}{3 \times 2 \times 1}}$$

$$= \frac{4}{1155}$$

35.

$$\frac{4}{3} + \frac{10}{9} + \frac{28}{27} + \ldots \text{ upto } n \text{ terms}$$

$$= \left(1 + \frac{1}{3}\right) + \left(1 + \frac{1}{9}\right) + \left(1 + \frac{1}{27}\right) + \ldots$$

$$\text{upto } n \text{ terms}$$

$$= n + \frac{1}{3}\left(1 + \frac{1}{3} + \frac{1}{3^2} + \ldots n \text{ terms}\right)$$

$$= n + \frac{\dfrac{1}{3}\left(1 - \dfrac{1}{3^n}\right)}{1 - \dfrac{1}{3}}$$

$$= \frac{2n + 1 - \dfrac{1}{3^n}}{2}$$

$$= \frac{3^n(2n + 1) - 1}{2(3^n)}$$

36.

In $\triangle ADC$,

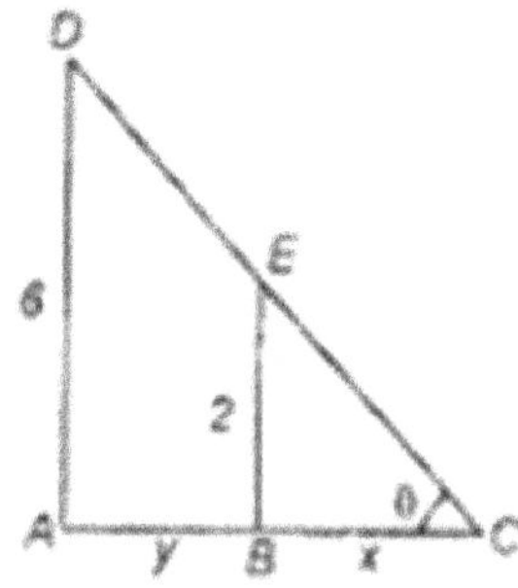

$$\tan\theta = \dfrac{6}{x+y}$$

and in $\triangle BCE$,

$$\tan\theta = \dfrac{2}{x}$$

$$\therefore \quad \dfrac{2}{x} = \dfrac{6}{x+y} \implies x+y = 3x$$

$$\implies \quad y = 2x$$

On differentiating w.r.t. t, we get

$$\dfrac{dy}{dt} = 2\dfrac{dx}{dt}$$

$$\implies \quad 6 = 2\dfrac{dx}{dt} \qquad \left(\because \dfrac{dy}{dt} = 6\,\text{given}\right)$$

$$\implies \quad \dfrac{dx}{dt} = 3\ \text{km/h}$$

37.

The given differential equation is

$$\dfrac{dy}{dx} = \dfrac{ax+h}{by+k}$$

On integrating both sides.

$$\int (by+k)\,dy = \int (ax+h)\,dx$$

$$\implies \quad \dfrac{by^2}{2} + ky = \dfrac{ax^2}{2} + hx + c$$

Thus, above equation represents a parabola, if

$$a = 0 \text{ and } b \neq 0$$

38.

$$\because\ y = a^x\,b^{2x-1}$$

Taking log on both sides, we get

$$\log y = x\log a + (2x-1)\log b$$

On differentiating w.r.t. x, we get

$$\dfrac{1}{y}\dfrac{dy}{dx} = \log a + \log b^2$$

$$\dfrac{dy}{dx} = y\log ab^2$$

Again differentiating, we get

$$\dfrac{d^2y}{dx^2} = \dfrac{dy}{dx}\log ab^2 = y\,(\log ab^2)^2$$

39.

The given equation is

$$x = 100t - \dfrac{25}{2}t^2$$

On differentiating w.r.t. t, we get

$$\dfrac{dx}{dt} = 100 - \dfrac{25}{2}\cdot(2t) = 100 - 25t$$

We know that the velocity of missile is zero at maximum height.

$$\therefore\ \text{On putting } \dfrac{dx}{dt} = 0,\ \text{we get}$$

$$100 - 25t = 0$$

$$\implies \quad t = 4$$

$$\therefore x = 100 \times 4 - \dfrac{25 \times 16}{2} = 400 - 200$$

$$= 200$$

40.

Any vector $\perp$ to $\vec{a}$ and coplanar to $\vec{b}$ and $\vec{c}$ is given by $\vec{a} \times (\vec{b} \times \vec{c})$

$\therefore$ Required vector is

$(2\hat{i} + \hat{j} + \hat{k}) \times [(\hat{i} + 2\hat{j} + \hat{k}) \times (\hat{i} + \hat{j} + 2\hat{k})]$

$$= (2\hat{i} + \hat{j} + \hat{k}) \times \begin{bmatrix} \hat{i} & \hat{j} & \hat{k} \\ 1 & 2 & 1 \\ 1 & 1 & 2 \end{bmatrix}$$

$= (2\hat{i} + \hat{j} + \hat{k}) \times (3\hat{i} - \hat{j} - \hat{k})$

$$= \begin{vmatrix} \hat{i} & \hat{j} & \hat{k} \\ 2 & 1 & 1 \\ 3 & -1 & -1 \end{vmatrix} = 5(\hat{j} - \hat{k})$$

41.

$n(U) = 20, n(A) = 12, n(B) = 9, n(A \cap B) = 4$

$\therefore \quad n(A \cup B) = n(A) + n(B) - n(A \cap B)$

$\qquad = 12 + 9 - 4 = 17$

Hence, $n[(A \cup B)^c] = n(U) - n(A \cup B)$

$\qquad = 20 - 17 = 3$

42.

$\because y = (1 - x)(2 - x)\dots(n - x)$

On taking log on both sides, we get

$\log y = \log(1 - x) + \log(2 - x) + \dots$

$\qquad\qquad\qquad + \log(n - x)$

$\dfrac{1}{y}\dfrac{dy}{dx} = \dfrac{1}{(1 - x)}(-1) + \dfrac{1}{(2 - x)}(-1) + \dots$

$\qquad\qquad\qquad + \dfrac{1}{(n - x)}(-1)$

$\dfrac{dy}{dx} = y\left[\dfrac{(2 - x)(3 - x)\dots(n - x)(-1) + \dots}{y}\right]$

$\left(\dfrac{dy}{dx}\right)_{x = 1} = 1 \cdot 2 \dots (n - 1)(-1)$

$\qquad\qquad = (-1)(n - 1)!$

43.

Let sides are $a = 13, b = 12, c = 5$

Now, $\qquad a^2 = b^2 + c^2$

$\Rightarrow \qquad (13)^2 = (12)^2 + 5^2$

$\Rightarrow \qquad 169 = 169$

$\Rightarrow \qquad \angle A = 90°$

We know, $R = \dfrac{a}{2\sin A}$

$\qquad R = \dfrac{13}{2 \cdot \sin 90°} = \dfrac{13}{2}$

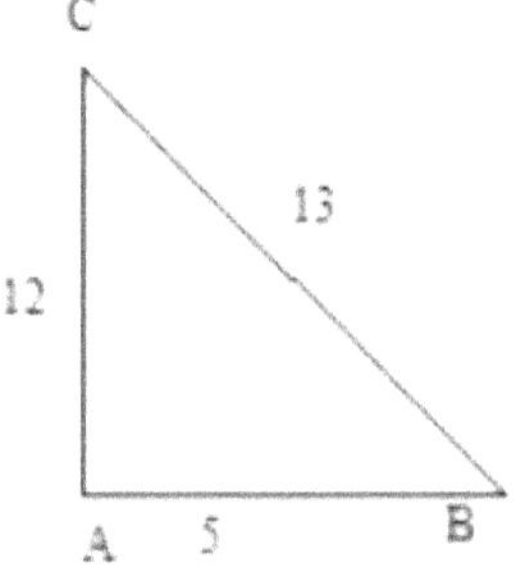

44.

Given that $\qquad {}^nC_{12} = {}^nC_6$

or $\qquad {}^nC_{n - 12} = {}^nC_6$

$\Rightarrow \qquad n - 12 = 6$

$\Rightarrow \qquad n = 18$

$\therefore \qquad {}^nC_2 = {}^{18}C_2 = \dfrac{18 \times 17}{2 \times 1}$

$\qquad\qquad = 153$

45.

Now, $\sqrt{2} + \sqrt{8} + \sqrt{18} + \sqrt{32} + \dots$

$= 1 \times \sqrt{2} + 2\sqrt{2} + 3\sqrt{2} + 4\sqrt{2} + \dots$

$= \sqrt{2}(1 + 2 + 3 + 4 + \dots \text{ upto 24 terms})$

$= \sqrt{2} \times \dfrac{24 \times 25}{2} = 300\sqrt{2} \left[\because \Sigma n = \dfrac{n(n + 1)}{2}\right]$

46.

Distance from centre (2, 1) to the line
$3x + 4y - 5$ = radius of circle

$$\Rightarrow \quad \frac{|3(2) + 4(1) - 5|}{\sqrt{3^2 + 4^2}} = r$$

$$\Rightarrow \quad \frac{5}{5} = r$$

$$\Rightarrow \quad r = 1$$

$\therefore$ Equation of circle is

$$(x - 2)^2 + (y - 1)^2 = 1^2$$

$$\Rightarrow \quad x^2 + y^2 - 4x - 2y + 4 + 1 = 1$$

$$\Rightarrow \quad x^2 + y^2 - 4x - 2y + 4 = 0$$

47.

Since the line $\dfrac{x}{\alpha} + \dfrac{y}{\beta} = 1$ touches the circle $x^2 + y^2 = a^2$.

$\therefore$ The perpendicular distance from centre $(0, 0)$ to the tangent = radius of the circle

$$\Rightarrow \quad \frac{|-1|}{\sqrt{\dfrac{1}{\alpha^2} + \dfrac{1}{\beta^2}}} = a$$

$$\Rightarrow \quad \frac{1}{a^2} = \frac{1}{\alpha^2} + \frac{1}{\beta^2}$$

The locus of $\left(\dfrac{1}{\alpha}, \dfrac{1}{\beta}\right)$ is

$$\frac{1}{a^2} = \frac{1}{x^2} + \frac{1}{y^2}$$

$\therefore$ It represents a circle.

48.

In ΔABC, $\tan 30° = \dfrac{BC}{AC}$

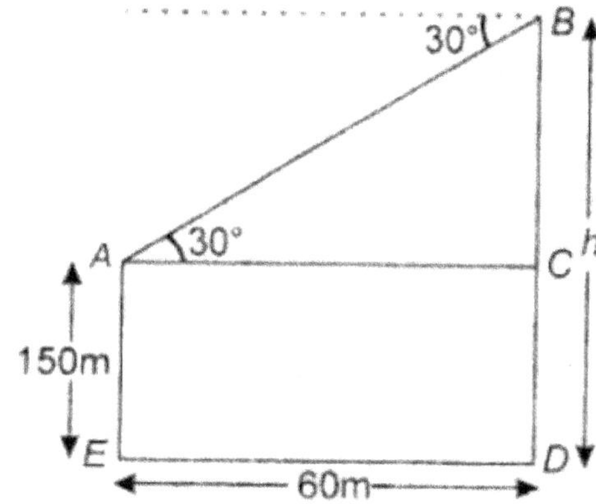

$$\Rightarrow \quad \frac{1}{\sqrt{3}} = \frac{h - 150}{60}$$

$$\Rightarrow \quad h - 150 = \frac{60}{\sqrt{3}}$$

$$\Rightarrow \quad h = (150 + 20\sqrt{3})\,\text{m}$$

49.

Given that,

$$\sin A + \cos B = a \qquad \qquad \dots(i)$$

and

$$\sin B + \cos A = b \qquad \qquad \dots(ii)$$

On squaring and adding Eqs. (i) and (ii), we get

$$\sin^2 A + \cos^2 B + 2\sin A \cos B + \sin^2 B$$

$$+ \cos^2 A + 2\sin B \cos A = a^2 + b^2$$

$$\Rightarrow \quad 2\sin(A + B) + 2 = a^2 + b^2$$

$$\Rightarrow \quad \sin(A + B) = \frac{a^2 + b^2 - 2}{2}$$

50.

$$\because f(x) = ax^2 + bx + c$$

and $\qquad g(x) = px^2 + qx$

Since, $g(1) = f(1)$

$\Rightarrow \qquad p + q = a + b + c \qquad \text{...(i)}$

and $\qquad g(2) - f(2) = 1$

$\Rightarrow \qquad 4p + 2q - 4a - 2b - c = 1 \qquad \text{...(ii)}$

also $\qquad g(3) - f(3) = 4$

$\Rightarrow \qquad 9p + 3q - 9a - 3b - c = 4 \qquad \text{...(iii)}$

From Eqs. (i) and (ii)

$$2p = 2a - c + 1$$

Now, $g(4) - f(4)$

$$= 16p + 4q - 16a - 4b - c$$
$$= 12p + 4(p + q) - 16a - 4b - c = 6 - 3c$$

51.

Let $I = \int e^x \left(\dfrac{1 + \sin x}{1 + \cos x} \right) dx$

$$= \int e^x \dfrac{\left(1 + 2 \sin \frac{x}{2} \cos \frac{x}{2} \right)}{2 \cos^2 \frac{x}{2}} dx$$

$$= \int \frac{1}{2} e^x \sec^2 \frac{x}{2} \, dx + \int e^x \tan \frac{x}{2} \, dx$$

$$= \frac{1}{2} \left[2e^x \tan \frac{x}{2} - \int 2e^x \tan \frac{x}{2} \, dx + \int e^x \tan \frac{x}{2} \, dx \right]$$

$$= e^x \tan \frac{x}{2} - \int e^x \tan \frac{x}{2} \, dx + \int e^x \tan \frac{x}{2} \, dx + c$$

$$= e^x \tan \frac{x}{2} + c$$

52.

On comparing given equation with $\dfrac{x^2}{a^2} - \dfrac{y^2}{b^2} = 1,$

we get

$$a^2 = \cos^2 \alpha \quad \text{and} \quad b^2 = \sin^2 \alpha$$

$$\therefore \qquad \sin^2 \alpha + \cos^2 \alpha = a^2 + b^2$$

$$\Rightarrow \qquad 1 = a^2 + b^2$$

Now, $\qquad e = \sqrt{\dfrac{a^2 + b^2}{a^2}}$

$$= \sqrt{\dfrac{1}{\cos^2 \alpha}} = \dfrac{1}{\cos \alpha}$$

Now, focus: $ae = \cos \alpha \cdot \dfrac{1}{\cos \alpha} = 1$

53.

The centre and radius of the first circle $x^2 + y^2 + 2x + 8y - 23 = 0$ are $C_1 (-1, -4)$ and $r_1 = \sqrt{40}$

Similarly, the centre and radius of second circle $x^2 + y^2 - 4x - 10y + 9 = 0$ are $C_2 (2, 5)$ and $r_2 = \sqrt{20}$

Now, $C_1 C_2 = \sqrt{(2 + 1)^2 + (5 + 4)^2}$

$$= \sqrt{9 + 81} = \sqrt{90}$$

and $\qquad r_1 + r_2 = \sqrt{40} + \sqrt{20}$

also $\qquad r_1 - r_2 = \sqrt{40} - \sqrt{20}$

Here, $r_1 - r_2 < C_1 C_2 < r_1 + r_2$

$\therefore$ Two common tangents can be drawn.

54.

Let $z = \dfrac{1 + 2i}{1 - (1 - i)^2}$

$$= \dfrac{1 + 2i}{1 - (1^2 + i^2 - 2i)} = \dfrac{1 + 2i}{1 + 2i}$$

$$= 1$$

$\therefore \quad |z| = 1$ and $\text{amp}(z) = \tan^{-1} \left(\dfrac{0}{1} \right) = 0$

55.

$$f(x) = \dfrac{|x|}{1 + |x|} = \begin{cases} \dfrac{x}{1 + x} & , \ x \geq 0 \\[2mm] \dfrac{-x}{1 - x} & , \ x < 0 \end{cases}$$

Graph of f(x)

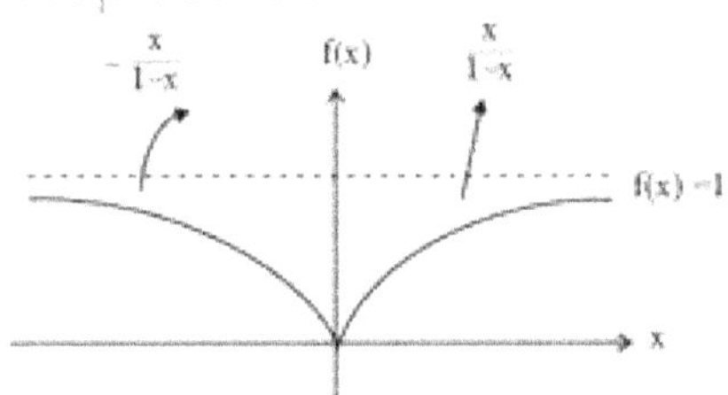

From graph we can see that, for two value of 'x', f(x) has same value so f(x) is not injective.

Also, range of f(x) is [0, 1)

So it is not surjective also.

56.

Let equation of the line through P(3, 8, 2) and parallel to the plane $3x + 2y - 2z + 15 = 0$ be

$$\frac{x-3}{A} = \frac{y-8}{B} = \frac{z-2}{C} \quad ...(i)$$

Then, $3A + 2B - 2C = 0$ ...(ii)

Let line (i) intersect $\dfrac{x-1}{2} = \dfrac{y-3}{4} = \dfrac{z-2}{3}$ at Q

then $\begin{vmatrix} x_1 - x_2 & y_1 - y_2 & z_1 - z_2 \\ a_1 & b_1 & c_1 \\ a_2 & b_2 & c_2 \end{vmatrix} = 0$

$$\Rightarrow \begin{vmatrix} 3-1 & 8-3 & 2-2 \\ A & B & C \\ 2 & 4 & 3 \end{vmatrix} = 0$$

$$\Rightarrow 15A - 6B - 2C = 0 \quad ...(iii)$$

From equation (ii) and equation (iii)

$$\frac{A}{\begin{vmatrix} 2 & -2 \\ -6 & -2 \end{vmatrix}} = \frac{B}{\begin{vmatrix} -2 & 3 \\ -2 & 15 \end{vmatrix}} = \frac{C}{\begin{vmatrix} 3 & 2 \\ 15 & -6 \end{vmatrix}}$$

$$\Rightarrow \frac{A}{2} = \frac{B}{3} = \frac{C}{6}$$

Substituting A, B and C in equation (i)

$$\frac{x-3}{2} = \frac{y-8}{3} = \frac{z-2}{6}$$

This is the equation of line PQ parallel to the plane $3x + 2y - 2z + 15 = 0$

Now, 'Q' is the point where this line cuts the line

$$\frac{x-1}{2} = \frac{y-3}{4} = \frac{z-2}{3}$$

So, point 'Q' will satisfy this line also

Any point 'Q' on line

$$\frac{x-3}{2} = \frac{y-8}{3} = \frac{z-2}{6} = \lambda$$

is Q$(2\lambda + 3, \; 3\lambda + 8, 6\lambda + 2)$

When this point also lies on $\dfrac{x-1}{2} = \dfrac{y-3}{4} = \dfrac{z-2}{3}$

$$\Rightarrow \frac{(2\lambda + 3) - 1}{2} = \frac{3\lambda + 8 - 3}{4} = \frac{6\lambda + 2 - 2}{3}$$

$$\Rightarrow \lambda = 1$$

Point Q = (5, 11, 8)

length of PQ $= \sqrt{(5-3)^2 + (11-8)^2 + (8-2)^2}$

$$= \sqrt{4 + 9 + 36}$$

$$= 7 \text{ unit}$$

57.

Let the centre be at $(0,0)$

Thus, the equation of the ellipse becomes

$$\frac{(x)^2}{a^2} + \frac{y^2}{b^2} = 1$$

Differentiating w.r.t x, we get

$$\Rightarrow \frac{2(x)}{a^2} + \frac{2y}{b^2} \cdot \frac{dy}{dx} = 0 \quad ....(1)$$

$$Thus, we\ get, \frac{dy}{dx} = -\left(\frac{x}{y}\right) \cdot \frac{b^2}{a^2}$$

$$Differntiating\ the\ equation\ 1\ w.r.t\ x$$

$$\Rightarrow \frac{2}{a^2} + \frac{2y}{b^2} \cdot \frac{d^2y}{dx^2} + \frac{2}{b^2} \cdot \left(\frac{dy}{dx}\right)^2 = 0$$

$$\Rightarrow \frac{b^2}{a^2} + y \cdot \frac{d^2y}{dx^2} + \left(\frac{dy}{dx}\right)^2 = 0$$

$$\Rightarrow -\frac{y}{x} \cdot \frac{dy}{dx} + y \frac{d^2y}{dx^2} + \left(\frac{dy}{dx}\right)^2 = 0$$

58.

Consider the triangle with sides 1, x and $\sqrt{1 + x^2}$

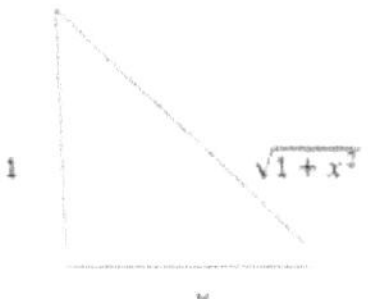

$$\sin\left(\cot^{-1}(x)\right) = \frac{1}{\sqrt{1 + x^2}}$$

$$\cos\left(\cot^{-1}(x)\right) = \frac{x}{\sqrt{1 + x^2}}$$

So,

$$\sqrt{1 + x^2}\left[\left\{\frac{x^2}{\sqrt{1 + x^2}} + \frac{1}{\sqrt{1 + x^2}}\right\}^2 - 1\right]^{\frac{1}{2}}$$

$$= \sqrt{1 + x^2}\left[1 + x^2 - 1\right]^{\frac{1}{2}}$$

$$= x\sqrt{1 + x^2}$$

59.

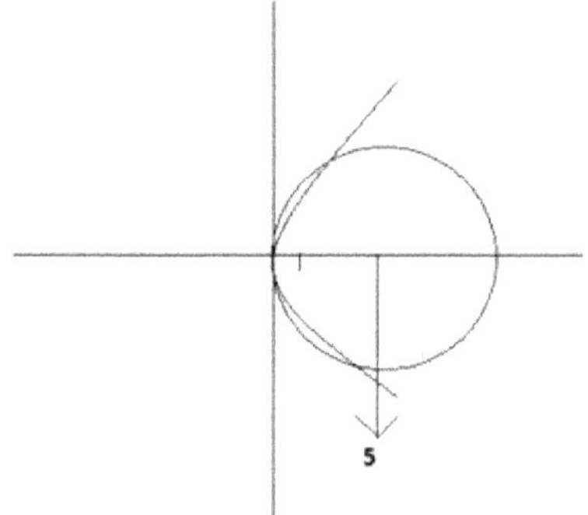

Now

$(x-5)^2 + y^2 = 25$ and $y^2 = 9x$

$(x-5)^2 + 9x = 25$

$\Rightarrow x^2 - 10x + 9x = 0$

$\Rightarrow x^2 - x = 0$

$x = \{0,1\}$

So area in one quadrant

$\int_0^1 Circle\,(y)dx - Parabola(y)dx$

$\Rightarrow \int_0^1 \sqrt{25 - (x-5)^2}\,dx - \sqrt{9x}\,dx$

$\Rightarrow \left| \left(\frac{x-5}{2}\right)\sqrt{25-(x-5)^2} + \frac{25}{2}\sin^{-1}\left(\frac{x-5}{5}\right) - \frac{3.2}{3}x^{\frac{3}{2}} \right|_0^1$

$\Rightarrow \left(-6 - \frac{25}{2}\sin^{-1}\left(\frac{4}{5}\right) - 2\right) - \left(0 - \frac{2}{2}\cdot\frac{\pi}{2}\right)$

$\Rightarrow \frac{2\pi}{4} - 8 - \frac{25}{2}\sin^{-1}\left(\frac{4}{5}\right)$

60.

Sum of odd coefficients of $(1+z)^5$ is $2^{5-1} = 2^4 = 16 = x$

$a+b+c+d = 16$ and $-16 < a < x$

Let $a = e-16$ then $e > 0$

$e - 16 + b + c + d = 16$

$e + b + c + d = 32$

Number of positive integral solutions $= (n+r-1)c_{r-1}$

$= (32+4-1)c_{4-1} = (35)c_3$

61. $2 + 2 + 4 = 8$

And $8 + 1 + 7 = 16$

Similarly,

$1 + 6 + 3 = 10$

And $4 + 9 + 7 = 20$

Here, the sum of the digits of the second group of numbers is twice the sum of the digits of the first group of numbers.

62.

The pattern is:

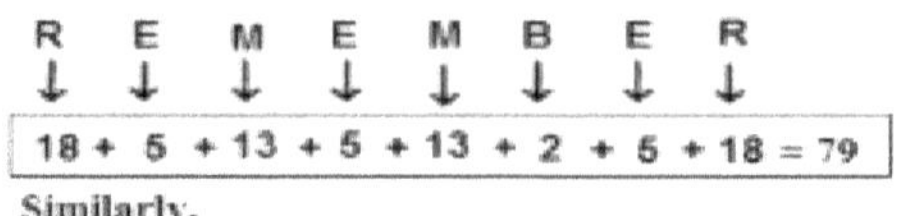

63. We found guns in arsenal. Similarly, we found contents in the Index.

64. The sequence of letters given is given below, which is the way-

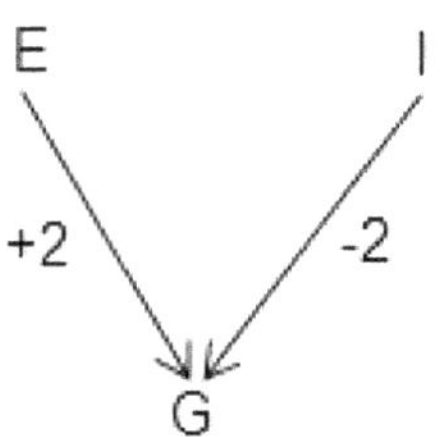

Similarly,

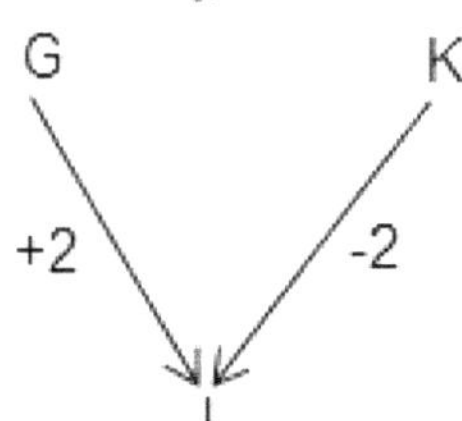

65. The sequence of the given numbers is as follows-

$14+1=15^2=225$

$21+1=22^2=484$

66. $4^3, 5^3, 225, 6^3$

67. Except 729, the sum of the digits of all other numbers is 12 while the sum of the digits of 729 is 18.

68. The pattern followed here is:

J (-4) → F

U (-4) → Q

P (-4) → L

But, X (-5) → S (thus, odd letters pair).

69. Except (165, 33), all others follow the same pattern as:

108/18=6

126/21=6

162/27=6

But, 165/33=5

70. 2367 → 2 + 3 + 6 + 7 = 18,

4374 → 4 + 3 + 7 + 4 = 18,

5319 → 5 + 3 + 1 + 9 = 18,

6182 → 6 + 1 + 8 + 2 = 17.

Thus 6182 is the odd one out.

71. Elephant belongs to the Herbivore group and Tiger is not related to either elephants or herbivores.

72. All these are independent.

73.

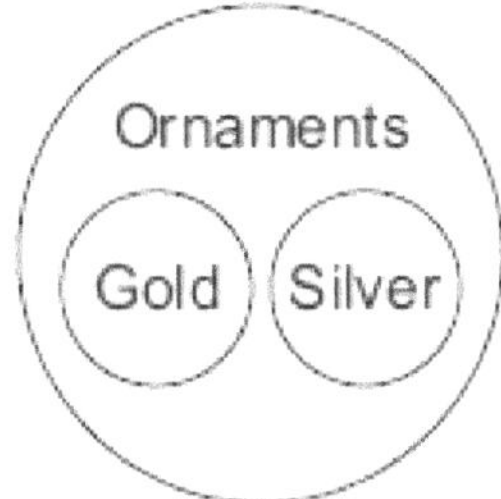

74.

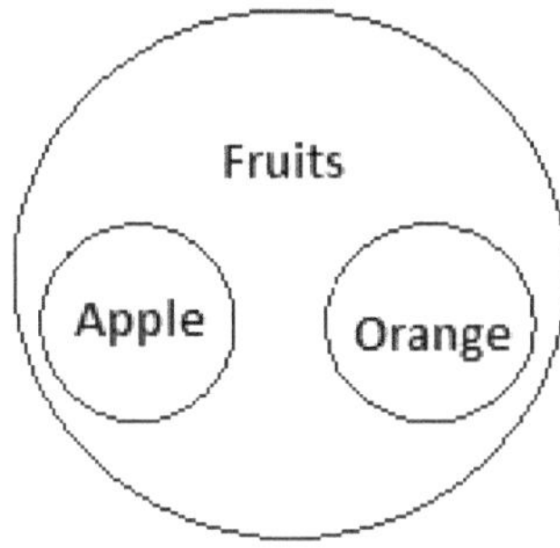

75. 6 and 9 are shown in Y so not a part of X.

76. Correct answer is (A)

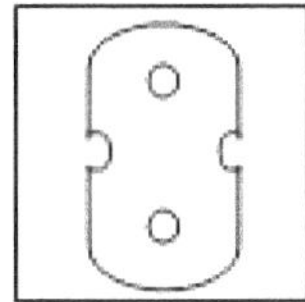

77. Option 2 represents the correct unfolded form of figure (Z)

78. Water image (B) is just reverse of Figure (X)

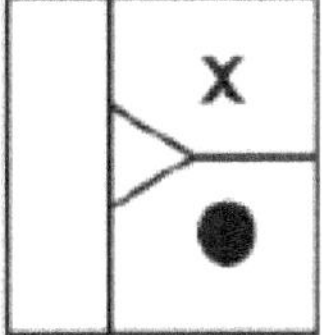

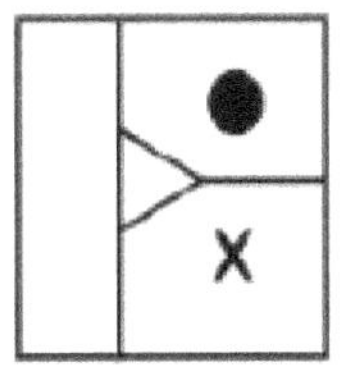

79. the correct answer figure is (C).

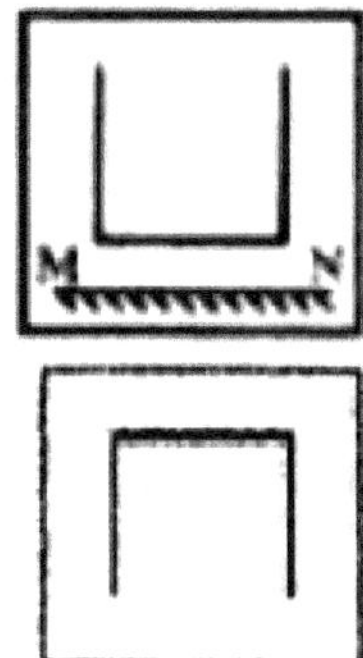

80.

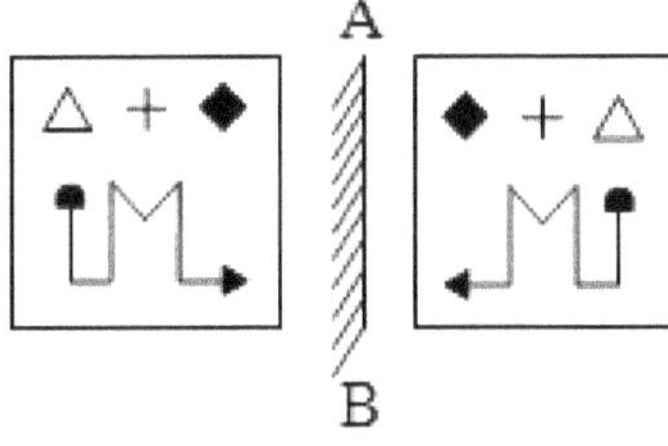

81. A Graphical User Interface is a computer interface that allows users to interact with a device through graphical elements such as pictures and animations, as opposed to text-based commands.

82. Input

83. Time during which a job is processed by the computer is Execution Time.

84. A flip-flop or latch is a circuit that has two stable states and can be used to store state information as Memory devices.

85. A real-time operating system (RTOS) is an operating system (OS) intended to serve real-time applications that process data as it comes in, typically without buffer delays. Processing time requirements (including any OS delay) are measured in tenths of seconds or shorter increments of time.

86. Multitasking, in an operating system, is allowing a user to perform more than one computer task (such as the operation of an application program) at a time. The operating system is able to keep track of where you are in these tasks and go from one to the other without losing information.

MS DOS does not implement the multitasking.

87. Microsoft Windows XP Professional x64 Edition, released on April 25, 2005, is an edition of Windows XP for x86-64 personal computers. It is designed to use the expanded 64-bit memory address space provided by the x86-64 architecture.

The primary benefit of moving to 64-bit is the increase in the maximum allocatable random-access memory (RAM

88. Authentication

89. End key. The End key is a key found on a computer keyboard that moves the cursor to the end of the line, document, page, cell, or screen of where your cursor is positioned.

90. Moves the cursor one Page Down

91. Moves the cursor one paragraph down

92. Moves the cursor one screen up

93. Click on Merge and Center tool on formatting toolbar

94. towards the bottom left corner

95. shows the name of cell or range currently working on

96. data sheet

97. 4

98. If you choose to select from the pre-made slide layouts, you cannot delete the objects in the layout

99. A PowerPoint template is a pattern or blueprint of a slide or group of slides that you save as a .potx file. Templates can contain layouts, theme colors, theme fonts, theme effects, background styles, and even content.

You can create your own custom templates and store them, reuse them, and share them with others. Additionally, you can find many different types of free templates built-in to PowerPoint. You can search for templates that are right for your presentation when you go to File > New in PowerPoint.

100. Each Microsoft PowerPoint theme includes a built-in color scheme to apply to your slides. If you don't like the available choices, you can create custom color schemes in PowerPoint to use in your presentation.

101. Sentences B and D hold the key to solving this question.

Sentence B says that at least in the rich world "that wasteful truth" has been overcome. What does this refer to?

Sentence A talks of elite American colleges now admitting men with lower grades just to even up the student numbers. Obviously this is not the "wasteful truth".

Sentence C quotes Stendhal and says that all geniuses born women are lost to public good. This is the "wasteful truth" referred to in sentence B. So B follows C.

Sentence D talks of a "monumental advance". Again, what does this refer to? The fact that geniuses born women are lost to public good has now been overcome in the rich word. So much so that, elite colleges are now admitting men with lower grades just to even up the numbers. So D follows A.

Hence, the answer is CBAD

102. Sentence A tells us what characterizes hate speech. Sentence C tells us what is not tantamount to hate speech. There is an obvious link here. A follows C.

Sentence D tells us that the student body's activism has been associated with hate speech by detractors. Again, we see a link with sentence C, which tells us that such an association is "spurious". So C follows D.

Sentence B, which discusses what the management ought to do provides a conclusion to the paragraph.

Hence, the answer is DCAB

103. Both sentences A and C look to be good opening sentences for the paragraph. So we need to look for clues that link the sentences.

Let us consider sentence B. It starts off with "that entailed" and discusses how the British tried to orchestrate a regional balance of power. This is obviously linked to sentence C. So B follows C.

We also note that sentence A declares commercial interests to be the driving force of the British Empire's global expansion. Sentence C refers to the factors that help realize commercial goals. So C follows A.

D makes a good concluding sentence.

Hence, the answer is ACBD

104. At the outset, both sentences A and B seem to offer a good choice to start the paragraph.

Sentence C states that if they are in a position to act, pilots can override "this mechanism". What can the mechanism refer to? The obvious answer is the code that opens the cockpit door discussed in sentence D. So C follows D.

Sentence D refers to exceptional circumstances when access to the cockpit can be obtained. Both situations discussed to here assume that the cockpit is no longer commandeered from within- i.e when the emergency affects the pilot or cockpit area, the crew can use a code to gain access. When the pilots are immobilized, the doors open automatically.

Sentence A refers to the search for a solution to the problem of access to the cockpit when the plane is still commandeered from within.

So A follows D.

However, we also know that C follows D. Considering sentences A and C, it is clear C is a better choice to immediately follow D than A, as it refers to the mechanism of overriding access to the cockpit.

Consider sentence B. This talks of flight safety efforts being focused on threats from the passenger side, leading to fortification of the cockpit. Sentence D talks of the exceptional circumstances when the fortified cockpit can be accessed. So D follows B.

Hence, the answer is BDCA

105. Sentence B suggests that a "fund-starved" country like India should not worry about foreign institutional investment which will come and go based on the external environment.

Sentence D talks of finding ways to protect the Indian economy from "external vicissitudes".

Sentence B offers a possible solution to the problem of foreign investment ebb and flow based on the environment outside. So B follows D, possibly immediately after.

Sentence D talks of a "new normal" kind of environment. Let us look at the other sentences to see what this could be referring to.

Sentence A talks of continued monetary easing by some nations and shrinking global trade.

Sentence C talks of how it is up to the political bosses to kick start the economy, as "everyone" is waiting for the other to act first.

Either of the two sentences above could be the "new normal" environment.

If we take the "new normal" environment to refer to the continued monetary easing and shrinking global trade, we have the sentence order ADB. The only answer option with this sequence is a) ADBC. This makes a cogent paragraph.

If we take the "new normal" environment to refer to "everyone waiting for the other to act first", we have the sentence order CDB. The answer option with this sequence is b) CDBA. This however, does not make a cogent paragraph, as there is no logic in sentence A following sentence B. In fact, considering just sentences A and B, it is clear B follows A. Sentence A sets a context. Sentence B suggests what should be done in this context.

Hence, the answer is ADBC

106. Criterion is singular and criteria, plural. The sentence given refers to only one criterion—evidence of misconduct. So, the options that use 'criteria' are wrong.

The usages 'criterion for determining' and 'criterion in determining' are both correct in the given context. 'To determine if a president gets impeached' mixes up tenses, and 'to determining the impeachment of a President' is incorrect usage.

Hence, the answer is option B

107. The modifier "by the president" is misplaced in the given sentence. The modifier should be close to the word it modifies, which, in this case, is the decision and not the Paris Agreement. The correct expression is "the decision by the president" or "the president's decision".

The second error is the use of the preposition "from". The correct usage is "pull out of".

The third error is the omission of the preposition 'in' before China. Where did the decision draw heavy criticism? Within the US, internationally, and specifically, in China.

Option (d) corrects all these errors.

Hence, the answer is option D

108. There are two verbs in the given sentence- 'occur' and 'are'. Let us look at each of these in turn to identify the subject associated with the verb.

'One of the problems' is singular, as it refers to one of many problems. So, the right verb to be used with this subject is 'is', not 'are'. The correct usage is "One of the problems........is...."

Now, consider the verb 'occur'. The subject that 'occur' is associated with is 'problems', not 'one of the problems'. So, the subordinate clause - the clause beginning with 'that'- takes a plural verb. Why is this so? The verb must agree with the subject of the clause, which is the relative pronoun 'that'. The pronoun has the same number as its antecedent, which is 'problems'. Since 'problems' is plural, 'that' is also plural, and so the verb associated with it must agree with 'problems'. Problems occur. So, the correct usage is "one of the problems that occur".

Another way to test this is to reword the sentence: Of the problems that occur, one is...

Also note that 'incidence' is the frequency of occurrence of something. As the sentence refers to the frequency of occurrence of a single metric- lung cancer- 'incidence' has to be used in singular.

Hence, the answer is option D

109. The given sentence has a faulty parallel structure. What follows 'and' must be parallel to what follows 'both'. But in the given sentence, 'both' is followed by 'to increase', while 'and' is followed by 'create'. The correct construction is— 'both to increase European military capacity within NATO and to create...'

Note here that 'both serves...' is also incorrect, as it is faulty parallelism.

Also, the article to be used with 'European' is 'a', not 'an', as 'European' begins with a consonant sound.

Hence, the answer is option D

110. The subject of the sentence is 'the sheer number'. This is singular, as the noun 'number' is singular. The verb 'has' relates to this, and not 'cars'.

The expression 'the number' indicates a single arithmetical value. So, it is followed by a singular verb. On the other hand, expression 'a number' serves as an indefinite pronoun meaning many. So, it is followed by a plural verb.

The adjective 'sheer' meaning utter or veritable is the correct word to be used in the given context.

Hence, the answer is option D

111. Statement a -There isn't more literary fraud in our age. More fraud is coming to light due to the Internet's surveillance.

True. The passage states the above.

Statement b - The line dividing novels and fake memoirs was never clear.

True. The author believes that the novel was born out of such "confusion".

Statement c - As long as the main or essential part of a memoir is correct, it does not matter if lesser details do not stand up to verification.

True. The author firmly believes that memoirs should not be held to journalistic standards of factuality.

Statement d - There exists now a widespread, diseased culture of literary fraud.

False. The passage argues more cases of fraud are coming to light, thanks to the internet.

Hence, the answer is D

112. Statement a - It was an unintentional deception but it stated the truth of human nature and was hence acceptable.

The deception by Richardson in 'Pamela' was clearly intentional, so this statement is not correct.

Statement b - It was just a ploy to capture the imagination of the readers with the truth of the possible.

Richardson's authorship of Pamela's letters was, according to the author, only a stratagem or ploy to captivate readers. Because the writing contained the truth of the possible- the truth of human nature- this was merely a lie and not a hoax. So statement b is correct.

Statement c - It was a deception perpetrated simply to make money.

A deception perpetrated to make money is a hoax. The author believes Richardson did not attempt a hoax. So we rule out this option.

Statement d - It was a mere prank, and did not generate public interest.

Again, we can rule out option d. We know from the passage that Richardson's authorship was revealed shortly after the novel was published and that he was "hailed as an innovator". Statement d also does not explain the author's comment.

Hence, the answer is B

113. Verisimilitude means the appearance of truth. It can refer to something that, as an assertion, has merely the appearance of truth. In the passage, this is the meaning that the word takes on, when the author talks of "hold them accountable for their verisimilitudes".

Of the choices given, the word 'absurdity' is the farthest removed from verisimilitude in meaning.

Hence, the answer is absurdity

114. Statement a - Before the 12th century BC, the use of syllabic writing existed in Ancient Greece.

We know this to be true from the passage, which talks of the Mycenaean fore-bearers of the Greeks using syllabic writing.

Statement b - Phoenician traders flourished in Greece at the time the Homeric epics were composed.

The passage states that the Phoenicians traders were much admired for their work during the time the Illiad was composed

and about a century later, when the Odyssey was composed, the Phoenicians did not enjoy much favor in Greece due to their competitive penetration of the Greek market.

Statement c - Greek, Roman and modern European literacy can be traced back to the Phoenicians.

This is stated in the passage and is true.

Statement d - Iliad and Odyssey are purely oral poetic speech, set to rhyme.

False. While these epics were composed in oral poetic speech, this was in the traditional meter of unrhymed dactylic hexameters. They are not set to rhyme.

Hence, the answer is D

115. The main idea of the passage is that the Iliad and Odyssey were composed by two distinct individuals differing in temperament and artistic accomplishment; probably both called Homer, practising the same traditional craft of oral composition and recitation.

Statement a - There could have been many Homers, old and often sightless wandering reciters of heroic legends.

While the above statement is true, this is not the main idea of the passage. The passage focuses on the 2 great epics in Western literature, Iliad and Odyssey and asserts that they were composed by two distinct individuals.

Statement b - Attributing the composition of the Iliad and Odyssey to one Homer is erroneous.

The above is clearly what the passage has been written to substantiate. This is the main idea of the passage.

Statement c - Both Iliad and Odyssey were created without recourse to writing.

The passage given discusses and proves this point. However, the author's intention in talking about this is to show that there was an "illiterate environment" in Greece at the time the epics were created, which explains why there is no historical record about the two different Homers who composed them.

Statement d - The Iliad and the Odyssey are of distinct literary types, physical structure and style.

Again, while the above is true and explained in the passage, it is one aspect of the author's argument that the epics ascribed to Homer were likely to have been composed by two different individuals of different temperaments and artistic style.

Hence, the answer is B

116. Blank (1): The word Homo after the blank tells us that the correct answer for this blank is genus, not genius.

Blank (2): The discovery of stone tools that predate any other tools found till now clearly tells us that what we have long presumed- that the genus Homo was first to craft stone tools- is wrong.

So the correct answer for blank (2) is however.

Hence, the answer is D

117. Blank (1): The sentence starts with "even in" the Nordic countries, household chores are "still" not evenly distributed. This leads us to egalitarian as the right choice for this blank, ruling out "elitist" and "prejudiced". Non-partisan meaning objective and not taking sides, is also not appropriate here.

Blank (2): Rebuked or admonished are choices here. Reprimand is rebuke by a formal authority, and condemned is too strong a word for this blank. Choice (b) with the words egalitarian and rebuked is hence the correct answer.

Hence, the answer is B

118. Blank (1): Except for "though", all other choices make sense in this blank. We need to look at the next sentence to finalize the choice for this blank.

Blank (2): We have 4 similar sounding word choices for this blank. The correct choice is factious, meaning dissentious or given to faction. Fractious, meaning unruly or quarrelsome, is also a possible choice, but ruled out because the first word with this option is "though", which does not make sense in blank (1). Facetious (frivolous) and factitious (artificial) do not make sense here.

Hence, the answer is C

119. Blank (1): The second sentence, which states that only seventeen percent of the government was actually shutdown, indicates the rhetoric referred to in blank (1) is not efficacious. Specious (apparently good but actually lacking merit), spurious (not genuine) and facile (superficial) all remain possibilities.

Blank (2): The obvious choices here are discord and disagreement. We have ruled out option A which has the word discord. So the correct answer is option B (specious, disagreement).

Hence, the answer is B

120. Blank (1): The correct choice here is "of".

Blank (2):The words "while" and "though" both fit in this blank.

The answer choice B which has the word "of" for blank 1 and "while" for blank 2 is hence the right answer.

Hence, the answer is B

Mathematics

Q.1

If $\frac{3\pi}{4} < \theta < \pi$ then $\sqrt{2 \cot \theta + \frac{1}{\sin^2 \theta}}$ is equal to

A. $1 + \cot \theta$

B. $-(1+\cot \theta)$

C. $1 - \cot \theta$

D. $-1 + \cot \theta$

Q.2 If the period of the function f(x) = sin (x/n) is 4π, then n is equal to then x is equal to

A. 1 **B.** 4 **C.** 8 **D.** 2

Q.3 If $\alpha + \beta = \pi/2$ and $\beta + \gamma = \alpha$, tan α equals

A. 2 (tan β + tan γ)

B. tan β + tan γ

C. tan β + 2 tan γ

D. 2 tan β + tan γ

Q.4 The value of sin 12° sin 48° sin 54° =

A. 2/3 **B.** 1/2 **C.** 1/8 **D.** 1/3

Q.5 The value of k for which (cos x + sin x)^2 + k sin x cos x − 1 = 0 is an identity is

A. -1 **B.** -2 **C.** 0 **D.** 1

Q.6

If cosec $\theta = \frac{p+q}{p-q}$, then cot $\left(\frac{\pi}{4} + \frac{\theta}{2} \right) =$

A. $\sqrt{\frac{p}{q}}$ **B.** $\sqrt{\frac{q}{p}}$ **C.** $\sqrt{pq}$ **D.** pq

Q.7 The number of all possible matrices of order 3 × 3 with each entry 0 or 1 is

A. 18 **B.** 512

C. 81 **D.** none of these

Q.8 k I$_2$ is the matrix

A. $\begin{bmatrix} k & k \\ 0 & 0 \end{bmatrix}$ **B.** $\begin{bmatrix} k & k \\ k & k \end{bmatrix}$

C. $\begin{bmatrix} 0 & k \\ k & 0 \end{bmatrix}$ **D.** $\begin{bmatrix} k & 0 \\ 0 & k \end{bmatrix}$

Q.9 If A is a matrix of order 3 ×4, then each row of A has

A. 3 elements **B.** 4 elements

C. 12 elements **D.** 7 elements

Q.10 If P is of order 2×3 and Q is of order 3×2, then PQ is of order

A. 2×3 **B.** 3×2 **C.** 3×3 **D.** 2×2

Q.11 If A and B are invertible matrices of the same order, then (AB)$^{-1}$ is equal to

A. A^{-1} B^{-1} **B.** A^{-1}B **C.** AB^{-1} **D.** B^{-1} A^{-1}

Q.12

If A = $\begin{bmatrix} 0 & 0 & 0 & 0 \\ 0 & 0 & 0 & 0 \\ 1 & 0 & 0 & 0 \\ 0 & 1 & 0 & 0 \end{bmatrix}$, then

A. A^3 = O **B.** A^2 = O

C. A^2 = I **D.** none of these

Q.13 If R is a relation from a non-empty set A to a non-empty set B, then

A. R = A $\cap$ B **B.** R = A $\cup$ B

C. R = A × B **D.** R $\subset$ A × B

Q.14 Let R be the relation on N defined as x R y iff x + 2y = 8. The domain of R is

A. {2, 4, 8} **B.** {2, 4, 6, 8}

C. {2, 4, 6} **D.** {1, 2, 3, 4}

Q.15 Which of the following is not an equivalence relation on I, then set of integers; x, y $\in$ I:

A. x R y $\Leftrightarrow$ x + y is an even integer

B. x R y $\Leftrightarrow$ x < y

C. x R y $\Leftrightarrow$ x − y is an even integer

D. x R y $\Leftrightarrow$ x = y

Q.16 Let A = {1, 2, 3} and R = {(1, 1), (2, 2), (1, 2), (2, 1), (2, 3)} be a relation on A, then R is

A. reflexive **B.** symmetric

C. antisymmetric **D.** none of these

Q.17 Let A = {1, 2, 3}. Which of the following is not an equivalence relation on A?

A. {(1, 1), (2, 2), (3, 3)}

B. {(1, 1), (2, 2), (3, 3), (1, 2), (2, 1)

C. {(1, 1), (2, 2), (3, 3), (2, 3), (3, 2)}

D. none of these

Q.18 If A and B are non-empty sets and A x B = B x A, then

A. A is a proper subset of B

B. B is a proper subset of A

C. A = B

D. None of these

Q.19 $\int 2^{2x} 2^x \, dx =$

A. $\dfrac{2^{2^x}}{(\log 2)^2} + C$ **B.** $\dfrac{2^{2^x}}{\log 2} + C$

C. $\dfrac{2^{2^x}}{\log_2 e} + C$ **D.** none of these

Q.20

$$\int_0^2 x\,[x]\,dx =$$

A. 1/2   **B.** 3/2
C. 5/2   **D.** none of these

Q.21

$$\int_0^{2\pi} (\cos x)^{2001}\,dx =$$

A. 2001   **B.** 2000
C. 1001   **D.** none of these

Q.22 The differential equation of all non-vertical line in a plane is
A. $d^2y/dx^2 = 0$ **B.** $d^2x/dy^2 = 0$
C. $dy/dx = 0$ **D.** $dx/dy = 0$

Q.23 The order of the differential equation whose general solution is
$y = A \cos x + B \sin x + Ce^{-x}$; A , B, C being arbitrary constants, is
A. 1   **B.** 2
C. 3   **D.** none of these

Q.24 The slope at any point of a curve y = f (x) is given by $dy/dx = 3x^2$ and it passes through (– 1, 1). The equation of the curve is
A. $y = x^3 + 2$ **B.** $y = -x^3 - 2$
C. $y = 3x^3 + 4$ **D.** $y = -x^3 + 2$

Q.25 If $\vec{a}$ is a proper vector, then number of unit vectors collinear with $\vec{a}$ is
A. 1   **B.** 2
C. 3   **D.** infinitely many

Q.26 If $\vec{a}$ and $\vec{b}$ are non-collinear proper vectors, then number of unit vectors at right angles to both $\vec{a}$ and $\vec{b}$ is
A. 1   **B.** 2
C. 4   **D.** infinitely many

Q.27

The vectors $2\hat{i} + 3\hat{j} - 6\hat{k}$ and $a\hat{i} + b\hat{j} + c\hat{k}$ are perpendicular when
A. a = 1, b = 2, c = 3   **B.** a = 3, b = 2, c = 1
C. a = 6, b = 2, c = 3   **D.** none of these

Q.28 If θ is the angle between vectors $\vec{a}$ and $\vec{b}$ such that $\vec{a} \cdot \vec{b} \geq 0$, then
A. $0 \leq \theta \leq \pi$ **B.** $\pi/2 \leq \theta \leq \pi$
C. $0 \leq \theta \leq \pi/2$ **D.** $0 < \theta < \pi/2$

Q.29

The magnitude of the resultant of vectors $\vec{a} = 2\hat{i} - \hat{j} + \hat{k}$ and $\vec{b} = \hat{i} + 2\hat{j} + 3\hat{k}$ is

A. $\sqrt{6}$ **B.** $\sqrt{34}$
C. $\sqrt{14}$ **D.** none of these

Q.30

The unit vector in the direction of sum of the vectors $\hat{i} + \hat{j} + \hat{k}$, $2\hat{i} - \hat{j} - \hat{k}$ and $2\hat{j} + 6\hat{k}$ is

A. $\dfrac{1}{7}(3\hat{i} + 2\hat{j} + 6\hat{k})$

B. $-\dfrac{1}{7}(3\hat{i} + 2\hat{j} + 6\hat{k})$

C. $\dfrac{1}{49}(3\hat{i} + 2\hat{j} + 6\hat{k})$

D. none of these

Q.31 The ratio in which the join of (1, –2, 3) and (4, 2, –1) is divided by the XOY plane is
A. 1 : 3   **B.** 3 : 1
C. –1 : 3   **D.** None of these.

Q.32 The direction cosines of the ray from p (1, –2, 4) to Q (–1, 1, –2) are
A. < –2, 3, –6 >   **B.** < 2, –3, 6>
C. < 2/7, –3/7, 6/7>   **D.** < – 2/7, 3/7, –6/7>

Q.33 The equation $|\vec{r}|^2(\vec{r} \cdot \vec{a}) + \lambda = 0$ represents a sphere if
A. $a^2 > \lambda$ **B.** $a^2 < \lambda$
C. $a^2 = \lambda$ **D.** None of these

Q.34 The line $x/1 = y/2 = z/3$ and the plane $2x - 4y + 2z = 3$ meet in
A. Only one point
B. No point
C. Infinitely many points
D. None of these.

Q.35 The radius of the sphere whose centre is the pointy
$C(3\hat{i} + 6\hat{j} - 2\hat{k})$ and which touches the plane $\vec{r} \cdot (2\hat{i} - 2\hat{j} - \hat{k}) = 10$ is
A. 7   **B.** 14/3
C. 14   **D.** None of these.

Q.36

Equation of any plane containing the line $\dfrac{x - x_1}{a} = \dfrac{y - y_1}{b} = \dfrac{z - z_1}{c}$ is
$A(x - x_1) + B(y - y_1) + C(z - z_1) = 0$, where
A. A/a=B/b=C/c   **B.** $Ax_1 + By_1 + Ca_1 = 0$
C. Aa + Bb + Cc = 0   **D.** $ax_1 + by_1 + cz_1 = 0$

Q.37 Solution set of the inequality x ≥ 0 is
A. half plane on the left of Y-axis
B. half plane on the right of Y-axis excluding the points on Y-axis
C. half plane on the right of Y –axis including the point on Y-axis
D. None of these

Q.38 Solution set of the inequality $y \leq 0$ is
A. half plane below the X-axis excluding the points on X-axis
B. half plane below the X-axis including the point on X – axis
C. half plane above the X-axis
D. None of these

Q.39 Region represented by the inequalities $x \geq 0$, $y \geq 0$ is
A. First quadrant
B. second quadrant
C. third quadrant
D. fourth quadrant

Q.40 Objective function of a L.P.P. is
A. a constant
B. a function to be optimized
C. a relation between the variables
D. None of these

Q.41 Which of the following sets is not convex?
A. $\{(x, y) : x + y \leq 1\}$
B. $\{(x, y) : x^2 + y^2 > 1\}$
C. $\{(x, y) : x^2 + y^2 \leq 1\}$
D. none of these

Q.42 Which of the following sets is convex?
A. $\{(x, y) : x^2 + y^2 \geq 1\}$
B. $\{(x, y) : 2x^2 + 3y^2 \leq 6\}$
C. $\{9x, y) : 4 \leq x^2 + y^2 \leq 9\}$
D. none of these

Q.43 A coin is tossed again and again. if tail appears on first three tosses, then the chance that head appears on fourth toss is
A. 1/16
B. 1/2
C. 1/8
D. None of these.

Q.44 If E_1 and E_2 are mutually exclusive events, then
A. $P(E_1) + P(E_2) \leq 1$
B. $P(E_1) + P(E_2) \geq 1$
C. $P(E_1) + P(E_2) = 1$
D. None of these

Q.45 A man speaks truth in 75% cases. He throws a dice and reports that it is a six. The probability that it is actually a six is
A. 3/8
B. 1/5
C. 3/24
D. None of these

Q.46 The probability that when 10 balls are distributed among 3 boxes, the first will contain 2 balls is
A. $2^8/3^{10}$
B. $^{10}C_2 2^8 /3^{10}$
C. $^{10}C^2/3^{10}$
D. None of these

Q.47 If A and are two mutually exclusive events, then $P(A + B)$ is equal to
A. $P(A)\, P(B)$
B. $P(A) + P(B)$
C. $P(A)\, P(B') + P(A')\, P(B)$
D. $P(A)\, P(B') - P(A')\, P(B)$.

Q.48 If E_1 and E_2 are two independent events, then $P(E_1 \cap E_2)$ is equal to
A. $P(E_1 \cap E_2) + P(E_2)$
B. $P(E_1) + P(E_2) + P(E_1 \cup E_2)$
C. $P(E_1)\, P(E_2)$
D. None of these.

Q.49 The value of λ, for which the sum of squares of the roots of the equation $x^2 - (\lambda + 2)x - \lambda + 1 = 0$ assumes the least value, is
A. 3
B. 1/3
C. -3
D. -1/3

Q.50
Solution set of the equation $\dfrac{2x-3}{x-1} + 1 = \dfrac{6x^2 - x - 6}{x-1}$ is
A. $\{1, -1/3\}$
B. $\{1\}$
C. $\{-1/3\}$
D. none of these

Q.51 The condition for the polynomial equation $ax^2 = bx = c = 0$ to be a quadratic is
A. $a > 0$
B. $a < 0$
C. $a \neq 0$
D. $a \neq 0, b \neq 0$

Q.52 Only one of the roots of $ax^2 + bx + c = 0$, $a \neq 0$ is zero if
A. $c = 0$
B. $c = 0, b \neq 0$
C. $b = 0, c = 0$
D. $b \neq 0, c \neq 0$

Q.53 The expression $ax^2 + bx + c$, $a > 0$ is positive for all real x only if
A. $b^2 - 4ac = 0$
B. $b^2 - 4ac \geq 0$
C. $b^2 - 4ac < 0$
D. $b^2 - 4ac > 0$

Q.54 The value (s) of p for which the equation $2x^2 - 2\sqrt{2}\, px + p = 0$ has equal roots is (are)
A. 0
B. 4
C. 0, 4
D. none of these

Q.55
$$\underset{x \to 0}{Lt}\ \frac{5^x - 4^x}{4^x - 3^x}\ \text{is equal to}$$
A. 0
B. $\log(5/4) / \log(4/3)$
C. 1
D. None of these

Q.56
$$\underset{x \to \infty}{Lt}\ \left(\frac{x+5}{x+1}\right)^{x+4}\ \text{is equal to}$$
A. e^4
B. e^5
C. e^3
D. none of these

Q.57
$$\text{The minimum value of } \sqrt{e^{x^4} - 1}\ \text{is}$$
A. 1
B. e
C. 0
D. none of these

Q.58
$$\underset{x \to 0}{Lt}\ \frac{1 - \cos x}{x}\ \text{is equal to}$$
A. 1/2
B. 0
C. 1
D. none of these

Q.59

$$Lt_{x \to 0} (1 + 2x)^{\frac{x+3}{x}} \text{ is equal to}$$

A. e^3 **B.** $e^{3/2}$
C. e^6 **D.** none of these

Q.60

$$Lt_{x \to 0} \frac{(1-x)^n - 1}{x} \text{ is}$$

A. $n!$ **B.** $(n-1)!$ **C.** $-n$ **D.** n

Analytical Ability & Logical Reasoning

Q.61 Common Information

In a survey conducted at a University, it was found that 51% of the students wanted to learn French as a foreign language, 48% wanted to learn German and 52% wanted to learn Russian.

Of the surveyed students, 21% wanted to learn both French and German, 23% wanted German and Russian and 24% wanted French and Russian. Only 12% wanted to learn all three languages. A total of 500 students were surveyed.

How many students wanted to learn only German?

A. 76   **B.** 80   **C.** 82   **D.** 90

Q.62 Common Information

In a survey conducted at a University, it was found that 51% of the students wanted to learn French as a foreign language, 48% wanted to learn German and 52% wanted to learn Russian.

Of the surveyed students, 21% wanted to learn both French and German, 23% wanted German and Russian and 24% wanted French and Russian. Only 12% wanted to learn all three languages. A total of 500 students were surveyed.

What is the number of students interested in French and Russian only?

A. 50   **B.** 55   **C.** 60   **D.** 65

Q.63 Common Information

In a survey conducted at a University, it was found that 51% of the students wanted to learn French as a foreign language, 48% wanted to learn German and 52% wanted to learn Russian.

Of the surveyed students, 21% wanted to learn both French and German, 23% wanted German and Russian and 24% wanted French and Russian. Only 12% wanted to learn all three languages. A total of 500 students were surveyed.

How many more students (apart from those who wanted to learn French and Russian only) were interested in either French or Russian?

A. 320   **B.** 325   **C.** 330   **D.** 335

Q.64 Common Information

In a survey conducted at a University, it was found that 51% of the students wanted to learn French as a foreign language, 48% wanted to learn German and 52% wanted to learn Russian.

Of the surveyed students, 21% wanted to learn both French and German, 23% wanted German and Russian and 24% wanted French and Russian. Only 12% wanted to learn all three languages. A total of 500 students were surveyed.

How many students were not interested in any of the languages?

A. 25   **B.** 30   **C.** 35   **D.** 40

Q.65 Common Information

In a survey conducted at a University, it was found that 51% of the students wanted to learn French as a foreign language, 48% wanted to learn German and 52% wanted to learn Russian.

Of the surveyed students, 21% wanted to learn both French and German, 23% wanted German and Russian and 24% wanted French and Russian. Only 12% wanted to learn all three languages. A total of 500 students were surveyed.

What is the ratio of the number of students interested in exactly two languages to those interested in only one language?

A. 30/51   **B.** 32/51   **C.** 40/51   **D.** 42/51

Q.66 Here are some words translated from an artificial language.

gorblflur means fan belt

pixngorbl means ceiling fan

arthtusl means tile roof

Which word could mean "ceiling tile"?

A. gorbltusl   **B.** flurgorbl   **C.** arthflur   **D.** pixnarth

Q.67 Here are some words translated from an artificial language.

hapllesh means cloudburst

srenchoch means pinball

resbosrench means ninepin

Which word could mean "cloud nine"?

A. leshsrench   **B.** ochhapl
C. haploch   **D.** haplresbo

Q.68 Here are some words translated from an artificial language.

agnoscrenia means poisonous spider

delanocrenia means poisonous snake

agnosdeery means brown spider

Which word could mean "black widow spider"?

A. deeryclostagnos   **B.** agnosdelano
C. agnosvitriblunin   **D.** trymuttiagnos

Q.69 Here are some words translated from an artificial language.

moolokarn means blue sky

wilkospadi means bicycle race

moolowilko means blue bicycle

Which word could mean "racecar"?

A. wilkozwet   **B.** spadiwilko
C. moolobreil   **D.** spadivolo

Q.70 Here are some words translated from an artificial language.

migenlasan means cupboard

lasanpoen means boardwalk

cuopdansa means pullman

Which word could mean "walkway"?

A. poenmigen   **B.** cuopeisel

C. lasandansa   **D.** poenforc

Q.71 Odometer is to mileage as compass is to

A. speed   **B.** hiking   **C.** needle   **D.** direction

Q.72 Marathon is to race as hibernation is to

A. winter   **B.** bear   **C.** dream   **D.** sleep

Q.73 Window is to pane as book is to

A. novel   **B.** glass   **C.** cover   **D.** page

Q.74 Cup is to coffee as bowl is to

A. dish   **B.** soup   **C.** spoon   **D.** food

Q.75 Yard is to inch as quart is to

A. gallon   **B.** ounce   **C.** milk   **D.** liquid

Q.76 In each of the following questions, two statements are given followed by three or four conclusions numbered I, II, III and IV. You have to take the given statements to be true even if they seem to be at variance from the commonly known facts and then decide which of the given conclusions logically follows from the given statements disregarding commonly known facts.

Statements: All branches are flowers. All flowers are leaves.

Conclusions:

I. All branches are leaves.

II. All leaves are branches.

III. All flowers are branches.

IV. Some leaves are branches.

A. None follows

B. Only I and IV follow

C. Only II and III follow

D. All follow

Q.77 In each of the following questions, two statements are given followed by three or four conclusions numbered I, II, III and IV. You have to take the given statements to be true even if they seem to be at variance from the commonly known facts and then decide which of the given conclusions logically follows from the given statements disregarding commonly known facts.

Statements: Some bags are pockets. No pocket is a pouch.

Conclusions:

I. No bag is a pouch.

II. Some bags are not pouches.

III. Some pockets are bags.

IV. No pocket is a bag,

A. None follows

B. Only I and III follow

C. Only II and III follow

D. Only either I or IV follows

Q.78 In each of the following questions, two statements are given followed by three or four conclusions numbered I, II, III and IV. You have to take the given statements to be true even if they seem to be at variance from the commonly known facts and then decide which of the given conclusions logically follows from the given statements disregarding commonly known facts.

Statements: All aeroplanes are trains. Some trains are chairs.

Conclusions:

I. Some aeroplanes are chairs.

II. Some chairs are aeroplanes.

III. Some chairs are trains.

IV. Some trains are aeroplanes.

A. None follows

B. Only I and II follow

C. Only II and III follow

D. Only III and IV follow

Q.79 In each of the following questions, two statements are given followed by three or four conclusions numbered I, II, III and IV. You have to take the given statements to be true even if they seem to be at variance from the commonly known facts and then decide which of the given conclusions logically follows from the given statements disregarding commonly known facts.

Statements: All politicians are honest. All honest are fair.

Conclusions:

I. Some honest are politicians.

II. No honest is politician.

III.Some fair are politicians.

IV. All fair are politicians.

A. None follows

B. Only I follows.

C. Only I and II follow.

D. Only I and III follow

Q.80 In each of the following questions, two statements are given followed by three or four conclusions numbered I, II, III and IV. You have to take the given statements to be true even if they seem to be at variance from the commonly known facts and then decide which of the given conclusions logically follows from the given statements disregarding commonly known facts.

Statements: Some clothes are marbles. Some marbles are bags.

Conclusions:

I. No cloth is a bag.

II. All marbles are bags.

III.Some bags are clothes.

IV. No marble is a cloth.

A. Only either I or IV follows

B. Only either I or II follows

C. None follows

D. Only either I or III follows

Computer Awareness

Q.81 Which one of the following is not an application software package?

A. Red Hat Linux　　　　**B.** Microsoft Office
C. Adobe Pagemaker　　**D.** Open Office

Q.82 Which of the following statement is wrong?

A. Photoshop is a graphical design tool by Adobe
B. Linux is free and open source software
C. Linux is owned and sold by Microsoft
D. Windows XP is an operating system

Q.83 An error is also known as:

A. Bug　　**B.** Debug　　**C.** Cursor　　**D.** Icon

Q.84 Microsoft Word is an example of

A. an operating system
B. Processing device
C. Application software
D. an input device

Q.85 Which of the following Operating systems is better for implementing a Client-Server network

A. MS DOS　　　　**B.** Windows 95
C. Windows 98　　**D.** Windows 2000

Q.86 My Computer was introduced from

A. Windows 3.1　　**B.** Windows 3.11
C. Windows 95　　**D.** Windows 98

Q.87 Which of the following Windows do not have Start button

A. Windows Vista　　**B.** Windows 7
C. Windows 8　　　　**D.** None of above

Q.88 Which is the latest version of MS Windows?

A. Windows 2007　　**B.** Windows 8.1
C. Windows 2008　　**D.** Windows 10

Q.89 Page Down Key is used to

A. Moves the cursor one line down
B. Moves the cursor one page down
C. Moves the cursor one screen down
D. Moves the cursor one paragraph down

Q.90 "Ctrl + PageUp" is used to

A. Moves the cursor one Page Up
B. Moves the cursor one Paragraph Up
C. Moves the cursor one Screen Up
D. Moves the cursor one Line Up

Q.91 "Ctrl + Up Arrow" is used to

A. Moves the cursor one page up
B. Moves the cursor one line up
C. Moves the cursor one screen up
D. Moves the cursor one paragraph up

Q.92 "Ctrl + Home" is used to

A. Moves the cursor to the beginning of Document
B. Moves the cursor to the beginning of Line
C. Moves the cursor to the beginning of Paragraph
D. All of the above

Q.93 You can merge the main document with data source in Excel. In mail merge operation, Word is usually

A. server　　**B.** source　　**C.** client　　**D.** none

Q.94 How can you update the values of formula cells if Auto Calculate mode of Excel is disabled?

A. F8　　**B.** F9　　**C.** F10　　**D.** F11

Q.95 You want to set such that when you type Baishakh and drag the fill handle, Excel should produce Jestha, Aashadh and so on. What will you set to effect that?

A. Custom List
B. Auto Fill Options
C. Fill Across Worksheet
D. Fill Series

Q.96 Where can you change automatic or manual calculation mode in Excel?

A. Double CAL indicator on status bar
B. Go to Tools >> Options >> Calculation and mark the corresponding radio button
C. Both of above
D. None of above

Q.97 What feature will you use to apply motion effects in between a slide exits and another enters?

A. Slide Transition　　**B.** Slide Design
C. Animation Objects　**D.** Animation Scheme

Q.98 The difference between Slide Design and Auto Content Wizard is

A. Both are same
B. Auto Content Wizard is just the wizard version of Slide Design
C. Slide Design does not provide sample content but Auto Content Wizard provides sample content too!
D. Slide Design asks your choice in steps but Auto Content Wizard does not let you make choices

Q.99 In which menu can you find features like Slide Design, Slide Layout etc.?

A. Insert Menu　　**B.** Format Menu
C. Tools Menu　　**D.** Slide Show Menu

Q.100 Which menu provides you options like Animation Scheme, custom Animation, Slide Transition?

A. Insert Menu　　**B.** Format Menu
C. Tools Menu　　**D.** Slide Show Menu

English

Q.101 1.1971 war changed the political geography of the subcontinent

2.Despite the significance of the event. There has been no serious book about the conflict

3.Surrender at Dacca aims to fill this gap

4.It also profoundly altered the geo-strategic situation in South-East Asia

A. 1324   **B.** 3142   **C.** 2143   **D.** 1423

Q.102 1). Nonetheless, Tocqueville was only one of the first of a long line of thinkers to worry whether such rough equality could survive in the face of a growing factory system that threatened to create divisions between industrial workers and a new business elite.

2)."The government of democracy brings the nation of political rights to the level of the humblest citizens. He wrote ," Just as the dissemination of wealth brings the notion of property within the reach of all the members of the community".

3). Tocqueville was far too shrewd an observer to be uncritical about the US, but his verdict was fundamentally positive.

4). No visitor to the US left a more enduring record of his travels and observations than the French writer and political theorist Alexis de Tocqueville, whose 'Democracy in America', first published in 1835, remains one of the most trenchant and insightful analyses of American social and political practises.

A. 4132   **B.** 2134   **C.** 4321   **D.** 4213

Q.103 1). The potential exchanges between the officials of IBBF and the Maharashtra Body-Building Association has all the trappings of a drama we are accustomed to.

2). In the case of sports persons, there is room for some sympathy, but the apathy of the administrators, which has even led to sanctions from international bodies, is unpardonable.

3). A case in the point is the hefty penalty of US $10,000 slapped on the Indian Body-Building Federation for not fulfilling its commitment for holding the Asian Championships in Mumbai in October.

4). It is a matter of deep regret and concern that the sports administrators often cause more harm to the image of the country than sportsmen and sportswomen do through their dismal performances.

A. 3124   **B.** 4231   **C.** 4123   **D.** 3421

Q.104 1). Over the years, I have had the opportunities to observe and understand the thought processes behind the ads that have been flooding both the print and the TV media.

2). Although there is a huge shift in the quality of ads that we come across on a daily basis-- thanks essentially to improvement in technology--I somehow can't help but feel that the quality of communication of the message has become diluted.

3). Proportionally, the number of ads that lack in quality, have gone up exponentially as well!!

4). There is an increasing attempt by most companies to be seen as cool and funky.

5). Another reason could be the burgeoning number of companies, which means an exponential increase in the number of ads that are being made.

A. 43125   **B.** 43512   **C.** 12453   **D.** 21435

Q.105 1). His political career came to an abrupt end with China's military operation.

2). He attracted as as repelled.

3). He was responsible for the debacle.

4). A man of paradoxes, Menon remained an enigma.

A. 4312   **B.** 1342   **C.** 4213   **D.** 4132

Q.106 On the surface, the conquest of the Aztec empire by Herman Cortes is one of the most amazing military accomplishments in history. With a small fighting force numbering in the hundreds, Cortes led the Spanish explorers into victory against an Aztec population that many believe topped 21 million. In light of such a seemingly impossible victory, the obvious question is: how did a small group of foreign fighters manage to topple one of the world's strongest, wealthiest, and most successful military empires?

Several factors led to Cortes' success. First, the Spanish exploited animosity toward the Aztecs among rival groups and convinced thousands of locals to fight. In one account of a battle, it is recorded that at least 200,000 natives fought with Cortes. Next, the Spanish possessed superior military equipment in the form of European cannons, guns, and crossbows, leading to effective and efficient disposal of Aztec defenses. For example, Spanish cannons quickly defeated large Aztec walls that had protected the empire against big and less technically advanced armies.

Despite the Spanish advantages, the Aztecs probably could have succeeded in defending their capital city of Tenochtitlan had they leveraged their incredible population base to increase their army's size and ensured that no rogue cities would ally with Cortes. In order to accomplish this later goal, Aztec leader Motecuhzoma needed to send envoys to neighboring cities telling their inhabitants about the horrors of Spanish conquest and the inevitability of Spanish betrayal.

In addition, the Aztecs should have exploited the fact that the battle was taking place on their territory. No reason existed for the Aztecs to consent to a conventional battle, which heavily favored the Spanish. Motecuhzoma's forces should have thought outside the box and allowed Cortes into the city, only to subsequently use hundreds of thousands of fighters to prevent escape and proceed in surprise "door-to-door" combat. With this type of battle, the Aztecs would have largely thwarted Spanish technological supremacy. However, in the end, the superior weaponry of the Spanish, the pent-up resentment of Aztec rivals, the failure of Aztec diplomacy, and the lack of an unconventional Aztec war plan led to one of the most surprising military outcomes in the past one thousand years.

Which of the following best characterizes the main point the author is trying to convey in the passage?

A. Aztec failure to fight an unconventional war led to an unnecessary defeat

B. Spanish victory was neither as impressive nor as surprising as it may first appear

C. Resentment toward the Aztecs led to their demise

D. Herman Cortes masterminded an amazing military accomplishment

Q.107 On the surface, the conquest of the Aztec empire by Herman Cortes is one of the most amazing military accomplishments in history. With a small fighting force numbering in the hundreds, Cortes led the Spanish explorers into victory against an Aztec population that many believe topped 21 million. In light of such a seemingly impossible victory, the obvious question is: how did a small group of

foreign fighters manage to topple one of the world's strongest, wealthiest, and most successful military empires?

Several factors led to Cortes' success. First, the Spanish exploited animosity toward the Aztecs among rival groups and convinced thousands of locals to fight. In one account of a battle, it is recorded that at least 200,000 natives fought with Cortes. Next, the Spanish possessed superior military equipment in the form of European cannons, guns, and crossbows, leading to effective and efficient disposal of Aztec defenses. For example, Spanish cannons quickly defeated large Aztec walls that had protected the empire against big and less technically advanced armies.

Despite the Spanish advantages, the Aztecs probably could have succeeded in defending their capital city of Tenochtitlan had they leveraged their incredible population base to increase their army's size and ensured that no rogue cities would ally with Cortes. In order to accomplish this later goal, Aztec leader Motecuhzoma needed to send envoys to neighboring cities telling their inhabitants about the horrors of Spanish conquest and the inevitability of Spanish betrayal.

In addition, the Aztecs should have exploited the fact that the battle was taking place on their territory. No reason existed for the Aztecs to consent to a conventional battle, which heavily favored the Spanish. Motecuhzoma's forces should have thought outside the box and allowed Cortes into the city, only to subsequently use hundreds of thousands of fighters to prevent escape and proceed in surprise "door-to-door" combat. With this type of battle, the Aztecs would have largely thwarted Spanish technological supremacy. However, in the end, the superior weaponry of the Spanish, the pent-up resentment of Aztec rivals, the failure of Aztec diplomacy, and the lack of an unconventional Aztec war plan led to one of the most surprising military outcomes in the past one thousand years.

The passage is sequentially organized in which of the following ways?

A. Introduce an enigma; explain the reasons for the enigma; discuss the inevitability of the enigma

B. Define a problem; explain the sources of the problem; offer a solution to the problem

C. Introduce a mystery; offer an explanation for the mystery; provide an alternative explanation for the mystery

D. Pose a question; offer an answer to the question; offer an alternative answer to the question

Q.108 On the surface, the conquest of the Aztec empire by Herman Cortes is one of the most amazing military accomplishments in history. With a small fighting force numbering in the hundreds, Cortes led the Spanish explorers into victory against an Aztec population that many believe topped 21 million. In light of such a seemingly impossible victory, the obvious question is: how did a small group of foreign fighters manage to topple one of the world's strongest, wealthiest, and most successful military empires?

Several factors led to Cortes' success. First, the Spanish exploited animosity toward the Aztecs among rival groups and convinced thousands of locals to fight. In one account of a battle, it is recorded that at least 200,000 natives fought with Cortes. Next, the Spanish possessed superior military equipment in the form of European cannons, guns, and

crossbows, leading to effective and efficient disposal of Aztec defenses. For example, Spanish cannons quickly defeated large Aztec walls that had protected the empire against big and less technically advanced armies.

Despite the Spanish advantages, the Aztecs probably could have succeeded in defending their capital city of Tenochtitlan had they leveraged their incredible population base to increase their army's size and ensured that no rogue cities would ally with Cortes. In order to accomplish this later goal, Aztec leader Motecuhzoma needed to send envoys to neighboring cities telling their inhabitants about the horrors of Spanish conquest and the inevitability of Spanish betrayal.

In addition, the Aztecs should have exploited the fact that the battle was taking place on their territory. No reason existed for the Aztecs to consent to a conventional battle, which heavily favored the Spanish. Motecuhzoma's forces should have thought outside the box and allowed Cortes into the city, only to subsequently use hundreds of thousands of fighters to prevent escape and proceed in surprise "door-to-door" combat. With this type of battle, the Aztecs would have largely thwarted Spanish technological supremacy. However, in the end, the superior weaponry of the Spanish, the pent-up resentment of Aztec rivals, the failure of Aztec diplomacy, and the lack of an unconventional Aztec war plan led to one of the most surprising military outcomes in the past one thousand years.

The author implies which of the following about the Aztec view toward an unconventional military confrontation of the Spanish?

A. The Aztecs did not consider it

B. The Aztecs considered it, but rejected it out of beliefs about how battles ought to be fought

C. The Aztecs considered this, but it was too late

D. The Aztecs were certain a victory could be achieved via traditional combat

Q.109 On the surface, the conquest of the Aztec empire by Herman Cortes is one of the most amazing military accomplishments in history. With a small fighting force numbering in the hundreds, Cortes led the Spanish explorers into victory against an Aztec population that many believe topped 21 million. In light of such a seemingly impossible victory, the obvious question is: how did a small group of foreign fighters manage to topple one of the world's strongest, wealthiest, and most successful military empires?

Several factors led to Cortes' success. First, the Spanish exploited animosity toward the Aztecs among rival groups and convinced thousands of locals to fight. In one account of a battle, it is recorded that at least 200,000 natives fought with Cortes. Next, the Spanish possessed superior military equipment in the form of European cannons, guns, and crossbows, leading to effective and efficient disposal of Aztec defenses. For example, Spanish cannons quickly defeated large Aztec walls that had protected the empire against big and less technically advanced armies.

Despite the Spanish advantages, the Aztecs probably could have succeeded in defending their capital city of Tenochtitlan had they leveraged their incredible population base to increase their army's size and ensured that no rogue cities would ally with Cortes. In order to accomplish this later goal, Aztec leader Motecuhzoma needed to send envoys to neighboring cities telling their inhabitants about the horrors of Spanish conquest and the inevitability of Spanish betrayal.

In addition, the Aztecs should have exploited the fact that the battle was taking place on their territory. No reason existed for the Aztecs to consent to a conventional battle, which heavily favored the Spanish. Motecuhzoma's forces should have thought outside the box and allowed Cortes into the city, only to subsequently use hundreds of thousands of fighters to prevent escape and proceed in surprise "door-to-door" combat. With this type of battle, the Aztecs would have largely thwarted Spanish technological supremacy. However, in the end, the superior weaponry of the Spanish, the pent-up resentment of Aztec rivals, the failure of Aztec diplomacy, and the lack of an unconventional Aztec war plan led to one of the most surprising military outcomes in the past one thousand years.

According to the passage, all of the following led to Cortes' success EXCEPT:

A. Advanced crossbows

B. Nimble military force

C. Local Spanish allies

D. Local tribal friction

Q.110 On the surface, the conquest of the Aztec empire by Herman Cortes is one of the most amazing military accomplishments in history. With a small fighting force numbering in the hundreds, Cortes led the Spanish explorers into victory against an Aztec population that many believe topped 21 million. In light of such a seemingly impossible victory, the obvious question is: how did a small group of foreign fighters manage to topple one of the world's strongest, wealthiest, and most successful military empires?

Several factors led to Cortes' success. First, the Spanish exploited animosity toward the Aztecs among rival groups and convinced thousands of locals to fight. In one account of a battle, it is recorded that at least 200,000 natives fought with Cortes. Next, the Spanish possessed superior military equipment in the form of European cannons, guns, and crossbows, leading to effective and efficient disposal of Aztec defenses. For example, Spanish cannons quickly defeated large Aztec walls that had protected the empire against big and less technically advanced armies.

Despite the Spanish advantages, the Aztecs probably could have succeeded in defending their capital city of Tenochtitlan had they leveraged their incredible population base to increase their army's size and ensured that no rogue cities would ally with Cortes. In order to accomplish this later goal, Aztec leader Motecuhzoma needed to send envoys to neighboring cities telling their inhabitants about the horrors of Spanish conquest and the inevitability of Spanish betrayal.

In addition, the Aztecs should have exploited the fact that the battle was taking place on their territory. No reason existed for the Aztecs to consent to a conventional battle, which heavily favored the Spanish. Motecuhzoma's forces should have thought outside the box and allowed Cortes into the city, only to subsequently use hundreds of thousands of fighters to prevent escape and proceed in surprise "door-to-door"

combat. With this type of battle, the Aztecs would have largely thwarted Spanish technological supremacy. However, in the end, the superior weaponry of the Spanish, the pent-up resentment of Aztec rivals, the failure of Aztec diplomacy, and the lack of an unconventional Aztec war plan led to one of the most surprising military outcomes in the past one thousand years.

Which of the following best characterizes the author's view about the inevitability of Aztec demise at the hands of the Spanish?

A. Absolutely Inevitable

B. Likely Inevitable

C. Ambivalent

D. Likely Not Inevitable

Q.111 You may wonder how the expert on fossils remain is able to trace descent through teeth, which seem _______ pegs upon which to hang whole ancestries.

A. Reliable   **B.** Inadequate

C. Novel   **D.** specious

Q.112 Seeing the pictures of our old home made me feel _______ and nostalgic.

A. fastidious   **B.** indignant

C. wistful   **D.** conciliatory

Q.113 Book publishing has long been _______ profession, partly because, for younger editors, the best way to win a raise or a promotion was to move on to another publishing house.

A. an innovative   **B.** a prestigious

C. an itinerant   **D.** a rewarding

Q.114 Part of the confusion in our societies _______ from our pursuit of efficiency and economic growth, in the _______ that these are the necessary ingredients of progress.

A. sterns, conviction

B. derives, evaluation

C. emerges, consideration

D. extends, planning

Q.115 War has been, throughout history, the chief _______ of social cohesion; and since science began, it has been the strongest _______ to technical progress.

A. Reason, encouragement

B. origin, boost

C. cause, provocation

D. source, incentive

Q.116 The people of the ancient Assyrian Empire were renowned warriors, although they also crafted some of the best-preserved ancient art.

A. were renowned warriors, although they also crafted

B. had been renowned warriors, although they also crafted

C. were renowned warriors, and also crafted

D. was renowned warriors, although they also crafted

Q.117 Sentence Correction

The administration discussed whether the number of students studying European languages was likely to decline when the senior lecturer retired.

A. whether the number of students studying European languages was likely

B. whether the number of students studying European languages were likely

C. if the students studying European languages were likely

D. if the number of European language students were likely

Q.118 With the advent of YouTube, Facebook, and Flickr, many savvy political consultants undertook revolutionary micro-targeting and get-out-the-vote techniques that enabled political candidates with cash-strapped budgets to be able to reach numerous likely voters and succeed in raising large numbers of money from enthusiastic and committed supporters in a short period of time.

A. cash-strapped budgets to be able to reach numerous likely voters and succeed in raising large numbers of money

B. cash-strapped budgets to reach numerous likely voters and be successful in raising large amounts of money

C. cash-strapped budgets to reach numerous likely voters, succeeding in raising large amounts of money

D. cash-strapped budgets to reach numerous likely voters and succeed in raising large amounts of money

Q.119 Among the litany of threats that many Israelis face, the potential for a nuclear-armed Iran is perhaps the more scary as this scenario could engulf the region in a violent war. This would likely result in historically unseen amounts of destruction, even for a region whose history is marred by perennial violence.

A. perhaps the more

B. perhaps the most

C. possibly, perhaps the most

D. possibly the greatest

Q.120 It is highly desirable that you furnish evidence of your expenses before you submit your final accounts.

A. It is highly desirable that you furnish evidence of your expenses

B. It is highly desirable that you should furnish evidence of your expenses

C. It is highly to be desired that you furnish evidences of your expenses

D. You must furnish evidence of your expenses

// Smart Answer Sheet //

Correct | Percentage of students who answered correctly. **Skipped** | Percentage of students who skipped.

Q.	Ans.	Correct / Skipped	Q.	Ans.	Correct / Skipped	Q.	Ans.	Correct / Skipped	Q.	Ans.	Correct / Skipped	Q.	Ans.	Correct / Skipped
1	B	84.04 % / 11.47 %	17	D	80.29 % / 16.26 %	33	A	76.45 % / 22.13 %	49	C	88.88 % / 10.83 %	65	B	82.5 % / 12.94 %
2	D	83.98 % / 12.81 %	18	C	81.06 % / 16.29 %	34	B	85.07 % / 14.81 %	50	C	88.74 % / 10.01 %	66	D	85.92 % / 11.19 %
3	C	88.18 % / 10.7 %	19	A	88.46 % / 10.41 %	35	B	77.36 % / 17.07 %	51	C	82.1 % / 12.89 %	67	D	84.76 % / 12.56 %
4	C	82.53 % / 16.45 %	20	B	87.62 % / 10.2 %	36	C	77.24 % / 13.18 %	52	B	87.98 % / 10.07 %	68	C	76.24 % / 11.42 %
5	B	78.57 % / 21.42 %	21	D	83.39 % / 16.12 %	37	C	84.69 % / 10.51 %	53	C	87.23 % / 12.53 %	69	D	85.95 % / 12.66 %
6	B	87.37 % / 10.37 %	22	A	81.57 % / 17.14 %	38	B	81.02 % / 18.35 %	54	C	77.88 % / 10.06 %	70	D	86.05 % / 13.58 %
7	B	89.23 % / 10.28 %	23	C	83.91 % / 11.39 %	39	A	76.2 % / 20.54 %	55	B	88.37 % / 11.58 %	71	D	78.14 % / 16.44 %
8	D	80.2 % / 17.28 %	24	A	79.49 % / 14.87 %	40	B	84.09 % / 13.49 %	56	A	89.41 % / 10.25 %	72	D	81.2 % / 10.27 %
9	B	79.59 % / 13.72 %	25	B	86.65 % / 11.8 %	41	C	84.04 % / 10.57 %	57	C	85.86 % / 11.41 %	73	D	85.36 % / 13.45 %
10	D	79.92 % / 17.19 %	26	B	84.04 % / 12.52 %	42	B	88.76 % / 11.13 %	58	B	78.37 % / 15.98 %	74	B	81.54 % / 12.93 %
11	D	89.04 % / 10.2 %	27	C	83.22 % / 16.46 %	43	B	80.58 % / 12.59 %	59	C	85.55 % / 13.83 %	75	B	76.87 % / 21.7 %
12	B	82.11 % / 14.51 %	28	C	76.21 % / 23.69 %	44	A	78.48 % / 11.39 %	60	C	85.63 % / 13.43 %	76	B	83.49 % / 16.39 %
13	D	83.11 % / 15.62 %	29	B	87.86 % / 10.85 %	45	A	77.43 % / 21.04 %	61	B	89.78 % / 10.13 %	77	C	81.53 % / 16.04 %
14	C	86.53 % / 11.6 %	30	A	83.65 % / 14.41 %	46	B	84.12 % / 12.55 %	62	C	79.18 % / 17.78 %	78	D	88.31 % / 10.6 %
15	B	76.52 % / 22.79 %	31	B	78.26 % / 12.29 %	47	B	82.5 % / 13.65 %	63	D	85.58 % / 14.24 %	79	D	83.65 % / 11.77 %
16	D	78.8 % / 19.68 %	32	D	76.23 % / 12.33 %	48	C	81.96 % / 17.5 %	64	A	83.13 % / 14.85 %	80	D	77.49 % / 21.29 %

Q.	Ans.	Correct / Skipped	Q.	Ans.	Correct / Skipped	Q.	Ans.	Correct / Skipped	Q.	Ans.	Correct / Skipped	Q.	Ans.	Correct / Skipped
81	A	85.8 % / 12.88 %	89	C	82.42 % / 10.07 %	97	A	79.57 % / 15.38 %	105	C	81.87 % / 12.93 %	113	C	88.87 % / 10.85 %
82	C	87.8 % / 10.47 %	90	A	83.2 % / 10.98 %	98	C	80.74 % / 16.67 %	106	B	83.61 % / 15.21 %	114	C	86.53 % / 10.76 %
83	A	77.61 % / 10.14 %	91	D	87.94 % / 11.87 %	99	B	85.41 % / 11.51 %	107	A	84.85 % / 14.95 %	115	D	79.67 % / 10.36 %
84	C	85.65 % / 12.55 %	92	A	83.07 % / 12.77 %	100	D	78.12 % / 17.6 %	108	A	86.6 % / 11.78 %	116	A	83.47 % / 15.67 %
85	D	89.33 % / 10.57 %	93	C	76.09 % / 10.46 %	101	D	86.31 % / 13.57 %	109	B	76.27 % / 20.53 %	117	A	88.53 % / 11.11 %
86	C	78.48 % / 19.44 %	94	B	79.0 % / 13.83 %	102	C	85.3 % / 10.12 %	110	D	81.85 % / 17.21 %	118	D	78.05 % / 18.7 %
87	C	88.56 % / 10.69 %	95	A	84.68 % / 13.64 %	103	B	79.6 % / 15.53 %	111	B	85.03 % / 14.66 %	119	B	76.82 % / 21.24 %
88	D	87.93 % / 10.16 %	96	B	83.07 % / 14.05 %	104	C	81.11 % / 18.31 %	112	C	85.16 % / 10.16 %	120	A	80.85 % / 10.3 %

//Hints and Solutions//

1.

$$\sqrt{2\cot\theta + \frac{1}{\sin^2\theta}} = \sqrt{2\cot\theta + \cos ec^2\theta}$$
$$= \sqrt{2\cot\theta + 1 + \cot^2\theta} = \sqrt{(1+\cot\theta)^2}$$
$$= |1+\cot\theta| = -(1+\cot\theta)$$
$$(\because \tfrac{3\pi}{4} < \theta < \pi,\ \therefore \cot\theta < -1 \Rightarrow 1+\cot\theta < 0)$$

2. Now, sin (x/n)

= sin (2π+x/n)

= sin (1/n(2nπ+x))

⇒ period of the function sin (x/n) is 2nπ

⇒ 2nπ = 4π ⇒ n = 2

3. tan α = tan (β + γ) =
$$\frac{\tan\beta + \tan\gamma}{1 - \tan\beta\,\tan\gamma}$$

⇒ tan α – tan α tan β tan γ = tan β + tan γ

⇒ tan α = tan α tan β tan γ + tan β + tan γ

= 1.tan γ + tan β + tan γ

(∵ tan α tan β = tan α tan (π/2−α) = tan α cot α = 1)

4.

sin 12° sin 48° sin 54° = $\frac{1}{2}$

{2 sin 48° sin 12°} sin (90° – 36°) = $\frac{1}{2}$

{cos 36° – cos 60°} cos 36° = $\frac{1}{2}\left\{\frac{\sqrt{5}+1}{4} - \frac{1}{2}\right\}\left(\frac{\sqrt{5}+1}{4}\right) = \frac{5-1}{32}$

5. Given

(cos x + sin x)² + k sin x cos x− 1 = 0 ∀ x

⇒ cos² x + sin² x + 2 cos x sin x + k sin x cos x− 1 = 0 ∀ x

(k +2) cos x sin x = 0 ∀

K + 2 = 0 ⇒ k = − 2

6.

Given $\cos ec\theta = \dfrac{p+q}{p-q} \Rightarrow \dfrac{1}{\sin\theta} = \dfrac{p+q}{p-q}$,

Apply componendo and dividendo

$$\frac{1+\sin\theta}{1-\sin\theta} = \frac{p+q+p-q}{p+q-p+q}$$

$$\Rightarrow \left\{\frac{\cos\frac{\theta}{2} + \sin\frac{\theta}{2}}{\cos\frac{\theta}{2} - \sin\frac{\theta}{2}}\right\}^2 = \frac{p}{q}$$

$$\Rightarrow \left\{\frac{1+\tan\frac{\theta}{2}}{1-\tan\frac{\theta}{2}}\right\}^2 = \frac{p}{q}$$

$$\Rightarrow \tan^2\left(\frac{\pi}{4} + \frac{\theta}{2}\right) = \frac{p}{q}$$

$$\Rightarrow \cot^2\left(\frac{\pi}{4} + \frac{\theta}{2}\right) = \frac{q}{p}$$

7. There are in total 9 entries and each entry can be selected in exactly 2 ways.

Hence, the total number of all possible matrices of the said type is 2^9.

8.

$$k\,I_2 = k\begin{bmatrix} 1 & 0 \\ 0 & 1 \end{bmatrix}$$

9. Each row of A contains 4 elements.

10. PQ is of order 2 × 2

11. $(AB)^{-1} = B^{-1} A^{-1}$

12. $A^2 = AA$

$$= \begin{bmatrix} 0 & 0 & 0 & 0 \\ 0 & 0 & 0 & 0 \\ 1 & 0 & 0 & 0 \\ 0 & 1 & 0 & 0 \end{bmatrix}\begin{bmatrix} 0 & 0 & 0 & 0 \\ 0 & 0 & 0 & 0 \\ 1 & 0 & 0 & 0 \\ 0 & 1 & 0 & 0 \end{bmatrix} = \begin{bmatrix} 0 & 0 & 0 & 0 \\ 0 & 0 & 0 & 0 \\ 0 & 0 & 0 & 0 \\ 0 & 1 & 0 & 0 \end{bmatrix}$$

13. A relation from a non-empty set A to a non-empty set B is defined as a subset of A × B

14. Domain of R = {x ∈N : x R y for some y ∈ N}| = {2, 4, 6}

$$\because x = 8 - 2y,\ y \in N = \left\{\begin{array}{l} 6\ when\ y = 1 \\ 4\ when\ y = 2 \\ 2\ when\ y = 3 \end{array}\right\}$$

Note that in this case

R = {(2, 3), (4, 2), (6, 1)}

∴

15. Since x , y does not imply y < x, therefore, x R y does not imply y R x. So the relation R is notsymmetric in this case

16. As (3, 3) ∉R , therefore, R is not reflexlive

As(2, 3) ∈ R but (3, 2) ∉ R, therefore, R is not symmetric

As both (1, 2) and (2, 1) are contained in R, therefore, R is not antisymmetric

(A relation R is antisymmetriciff x R y and y R x ⇒ x = y)

17. All the subsets of A× A, given in (a), (b) and (c) are equivalence relation on A, as they arereflexive, symmetric and transitive

18. Let x ∈ A, y ∴ B be arbitrary, then (x, y) ∈ A × B

⇒ (x, y) ∈ B × A (∵ A × B = B × A)

⇒x∈ B and y ∈ A

Hence A ⊂ B and B ⊂ A ⇒A = B

19.

$$\text{Substitute } 2^x = t$$

$$2^x \log 2 = \frac{dt}{dx} \Rightarrow 2^x \log 2 \, dx = dt$$

$$\int 2^{2^x} 2^x \, dx = \int 2^t \frac{dt}{\log 2}$$

$$= \frac{1}{\log 2} \int 2^t dt = \frac{1}{\log 2} \cdot \frac{2^t}{\log 2} + C$$

$$= \frac{2^{2^x}}{(\log 2)^2} + C$$

20.

$$\text{For } 0 \le x < 1, \ [x] = 0$$

$$\text{and for } 1 \le x < 2, \ [x] = 1$$

$$\text{Hence } \int_0^2 x[x] \, dx = \int_0^1 x[x] \, dx + \int_1^2 x[x] \, dx$$

$$= 0 + \int_1^2 x(1) \, dx = \left[\frac{x^2}{2}\right]_1^2$$

$$= \frac{1}{2}(2^2 - 1^2) = \frac{3}{2}.$$

21.

$$\text{Let } I = \int_0^{2\pi} (\cos x)^{2001} dx$$

$$= 2 \int_0^{\pi} (\cos x)^{2001} dx$$

$$(\because (\cos x)^{2001} = \cos^{2001}(2\pi - x))$$

$$= 0 \ (\because \cos^{2001}(\pi - x) = -\cos^{2001}x)$$

We have used the results $\int_0^{2a} f(x) \, dx$

$$= \begin{cases} 2\int_0^a f(x) \, dx \ if \ f(2a - x) = f(x) \\ \\ 0 \ if \ (2a - x) = -f(x) \end{cases}$$

22. Equation of any non-vertical line in a given plane is of the form y = mx + c, where m, c are

arbitrary constants. Differentiating twice w.r.t. x (to eliminate c, m), we get d²y/dx² = 0

23. since the general solution contains three arbitrary constants,

therefore, the differential equationin reference must be of order3.

24. Given dy/dx= 3x² ⇒ y = x³ + C

since (− 1, 1) lies on the curve, therefore,

1 = (− 1)³ + C ⇒ C = 2

25. As a⃗ is a non-zero vector

$$\hat{a} = \frac{\vec{a}}{|\vec{a}|} \quad and \quad - \hat{a}$$

are two unit vectors collinear with a⃗ .

26.

Since $\vec{a}$ and $\vec{b}$ are non –zero collinear vectors.

therefore, $\vec{a} \times \vec{b}$ is a non zero vector at right angles to both $\vec{a}$ and $\vec{b}$. Hence

$\frac{\vec{a} \times \vec{b}}{|\vec{a} \times \vec{b}|}$ and $- \frac{\vec{a} \times \vec{b}}{|\vec{a} \times \vec{b}|}$ are the two unit vectors perpendicular to both $\vec{a}$ and $\vec{b}$

27.

$$\text{Vectors} \left(2\hat{i} + 3\hat{j} - 6\hat{k}\right) . \left(a\hat{i} + \hat{b} + \hat{c}\right) = 0$$

if 2a + 3b − 6c = 0

28. a⃗ ·b⃗ ⩾0 ⇒ ab cos θ ≥ 0

⇒ cos θ ≥ 0 ⇒ 0 ≤ π/2

29.

Resultant of $\vec{a}$ and $\vec{b}$ means $\vec{a} + \vec{b}$.

$$\text{Here } \vec{a} + \vec{b} = \left(2\hat{i} + \hat{j} + \hat{k}\right) + \left(\hat{i} + 2\hat{j} + 3\hat{k}\right)$$

$$= 3\hat{i} + 3\hat{j} + 4\hat{k}$$

$$\therefore |\vec{a} + \vec{b}| = \sqrt{3^2 + 3^2 + 4^2} = \sqrt{9 + 9 + 16}$$

$$= \sqrt{34}$$

30.

Sum of the given vectors

$$= \left(\hat{i} + \hat{j} + \hat{k}\right) + \left(2\hat{i} - \hat{j} - \hat{k}\right) + \left(2\hat{j} + 6\hat{k}\right)$$

$$= 3\hat{i} + 2\hat{j} + 6\hat{k}$$

∴ The unit vector in the direction of the sum of the given vectors

$$= \frac{3\hat{i} + 2\hat{j} + 6\hat{k}}{|3\hat{i} + 2\hat{j} + 6\hat{k}|} = \frac{3\hat{i} + 2\hat{j} + 6\hat{k}}{\sqrt{3^2 + 2^2 + 6^2}}$$

$$= \frac{1}{7}\left(3\hat{i} + 2\hat{j} + 6\hat{k}\right)$$

31.

Let A (1, −2, 3) and B(4, 2, −1). Let the plane XOY meet the line AB in the point C such that C divides [AB] in the ratio k : 1, then

$C \equiv \left(\frac{4k+1}{k+1}, \frac{2k-2}{k+1}, \frac{-k+3}{k+1}\right)$.

Since C lies on the plane XOY i.e. the plane

z = 0, therefore, $\frac{-k+3}{k+1} = 0 \Rightarrow k = 3$

32. {{1.PNG}}

33.

The given equation is $|\hat{r}|^2 - 2(\hat{r} \bullet \hat{a}) + \lambda = 0 \Rightarrow |r|^2 - 2(\vec{r} \bullet \vec{a}) + |\vec{a}|^2 + \lambda - |\vec{a}|^2 = 0 \Rightarrow (\vec{r} - \vec{a})^2 = |\vec{a}|^2 - \lambda$
$|\vec{r} - \vec{a}|^2 = a^2 - \lambda.$
This represents a sphere only if $a^2 - \lambda > 0$.
i.e. if $a^2 \lambda$.

34. Any point on the given line is (t,2t,3 t). if lies in the given pane if 2(t) − 4 (2 t) +2 (3t)

i.g. if 0 t = 3, which is not true for any t ∈R. Hence, the given line and the given plane do not meet any point.

35.

Since the sphere in reference touches the given plane $\vec{r} \bullet (2\hat{i} - 2\hat{j} - \hat{k}) = 10$
i.e. the plane 2x- 2y –z -10 =0, therefore, radius = length of perpendicular from the centre C (3.6, -2) upon the tangent plane
$= \dfrac{|2\times 3 - 2\times 6 - (-2) - 10|}{\sqrt{2^2 + (-2)^2 + 1^2}} = \dfrac{14}{3}.$

36. When a line lies in a plane, then it is at right angles to the normal to the plane. Here, d.n, of the line are < a,b,c,> and attitude numbers fof the plane are being taken as . So, we must have aA +bB + cC = 0.

37. Solution set of the given inequality is {(x, y) : x ≥ 0} i.e. the set of all points whose abscissae are

non – negative. All these points lie either on Y – axis or on the right of Y – axis.

38. Solution set of the given inequality is {(x, y): y ≤ 0} i.e. the set of all points whose ordinates are

non – positive. All these points lie either on X – axis or below X – axis.

39. Solution set of the given inequalities is

{(x, y) : x ≥ 0} ∩ {(x, y) : y ≥ 0} = {(x, y) : x ≥ 0, y ≥ 0} i.e. the set of all those points whose both coordinates are non – negative. All these points lei in the first quadrant (including points on +ve X – axis, + ve Y – axis and the origin).

40. Objective function is a linear function (of the variables involved) whose maximum or minimum value is to be found.

41. The set {(x, y) : 1 ≤ x2 + y2 ≤ 3} is not convex as is clear from the adjoining figure. The segment

A B is not contained in the set through the points A and B are contained in the set.

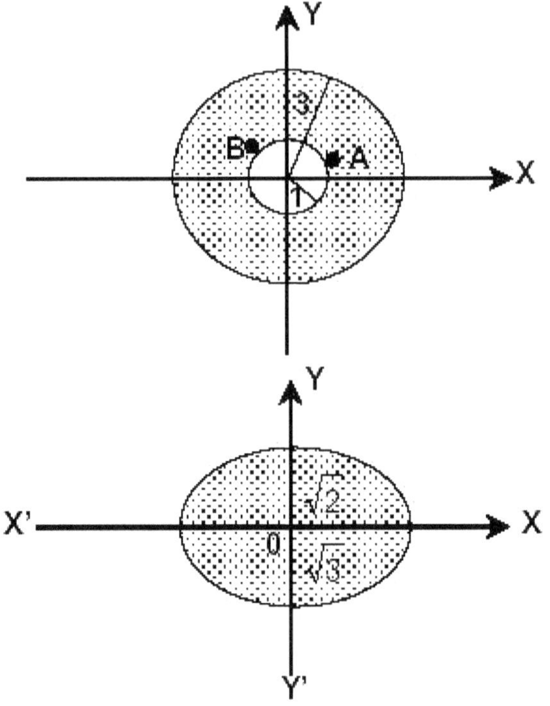

42. The set {(x, y) : 2x^2 + 3y^2 ≤ 6} = {(x, y): x^2/3+y^2/2⩽1} is the set of all points on and inside the ellipse

x^2/3+y^2/2=1

43. Since the outcomes of successive throws of a coin are independent, therefore, the chance of

occurrence or non-occurrence of head o fourth toss does not depend on the outcomes of first three

tosses.

Hence, the required probability = 1/2.

44. As E$_1$ and e$_2$ are mutually exclusive, therefore,

E$_1$ ∩ e$_2$ = ∅ ⇒ E$_1$ ⊂ E ^{c}$_2$and E$_2$ ⊂ E ^{c}$_1$

P (E$_1$) ≤ P (E ^{c}$_2$)

P (E$_1$) ≤ P 1 − P (E$_2$)

P (E$_1$) + P (E$_2$) ≤ 1.

45.

Let E_1 : 'dice shows up a six' and E_2 : 'dice does not show up a six', then E_1 and E_2 are mutually exclusive and exhaustive. Also, $P(E_1) = \frac{1}{6}$ and $P(E_2) = \frac{5}{6}$.
Let E : the man reports that. a six has come up then $P(E/E_1) = \frac{23}{4}$ and $P(E/E_2) = \frac{1}{4}$. By Bye's theorem
$$P(E_1/E) = \frac{P(E/E_1)\, P(E_1)}{P(E/E_1)\, P(E_1) + P(E/E_2)\, P(E_2)}$$
$$= \frac{\frac{3}{4}\times\frac{1}{6}}{\frac{3}{4}\times\frac{1}{6} + \frac{1}{4}\times\frac{5}{6}} = \frac{3}{3+5} = \frac{3}{8}.$$

46. Each ball can be put in any one of the three boxes, therefore, the total number of ways in which

all the balls can be put into three boxes is 3$^{10.}$

Tow balls can by chosen out of 10 in ^{10}C$_2$ ways. When these balls are put into the first box, the remaining 8 balls can be put into the remaining two boxes in 2^8 ways. Hence, the number of ways in

which the first box contains 2 balls = $^{10}C_2\, 2^8$.

∴ Required probability = $^{10}C_2 \times 2^8 / 3^{10}$.

47. Given $A \cap B = \emptyset \Rightarrow P(A \cap B) = 0$

$P(A \cup B) = P(A) + P(B) - P(A \cap B)$

$= P(A) + P(B)$.

48. E_1 and E_2 are independent

$P(E_1 \cap E_2) = P(E_1)\, P(E_2)$. (By definition)

49. If the roots of the given equation are $\alpha\beta$, then $\alpha + \beta = \lambda + 2$ and $\alpha\beta = 1 - \lambda$

Hence, $\alpha^2 + \beta^2 = (\alpha + \beta)^2 - 2\alpha\beta$

$= (\lambda + 2)^2 - 2(1 - \lambda)$

$= \lambda^2 + 4\lambda + 4 - 2 + 2\lambda$

$= \lambda^2 + 6\lambda + 9 - 7$

$= (\lambda + 3)^2 - 7$

Clearly, $\alpha^2 + \beta^2$ is least when $\lambda + 3 = 0$ i.e. when $\lambda = -3$

50.

Given equation can be written as $2x - 3 + x - 1 = 6x^2 - x - 6,\ x \ne 1$

or $6x^2 - 4x - 2 = 0$

or $3x^2 - 2x - 1 = 0,\ x \ne 1$

$\Rightarrow x = \dfrac{2 \pm \sqrt{4 + 12}}{6} = \dfrac{2 \pm 4}{6} = 1,\ -\dfrac{1}{3}$, but $x \ne 1$, therefore, the only solution is $x = -\dfrac{1}{3}$.

51. The equation $ax^2 + bx + c = 0$ is a quadratic equation only if a $\ne 0$, for if $a = 0$ then the equation

becomes $bx + c = 0$, which is not of second degree

52. When one roots is 0 and the other is non zero, then sum of the roots is no-zero and product is

zero

$\Rightarrow -b/a \ne 0$ and $c/a = 0$

$\Rightarrow b \ne 0$ and $c = 0$

53.

$ax^2 + bx + c = \left\{ x^2 + \dfrac{b}{a}x + \dfrac{c}{a} \right\}$

$= a\left\{ \left(x + \dfrac{b}{2a}\right)^2 + \dfrac{c}{a} - \dfrac{b^2}{4a^2} \right\},\ a > 0$

$= a\left\{ \left(x + \dfrac{b}{2a}\right)^2 + \dfrac{4ac - b^2}{4a^2} \right\} > 0$

For all real x only if $\dfrac{4ac - b^2}{4a^2} > 0$

i.e. if $b^2 - 4ac < 0$

54. For equal roots disc = 0

$\Rightarrow (\sqrt{2}\, p)^2 - 4.2.p = 0 \Rightarrow 2p(p - 4) = 0$

55.

$$\underset{x \to 0}{Lt}\ \frac{5^x - 4^x}{4^x - 3^x}$$

$$= \underset{x \to 0}{Lt}\ \frac{\left(\frac{5^x - 1}{x}\right) - \left(\frac{4^x - 1}{x}\right)}{\left(\frac{4^x - 1}{x}\right) - \left(\frac{3^x - 1}{x}\right)}$$

$$= \frac{\log 5 - \log 4}{\log 4 - \log 3} = \frac{\log (5/4)}{\log (4/3)}$$

56.

$$\underset{x \to \infty}{Lt}\ \left(\frac{x+5}{x+1}\right)^{x+4}$$

$$= \underset{x \to \infty}{Lt}\ \left\{ \left(1 + \frac{4}{x+1}\right)^{\frac{x+1}{4}} \right\}^{\frac{4(x+4)}{x+1}} = e^4$$

$$\left(\because\ \underset{x \to \infty}{Lt}\ \left(1 + \frac{4}{x+1}\right)^{\frac{x+1}{4}} = e \text{ as } x \to \infty \Rightarrow \frac{4}{x+1} \to 0 \right.$$

and $\underset{x \to \infty}{Lt}\ \dfrac{(x+4)4}{x+1} = \underset{x \to \infty}{Lt}\ \dfrac{4\left(1 + \frac{4}{x}\right)}{1 + \frac{1}{x}} = 4 \Big)$

57.

Note that 0 for each $x \in R$ and $-1 = 0$. Here $\sqrt{e^{x^2}} - 1$ acquires the minimum value 0 at $x = 0$

58.

$$\underset{x \to 0}{Lt}\ \frac{1 - \cos x}{x} = \underset{x \to 0}{Lt}\ \frac{(1 - \cos x)(1 + \cos x)}{x(1 + \cos x)}$$

$$= \underset{x \to 0}{Lt}\ \frac{\sin x}{x} \cdot \frac{\sin x}{1 + \cos x} = 0$$

59.

$$\underset{x \to 0}{Lt}\ (1 + 2x)^{\frac{x+3}{x}} = \underset{x \to 0}{Lt}\ (1 + 2x)^1\, (1 + 2x)^{3/x}$$

$$\lim_{x \to 0} (1 + 2x)^{\frac{3}{x}} = \lim_{2x \to 0} \left\{ (1 + 2x)^{\frac{1}{2x}} \right\}^6 = e^6$$

60.

$$\underset{x \to 0}{Lt}\ \frac{(1 - x)^n - 1}{x} = \frac{n(1 - x)^{n-1}(-1) - 0}{1}$$

$= n(1 - 0)(-1) = -n$ (L–Hopital's rule)

61.

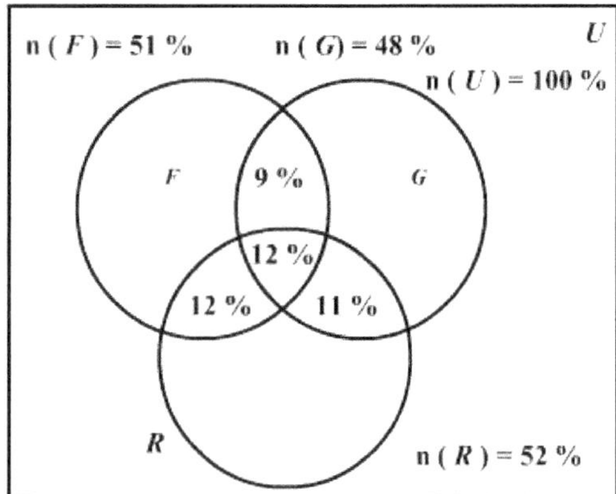

Therefore, the number students who wanted to learn German only,

$=0.16 \times 500$

$=80$

62.

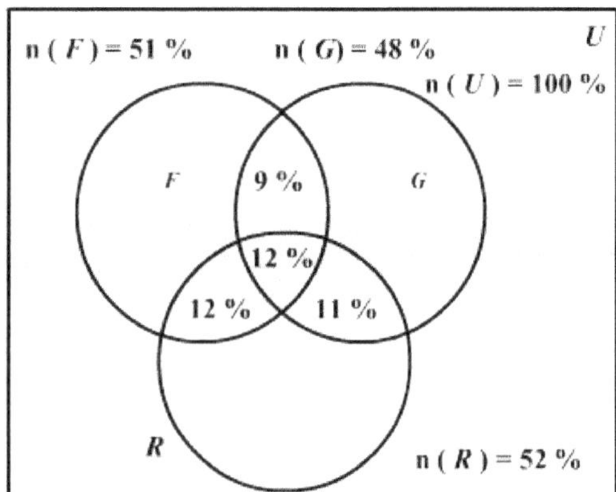

Therefore, the number of students who wanted to learn R and F only

$=0.12 \times 500$

$=60$

63.

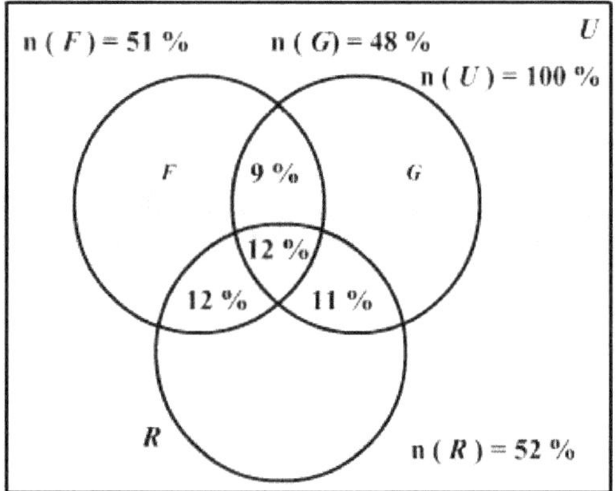

Therefore, 395 - 60 = 335 more students were interested in either French or Russian.

64. The percentage of students not interested in any of the languages = 100% - (the percentage of students interested in any one language only) - (the percentage of students interested in any two languages only) - (the percentage of students interested in all three languages)

Percentage of students interested in F only,

$=51-9-12-12$

$=18\%$

Similarly we can find that the percentage of students interested in only Russian and German is 17% and 16% respectively.

∴ The percentage of students not interested in any of the languages

$=100\% \ -(18+17+16)\% \ -(9+12+11)\% \ -12\%$

$=5\%$

Therefore, the number of students not interested in any language,

$=0.05 \times 500$

$=25$

65.

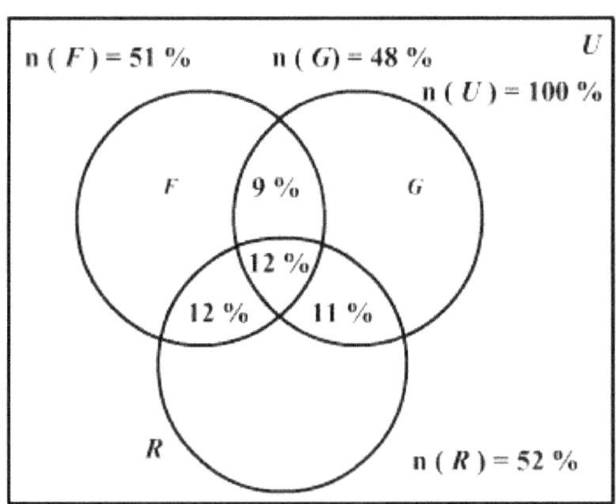

The required ratio is given by:

$=\%$ of students interested in any two languages only% of students interested in any one language only

$=(9+12+11)\%(18+17+16)\%$

$=3251$

66. Gorbl means fan; flur means belt; pixn means ceiling; arth means tile; and tusl means roof. Therefore, pixnarth is the correct choice.

67. Hapl means cloud; lesh means burst; srench means pin; och means ball; and resbo means nine. Leshsrench (choice a) doesn't contain any of the words needed for cloud nine. We know that och means ball, so that rules out choices b and c. When you combine hapl (cloud) with resbo (nine), you get the correct answer

68. In this language, the noun appears first and the adjectives follow. Since agnos means spider and should appear first, choices a and d can be ruled out. Choice b can be ruled out because delano means snake.

69. From wilkospadi, you can determine that wilko means bicicyle and spadi means race. Therefore, the first part of the word that means racecar should begin with spadi. That limits your choices to b and d. Choice b, spadiwilko, is incorrect because we have already determined that wilkomeans bicycle. Therefore, the answer must be choice d, spadivolo.

70. Migen means cup; lasan means board; poen means walk; cuop means pull; and dansa means man. The only possible choices, then, are choices a and d. Choice a can be ruled out because migen means cup.

71. An odometer is an instrument used to measure mileage. A compass is an instrument used to determine direction. Choices a, b, and c are incorrect because none is an instrument.

72. A marathon is a long race and hibernation is a lengthy period of sleep. The answer is not choice a or b because even though a bear and winter are related to hibernation, neither completes the analogy. (Choice c) is incorrect because sleep and dream are not synonymous.

73. A window is made up of panes, and a book is made up of pages. The answer is not (choice a) because a novel is a type of book. The answer is not (choice b) because glass has no relationship to a book. (Choice c) is incorrect because a cover is only one part of a book; a book is not made up of covers.

74. Coffee goes into a cup and soup goes into a bowl. Choices a and c are incorrect because they are other utensils. The answer is not choice d because the word food is too general.

75. A yard is a larger measure than an inch (a yard contains 36 inches). A quart is a larger measure than an ounce (a quart contains 32 ounces). Gallon (choice a) is incorrect because it is larger than a quart. Choices c and d are incorrect because they are not units of measurement.

76. Since both the premises are universal and affirmative, the conclusion must be universal affirmative and should not contain the middle term. So, it follows that 'All branches are leaves'. Thus, I follows. IV is the converse of this conclusion and so it also holds.

77. Since one premise is particular and the other negative, the conclusion must be particular negative and should not contain the middle term. So, II follows. III is the converse of the first premise and thus it also holds.

78. Since the middle term 'trains' is not distributed even once in the/premises, no definite conclusion follows. However, III is the converse of the second premise while IV is the converse of the first premise. So, both of them hold.

79. Clearly, it follows that 'All politicians are fair'. I is the converse of the first premise, while III is the converse of the above conclusion. So, both I and III hold.

80. Since both the premises are particular, no definite conclusion follows. However, I and III involve only the extreme terms and form a complementary pair. Thus, either I or III follows.

81. Red Hat Linux is one of the highly used Enterprise Operating System in the Linux Market.

82. Linux is free and open source software it is not sold by Microsoft or any other company.

83. An error in computer program is known as Bug and process of fixing Bugs are known as Debug.

84. Microsoft Word or MS-WORD (often called Word) is a graphical word processing program that users can type with. It is made by the computer company Microsoft. Its purpose is to allow users to type and save documents. Similar to other word processors, it has helpful tools to make documents.

85. Windows 2000

86. Windows 95

87. Windows 8

88. Windows 10

89. Moves the cursor one screen down

90. Moves the cursor one Page Up

91. Moves the cursor one paragraph up

92. Moves the cursor to the beginning of Document

93. client

94. F9

95. Custom List

96. Go to Tools >> Options >> Calculation and mark the corresponding radio button

97. Slide transitions are the effects that occur when you move from one slide to the next during a presentation. You can control the speed, add sound, and customize the properties of transition effects.

98. Slide Design does not provide sample content but Auto Content Wizard provides sample content too!

99. Format Menu

100. Slide Show Menu

101. We can see that Option 1 is most likely the starting sentence. Now that we know that 1 is the starting sentence we can eliminate choice B and C as they start with 3 and 2 respectively and not with sentence 1.

This narrows down our possibilities to option A and option D.

Now we can see in option A 3 follows sentence 1 but the gap spoken of in sentence 3 has no correlation with political geography of the subcontinent spoken of in sentence 1 , so we can rule out Option A.

Therefore answer has to be option D, as we can also see it elaborates on the change mentioned in sentence 1.

102. 3 logically follows 4 as it further describes the writer mentioned in 4. 1 follows 2 as it concludes 'Nonetheless' despite everything mentioned in 2.

103. Here sentence 3 is an example of sentence 4. Therefore 3 will come after 4.

Now as we go by elimination method only option B and C remains.

Now go by ACRONYM Method IBBF in sentence 1 and Indian Body-Building Federation in sentence 3. Therefore sentence 3 will come before 1 as full form of the acronym is stated in sentence 3 and only afterwards short form is used in sentence 1. Hence only option B remains which is the correct answer.

104. As it is an individual explaining his perceptions, it should begin with 1.

105. 'A man of paradoxes' is logically continued by 'repelled ' and 'attracted'. Subsequently, 'the' debacle refers to China's flopped military operation and hence choice C.

106. In order to ascertain the main point that the author is trying to make, it is important to examine logical flow of the passage.

1st Paragraph: Explain a seemingly amazing accomplishment and ask whether it really is as impressive as it first appears.

2nd Paragraph: Explain factors that made the impressive accomplishment not as impressive.

3rd Paragraph: Explain how the seemingly amazing accomplishment didn't have to turn out the way it did.

4th Paragraph: Explain how the seemingly amazing accomplishment didn't have to turn out the way it did.

A.The Aztec failure to fight in an unconventional manner is discussed only in the last paragraph and is mentioned only to make a larger point: the fall of the Aztec was not as impressive as it originally appeared.

B.This encapsulates the logical flow and main points of the passage.

C.This topic is only discussed during part of the second paragraph and is mentioned only to make a larger point: the fall of the Aztec was not as impressive as it originally appeared.

D.The main point of the passage is to challenge this common belief and point out that it was not as amazing as is often asserted.

E.The passage never even mentions that the Aztec had myopic vision let alone makes this the main focus.

107. In order to see the sequential ordering, break down the logical flow of the passage.

1st Paragraph: Introduce something that looks very impressive on the surface and ask how it happened.

2nd Paragraph: Offer several factors that help explain what seemed so impressive and unbelievable.

3rd Paragraph: Provide several ways that the seemingly unbelievable was not inevitable.

4th Paragraph: Continue with paragraph 3. Conclude by noting that the seemingly unbelievable and unexplainable was both explainable and not inevitable.

To summarize the sequential organization:

Introduce an enigma ("how did a small group of foreign fighters manage to topple one of the world's strongest, wealthiest, and most successful military empires?")

Explain reasons for the enigma (2nd paragraph)

Discuss the inevitability of the enigma (3rd and 4th paragraphs)

A.This matches the sequential order explained above.

B.The third and fourth paragraphs are not offering a solution to a problem but rather discussing the inevitability of an outcome.

C.The third and fourth paragraphs are not providing an alternative explanation for the mystery but rather discussing the inevitability of the mystery.

D.The third and fourth paragraphs are not providing an alternative answer to the question but rather discussing the inevitability of the mystery.

E.The second paragraph does not discuss the likelihood of the problem but rather explains the sources of the problem (i.e., the sources for the seemingly incredible victory of Cortes). The passage makes no mention of the consequences of the invasion, its success, or its seemingly impressive status etc.

108. The author never mentions that the Aztecs had a view toward an unconventional military conflict with the Spanish. The topic is mentioned only as the author notes that the Aztecs should have pursued this type of a confrontation with the Spanish. Further, when the author did mention unconventional combat, he prefaced it with the statement: "Motecuhzoma's forces should have thought outside the box..." Based upon these facts, our best inference is that the Aztecs did not ever consider an unconventional military confrontation with Cortes.

A.This seems to be implied in the author's suggestion that "Motecuhzoma's forces should have thought outside the box..."

B.The passage never mentions nor implies that the Aztecs considered an unconventional military confrontation with the Spanish.

C.The passage never mentions nor implies that the Aztecs considered an unconventional military confrontation with the Spanish.

D.The passage never mentions nor implies that the Aztecs were certain they could achieve victory in a traditional means.

E.The passage never mentions nor implies that the Aztecs considered an unconventional military confrontation, let alone how it would be influenced by the geography of Tenochtitlan.

109. A.The passage mentions this as a source of success: "the Spanish possessed superior military equipment in the form of European cannons, guns, and crossbows"

B.Although the passage mentions that Cortes' army was small, it implies that this as a weakness. The passage never states that the military was nimble nor does it mention this as a source of success.

C.The passage mentions this as a source of success: "In one account of a battle, it is recorded that at least 200,000 natives fought with Cortes."

D.The passage mentions this as a source of success: "animosity toward the Aztecs among rival groups"

E.The passage mentions this as a source of success: "Spanish cannons quickly defeated large Aztec walls"

110. The relevant portion of the passage is: "Despite the Spanish advantages, the Aztecs probably could have succeeded in defending their capital city of Tenochtitlan"

A.This does not match with the passage: "the Aztecs probably could have succeeded in defending their capital"

B.This does not match with the passage: "the Aztecs probably could have succeeded in defending their capital"

C.This does not match with the passage: "the Aztecs probably could have succeeded in defending their capital"

D.This does match with the passage: "the Aztecs probably could have succeeded in defending their capital"

E.This does not match with the passage: "the Aztecs probably could have succeeded in defending their capital"

111. Specious = false and misleading

Novel = marvellous in a new way.

112. Wistful means sad about something past.

(fastidious = choosy and difficult to please.

Indignant = Angry, Conciliatory = making compromise or befriending.)

113. The key phrase here is 'move on'. If editors have to travel from firm to firm to succeed in their field, then publishing can be classified as itinerant profession, a profession marked by traveling.

114. Emerges means comes out. Confusion cannot be derived from the situation.

To stem is to stop something, which the sentence is not pointing to.

Therefore, options (a) and (b) are incorrect.

Option (d) is incorrect as in the second filler 'planning' can't be used.

115. In the given space of time i.e. 'throughout history' there can be only source. Reason and cause or origin can be a particular event.

Boost, Encouragement and Incentive mean the same.

116. The subject (people, which is plural) must agree with the verb (were, which is plural).

The two verbs (were and crafted) should be in the same tense since both happened at the same time in the past.

A.This correct sentence is written such that the subject and verb agree

B.had been renowned is improperly constructed in the past perfect tense, implying that the Assyrian Empire stopped being known for renown warriors before its people crafted well-preserved art

C.The comma improperly splits the sentence, creating a comma splice

D.The subject (people, which is plural) does not agree with the verb (was, which is singular)

E.The use of the participle crafting is improper and should be replaced by a verb

117. "Whether" is correct because the question concerns a choice not a condition. With the expression "the number of" a singular verb is needed and hence "was" is correct. "Liable" is used in expressions such as "liable to prosecution" and not for expressions of possibility.

118. (1) The sentence must be constructed such that corresponding consequences of an action are parallel. Specifically, the sentence should read enabled political candidates with cash-strapped budgets to x and y where x and y are parallel.

(2) The phrase to be able to z is redundant and should be replaced by to z

(3) The phrase numbers of money should be amounts of money since number is only used when the object in question can be counted and money cannot be counted (i.e., you do not say 1 money, 2 money, 3 money). Note: By comparison, dollars can be counted (i.e., you would say 1 dollar, 2 dollars, 3 dollars) and as a result, we would say: the number of dollars.

A.the phrase to be able to reach is redundant and can be shortened as follows: to reach; large numbers of money is not grammatically correct since money itself cannot be counted and, as a result, amount should be used instead

B.the phrase to reach...and be successful is not parallel

C.this sentence is set up such that succeeding modifies reaching voters instead of being a separate action on its own

D.the phrase is parallel (i.e., to reach...[to] succeed); to be able to reach is replaced by the shorter to reach

E.the phrase to be able to reach is redundant and should be replaced by to reach

119. The superlative form most scary must be used instead of the comparative form more scary since the author is indicating that among all the threats, a specific threat is the most scary.

A.more must be replaced by most as the superlative form (most) must be used since the author is not comparing threats but stating that a single threat is the scariest

B.The superlative form is correctly used

C.Although the superlative form is correctly used, this choice makes the sentence unduly long; the phrase possibly, perhaps is awkward and not idiomatically correct

D.While a superlative is used, the sentence is exceedingly awkward as the phrasepossibly the greatest scary is not idiomatic

E.The superlative form is not used; the phrase possibly the great
scary as this scenariois awkward and not idiomatic

120. No error.

Mathematics

Q.1

$$\text{If } A = \begin{bmatrix} 0 & 0 & 0 \\ 0 & 0 & 0 \\ 0 & 1 & 0 \end{bmatrix}, \text{ then A is}$$

A. an invertible matrix
B. an idempotent matrix
C. a nilpotent matrix
D. none of these

Q.2 If A and B are symmetric matrices of the same order, then
A. AB is symmetric matrix
B. A−B is a skew-symmetric matrix
C. AB + BA is a symmetric matrix
D. AB − BA is a symmetric matrix

Q.3 If A is any square matrix, then
A. $A + A^t$ is skew-symmetric
B. $A - A^t$ is symmetric
C. AA^t is symmetric
D. none of these

Q.4 Each diagonal element of a skew-symmetric matrix is
A. zero   B. positive   C. non-real   D. negative

Q.5 If I_n is the identity matrix of order n, then $(I_n)^{-1}$
A. does not exist
B. $= I_n$
C. $= O$
D. $n\, I_n$

Q.6 A square matrix $A = [a_{ij}]_{n \times n}$ is called a diagonal matrix if $a_{ij} = 0$ for
A. $i = j$ B. $i < j$ C. $i > j$ D. $i \neq j$

Q.7 The centre of the circle given by
$X^2 + y^2 + z^2 - 2y - 4z + 1 = 0, X + 2Y + 2Z - 15 - 0$ is
A. $(1, -3, 4)$
B. $(-1, 3, 4)$
C. $(1, 3, -4)$
D. $(1, 3, 4)$.

Q.8 The distance of the point (3,4,5) from X-axis is
A. 3   B. 5   C. $\sqrt{34}$ D. $\sqrt{41}$

Q.9 The direction cosines of X-axis are
A. $< 0,0,1 >$
B. $< 1,0,0 >$
C. $< 0,1,0 >$
D. $< 0,1,1 >$.

Q.10 The medians of a triangle are concurrent at the point called
A. Circumcentre
B. Orthocentre
C. Centroid
D. Incentre

Q.11 The direction cosines of any normal to the XY plane are
A. $< 1, 0,0 >$
B. $< 0,1,0 >$
C. $< 1, 1,0 >$
D. $< 0, 0,1 >$

Q.12 The numbers 3, 4,5 can be
A. Direction cosines of a line space
B. Direction number of a line space
C. Co-ordinate of a point on the line y = 4, z= 0.
D. Co-ordinates of a point in the pane x+ y −z =c.

Q.13 The function $f(x) = x^2 e^{-x}$ strictly increases on
A. $[0, 2]$
B. $(0, \infty)$
C. $(-\infty, 0] \cup [2, \infty)$
D. none of these.

Q.14 For the curve $x = t^2 - 1$, $y = t^2 - t$ tangent is parallel to X-axis where
A. $t = 0$
B. $t = 1/\sqrt{3}$
C. $t = 1/2$
D. $t = -1/\sqrt{3}$

Q.15 At $(0,0)$, the curve $y^2 = x^3 + x^2$
A. touches X-axis
B. bisects the angle between the axes
C. makes an angle of 60° with OX
D. none of these

Q.16 Let $f(x) = x^{25}(1-x)^{75}$ for all $x \in [0, 1]$, then f(x) assumes its maximum value at
A. 0   B. 1/4   C. 1/2   D. 1/3

Q.17 Minimum value of the function
$f(x) = x^2 + x + 1$ is
A. 1
B. 3
C. 3/4
D. none of these

Q.18 The equation of the normal to the curve $y = \sin x$ at (0,0) is
A. $x = 0$ B. $x + y = 0$ C. $y = 0$ D. $x - y = 0$

Q.19 The differential equation of the family of all circles with centres at origin is
A. $x + y_1 = 0$
B. $x + y\, y_1 = 0$
C. $x - y\, y_1 = 0$
D. none of these

Q.20 If $dy/dx = e^{-2y}$ and y = 0, when x = 5, then the value of x when y = 3 is
A. e^5
B. $e^6 + 1$
C. $\dfrac{e^6 + 9}{2}$
D. $\log_e 6$

Q.21 The equation of the curve, whose slope at any point different from origin is y + y/x, is
A. $y = x\, e^x + C, C \neq 0$
B. $y = x\, e^x$
C. $x\, y = e^x$
D. $y + x\, e^x = C$

Q.22 The general solution of the differential equation

$$\frac{d^3 y}{dx^3} = 0 \text{ is}$$

A. $ax^3 + bx^2 + cx$

B. $ax^2 = bx + c$

C. $x^3 + x^2 + c$

D. none of these

Q.23 Solution of the differential equation

dy/dx= 1 + x y is

A. $y = c\, e^{-x^2/2}$

B. $y = c\, e^{x^2/2}$

C. $y = (x + c)\, e^{-x^2/2}$

D. none of these

Q.24 The degree of the differential equation

$$\left(\frac{d^2 y}{dx^2}\right)^2 + \left(\frac{dy}{dx}\right)^2 - xy = 0 \text{ is}$$

A. 1   **B.** 2   **C.** 3   **D.** 4

Q.25 If E and F are independent events such that 0> p (E) <1 and 0 > P (F) < 1 then

A. E and F are mutually exclusive

B. E^c and F are not independent

C. E and F^c are not independent

D. E^c and F^c are independent.

Q.26 If A ad B are any two events associated with an experiment then A-B is not equal to

A. $A \cap B^c$

B. $A - (A \cap B)$

C. $(A^c \cup B)^c$

D. None of these.

Q.27 An unbiased dice is rolled four times. The probability that the minimum number on any toss is not less than 3 is

A. 16/81   **B.** 1/81   **C.** 65/81   **D.** 80/81

Q.28 The probability that a man will live for 10 more years is 1/4 and that his wife will live 10 more years is 1/3.The probability that neither will be alive in 10 years is

A. 5/12   **B.** 1/2   **C.** 7/12   **D.** 11/12

Q.29 The probability of having atleast one tail in five throws with a coin is

A. 31/32   **B.** 1/32   **C.** 1/5   **D.** 1.

Q.30 If E is any event associated with an experiment, then

A. P (E) ≤ 0

B. P (E) ≥ 1

C. P (E) ≥ 0

D. 0 ≤ P (E) ≤ 1.

Q.31 If x < 0, maximum value of

$$x + \frac{1}{x} \text{ is}$$

A. 0   **B.** -1   **C.** – 2   **D.** – 4

Q.32 If x ∈ R, minimum value of $x^2 + x + 1$ is

A. 1

B. 3/4

C. 3

D. none of these

Q.33 If x ∈ R, maximum value of $x - x^2$ is

A. 0

B. – 1

C. 3

D. none of these

Q.34 If x ∈ R, minimum value of $3x^2 + 7x + 10$ is

A. 10   **B.** 10/3   **C.** 3/10   **D.** 71/12

Q.35 For θ ∈ R*, | sec θ + cos θ| cannot be less then

A. 2

B. 4

C. 4/√3

D. none of these

Q.36 If a, b, c are positive real numbers, then (a + b) (b + c) (c + a) is greater than

A. a + b + c

B. 8 abc

C. 2 (a + b + c)

D. 6 abc

Q.37 If a, b, c are distinct positive real numbers, then (a + b) (b + c) (c + a) is greater then

A. a + b + c

B. 8 abc

C. 2 (a + b + c)

D. 6 abc

Q.38 Which of the following is not a vector quantity?

A. force   **B.** mass   **C.** weight   **D.** velocity

Q.39 A vector with magnitude zero is called a

A. free vector

B. localized vector

C. position vector

D. null vector

Q.40 The magnitude of a vector can never be

A. negative

B. zero

C. positive

D. none of these

Q.41

Let $\vec{a}$ be a non-zero vector then $\dfrac{\vec{a}}{|\vec{a}|}$ is a

A. null vector

B. scalar

C. unit vector parallel to $\vec{a}$

D. unit vector perpendicular to $\vec{a}$

Q.42 For any two vectors

$\vec{a}$ and $\vec{b}$ which of the following is true?

A. $|\vec{a} + \vec{b}| \geq |\vec{a}| + |\vec{b}|$

B. $|\vec{a} + \vec{b}| = |\vec{a}| + |\vec{b}|$

C. $|\vec{a} + \vec{b}| < |\vec{a}| + |\vec{b}|$

D. $|\vec{a} + \vec{b}| \leq |\vec{a}| + |\vec{b}|$

Q.43
If $\hat{a}$ is a unit vector and $\vec{b}$, a non-zero vector not parallel to $\hat{a}$, then the vector $\vec{b} - (\hat{a} \cdot \vec{b}) \hat{a}$ is

A. parallel to $\vec{b}$

B. at right angles to $\hat{a}$

C. parallel to $\hat{a}$

D. at right angles to $\vec{b}$

Q.44 If $\alpha\beta$ are the roots of the equation $3x2 - 6x - 5 = 0$, then the equation whose roots are $\alpha + \beta$ and

$$\frac{2}{\alpha + \beta}$$

A. $x^2 + 3x - 1 = 0$
B. $x^2 + 3x + 2 = 0$
C. $x^2 - 3x - 2 = 0$
D. $x^2 - 3x + 2 = 0$

Q.45 If the roots of the equation

$$px^2 + 2qx + r = 0 \text{ and } qx^2 - 2\sqrt{pr}\, x + q = 0$$

are simultaneously real, then

A. $p = q, r \neq 0$
B. $2q = \pm \sqrt{pr}$
C. $\dfrac{p}{q} = \dfrac{q}{r}$
D. $q = r \neq 0$

Q.46 The number of the solution of $x^2 = 3\,|x| + 2 = 0$ is
A. 0
B. 2
C. 4
D. 1

Q.47
If $x = \sqrt{20 + \sqrt{20 + \sqrt{20 + \ldots}}}$ to ∞, then x

A. is an irrational number
B. $4 < x < 5$
C. $x = 5$
D. $x > 5$

Q.48 The roots of the equation $(b - c) x^2 + (c - a) x + (a - b) = 0$ are (a, b, c are distinct real numbers);

A. $1, \dfrac{a-b}{b-c}$
B. $1, \dfrac{c-a}{b-c}$
C. $\dfrac{a-b}{b-c}, \dfrac{c-a}{b-c}$
D. $1, \dfrac{b-c}{a-b}$

Q.49 The number of roots of the equation $x^6 - 7x^3 - 8 = 0$ is
A. 1
B. 2
C. 3
D. 6

Q.50
If in a triangle ABC a $\cos^2\left(\frac{C}{2}\right) + c\cos^2\left(\frac{A}{2}\right) = \frac{3b}{2}$, then the sides a, b and c

A. satisfy a + b = c
B. are in A.P.
C. are in G.P.
D. are in H.P.

Q.51 The sides of a triangle are in the ratio 1:√3:2, then angles of the triangle are in the ratio
A. 1:3:5
B. 2:3:4
C. 3:2:1
D. 1:2:3

Q.52 If θ and ϕ are acute angles, $\sin\theta = 1/2$, $\cos\phi = 1/3$, then the value of $\theta + \phi$ lies in

A. $\left(\dfrac{\pi}{3}, \dfrac{\pi}{2}\right]$
B. $\left(\dfrac{\pi}{2}, \dfrac{2\pi}{3}\right]$
C. $\left(\dfrac{2\pi}{3}, \dfrac{5\pi}{6}, \pi\right]$
D. $\left(\dfrac{5\pi}{6}, \pi\right]$

Q.53 $\sin 20°\,(\tan 10° + \cot 10°)$ is equal to
A. 0
B. 1/2
C. 1
D. 2

Q.54 $\cot 36° \cot 72°$ is equal to
A. 1/5
B. 1/√5
C. 1
D. none of these

Q.55
If $\sin \alpha = \dfrac{1}{2} \sin (\alpha + 2\beta)$, then $\dfrac{\tan(\alpha+\beta)}{\tan \beta} =$

A. 5/3
B. 1/3
C. 3
D. 3/5

Q.56 A − B = B − A iff
A. $A \subset B$
B. $B \subset A$
C. $A = B$
D. $A \cap B = \phi$

Q.57 If A, B, C are any three sets, then $A \cup (B \cap C)$ is equal to
A. $(A \cup B) \cap (A \cup C)$
B. $(A \cup B) \cup (A \cup C)$
C. $(A \cap B) \cup (A \cap C)$
D. none of these

Q.58 $(A \cup B)^c$ is equal to
A. $A^c \cup B^c$
B. $A^c \cap B^c$
C. $A \cap B$
D. none of these

Q.59 If A is a finite set containing n distinct elements, then the number of relations on A is equal to
A. 2^n
B. 2^{n2}
C. n^2
D. none of these

Q.60 Number of relations that can be defined on the set A = {a, b, c, d} is
A. 24
B. 16
C. 4^4
D. 2^{16}

Analytical Ability & Logical Reasoning

Q.61 Look at this series: 2, 1, (1/2), (1/4), … What number should come next?
A. (1/3)
B. (1/8)
C. (2/8)
D. (1/16)

Q.62 Look at this series: 7, 10, 8, 11, 9, 12, … What number should come next?
A. 7
B. 10
C. 12
D. 13

Q.63 SCD, TEF, UGH, ___, WKL

A. CMN   **B.** UJI   **C.** VIJ   **D.** IJT

Q.64 B$_2$CD, ____, BCD$_4$, B$_5$CD, BC$_6$D

A. B$_2$C$_2$D   **B.** BC$_3$D   **C.** B$_2$C$_3$D   **D.** BCD$_7$

Q.65 FAG, GAF, HAI, IAH, ___

A. JAK   **B.** HAL   **C.** HAK   **D.** JAI

Q.66 Here are some words translated from an artificial language.

gorblflur means fan belt

pixngorbl means ceiling fan

arthtusl means tile roof

Which word could mean "ceiling tile"?

A. gorbltusl   **B.** flurgorbl   **C.** arthflur   **D.** pixnarth

Q.67 Here are some words translated from an artificial language.

hapllesh means cloudburst

srenchoch means pinball

resbosrench means ninepin

Which word could mean "cloud nine"?

A. leshsrench   **B.** ochhapl

C. haploch   **D.** haplresbo

Q.68 Here are some words translated from an artificial language.

agnoscrenia means poisonous spider

delanocrenia means poisonous snake

agnosdeery means brown spider

Which word could mean "black widow spider"?

A. deeryclostagnos   **B.** agnosdelano

C. agnosvitriblunin   **D.** trymuttiagnos

Q.69 Here are some words translated from an artificial language.

moolokarn means blue sky

wilkospadi means bicycle race

moolowilko means blue bicycle

Which word could mean "racecar"?

A. wilkozwet   **B.** spadiwilko

C. moolobreil   **D.** spadivolo

Q.70 Here are some words translated from an artificial language.

migenlasan means cupboard

lasanpoen means boardwalk

cuopdansa means pullman

Which word could mean "walkway"?

A. poenmigen   **B.** cuopeisel

C. lasandansa   **D.** poenforc

Q.71 Statement and Conclusion-

Soldiers serve their country.

A.   Men generally serve their country.

B.   Those who serve their country are soldiers.

C.   Some men who are soldiers serve their country.

D.   Women do not serve their country because they are not soldiers.

Q.72 Statement and Conclusion-

A factory worker has five children. No one else in the factory has five children.

A.   All workers in the factory have five children each.

B.   Everybody in the factory has children.

C.   Some of the factory workers have more than five children.

D.   Only one worker in the factory has exactly five children.

Q.73 Statement and Conclusion-

Television convinces viewers that the likelihood of their becoming the victim of a violent crime is extremely high; at the same time by its very nature, TV persuades viewers to passively accept whatever happens to them.

A.   TV viewing promotes criminal behaviour.

B.   TV viewers are most likely to be victimized than others.

C.   People should not watch TV.

D.   TV promotes a feeling of helpless vulnerability in viewers.

Q.74 Statement and Conclusion-

A forest has as many sandal trees as it has Ashoka trees. Three-fourth of the trees are old ones and half of the trees are at the flowering stage.

A.   All Ashoka trees are at the flowering stage.

B.   All sandal trees are at the flowering stage.

C.   At least one-half of the Ashoka trees are old.

D.   None of these

Q.75 Statement and Conclusion-

The government is soon going to introduce a bill which would permit the instituting of private universities under very strict directions

A.   We have some private universities in our country even now.

B.   The demand for more universities is being stepped up.

C.   Such directions can also be issued without informing the Parliament.

D.   The government gives directions to establish anything in private sector.

Q.76 Which word does NOT belong with the others?

A. wing   **B.** fin   **C.** beak   **D.** rudder

Q.77 Which word does NOT belong with the others?

A. core   **B.** seeds   **C.** pulp   **D.** slice

Q.78 Which word does NOT belong with the others?

A. peninsula   **B.** island

C. bay   **D.** cape

Q.79 Which word does NOT belong with the others?

A. fair   **B.** just

C. equitable   **D.** favorable

Q.80 Which word does NOT belong with the others?

A. unique   **B.** beautiful

C. rare   **D.** exceptional

Computer Awareness

Q.81 A light sensitive device that converts drawing, printed text or other images into digital form is

A. Keyboard   **B.** Plotter
C. Scanner   **D.** OMR

Q.82 Which protocol provides e-mail facility among different hosts?

A. FTP   **B.** SMTP
C. TELNET   **D.** SNMP

Q.83 The basic architecture of computer was developed by

A. John Von Neumann   **B.** Charles Babbage
C. Blaise Pascal   **D.** Garden Moore

Q.84 In order to tell Excel that we are entering a formula in cell, we must begin with an operator such as

A. $ **B.** @   **C.** +   **D.** =

Q.85 In how many generations a computer can be classified?

A. 3   **B.** 4   **C.** 5   **D.** 6

Q.86 World Wide Web is being standard by

A. Worldwide corporation
B. W3C
C. World Wide Consortium
D. World Wide Web Standard

Q.87 If there are multiple recycle bin for a hard disk

A. You can set different size for each recycle bin
B. You can choose which recycle bin to use to store your deleted files
C. You can make any one of them default recycle bin
D. None of above

Q.88 Identify false statement

A. You can find deleted files in recycle bin
B. You can restore any files in recycle bin if you ever need
C. You can increase free space of disk by sending files in recycle bin
D. You can right click and choose Empty Recycle Bin to clean it at once

Q.89 If the displayed system time and date is wrong, you can reset it using

A. Write   **B.** Calendar
C. Write file   **D.** Control panel

Q.90 You should save your computer from?

A. Viruses   **B.** Time bombs
C. Worms   **D.** All of the above

Q.91 The ability to combine name and addresses with a standard document is called ________

A. document formatting
B. database management
C. mail merge
D. form letters

Q.92 Which enables us to send the same letter to different persons?

A. macros   **B.** template
C. mail merge   **D.** none

Q.93 A word processor would most likely be used to do

A. keep an account of money spent
B. do a computer search in media center
C. maintain an inventory
D. type a biography

Q.94 What is gutter margin?

A. Margin that is added to the left margin when printing
B. Margin that is added to right margin when printing
C. Margin that is added to the binding side of page when printing
D. Margin that is added to the outside of the page when printing

Q.95 Which can be used for quick access to commonly used commands and tools?

A. Status bar   **B.** Tool bar
C. Menu bar   **D.** Title bar

Q.96 Which of the following format you can decide to apply or not in AutoFormat dialog box?

A. Number format   **B.** Border format
C. Font format   **D.** All of above

Q.97 How can you remove borders applied in cells?

A. Choose None on Border tab of Format cells
B. Open the list on Border tool in Formatting toolbar then choose first tool (no border)
C. Both of above
D. None of above

Q.98 Where can you set the shading color for a range of cells in Excel?

A. Choose required color form Patterns tab of Format Cells dialog box
B. Choose required color on Fill Color tool in Formatting toolbar
C. Choose required color on Fill Color tool in Drawing toolbar
D. All of above

Q.99 Which tab is not available on left panel when you open a presentation?

A. Outline
B. Slides
C. Notes
D. All of above are available

Q.100 Which of the following section does not exist in a slide layout?

A. Titles   **B.** Lists
C. Charts   **D.** Animations

English

Q.101 Rajeev failed in the examination because none of his answers were _______ to the questions asked.

A. allusive   **B.** revealing

C. pertinent   **D.** referential

Q.102 There are _______ views on the issue of giving bonus to the employees.

A. independent   **B.** divergent

C. modest   **D.** adverse

Q.103 Man who has committed such an _______ crime must get the most severe punishment.

A. injurious   **B.** injurious

C. unworhty   **D.** abominable

Q.104 He has _______ people visiting him at his house because he fears it will cause discomfort to neighbours

A. curtailed   **B.** requested

C. stopped   **D.** warned

Q.105 Although he never learn to read, his exceptional memory and enquiring mind eventually made him a very _______ man.

A. dedicated   **B.** erudite

C. pragmatic   **D.** benevolent

Q.106 Kiran asked me, "Did you see the Cricket match on television last night?"

A. Kiran asked me whether I saw the Cricket match on television the earlier night

B. Kiran asked me whether I had seen the Cricket match on television the earlier night.

C. Kiran asked me did I see the Cricket match on television the last night.

D. Kiran asked me whether I had seen the Cricket match on television the last night.

Q.107 David said to Anna, "Mona will leave for her native place tomorrow."

A. David told Anna that Mona will leave for her native place tomorrow.

B. David told Anna that Mona left for her native place the next day

C. David told Anna that Mona would be leaving for her native place tomorrow.

D. David told Anna that Mona would leave for her native place the next day.

Q.108 I said to him, "Why are you working so hard?"

A. I asked him why he was working so hard.

B. I asked him why was he working so hard.

C. I asked him why had he been working so hard.

D. I asked him why he had been working so hard.

Q.109 He said to her, "What a cold day!"

A. He told her that it was a cold day.

B. He exclaimed that it was a cold day.

C. He exclaimed sorrowfully that it was a cold day.

D. He exclaimed that it was a very cold day.

Q.110 The tailor said to him, "Will you have the suit ready by tomorrow evening?"

A. The tailor asked him that he will have the suit ready by the next evening.

B. The tailor asked him that he would had the suit ready by the next evening

C. The tailor asked him if he would have the suit ready by the next evening

D. The tailor asked him if he will like to the suit ready by the next evening.

Q.111 Our task had been completed before sunset.

A. We completed our task before sunset.

B. We have completed our task before sunset.

C. We complete our task before sunset.

D. We had completed our task before sunset.

Q.112 The boy laughed at the beggar.

A. The beggar was laughed by the boy.

B. The beggar was being laughed by the boy.

C. The beggar was being laughed at by the boy.

D. The beggar was laughed at by the boy.

Q.113 The boys were playing Cricket.

A. Cricket had been played by the boys.

B. Cricket has been played by the boys.

C. Cricket was played by the boys.

D. Cricket was being played by the boys.

Q.114 They drew a circle in the morning.

A. A circle was being drawn by them in the morning.

B. A circle was drawn by them in the morning.

C. In the morning a circle have been drawn by them.

D. A circle has been drawing since morning.

Q.115 They will demolish the entire block.

A. The entire block is being demolished.

B. he block may be demolished entirely.

C. The entire block will have to be demolished by the

D. The entire block will be demolished.

Q.116 S_1: A force of exists between everybody in the universe.

P : Normally it is very small but when the one of the bodies is a planet, like earth, the force is considerable.

Q : It has been investigated by many scientists including Galileo and Newton.

R : Everything on or near the surface of the earth is attracted by the mass of earth.

S : This gravitational force depends on the mass of the bodies involved.

S_6: The greater the mass, the greater is the earth's force of attraction on it. We can call this force of attraction gravity.

The Proper sequence should be:

A. PRQS   **B.** PRSQ   **C.** QSRP   **D.** QSPR

Q.117 S^1: Calcutta unlike other cities kepts its trams.

P : As a result there horrendous congestion.

Q : It was going to be the first in South Asia.

R : They run down the centre of the road.

S : To ease in the city decided to build an underground railway line.

S⁶: The foundation stone was laid in 1972.

The Proper sequence should be:

A. PRSQ   **B.** PSQR   **C.** SQRP   **D.** RPSQ

Q.118 S₁: For some time in his youth Abraham Lincoln was manager for a shop.

P : Then a chance Customer would come.

Q : Young Lincoln way of keeping shop was entirely unlike anyone else's.

R : Lincoln would jump up and attend to his needs and then revert to his reading.

S : He used to lie full length on the counter of the shop eagerly reading a book.

S₆: Never before had Lincoln had so much time for reading as had then.

The Proper sequence should be:

A. SRQP   **B.** QSPR   **C.** SQRP   **D.** QPSR

Q.119 S₁: All the land was covered by the ocean.

P : The leading god fought the monster, killed it and chopped its body in to two halves.

Q : A terrible monster prevented the gods from separating the land from the water.

R : The god made the sky out of the upper part of the body and ornamented it with stars.

S : The god created the earth from the lower part, grew plants on it and populated it with animals.

S₆: The god moulded the first people out of clay according to his own image and mind.

The Proper sequence should be:

A. PQRS   **B.** PQSR   **C.** QPSR   **D.** QPRS

Q.120 S₁: Smoke oozed up between the planks.

P : Passengers were told to be ready to quit the ship.

Q : The rising gale fanned the smouldering fire.

R : Everyone now knew there was fire on board.

S : Flames broke out here and there.

S₆: Most people bore the shock bravely.

The Proper sequence should be:

A. SRQP   **B.** QPSR   **C.** RSPQ   **D.** QSRP

// Smart Answer Sheet //

Correct — Percentage of students who answered correctly. **Skipped** — Percentage of students who skipped.

Q.	Ans.	Correct / Skipped
1	C	81.91 % / 13.62 %
2	C	86.77 % / 10.56 %
3	C	86.31 % / 11.2 %
4	A	82.61 % / 11.11 %
5	B	78.05 % / 12.21 %
6	D	82.62 % / 13.72 %
7	D	89.41 % / 10.24 %
8	D	81.64 % / 11.82 %
9	B	86.22 % / 13.29 %
10	C	78.36 % / 12.01 %
11	D	82.38 % / 12.7 %
12	B	86.98 % / 12.38 %
13	A	88.58 % / 10.53 %
14	D	80.62 % / 11.0 %
15	B	77.54 % / 16.54 %
16	B	82.06 % / 17.62 %
17	C	83.88 % / 12.07 %
18	B	82.48 % / 13.39 %
19	B	77.11 % / 22.02 %
20	C	84.33 % / 11.39 %
21	B	88.57 % / 10.5 %
22	B	82.96 % / 11.54 %
23	D	89.14 % / 10.56 %
24	B	84.17 % / 13.92 %
25	D	89.66 % / 10.15 %
26	D	76.22 % / 19.15 %
27	A	81.17 % / 13.99 %
28	B	76.83 % / 17.74 %
29	A	80.37 % / 11.96 %
30	D	83.49 % / 16.31 %
31	C	80.62 % / 19.32 %
32	B	89.08 % / 10.44 %
33	C	84.49 % / 14.53 %
34	D	83.27 % / 14.44 %
35	A	86.1 % / 11.63 %
36	D	83.62 % / 11.75 %
37	B	79.81 % / 18.3 %
38	B	83.27 % / 10.15 %
39	D	77.8 % / 15.56 %
40	A	80.55 % / 16.29 %
41	C	84.06 % / 10.06 %
42	D	84.35 % / 15.52 %
43	B	79.21 % / 11.51 %
44	D	80.03 % / 15.54 %
45	C	79.63 % / 15.43 %
46	A	80.14 % / 18.35 %
47	C	85.74 % / 10.53 %
48	A	76.21 % / 23.57 %
49	D	88.31 % / 11.69 %
50	B	86.08 % / 11.16 %
51	D	80.13 % / 19.05 %
52	B	81.47 % / 12.76 %
53	D	85.09 % / 11.12 %
54	B	76.8 % / 11.84 %
55	C	77.18 % / 21.73 %
56	C	87.67 % / 10.0 %
57	A	83.2 % / 14.24 %
58	B	81.33 % / 13.32 %
59	C	85.15 % / 12.65 %
60	D	80.42 % / 12.04 %
61	B	83.86 % / 14.84 %
62	B	87.46 % / 10.81 %
63	C	84.58 % / 14.7 %
64	B	80.07 % / 19.04 %
65	B	76.75 % / 10.23 %
66	D	76.29 % / 19.93 %
67	D	83.88 % / 15.35 %
68	C	86.3 % / 11.09 %
69	D	83.34 % / 13.26 %
70	D	78.6 % / 11.83 %
71	C	83.5 % / 14.16 %
72	D	85.85 % / 12.64 %
73	D	84.88 % / 10.3 %
74	D	79.35 % / 12.64 %
75	B	80.34 % / 10.2 %
76	C	89.24 % / 10.15 %
77	D	78.3 % / 11.45 %
78	C	84.02 % / 14.35 %
79	D	87.33 % / 10.93 %
80	B	77.68 % / 15.4 %

Q.	Ans.	Correct / Skipped	Q.	Ans.	Correct / Skipped	Q.	Ans.	Correct / Skipped	Q.	Ans.	Correct / Skipped	Q.	Ans.	Correct / Skipped
81	C	86.59 % / 12.5 %	89	D	76.89 % / 12.55 %	97	C	87.27 % / 12.6 %	105	B	81.49 % / 14.16 %	113	D	86.38 % / 10.08 %
82	B	81.16 % / 18.15 %	90	D	77.77 % / 14.3 %	98	D	76.48 % / 18.01 %	106	B	89.84 % / 10.1 %	114	B	87.21 % / 11.35 %
83	A	77.02 % / 20.6 %	91	C	76.05 % / 16.81 %	99	C	76.26 % / 17.45 %	107	D	78.22 % / 14.58 %	115	D	89.63 % / 10.15 %
84	D	78.66 % / 20.75 %	92	C	87.12 % / 10.81 %	100	D	83.29 % / 13.31 %	108	B	76.39 % / 12.14 %	116	D	77.97 % / 12.5 %
85	C	84.98 % / 13.46 %	93	D	79.72 % / 13.76 %	101	C	88.83 % / 10.43 %	109	D	89.1 % / 10.87 %	117	D	84.73 % / 13.46 %
86	B	81.66 % / 12.09 %	94	C	80.3 % / 15.87 %	102	B	77.03 % / 13.38 %	110	C	87.75 % / 11.88 %	118	B	88.7 % / 10.85 %
87	A	77.42 % / 21.66 %	95	B	84.75 % / 14.63 %	103	D	86.24 % / 11.72 %	111	D	89.41 % / 10.49 %	119	D	77.81 % / 14.96 %
88	C	88.45 % / 11.23 %	96	D	84.96 % / 11.36 %	104	C	80.5 % / 11.27 %	112	D	78.17 % / 13.03 %	120	A	83.86 % / 12.69 %

//Hints and Solutions//

1. An idempotent matrix A is a square matrix such that $A^2 = A$ and a nilpotent matrix A is a

square matrix such that $A^r = O$ for some +ve integer r (naturally, not greater than the order of the matrix).

In this case, we have $A^2 = O$.

2. $(AB + BA)^t = (AB)^t + (BA)^t$

$= B^t A^t + A^t B^t = BA + AB = AB + BA$

$(\because A^t = A$ and $B^t = B)$

3. $(AA^t)^t = (A^t)^t A^t = AA^t$

$\Rightarrow AA^t$ is symmetric.

4. Each diagonal entry of a skew symmetric matrix is 0 as for a skew symmetric matrix $A = [a_{ij}]_{n \times n}$

$a_{ij} = -a_{ji} \Rightarrow a_{ii} = -a_{ii} -a_{ii}$ for $j = i \Rightarrow a_{ii} = 0$.

5. $\because I_n I_n = I_n, \therefore (I_n)^{-1} = I_n$

6. $A = [a_{ij}]_{n \times n}$ is a diagonal matrix iff all non-diagonal entries are 0 i.e. iff $a_{ij} = 0$ for $i \neq j$.

7.
The centre of the circle in reference lies on a line perpendicular to the place x+ 2y + 2z − 15 = 0 and passing through the centre of the sphere
$x^2 + y^2 + z^2 - 2y - 4z + 1 = 0$
i.e. the point (0,1,2).
So, the centre of the circle lies on the lice
$\frac{x-0}{1} = \frac{y-1}{2} = \frac{z-2}{2}$
Any point on this line is (t, 2t, +1, 2t + 2)
This point lies in the plane x+ 2y + 2z -15 = 0
If t + 2 (2 t +1) + 2 (2t + 2) − 15 = 0
i.e. if 9 i.e. t = 1.
Hence, the required centre is
(1, 2 + 1, +2) = (1,3,4).

8.
The foot of perpendicular form (3,4,5) on X-axis is (3,0,0).
Hence, the required distance
$= \sqrt{(3-3)^2 + (4-0)^2 + (5-0)^2} = \sqrt{41}$

9. The direction cosines of X-axis are $< \cos 0^0, \cos 90° >$ i.e.$< 1,00 >$.

10. The point of concurrence of he medians of a triangle is called centroid of the triangle.

11. The equation of XY-plane is z =0

i.e. 0x + 0y +1 z = 0.

12. $< 3, 4, 5 >$ can be direction number of a line in space

13.
Here, $f'(x) = \frac{d}{dx}\left(x^2 e^{-x}\right)$
$= x^2 e^{-x}(-1) + e^{-x} 2x$
$\Rightarrow f'(x) = e^{-x}(2x - x^2) > 0$
if $2x - x^2 > 0$ i.e. if $x(x - 2) < 0$
i.e. if $0 < x < 2$. Hence f is strict increasing on [2, 0]

14.
$\frac{dy}{dx} = 0 \Rightarrow \frac{dy}{dx} = 0 \Rightarrow 2t - 1 = 0 \Rightarrow t = \frac{1}{2}$

15.
$\left(\frac{dy}{dx}\right)_{(0,0)} = 1$ and hence the tangent to the curve at (0, 0) makes an angle of $\frac{\pi}{4}$ with + ve X– axis

16.
$f'(x) = x^{25} \times 75(1 - x)^{74}(-1) + (1 - x)^{75} \times 25 x^{24}$
$= 25x^{24}(1 - x)^{74}\{-3x + (1 - x)\} \forall x \in R$
$\Rightarrow f'(x) = 0 \Rightarrow x = \frac{1}{4} \in (0, 1)$
Note that $f(0) = f(1) = 0$
and $f\left(\frac{1}{4}\right) = \frac{3^{75}}{4^{100}}$
So f(x) is maximum at $x = \frac{1}{4}$

17.
$f(x) = x^2 + x + 1 = \left(x + \frac{1}{2}\right)^2 + \frac{3}{4} \geqslant \frac{3}{4} \forall x \in R$

18.
Since $\frac{dy}{dx} = \cos x$, therefore slope of tangent at (0, 0) = cos 0 = 1 and hence slope of normal at (0, 0) is − 1

19. Equation of any circle with centre at origin is $x^2 + y^2 = r^2$; differentiating w.r.t. x, we get $2x + 2y\, y_1 = 0$ or $x + yy_1 = 0$

20.

Given $\frac{dy}{dx} = e^{-2y} \Rightarrow e^{2y}\, dy = dx$

$\int e^{2y}\, dy = \int dx + C$

$\frac{e^{2y}}{2} = x + C$ ....(1)

when x = 5, y = 0, therefore, $\frac{1}{2} = 5 + C$

$C = -\frac{9}{2}$ and hence from (1)

$\frac{e^{2y}}{2} = x - \frac{9}{2}$ ....(2)

when y = 3, we get

$\frac{e^6}{2} = x - \frac{9}{2} \Rightarrow x = \frac{e^6 + 9}{2}$

21.

Given $\frac{dy}{dx} = y + \frac{y}{x} \Rightarrow \frac{1}{y}\, dy\left(1 + \frac{1}{x}\right) dx$

$\log y = x + \log x + c \Rightarrow y = x\, e^{x + c}$

The curve in reference corresponds to c = 0.

22.

$$\frac{d^3y}{dx^3} = 0 \Rightarrow \left(\frac{d^2y}{dx^2}\right) = 0 \Rightarrow \frac{d^2y}{dx^2} = A$$

$$\Rightarrow \frac{d}{dx}\left(\frac{dy}{dx}\right) = A \Rightarrow \frac{dy}{dx} = Ax + B$$

$$y = \frac{Ax^2}{2} + Bx + C$$

$y = ax^2 + bx + c;\ a = \frac{A}{2},\ b = B,\ c = C$

23.

Given differential equation is $\frac{dy}{dx} = 1 + xy$ i.e. $\frac{dy}{dx} + (-x)y = 1$, which is a linear differential equation. An integrating factor is $e^{\int x\,dx}$ = and hence solution is given by

= ∫ 1. dx + C.

1.

24.

In the given differential equation, highest order derivative is $\frac{d^2y}{dx^2}$ and its highest power is $\left(\frac{d^2y}{dx^2}\right)^2$. Hence the degree of the given differential equation is 2.

25. If two events are independent, then their complements are also independent.

26. Note that $A - B = A \cap B^c = ((A \cap B^c)^c)^c = (A^c \cup B)^c$. Also, $A - B = A - A \cap B$.

27. required probability = $(4/6)^4$.

($\because$ 3, 4, 5, 6 are favourable outcomes when a dice is rolled once)

28. Required probability =

$$\left(1 - \frac{1}{4}\right) \times \left(1 - \frac{1}{3}\right).$$

29.

It is a case of Bernoullian trials where success is "a tail comes up". Here, $p = \frac{1}{2}$ and $q = \frac{1}{2}$. Required probability = $1 - p(0) = 1 - {}^5C_0\left(\frac{1}{2}\right)^5$.

30. By definition of probability, $0 \leq p(E) \leq 1$.

31.

Now, $x + \frac{1}{x} = -y - \frac{1}{y}$ where $y = -x > 0$

$$\Rightarrow x + \frac{1}{x} = -\left\{y + \frac{1}{y}\right\}$$

$$= \left\{\left(\sqrt{y} - \frac{1}{\sqrt{y}}\right)^2 + 2\right\} \leq -2 \text{ for all } x < 0.$$

Note that $x + \frac{1}{x} = -2$ for $x = -1$.

32.

Here, $x \in r$ and hence $x^2 + x + 1$

$$= \left(x + \frac{1}{2}\right)^2 + \left(1 - \frac{1}{4}\right)$$

$$= \left(x + \frac{1}{2}\right)^2 + \frac{3}{4}$$

$$\Rightarrow x^2 + x + 1 \geq \frac{3}{4} \text{ for all real } x.$$

Note that $x^2 + x + 1 = \frac{3}{4}$ for $x = -\frac{1}{2}$

(i.e. when $x + \frac{1}{2} = 0$)

33.

Now, $x - x^2 = -(x^2 - x)$

$$= -\left(x^2 - x + \frac{1}{4}\right) + \frac{1}{4}$$

$$\Rightarrow x - x^2 = -\left(x - \frac{1}{2}\right)^2 + \frac{1}{4} \leq \frac{1}{4} \text{ for all } x \in R.$$

Note that $x - x^2 = \frac{1}{4}$ when $x = \frac{1}{2}$.

34.

Here, $x \in R$ and

$3x^2 + 7x + 10 = 3\left\{x^2 + \frac{7}{3}x\right\} + 10$

$$= \left\{x^2 + \frac{7}{3}x + \left(\frac{7}{6}\right)^2\right\} + 10 - 3\left(\frac{7}{6}\right)^2$$

$$= 3\left(x + \frac{7}{6}\right)^2 + \frac{12 \times 10 - 49}{12}$$

$$= 3\left(x + \frac{7}{6}\right)^2 + \frac{71}{12}$$

$$\Rightarrow 3x^2 + 7x + 10 = 3\left(x + \frac{7}{6}\right)^2 + \frac{71}{12} \geq \frac{71}{12} \text{ for all } x \in R.$$

Note that $3x^2 + 7x + 10 = \frac{71}{12}$ for $x = \frac{-7}{6}$.

35. As $|\sec\theta + \cos\theta|^2 = (\sec\theta + \cos\theta)^2$

$= \sec^2\theta + \cos^2\theta + 2$

$= (\sec\theta - \cos\theta)^2 + 2 + 2,$

therefore, $|\sec\theta + \cos\theta|^2 \geq 4$

$\Rightarrow |\sec\theta + \cos\theta| \geq 2.$

36.

Since a, b and c are positive reals, therefore,

$\frac{a+b}{2} \geq \sqrt{ab}, \frac{b+c}{2} \geq \sqrt{bc}$

and $\frac{c+a}{2} \geq \sqrt{ca}$ ($\because A.M. \geq G.M.$)

$\Rightarrow a + b \geq 2\sqrt{ab}, b + c \geq 2\sqrt{bc}$

and $c + a \geq 2\sqrt{ca}$

$\Rightarrow (a + b)(b + c)(c + a) \geq 8\,abc > 6\,abc.$

37.

Since a, b and c are distinct positive real numbers, therefore,

$\frac{a+b}{2} > \sqrt{ab}, \frac{b+c}{2} > \sqrt{bc}$ and $\frac{c+a}{2} > \sqrt{ca}$

$\Rightarrow a + b > 2\sqrt{ab}, b + c > 2\sqrt{bc}$

and $c + a > 2\sqrt{ca}$

$\Rightarrow (a + b)(b + c)(c + a) > 8\,abc.$

38. Mass is not a vector quantity.

39. A vector with magnitude zero is called a null vector.

40. Magnitude of a vector can never be negative.

41.

$$\left|\frac{\vec{a}}{|\vec{a}|}\right| = \frac{1}{|\vec{a}|}|\vec{a}| = 1 \Rightarrow \frac{\vec{a}}{|\vec{a}|} \text{ is a unit}$$

vector in the direction of $\vec{a}$.

42.

$|\vec{a} + \vec{b}| \leq |\vec{a}| + |\hat{a} \bullet (\vec{b} - (\hat{a} \bullet \hat{b})\hat{a})|$ is the only true result.

43.

$$\hat{a} \bullet (\vec{b} - (\hat{a} \bullet \hat{b})\hat{a})$$
$$= \hat{a} \bullet \hat{b} - (\hat{a} \bullet \hat{b})(\hat{a} \bullet \hat{a})$$
$$= \hat{a} \bullet \hat{b} - (\hat{a} \bullet \hat{b})1^2 = 0$$

44.

$$\alpha + \beta + \frac{2}{\alpha + \beta} = 2 + \frac{2}{2} = 3$$
$$\text{and } (\alpha + \beta)\frac{2}{\alpha + \beta} = 2$$

45.

$(2q)^2 - 4pr \geq 0$ and $(-2\sqrt{pr})^2 - 4q \cdot q \geq 0$
$\Rightarrow q^2 - pr \geq 0$ and $pr - q^2 \geq 0$
$\Rightarrow q^2 - pr \geq 0$ and $q^2 - pr \leq 0$
$\Rightarrow q^2 = pr \Rightarrow \frac{p}{q} = \frac{q}{r}$

46. $x^2 = 3|x| + 2 = 0 \Rightarrow |x| = -1, -2$, which is not true for any real x.

47.

$$x = \sqrt{20 + x}$$
$$\Rightarrow x^2 = 20 = x, x > 0$$
$$\Rightarrow x^2 - x - 20 = 0, x < 0$$

48. Here, sum of coefficients is 0, therefore, 1 is a root and product of roots =

$$\frac{a - b}{b - c}$$

49. A polynomial equation of degree n has n roots (real or complex). Hence, in this case, the number of roots is 6

50.

$$a\cos^2\frac{C}{2} + c\cos^2\frac{A}{2} = \frac{3b}{2}$$
$$\Rightarrow \frac{a(1+\cos C)}{2} + \frac{c(1+\cos A)}{2} = \frac{3b}{2}$$

$a + c + (a\cos C + c\cos A) = 3b$

$a + c + b = 3b \Rightarrow a + c = 2b$

a, b, c are in A.P.

51.

Let the sides be $a = x$, $b = \sqrt{3}x$, $c = 2x$,

then $\cos C = \frac{a^2 + b^2 - c^2}{2ab} = 0$

$\Rightarrow C = 90°$

$\Rightarrow A + B = 180° - C = 90°$

Also $\frac{a}{\sin A} = \frac{b}{\sin B}$

$\Rightarrow \frac{x}{\sin A} = \frac{\sqrt{3}x}{\sin(90° - A)}$

$\Rightarrow \tan A = \frac{1}{\sqrt{3}}$

$\Rightarrow A = 30°$

Consequently B = 60°.

52.

Now $\sin\theta = \frac{1}{2}$

$\Rightarrow \theta = \frac{\pi}{6}$

and $\cos\varphi = \frac{1}{3}$

$\Rightarrow \frac{\pi}{3}$

$\frac{\pi}{3} < \varphi < \frac{\pi}{2}$

$\left(\because \frac{1}{2} > \frac{1}{3} > 0 \, i.e. \cos\frac{\pi}{3} > \cos\phi > \cos\frac{\pi}{2}\right)$

$\Rightarrow \frac{\pi}{6} + \frac{\pi}{3} < \theta + \phi < \frac{\pi}{6} + \frac{\pi}{2}$

or $\frac{\pi}{2} < \theta + \phi < \frac{2\pi}{3}$

53. $\sin 20° (\tan 10° + \cot 10°) = \sin 20° (2\,\mathrm{cosec}\,20°) = 2$

$(\because \tan\theta + \cot\theta = 2\,\mathrm{cosec}\,2\theta)$

54.

$$\cot 36° \cot 72° = \frac{2\cos 72° \cos 36°}{2\sin 72° \sin 36°}$$
$$= \frac{\cos(72°+36°) + \cos(72°-36°)}{\cos(72°-36°) - \cos(72°+36°)}$$
$$= \frac{\cos 108° + \cos 36°}{\cos 36° - \cos 108°} = \frac{-\sin 18° + \cos 36°}{\cos 36° + \sin 18°}$$
$$= \frac{-\frac{\sqrt{5}-1}{4} + \frac{\sqrt{5}+1}{4}}{\frac{\sqrt{5}+1}{4} + \frac{\sqrt{5}-1}{4}}$$
$$= \frac{2}{2\sqrt{5}} = \frac{1}{\sqrt{5}}$$

55.

Given $\dfrac{\sin(\alpha+2\beta)}{\sin\alpha} = \dfrac{2}{1}$,

apply componendo and dividendo

$$\dfrac{\sin(\alpha+2\beta)+\sin\alpha}{\sin(\alpha+2\beta)-\sin\alpha} = \dfrac{2+1}{2-1}$$

$$\Rightarrow \dfrac{2\sin(\alpha+\beta)\cos\beta}{2\cos(\alpha+\beta)\sin\beta} = 3$$

56. A − B and B − A are always disjoint and hence A − B = B − A only if either of these is φ i.e. if A ⊂ B and B ⊂ A i.e. if A= B

57. A ∪ (B ∩ C) = (A ∪ B) ∩ (A ∪ C) (Distributive law)

58. (A ∪ B)^C = A^C ∩ B^C |De Morgan's law's

59. The number of elements in A ×A is n ×n = n^2

60. Since n (A) = 4, therefore, n(A × A) = 16. Hence number of subsets of A × A = 2^{16}. So, number

of relations on A = 2^{16}.

61. This is a simple division series; each number is one-half of the previous number.

In other terms to say, the number is divided by 2 successively to get the next result.

4/2 = 2

2/2 = 1

1/2 = 1/2

(1/2)/2 = 1/4

(1/4)/2 = 1/8 and so on.

62. This is a simple alternating addition and subtraction series. In the first pattern, 3 is added; in the second, 2 is subtracted.

63. There are two alphabetical series here. The first series is with the first letters only: STUVW. The second series involves the remaining letters: CD, EF, GH, IJ, KL.

64. Because the letters are the same, concentrate on the number series, which is a simple 2, 3, 4, 5, 6 series, and follows each letter in order

65. The middle letters are static, so concentrate on the first and third letters. The series involves an alphabetical order with a reversal of the letters. The first letters are in alphabetical order: F, G, H, I , J. The second and fourth segments are reversals of the first and third segments. The missing segment begins with a new letter.

66. Gorbl means fan; flur means belt; pixn means ceiling; arth means tile; and tusl means roof. Therefore, pixnarth is the correct choice.

67. Hapl means cloud; lesh means burst; srench means pin; och means ball; and resbo means nine. Leshsrench (choice a) doesn't contain any of the words needed for cloud nine. We know that och means ball, so that rules out choices b and c. When you

combine hapl (cloud) with resbo (nine), you get the correct answer

68. In this language, the noun appears first and the adjectives follow. Since agnos means spider and should appear first, choices a and d can be ruled out. Choice b can be ruled out because delano means snake.

69. From wilkospadi, you can determine that wilko means bicycle and spadi means race. Therefore, the first part of the word that means racecar should begin with spadi. That limits your choices to b and d. Choice b, spadiwilko, is incorrect because we have already determined that wilkomeans bicycle. Therefore, the answer must be choice d, spadivolo.

70. Migen means cup; lasan means board; poen means walk; cuop means pull; and dansa means man. The only possible choices, then, are choices a and d. Choice a can be ruled out because migen means cup.

71. Some men who are soldiers serve their country.

72. Only one worker in the factory has exactly five children.

73. TV promotes a feeling of helpless vulnerability in viewers.

74. None of these

75. The demand for more universities is being stepped up.

76. The wing, fin, and rudder are all parts of an airplane.

77. The core, seeds, and pulp are all parts of an apple. A slice would be a piece taken out of an apple.

78. A peninsula, island, and cape are all landforms; a bay is a body of water

79. Fair, just, and equitable are all synonyms meaning impartial. Favorable means expressing approval.

80. Unique, rare, and exceptional are all synonyms. Beautiful has a different meaning.

81. A scanner is a device that captures images from photographic prints, posters, magazine pages, and similar sources for computer editing and display. Scanners come in hand-held, feed-in, and flatbed types and for scanning black-and-white only, or color. Very high resolution scanners are used for scanning for high-resolution printing, but lower resolution scanners are adequate for capturing images for computer display. Scanners usually come with software, such as Adobe's Photoshop product, that lets you resize and otherwise modify a captured image.

82. SMTP (Simple Mail Transfer Protocol) is a TCP/IP protocol used in sending and receiving e-mail. However, since it is limited in its ability to queue messages at the receiving end, it is usually used with one of two other protocols, POP3 or IMAP that let the user save messages in a server mailbox and download them periodically from the server. SMTP usually is implemented to operate over Internet port 25.

Many mail servers now support Extended Simple Mail Transfer Protocol (ESMTP), which allows multimedia files to be delivered as e-mail

83. In 1945, Professor J. von Neumann, who was then working at the Moore School of Engineering in Philadelphia, where the

E.N.I.A.C. had been built, issued on behalf of a group of his co-workers, a report on the logical design of digital computers.

84. In MS Excel, formulas are equations that perform various calculations in your worksheets. Though Microsoft has introduced a handful of new functions over the years, the concept of Excel spreadsheet formulas is the same in all versions of Excel 2016, Excel 2013, Excel 2010, Excel 2007 and lower.

All Excel formulas begin with an equal sign (=).

85. There is 5 generation of computer available till now.

1st Generation of Computer = The period of first generation: 1946-1959. Vacuum tube based.

2nd Generation of Computer = The period of second generation: 1959-1965. Transistor based.

3rd Generation of Computer = The period of third generation: 1965-1971. Integrated Circuit based.

4th Generation of Computer = The period of fourth generation: 1971-1980. VLSI microprocessor based.

5th Generation of Computer = The period of fifth generation: 1980-onwards. ULSI microprocessor based.

86. The World Wide Web Consortium is the main international standards organization for the World Wide Web.

87. If there are multiple recycle bin for a hard disk You can set different size for each recycle bin

88. That kind of a delete, which is a manual delete (you're clearly doing it in Windows Explorer), actually just moves the file into the Recycle Bin and doesn't free up any space until you empty the Recycle Bin.

Once you empty the Recycle Bin:

All of the files within it are then removed from the hard disk.

And the space is freed up.

89. If the displayed system time and date is wrong, you can reset it using Control panel

90. You should save your computer from-

Viruses

Time bombs

Worms

91. The automatic addition of names and addresses from a database to letters and envelopes in order to facilitate sending mail, especially advertising, to many addresses.

92. The automatic addition of names and addresses from a database to letters and envelopes in order to facilitate sending mail, especially advertising, to many addresses.

93. A word processor is software or a device that enables users to create, edit, and print documents.

It allows you to type and write text, store it electronically in pc memory, display it on a screen of a monitor, modify the content by entering commands and characters from the keyboard, and at last print it.

Word processing is the most common of all the computer software.

94. The gutter margin is a typographical term used to designate an additional margin added to a page layout to compensate for the part of the paper made unusable by the binding process. In a facing pages layout (Word refers to this type of layout as "mirror margins"), the gutter margin is on the very inside of both pages.

95. In computer interface design, a toolbar (originally known as ribbon) is a graphical control element on which on-screen buttons, icons, menus, or other input or output elements are placed. Toolbars are seen in many types of software such as office suites, graphics editors and web browsers.

96. In AutoFormat dialog box you can decide to apply-

Number format
Border formatFont format

97. You can remove borders applied in cells by Choose None on Border tab of Format cells and Open the list on Border tool in Formatting toolbar then choose first tool (no border)

98. You can set the shading color for a range of cells in Excel following ways-

- Choose required color form Patterns tab of Format Cells dialog box

- Choose required color on Fill Color tool in Formatting toolbar

- Choose required color on Fill Color tool in Drawing toolbar

99. Notes tab is not available on left panel when you open a presentation

100. Animations does not exist in a slide layout.

101. Rajeev failed in the examination because none of his answers were **pertinent** to the questions asked.

102. divergent means **tending to be different or develop in different directions.**

103. Abominable means very bad or terrible.

104. He has **stopped** people visiting him at his house because he fears it will cause discomfort to neighbours

105. Although he never learn to read, his exceptional memory and enquiring mind eventually made him a very **erudite** man.

106. Kiran asked me whether I had seen the Cricket match on television the earlier night.

107. David told Anna that Mona would leave for her native place the next day.

108. I asked him why he was working so hard.

109. He exclaimed that it was a very cold day.

110. The tailor asked him if he would have the suit ready by the next evening.

111. We had completed our task before sunset.

The given sentence is in passive voice and it is in Past Perfect Tense.

To convert it into active voice, we just remove **been** from the given sentence and object (our)will be change into subject (We).

Rule :

 Subject + had + V³ + Other agents.

112. The beggar was laughed at by the boy.

Given sentence is in Past indefinite (Past simple) tense and it is in the active voice. To change it into Passive voice Object (the boy) will become subject and subject (The beggar) will be object. We also use helping verb of past simple tense was with V³ form of the main verb. Keep it in mind that the preposition at must be retained with the verb.

Rule :

Subject + (was /were) + V³ + Other Agents.

113. Cricket was being played by the boys.

The given sentence is in Past Continuous Tense and it is in active voice. We need to change it into Passive voice.

Rule :

Subject + (was /were) + being + V³ + Optional Agents.

114. A circle was drawn by them in the morning.

Given sentence is in Past simple tense and it is in active voice, we need to change it into passive voice.

Rule :

Subject + (was / were) + V³ + Optional Agents.

115. The entire block will be demolished.

The given sentence contains one of Model verb **(Model Verb = will, shall, can, may, might, could, might, must, would)**. It is in active voice.

Rule :

Subject + Model verb + be + V3 + Optional Objects.

116. It has been investigated by many scientists including Galileo and Newton. This gravitational force depends on the mass of the bodies involved. Normally it is very small but when the one of the bodies is a planet, like earth, the force is considerable. Everything on or near the surface of the earth is attracted by the mass of earth.

117. They run down the centre of the road. As a result there horrendous congestion. To ease in the city decided to build an underground railway line. It was going to b the first in South Asia.

118. Young Lincoln way of keeping shop was entirely unlike anyone else's. He used to lie full length on the counter of the shop eagerly reading a book. Then a chance customer would come. Lincoln would jump up and attend to his needs and then revert to his reading.

119. A terrible monster prevented the gods from separating the land from the water. The leading god fought the monster, killed it and chopped its body into two halves. The god made the sky out of the upper part of the body and ornamented it with stars. The god created the earth from the lower part, grew plants on it and populated it with animals.

120. Through the ages, plants have evolved from simple to more complex forms. First there were water plants then land plants appeared during the Paleozoic era. Records of the history of the world are contained in fossils. But since the fossil remains appear locked in rock layers, they are closely related to the geologist area of investigation.

Mathematics

Q.1 The degree of the differential equation

$$\left[1 + \left(\frac{dy}{dx}\right)^2\right]^{3/2} = \frac{d^2 y}{dx^2} \text{ is}$$

A. 1   **B.** 2   **C.** 3   **D.** 4

Q.2 The degree of the differential equation

$$\left[1 + \left(\frac{dy}{dx}\right)^2\right]^{5/3} = \frac{d^2 y}{dx^2} \text{ is}$$

A. 1   **B.** 3   **C.** 5   **D.** 4

Q.3 The complete solution of the differential equation $dy/dx = 2x + 5$ is

A. 1   **B.** 3   **C.** 5   **D.** 4

Q.4 The general solution of the differential equation

$$\frac{d^2 y}{dx^2} = e^{-2x} \text{ is}$$

A. $y = \frac{1}{4}e^{-2x} + C$

B. $y = e^{-2x} + cx + d$

C. $y = \frac{1}{4}e^{-2x} + cx^2 + d$

D. $y = \frac{1}{4}e^{-2x} + cx + d$

Q.5 The general solution of the differential equation $(1+y^2)\,dx + y(1+x^2)\,dy = 0$ is (C an arbitrary constant)

A. $(1 + x^2)(1 + y^2) = 0$
B. $(1 + x^2)(1 + y^2) = C,$
C. $(1 + x^2) = C(1 + y^2)$
D. $(1 + y^4) = C(1 + x^2).$

Q.6 Given that $dy/dx = y\, e^x$ such that wne $x = 0$, $y = e$. The value of y ($y > 0$) when $x = 1$ will be

A. e   **B.** 1/e
C. e^e **D.** none of these

Q.7 Let A be any $m \times n$ matrix, then A^2 can be found only when

A. $m < n$ **B.** $m > n$
C. $m = n$ **D.** none of these

Q.8 If A and B are any two matrices, then

A. AB = BA
B. AB = I
C. AB = O
D. AB may or may not be defined

Q.9 A square matrix A is called idempotent if

A. $A^2 = I$ **B.** $A^2 = O$ **C.** $2A = I$ **D.** $A^2 = A$

Q.10 A square matrix $A = [a_{ij}]_{n \times n}$ is called a lower triangular matrix if $a_{ij} = 0$ for

A. i = j   **B.** i < j
C. i > j   **D.** none of these

Q.11 A square matrix $A = [a_{ij}]_{n \times n}$ is called an upper triangular if $a_{ij} = 0$ for

A. i = j   **B.** i < j
C. i > j   **D.** none of these

Q.12 If A and B are square matrices of the same order, then $(A+B)^2 = A^2 + 2AB + B^2$ implies

A. AB = BA   **B.** AB = O
C. AB + BA = O   **D.** none of these

Q.13

If $A(\vec{a})$, $B(\vec{b})$ and $C(\vec{C})$ are the vertices of an equilateral triangle whose orthocentre is at the origin, then

A. $\vec{a} + \vec{b} = \vec{c}$ **B.** $a^2 + b^2 = c^2$

C. $\vec{a} + \vec{b} + \vec{c} = \vec{0}$ **D.** none of these

Q.14

If I is the incentre of triangle ABC, then $|BC|\,|I\vec{A}| + |CA|\,I\vec{B} + |AB|\,I\vec{C}$ is equal to

A. $\dfrac{I\vec{A} + I\vec{B} + I\vec{C}}{3}$

B. $|\vec{A} + I\vec{B} + I\vec{C}$

C. $\vec{0}$

D. none of these

Q.15

If $\hat{a}$ and $\hat{b}$ are unit vectors such that $\hat{a} - 4\hat{b}$ is at right angles to $7\hat{a} - 2\hat{b}$, then the angle between $\hat{a}$ and $\hat{b}$ is

A. $\pi/2$ **B.** $\pi/3$ **C.** $\pi/6$ **D.** $\pi/4$

Q.16

If $\vec{a}, \vec{b}, \vec{c}$ are three mutually perpendicular unit vectors then $|\vec{a} + \vec{b} + \vec{c}|$ is equal to

A. 1   **B.** $\sqrt{3}$
C. 3   **D.** none of these

Q.17

If $\hat{a}, \hat{b}, \hat{c}$ are mutually perpendicular vectors of equal magnitude, then the angle θ which $\vec{a} + \vec{b} + \vec{c}$ makes with any of these three vectors vector is given by

A. $\cos^{-1}\left(\dfrac{1}{3}\right)$ **B.** $\cos^{-1}\left(\dfrac{1}{\sqrt{3}}\right)$

C. $\cos^{-1}\left(\dfrac{2}{\sqrt{3}}\right)$ **D.** $\cos^{-1}\left(\dfrac{2}{3}\right)$

Q.18

If $\vec{a} = \hat{i} + \hat{j} + \hat{k}, \vec{b} = 4\hat{i} + 3\hat{j} + 4\hat{k}$ and $\vec{c} = \hat{i} + \alpha\hat{j} + \beta\hat{k}$ are linearly dependent vectors and $|\vec{c}| = \sqrt{3}$, then

A. $\alpha = 1, \beta = -1$ **B.** $\alpha = 1, \beta = \pm 1$
C. $\alpha = -1, \beta = \pm 1$ **D.** $\alpha = \pm 1, \beta = 1$

Q.19

The value of $\sin\left(2\cos^{-1}\left(-\dfrac{3}{5}\right)\right)$ is

A. 24/25   **B.** -24/25
C. 7/25   **D.** none of these

Q.20 $\tan(\sin^{-1} x)$ is equal to

A. $\dfrac{x}{\sqrt{1-x^2}}$ **B.** $\dfrac{-x}{\sqrt{1-x^2}}$

C. $\dfrac{|x|}{\sqrt{1-x^2}}$ **D.** none of these

Q.21 $\cot(\cos^{-1}x)$ is equal to

A. $\dfrac{|x|}{\sqrt{1-x^2}}$ **B.** $\dfrac{x}{\sqrt{1-x^2}}$

C. $\dfrac{-x}{\sqrt{1-x^2}}$ **D.** none of these

Q.22 $\cos(\tan^{-1}x)$ is equal to

A. $\dfrac{1}{\sqrt{1+x^2}}$ **B.** $-\dfrac{1}{\sqrt{1+x^2}}$

C. $\dfrac{\sqrt{1+x^2}}{x}$ **D.** none of these

Q.23 If $2\tan^{-1}(\cos x) = \tan^{-1}(2\csc x)$, then $x =$
A. $\pi/6$ **B.** $\pi/3$
C. $\pi/4$ **D.** none of these

Q.24

$\cos^{-1}\left(\cos\dfrac{5\pi}{4}\right)$ is equal to

A. $5\pi/4$ **B.** $-\pi/4$
C. $3\pi/4$ **D.** none of these

Q.25

If E is an even, then $P(\overline{E})$ is equal to

A. P (E)   **B.** 1– P (E)   **C.** – P (E)   **D.** 1+ P (E).

Q.26 The probability that a teacher will give an unannounced test during any class is 1/5.If a student is absent twice, then the probability that he misses atleast one test is
A. 2/5   **B.** 4/5   **C.** 7/25   **D.** 9/25

Q.27 If the probability for a to fail in an examination is 0.2 and that for B is 0.3, then the probability that either A fails or B fails is
A. 0.5   **B.** 0.44
C. 0.06   **D.** none of these

Q.28 In a single throw of two dice, the probability of getting a total of 7 or 9 is
A. 4/18   **B.** 1/3
C. 5/18   **D.** none of these

Q.29

A and B are two events such that P (A) = 0.3 and P (A ∪ B) = 0.8. If A and B are independent,
P (B) is

A. 2/3   **B.** 3/8
C. 2/7   **D.** none of these

Q.30 Let A and B be two independent events. The probability that A and B occur is 1/12 and the probability that neither A nor B occurs is 1/2. The respective probabilities of A and B are
A. 1/6 and 1/2
B. 1/2 and 1/6
C. 1/3 and 1/4 or 1/4 and 1/3
D. none of these

Q.31 If $X_1 = (x_1, y_1)$ and $X_2 = (x_2, y_2)$ are two optimal solutions of a L.P.P., then
A. $\lambda X_1 + (1 - \lambda) X_2, \lambda \in R$ is also an optimal solution
B. $\lambda X_1 + (1 + \lambda) X_2, \lambda \in R$ is also an optional solution
C. $\lambda X_1 + (1 + \lambda) X_2, 0 \leq \lambda \leq 1$ is also an optimal solution
D. $\lambda X_1 + (1 - \lambda) X_2, 0 \leq \lambda \leq 1$ is also an optimal solution

Q.32 The graph of the inequality 2x + 3y > 6 is
A. half plane that containing the origin
B. half plane not containing the origin excluding the points on the line 2x + 3y = 6
C. whole XOY –plane excluding the points on the line 2x + 3y = 6
D. none of these

Q.33 Which of the following statements is correct?
A. Every L.P.P. has atleast one optical solution
B. Every L.P.P. has a unique optimal solution
C. If an L.P.P. has two optical solutions then it has infinitely many solutions
D. none of these

Q.34 The optimal value of the objective function is attained at the points
A. On X –axis
B. On Y-axis
C. which are corner-points of the feasible region
D. none of these

Q.35 In solving the following L.P.P.: "minimize f = 6x + 10y subject to x ≥ 6, y ≥ 2: 2x + y ≥ 10: x ≥ 0, y ≥ 0" redundant constrains are

A. x ≥ 6, y ≥ 2
B. 2x + y ≥ 10, x ≥ 0, y ≥ 0
C. x ≥ 6
D. none of these

Q.36 If x > 0, minimum values of x + 1/x is

A. 1   **B.** 0   **C.** 4   **D.** 2

Q.37 The value of λ, for which the sum of squares of the roots of the equation $x^2 - (λ + 2)x - λ + 1 = 0$ assumes the least value, is

A. 3   **B.** 1/3   **C.** -3   **D.** -1/3

Q.38

Solution set of the equation $\frac{2x-3}{x-1} + 1 = \frac{6x^2 - x - 6}{x-1}$ is

A. $\left\{ 1, -\frac{1}{3} \right\}$ **B.** {1}

C. $\left\{ -\frac{1}{3} \right\}$ **D.** none of these

Q.39 The condition for the polynomial equation $ax^2 = bx = c = 0$ to be a quadratic is

A. a > 0
B. a < 0
C. a ≠ 0
D. a ≠ 0, b ≠ 0

Q.40 Only one of the roots of $ax^2 + bx + c = 0$, a ≠ 0 is zero if

A. c = 0
B. c = 0, b ≠ 0
C. b = 0, c = 0
D. b ≠ 0, c ≠ 0

Q.41 The expression $ax^2 + bx + c$, a > 0 is positive for all real x only if

A. $b^2 - 4ac = 0$
B. $b^2 - 4ac ≥ 0$
C. $b^2 - 4ac < 0$
D. $b^2 - 4ac > 0$

Q.42 The value (s) of p for which the equation $2x^2 - 2\sqrt{2}\,px + p = 0$ has equal roots is (are)

A. 0
B. 4
C. 0,4
D. none of these

Q.43 f ∫ f(x) dx = g (x) and also ∫f(x) dx = h (x), then

A. h (x) + g (x) = constant
B. g(x) h (x) = constant
C. g (x) −h (x) = constant
D. g (x) = h (x)

Q.44

$\int \frac{e^x (x+1)}{\cos^2 (x\,e^x)} dx$ is equal to

A. tan (x eˣ) + C
B. tan (x² eˣ) + C
C. cot (x eˣ) + C
D. sin² (x eˣ) + C

Q.45 d/dx (∫ f(x) dx) is equal to

A. f'(x)
B. (f(x)²/2
C. f(x)
D. none of these

Q.46 An anti-derivative of x/cos² x is

A. x tan x
B. log |cos x|
C. x tan x + log |cos x|
D. cot x

Q.47

Which of the following is not equal to $\int \frac{1}{\sqrt{1-x^2}} dx$

A. sin⁻¹ x
B. −cos⁻¹ x
C. π/2−cos⁻¹x
D. none of these

Q.48 The next term of the sequence 1, 2, 4, 7, 11,.....is

A. 15   **B.** 16   **C.** 17   **D.** 18

Q.49 The next term of the sequence 2, 6, 12, 20, ...is

A. 30   **B.** 24   **C.** 40   **D.** 28

Q.50 The 10ᵗʰ term of the sequence √3, √12, √27 ,..... is

A. √243   **B.** √300   **C.** √363   **D.** √432

Q.51

The next term of the series $\frac{3}{2} + \frac{5}{4} + \frac{9}{8} + \frac{17}{16}$ ....is

A. 25/32   **B.** 29/32   **C.** 37/32   **D.** 33/32

Q.52 If $a_1 = a_2$, $a_n = a_{n-1} - 1$ (n > 2), then a_5 is

A. 1   **B.** 0   **C.** -1   **D.** -2

Q.53 If a, 4, b are in A.P.; a, 2, b are in G.P.; then a, 1, b are in

A. H.P.
B. A.P.
C. G.P.
D. none of these

Q.54 The function $f(x) = x^2$, for all real x, is

A. decreasing
B. increasing
C. neither decreasing nor increasing
D. none of these

Q.55 The function f(x) = mx + c where m, c are constants, is strict decreasing function for all x ∈ R if

A. m = 0   **B.** m > 0   **C.** m < 0   **D.** m ≥ 0

Q.56 The function $f(x) = \tan^{-1} x$ is

A. strict increasing
B. strict decreasing
C. neither increasing nor decreasing
D. differentiable nowhere.

Q.57 Rolle's Theorem is not applicable to the function f (x) = | x | for − 2 ≤ x ≤ 2 because

A. f (x) is continuous for − 2 ≤ x ≤ 2
B. f (x) is not derivable for x = 0
C. f (− 2) = f (2)
D. none of these.

Q.58 Let $f(x) = x^3 - 6x^2 + 9x + 8$, then f (x) is decreasing in

A. (− ∞ , 1)
B. [1, 3]
C. [3, ∞)
D. (− ∞ , 1) ∪ (3, ∞).

Q.59 The function $f(x) = x^2$ has a stationary point at

A. x = e   **B.** x = 1/e   **C.** x = 1   **D.** x = √e.

Q.60 Let f(x) = x − cos x, x ∈ R then f is

A. a decreasing function
B. an odd function
C. an increasing function
D. none of these

Analytical Ability & Logical Reasoning

Q.61 How many pairs of letters are there in the word " CASTRAPHONE" which have as many letters between them in the word as in the alphabet?

A. 3   **B.** 4   **C.** 5   **D.** 6

Q.62 A B C D E F G H I J K L M N O P Q R S T U V W X Y Z .
Which letter in this alphabet is the eighth letter to the right of the letter and which is tenth letter to the left of the last but one letter of the alphabet?

A. X   **B.** W   **C.** I   **D.** H

Q.63 How many meaningful English words can be formed with the letters ESRO using each letter only once in each word?

A. None   **B.** One   **C.** Two   **D.** Three

Q.64 Arrange these words in alphabetical order and tick the one that comes last

1. Abandon 2. Actuate 3. Accumulate 4. Acquit 5. Achieve

A. Actuate   **B.** Accumulate
C. Acquit   **D.** Achieve

Q.65 If the first and second letters in the word DEPRESSION' were interchanged, also the third and the fourth letters, the fifth and the sixth letters and so on, which of the following would be the seventh letter from the right ?

A. R   **B.** O   **C.** S   **D.** P

Q.66 A is B's sister. C is B's mother. D is C's father. E is D's mother. Then, how is A related to D?

A. Grandfather   **B.** Grandmother
C. Daughter   **D.** Granddaughter

Q.67 A girl introduced a boy as the son of' the daughter of the father of her uncle. The boy is girl's

A. Brother   **B.** Son
C. Uncle   **D.** Son-in-law

Q.68 Pointing to a person, a man said to a woman, "His mother is the only daughter of your father." How was the woman related to the person ?

A. Aunt   **B.** Mother
C. Wife   **D.** Daughter

Q.69 P is the brother of Q and R. S is R's mother. T is P's father. Which of the following statements cannot be definitely true ?

A. T is Q's father   **B.** S is P's mother
C. P is S's son   **D.** Q is T's son

Q.70 Pointing out to a lady, a girl said, "She is the daughter-in-law of the grandmother of my father's only son." How is the lady related to the girl ?

A. Sister-in-law   **B.** Mother

C. Aunt   **D.** Can't be determined

Q.71 In a certain code language COMPUTER is written as RFUVQNPC. How will MEDICINE be written in that code language?

A. MFEDJJOE   **B.** EOJDEJFM
C. MFEJDJOE   **D.** EOJDJEFM

Q.72 In a certain code language,
'134' means 'good and tasty';
'478' means 'see good pictures' and
'729' means 'pictures are faint'.
Which of the following digits stands for 'see'?

A. 9   **B.** 2   **C.** 1   **D.** 8

Q.73 In a certain code, MONKEY is written as XDJMNL. How is TIGER written in that code ?

A. SHFDQ   **B.** HFDSQ   **C.** RSAFD   **D.** QDFHS

Q.74 If FRIEND is coded as HUMJTK, how is CANDLE written in that code ?

A. EDRIRL   **B.** DCQHQK
C. ESJFME   **D.** DEQJQM

Q.75 If Z = 52 and ACT = 48, then BAT will be equal to

A. 39   **B.** 41   **C.** 44   **D.** 46

Q.76 In a certain code '13' means 'stop smoking' and '59' means 'injurious habit'. What is the meaning of '9' and '5' respectively in that code ?

I. '157' means 'stop bad habit'.

II. '839' means 'smoking is injurious'.

A. If the data in statement I alone are sufficient to answer the question

B. If the data in statement II alone are sufficient answer the question

C. If the data either in I or II alone are sufficient to answer the question;

D. If the data even in both the statements together are not sufficient to answer the question

Q.77 Among five friends who is the tallest ?

I. D is taller than A and C.

II. B is shorter than E but taller than D.

A. If the data in statement I alone are sufficient to answer the question

B. If the data in statement II alone are sufficient answer the question

C. If the data either in I or II alone are sufficient to answer the question;

D. If the data in both the statements together are needed.

Q.78 What is Reena's rank in the class ?

I. There are 26 students in the class.

II. There are 9 students who have scored less than Reena.

A. If the data in statement I alone are sufficient to answer the question

B. If the data in statement II alone are sufficient answer the question

C. If the data either in I or II alone are sufficient to answer the

question;

D. If the data in both the statements together are needed.

Q.79 In which year was Rahul born ?

I. Rahul at present is 25 years younger to his mother.

II. Rahul's brother, who was born in 1964, is 35 years younger to his mother.

A. If the data in statement I alone are sufficient to answer the question

B. If the data in statement II alone are sufficient answer the question

C. If the data either in I or II alone are sufficient to answer the question;

D. If the data in both the statements together are needed.

Q.80 In what proportion would Raj, Karan and Altaf distribute profit among them ?

I. Raj gets two-fifth of the profit.

II. Karim and Altaf have made 75% of the total investment.

A. If the data in statement I alone are sufficient to answer the question

B. If the data in statement II alone are sufficient answer the question

C. If the data either in I or II alone are sufficient to answer the question;

D. If the data even in both the statements together are not sufficient to answer the question

Computer Awareness

Q.81 Graphical pictures that represent an object like file, folder etc are:

A. Task bar
B. Windows
C. Icons
D. Desktop

Q.82 Which of the following is not an advantage of magnetic disk storage?

A. The access time of magnetic disk is much less than that of magnetic tape

B. Disk storage is less expensive than tape storage

C. Disk storage is longer lasting than magnetic tape

D. None of the above

Q.83 The 0 and 1 in the binary numbering system are called Binary Digits or

A. Bytes
B. Kilobytes
C. Decimal bytes
D. Bits

Q.84 Which of the following does not support more than one program at a time?

A. DOS
B. Linux
C. Windows
D. Unix

Q.85 Which of the following is not an operating system?

A. DOS
B. Linux
C. Windows
D. Oracle

Q.86 Linux is a(n) .... operating system

A. Open source
B. Microsoft
C. Windows
D. Mac

Q.87 Which operating system can you give smallest file name?

A. Ps/2
B. Dos
C. Windows
D. Windows NT

Q.88 Which of the following are word processing software?

A. WordPerfect
B. Wordpad
C. MS Word
D. All of above

Q.89 Which file starts MS Word?

A. winword.exe
B. word.exe
C. msword.exe
D. word2003.exe

Q.90 Ctrl + N is used to

A. Save Document
B. Open Document
C. New Document
D. Close Document

Q.91 To exit from the Resume Wizard and return to the document window without creating a resume, click the _____ button in any panel in the Resume Wizard dialog box.

A. Cancel
B. Back
C. Next
D. Finish

Q.92 Which of the following Excel screen components can NOT be turned on or off?

A. Formula Bar
B. Status Bar
C. Tool Bar
D. None of above

Q.93 What happens when you press Ctrl + X after selecting some cells in Excel?

A. The cell content of selected cells disappear from cell and stored in clipboard

B. The cells selected are marked for cutting

C. The selected cells are deleted and the cells are shifted left

D. The selected cells are deleted and cells are shifted up

Q.94 Which of the following option is not available in Paste Special dialog box?

A. Add
B. Subtract
C. Divide
D. SQRT

Q.95 Which command will you choose to convert a column of data into row?

A. Cut and Paste

B. Edit >> Paste Special >> Transpose

C. Both of above

D. None of above

Q.96 Which short cut key inserts a new slide in current presentation?

A. Ctrl+N
B. Ctrl+M
C. Ctrl+S
D. All of above

Q.97 What happens if you select first and second slide and then click on New Slide button on toolbar?

A. A new slide is inserted as first slide in presentation

B. A new slide is inserted as second slide in presentation

C. A new slide is inserted as third slide in presentation

D. None of above

Q.98 Which of the following method can insert a new slide in current presentation?

A. Right click on the Slide panel and choose New Slide

B. From Insert menu choose New Slide

C. Click on New Slide button on toolbar

D. All of above

Q.99 Which of the following is not a part of Slide Design

A. Design Template   **B.** Color Scheme

C. Animation Scheme   **D.** Slide Layout

Q.100 What is the best way to create another copy of a slide?

A. Click the slide then press Ctrl+A and paste in new slide

B. From Insert Menu choose Duplicate Slide

C. Redo everything on a new slide that you had done on previous slide

D. None of above

English

Q.101 Find the correct spelt word.

A. Cacophone   **B.** Cacophoney

C. Cacophoni   **D.** Cacophony

Q.102 Find the correct spelt word.

A. Capricious   **B.** Cappricious

C. Caprisious   **D.** Carisuous

Q.103 Find the correct spelt word.

A. Centrefuge   **B.** Centrifuse

C. Centifuse   **D.** Centrifuge

Q.104 Find the correct spelt word.

A. Chauvinist   **B.** Chaubinist

C. Chauviniste   **D.** Chaubenist

Q.105 Find the correct spelt word.

A. Compendioum   **B.** Compendium

C. Compandium   **D.** Commppendium

Q.106 He said,"I cannot help you at present because I am myself in difficulty."

A. He said that I cannot help you at present because I myself in difficulty.

B. He said that he could not help me at present because he was himself in difficulty.

C. He told that he could not help you at present because he was himself in difficulty.

D. He asked that he could not help you at present because he was himself in difficulty.

Q.107 He told her, "I want to meet your father":

A. He told her that I want to meet your father.

B. He told her that he wanted to meet her father.

C. He told her that he wanted to meet your father.

D. He told her that she wanted to meet her father.

Q.108 He says, "I don't want to play any more."

A. He says that he doesn't want to play any more.

B. He says that I don't want to play any more.

C. He says that I didn't want to play any more.

D. He says that he didn't want to play any more.

Q.109 The government has announced, "Taxes will be raised":

A. The government has announced that taxes would be raised.

B. The government has announced that taxes would raised.

C. The government has announced that taxes will be raised.

D. The government has announced taxes will be raised.

Q.110 Mohan said, "We shall go to see the Taj in the moonlit night":

A. Mohan said that we shall go to see the Taj in the moonlit night.

B. Mohan told that we shall go to see the Taj in moonlit night.

C. Mohan told that we should go to see the Taj in the moonlit night.

D. Mohan said that they should go to see the Taj in moonlit night.

Q.111 This is a good ...... for a picnic.

A. plot   **B.** spot

C. scene   **D.** landscape

Q.112 The .... of private limited companies is in the hands of its directors.

A. managers   **B.** adminstrators

C. management   **D.** deparment

Q.113 Ram the prince of Ayodhya .... his siblings.

A. adorned   **B.** adored

C. vitiated   **D.** endangered

Q.114 The Christmas tree was.......... with stars and other decorative items.

A. adorned   **B.** endowed   **C.** encased   **D.** enticed

Q.115 The .... of the state is efficient.

A. administration   **B.** democracy

C. policy   **D.** autocracy

Q.116 Find out whether there is any grammatical error in below sentence.

According to the Bible / it is meek and humble / who shall inherit the earth.

A. According to the Bible

B. it is meek and humble

C. who shall inherit the earth

D. No error

Q.117 Find out whether there is any grammatical error in below sentence.

Do the roses in your garden smell / more sweetly / than those in ours?

A. Do the roses in your garden smell

B. more sweetly

C. than those in ours

D. No error

Q.118 Find out whether there is any grammatical error in below sentence.

Block of Residential flats / are coming up / near our house.

A. Block of Residential flats

B. are coming up

C. near our house
D. No error

Q.119 Find out whether there is any grammatical error in below sentence.

You can get / all the information that you want / in this book.

A. You can get
B. all the information that you want
C. in this book
D. No error

Q.120 Find out whether there is any grammatical error in below sentence.

The students were / awaiting for / the arrival of the chief guest.

A. The students were
B. awaiting for
C. the arrival of the chief guest
D. No error

// Smart Answer Sheet //

Correct Percentage of students who answered correctly. **Skipped** Percentage of students who skipped.

Q.	Ans.	Correct / Skipped	Q.	Ans.	Correct / Skipped	Q.	Ans.	Correct / Skipped	Q.	Ans.	Correct / Skipped	Q.	Ans.	Correct / Skipped
1	B	78.17 % / 17.42 %	17	B	83.93 % / 10.12 %	33	C	80.76 % / 10.89 %	49	A	86.46 % / 10.05 %	65	D	77.32 % / 15.33 %
2	B	78.22 % / 18.33 %	18	D	81.48 % / 16.39 %	34	C	89.43 % / 10.55 %	50	B	78.25 % / 20.92 %	66	D	79.41 % / 11.19 %
3	D	89.79 % / 10.05 %	19	B	82.25 % / 14.21 %	35	B	86.93 % / 11.72 %	51	D	80.67 % / 16.93 %	67	A	85.71 % / 13.19 %
4	D	83.58 % / 12.55 %	20	A	78.9 % / 14.27 %	36	D	86.47 % / 10.24 %	52	C	85.95 % / 11.55 %	68	A	90.0 % / 10.0 %
5	B	83.97 % / 10.54 %	21	B	79.6 % / 15.37 %	37	C	77.76 % / 15.8 %	53	A	84.03 % / 11.16 %	69	D	89.7 % / 10.14 %
6	C	77.36 % / 19.94 %	22	A	78.33 % / 17.8 %	38	C	83.6 % / 15.32 %	54	C	80.8 % / 15.95 %	70	D	79.42 % / 12.54 %
7	C	78.37 % / 16.21 %	23	C	88.51 % / 11.27 %	39	C	85.55 % / 11.09 %	55	C	82.33 % / 12.98 %	71	D	83.73 % / 13.45 %
8	D	84.24 % / 12.7 %	24	C	81.07 % / 10.4 %	40	B	81.73 % / 10.29 %	56	C	86.52 % / 10.61 %	72	D	88.78 % / 10.35 %
9	D	89.1 % / 10.61 %	25	B	80.7 % / 13.22 %	41	C	82.69 % / 10.46 %	57	B	87.63 % / 10.26 %	73	D	87.26 % / 10.61 %
10	B	85.59 % / 10.82 %	26	D	76.96 % / 17.58 %	42	C	86.63 % / 11.12 %	58	B	88.95 % / 10.99 %	74	A	89.75 % / 10.23 %
11	C	81.9 % / 10.8 %	27	B	85.31 % / 12.03 %	43	C	77.31 % / 19.76 %	59	B	78.15 % / 15.2 %	75	D	77.64 % / 11.58 %
12	A	89.05 % / 10.74 %	28	C	81.14 % / 15.42 %	44	A	84.97 % / 13.3 %	60	C	78.29 % / 15.3 %	76	C	80.35 % / 16.61 %
13	C	83.12 % / 13.61 %	29	C	88.85 % / 11.02 %	45	C	85.84 % / 11.74 %	61	D	79.71 % / 19.67 %	77	D	82.42 % / 11.61 %
14	C	87.1 % / 10.67 %	30	C	86.71 % / 11.3 %	46	C	85.18 % / 14.26 %	62	B	80.07 % / 15.8 %	78	D	83.65 % / 11.56 %
15	B	78.0 % / 11.0 %	31	D	81.44 % / 14.78 %	47	D	86.83 % / 12.51 %	63	D	85.89 % / 11.24 %	79	D	81.6 % / 14.22 %
16	B	84.11 % / 10.62 %	32	B	84.27 % / 14.92 %	48	B	77.38 % / 21.62 %	64	A	85.58 % / 11.48 %	80	D	81.08 % / 15.42 %

Q.	Ans.	Correct		Q.	Ans.	Correct		Q.	Ans.	Correct		Q.	Ans.	Correct		Q.	Ans.	Correct
		Skipped				Skipped				Skipped				Skipped				Skipped
81	C	88.16 %		89	A	80.43 %		97	C	85.11 %		105	B	81.78 %		113	B	81.18 %
		10.63 %				18.29 %				11.19 %				14.61 %				15.73 %
82	D	81.54 %		90	C	78.42 %		98	D	76.78 %		106	B	81.41 %		114	A	80.68 %
		15.18 %				16.76 %				17.29 %				13.62 %				11.49 %
83	D	77.23 %		91	D	77.65 %		99	D	84.92 %		107	B	88.18 %		115	A	77.46 %
		21.33 %				21.61 %				11.39 %				11.14 %				16.41 %
84	A	89.85 %		92	D	85.74 %		100	B	86.02 %		108	A	79.69 %		116	B	79.41 %
		10.0 %				13.97 %				12.74 %				11.73 %				13.25 %
85	D	81.92 %		93	B	86.06 %		101	D	84.66 %		109	C	76.07 %		117	B	88.27 %
		14.53 %				12.79 %				10.3 %				21.06 %				11.6 %
86	A	81.31 %		94	D	81.21 %		102	A	81.28 %		110	D	85.22 %		118	A	77.21 %
		17.5 %				11.02 %				12.6 %				12.7 %				13.19 %
87	B	86.36 %		95	B	84.61 %		103	D	83.4 %		111	B	89.77 %		119	B	86.46 %
		11.05 %				14.94 %				13.43 %				10.13 %				13.35 %
88	D	78.32 %		96	B	88.6 %		104	A	79.85 %		112	C	83.49 %		120	B	84.93 %
		14.41 %				10.39 %				19.74 %				14.04 %				12.56 %

//Hints and Solutions//

1. For, finding the degree of the given differential equation, square the two sides to obtain

$$\left\{1 + \left(\frac{dy}{dx}\right)^2\right\}^3 = \left(\frac{d^2y}{dx^2}\right)^2 \text{ so}$$

that the degree of the differential equation is 2.

2. Cubing both sides of the given differential equation, we obtain

$$\left\{1 + \left(\frac{dy}{dx}\right)^2\right\}^5 = \left(\frac{d^2y}{dx^2}\right)^3 \Rightarrow$$

the degree of the given differential equation is 3.

3. Given differential equation is dy/dx = 2 x + 5 ; integrating we get, y = x^2 + 5x + C, C being any constant.

4.

$\frac{d^2y}{dx^2} = e^{-2x}$, integrating we get.

$\frac{dy}{dx} = \frac{e^{-2x}}{-2} + c$, again intergrating

$y = \frac{e^{-2x}}{(-2)(-2)} + cx + d$

or y = $\frac{1}{4}e^{-2x}$ + cx + d where c and d are arbitrary constants.

5.

Given differential equation is

x (1 + y^2) dx + y (1 + x^2) dy = 0

$\Rightarrow \frac{x}{1+x^2} dx + \frac{y}{1+y^2} dy = 0$

Integrating, we get

$\frac{1}{2}$ log (1 + x^2) + $\frac{1}{2}$ log (1 = y^2) = k

log (1 + x^2) (1 + y^2) = 2 k

(1 + x^2) (1 + y^2) e^{2k} = C

6.

$\frac{dy}{dx}$ = y e^x $\Rightarrow$ $\frac{1}{y} \frac{dy}{dx}$ = e^x $\Rightarrow$ log y = e^x + c,

for x = 0, y = e

log e = e^0 + c $\Rightarrow$ c = 0.

Hence log y = e^x + 0 $\Rightarrow$ log y = e^x.

For x = 1, log y = e^1 $\Rightarrow$ y = e^e.

7. A^2 = AA is meaningful only if number of columns in a is equal to the number of rows in it i.e. if m = n.

8. In general AB ≠ BA, AB ≠ O, AB may or may not be defined.

9. A square matrix A is idempotent; iff A^2 = A.

10. A = $[a_{ij}]_{n \times n}$ is lower triangular iff all entries above the diagonal vanish i.e. iff a_{ij} = 0 for i < j.

11. A square matrix A = $[a_{ij}]_{n \times n}$ is called upper triangular iff all entries below the diagonal vanish i.e. iff a_{ij} = 0 for i > j.

12. $(A + B)^2$ = A^2 + 2 AB + B^2

(A + B) (A + B) = A^2 + 2 AB + B^2

A^2 + AB + BA + B^2 = A^2 + 2 AB + B^2

BA = AB.

13.

Since the triangle is equilateral, orthocentre coincides with the centroid.

P.V. of orthocentre = P.V. of centroid = $\vec{0}$

$\Rightarrow \frac{\vec{a} + \vec{b} + \vec{c}}{3} = \vec{0} = \vec{a} + \vec{b} + \vec{c} = \vec{0}$

14.

Taking I, the incentre of the triangle as origin, we have

P.V. of I = $\dfrac{|BC|\,\vec{IA} + |CA|\,\vec{IB} + |AB|\,\vec{IC}}{|BC| + |CA| + |AB|}$

(Using incentre formula)

$\Rightarrow \vec{0} = \dfrac{|BC|\,\vec{IA} + |CA|\,\vec{IB} + |AB|\,\vec{IC}}{|BC| + |CA| + |AB|}$

$|BC|\,\vec{IA} + |CA|\,\vec{IB} + |AB|\,\vec{IC} = \vec{0}$

15.

Given $\left(\hat{a} - 4\hat{b}\right) \cdot \left(7\hat{a} - 2\hat{b}\right) \perp \left(7\hat{a} - 2\hat{b}\right)$

$\Rightarrow \left(\hat{a} - 4\hat{b}\right) \cdot \left(7\hat{a} - 2\hat{b}\right) = 0$

$7\hat{a} \cdot \hat{a} - 2\hat{a} \cdot \hat{b} - 28\hat{b} \cdot \hat{a} + 8\hat{b} \cdot \hat{b} = 0$

$\hat{a} \cdot \hat{b} = \frac{15}{30} = \frac{1}{2}$

cos θ = $\frac{1}{2}$, θ being the angle between $\hat{a}$ and $\hat{b}$

θ = $\frac{\pi}{3}$

16.

$|\vec{a} + \vec{b} + \vec{c}|^2 = (\vec{a} + \vec{b} + \vec{c}) \cdot (\vec{a} + \vec{b} + \vec{c}) \cdot (\vec{a} + \vec{b} + \vec{c})$

$= \vec{a} \cdot \vec{a} + \vec{b} \cdot \vec{b} + \vec{c} \cdot \vec{c} + 2 (\vec{a} \cdot \vec{b} + \vec{b} \cdot \vec{c} + \vec{c} \cdot \vec{a})$

$= |\vec{a}|^2 + |\vec{b}|^2 + |\vec{c}|^2 + 0$

$(\vec{a} \cdot \vec{b} = \vec{b} \cdot \vec{c} = \vec{c} \cdot \vec{a} = 0$ as $\vec{a}, \vec{b}, \vec{c}$ are mutually orthogonal)

$= 1^2 + 1^2 + 1^2 = 3$

$= |\vec{a} + \vec{b} + \vec{c}| = \sqrt{3}$

17.

Let $|\vec{a}| = |\vec{b}| = |\vec{c}| = k$ (say),

then $|\vec{a} + \vec{b} + \vec{c}|$

$= \sqrt{(\vec{a} + \vec{b} + \vec{c}) \bullet (\vec{a} + \vec{b} + \vec{c})}$

$= \sqrt{k^2 + k^2 + k^2} = \sqrt{3}\,K$

(Note that $\vec{a} \bullet \vec{b} = \vec{b} \bullet \vec{c} = \vec{c} \bullet \vec{a} = 0$)

If θ is the angle between $\vec{a}$ and $\vec{a} + \vec{b} + \vec{c}$, then

$\cos\theta = \dfrac{\vec{a} \bullet (\vec{a} + \vec{b} + \vec{c})}{|\vec{a}|\,|\vec{a} + \vec{b} + \vec{c}|}$

$= \dfrac{\vec{a} \bullet \vec{a} + \vec{a} \bullet \vec{b} + \vec{a} \bullet \vec{c}}{k\,(\sqrt{3}\,k)}$

$= \dfrac{|\vec{a}|^2}{k\,(\sqrt{3}\,k)} \quad (\vec{a} \bullet \vec{b} = \vec{a} \bullet \vec{c} = 0)$

$= \dfrac{k^2}{\sqrt{3}\,k^2} = \dfrac{1}{\sqrt{3}} \Rightarrow \theta = \cos^{-1}\left(\dfrac{1}{\sqrt{3}}\right)$

18.

Since $\vec{a}, \vec{b}, \vec{c}$ are linear dependent, therefore, they are coplanar. Hence $[\vec{a}\,\vec{b}\,\vec{c}] = 0$

$\Rightarrow \begin{vmatrix} 1 & 1 & 1 \\ 4 & 3 & 4 \\ 1 & \alpha & \beta \end{vmatrix} = 0$

$3\beta - 4\alpha - (4\beta - 4) + 4\alpha - 3 = 0$

$\ldots - \beta = -1 \Rightarrow \beta = 1$

Also. $|\vec{c}| = \sqrt{3}. \Rightarrow |\vec{c}|^2 = 3$

$1^2 + \alpha^2 + \beta^2 = 3$

$1 + \alpha^2 + 1 = 3 \Rightarrow \alpha^2 = 1 \Rightarrow \alpha = \pm 1$

19.

$\sin\left(2\cos^{-1}\left(-\dfrac{3}{5}\right)\right)$

$= 2\sin\left(\cos^{-1}\left(-\dfrac{3}{5}\right)\right)\cos\left(\cos^{-1}\left(-\dfrac{3}{5}\right)\right)$

$= 2\sqrt{1 - \left(-\dfrac{3}{5}\right)^2}\left(-\dfrac{3}{5}\right) = -\dfrac{24}{25}$

20.

$\tan(\sin^{-1}x) = \dfrac{\sin(\sin^{-1}x)}{\cos(\sin^{-1}x)} = \dfrac{x}{\sqrt{1 - x^2}}$

21.

$\cos(\cos^{-1}x) = \dfrac{\cos(\cos^{-1}x)}{\sin(\cos^{-1}x)}$

$= \dfrac{x}{\sqrt{1 - x^2}}$

22.

Let $\tan^{-1}x = \theta \Rightarrow x = \tan\theta, -\dfrac{\pi}{2} < \theta < \dfrac{\pi}{2}$

$\therefore \cos(\tan^{-1}x) = \cos\theta = \dfrac{1}{\sec\theta}$

$= \dfrac{1}{\sqrt{1 + \tan^2\theta}} = \dfrac{1}{\sqrt{1 + x^2}}$

23.

$2\tan^{-1}(\cos x) = \tan^{-1}(2\cosec x)$

$\Rightarrow \tan^{-1}\left(\dfrac{2\cos x}{1 - \cos^2 x}\right) = \tan^{-1}(2\cosec x)$

$\left(\because 2\tan^{-1}x = \tan^{-1}\dfrac{2x}{1 - x^2} \text{ for } |x| < 1\right)$

$\Rightarrow \dfrac{2\cos x}{\sin^2 x} = \dfrac{2}{\sin x} \Rightarrow \cot x = 1$

$\Rightarrow x = \dfrac{\pi}{4}$

24.

$\cos^{-1}\left(\cos\dfrac{5\pi}{4}\right) = \cos^{-1}\left(\cos\left(\pi + \dfrac{\pi}{4}\right)\right)$

$= \cos^{-1}\left(-\cos\dfrac{\pi}{4}\right)$

$= \cos^{-1}\left(\cos\left(\pi - \dfrac{\pi}{4}\right)\right) = \dfrac{3\pi}{4}$

$(\because 0 \le \cos^{-1}x \le \pi)$

25.

E and $\bar{E}$ are M, and exhaustive, therefore, P (E) + P = 1.

26. required probability = 1 − p (student does not both test) = 1 − P (the teacher does not give test on both days)

$1 - \left(1 - \dfrac{1}{5}\right)\left(1 - \dfrac{1}{5}\right) = 1 - \dfrac{16}{25} = \dfrac{9}{25}.$

27. Required probability = 1− (neither A nor B fails)

= 1− P (both A and B are successful)

= 1 − (1− 0.2) (1− 0.3) = 1 − 0.8 0.7 = 0.44.

28. P (a total of 7 or 9) = P (a total of 7) + P (a total or 9)

= 6/36 + 4/36 (a total of 7 and a of 9 cannot occur simultaneously)

29.

$P(A \cup \bar{B}) = 0.8$

$P(A) = P(\bar{B} - P(A \cap \bar{B}) = 0.8$

$P(A) + 1 - x - P(A)(1 - x) = 0.8$, where $x = P(B)$.

30.

If P (A) = x and P (B) = y, then

$P(A \cap B) = \dfrac{1}{12} \Rightarrow P(A)\,P(B) = \dfrac{1}{2}$ or $xy = \dfrac{1}{12}$ and

P (neither A nor B occurs)

$= P(A')\,P(B') = \dfrac{1}{2} \Rightarrow P(A')\,P(B') = \dfrac{1}{2}$ or $(1 - x)(1 - y) = \dfrac{1}{2}$

31.

If $f = ax + by$ is the objective function and $f' = ax_1 + by_1 = ax_2 + by_2$ is the optimum value of f, attained at two points $X_1 = (x_1, y_1)$ and $X_2 (x_2, y_2)$ then the value of f at the point $\lambda X_1 + (1 - \lambda)X_2$

$= (\lambda x_1 + (1 - \lambda)x_2, \lambda y_1 + (1 - \lambda)y_2)$

$= a\{\lambda x_1 + (1 - \lambda)x_2\} + b\{\lambda y_1 + (1 - \lambda)y_2\}$

$= \lambda(ax_1 + by_1) + (1 - \lambda)(ax_2 + by_2)$

$= (ax_1 + by_1)(\lambda + 1 - \lambda)$

$(ax_2 + by_2 = ax_1 + by_1)$

$= ax_1 + by_1 = f'$, the optimum value of f.

32. Note that the origin i.e. (0, 0) does not satisfy the inequality $2x + 3y > 6$ ($2.0 + 3.0 < 6$)

So, the graph of $2x + 3y > 6$ is the half plane not containing the origin. Also, the points on the line $2x + 3y > 6$, therefore, graph does not contain the points of the line $2x + 3y = 6$.

33. We know that if $X_1 = (x_1, y_1)$ and $X_2 = (x_2, y_2)$ are two optimal solutions of a L.P.P., then for all $\lambda \in [0, 1]$, $\lambda X_1 + (1 - \lambda) X_2$ is also an optimal solution. So, alternative (c) is correct.

34. The optimal value of the objective function is attained at the corner points of the feasible region.

35. For $x \geq 6$, $y \geq 2$; $2x + y \geq 2 \times 6 + 2$ and hence the constraint $2x + y \geq 10$ is also automatically

satisfied by every point of the graph of the inequalities $x \geq 6$, $y \geq 2$. Also, graph of $x \geq 6$, $y \geq 2$ is a subset

of the graph of the inequalities $x \geq 0$, $y \geq 0$.

36.

$$\text{Now, } x + \frac{1}{x} = \left(\sqrt{x} - \frac{1}{\sqrt{x}}\right)^2 + 2 \geq 2 \text{ for all } x > 0$$

Note that $x + \frac{1}{x} = 2$ for $x = 1$.

37.

If the roots of the given equation are $\alpha\beta$, then $\alpha + \beta = \lambda + 2$ and $\alpha\beta = 1 - \lambda$
Hence, $\alpha^2 + \beta = (\alpha + \beta)^2 - 2\alpha\beta$
$= (\lambda + 2)^2 - 2(1 - \lambda)$
$= \lambda^2 + 4\lambda + 4 - 2 + 2\lambda$
$= \lambda^2 + 6\lambda + 9 - 7$
$= (\lambda + 3)^2 - 7$
Clearly, $\alpha^2 + \beta^2$ is least when $\lambda + 3 = 0$ i.e. when $\lambda = -3$

38.

Given equation can be written as $2x - 3 + x - 1 = 6x^2 - x - 6$, $x \neq 1$
or $6x^2 - 4x - 2 = 0$
or $3x^2 - 2x - 1 = 0$, $x \neq 1$
$\Rightarrow x = \frac{2 \pm \sqrt{4 + 12}}{6} = \frac{2 \pm 4}{6} = 1, -\frac{1}{3}$, but $x \neq 1$, therefore, the only solution is $x = -\frac{1}{3}$.

39. The equation $ax^2 + bx + c = 0$ is a quadratic equation only if a $\neq 0$, for if a = 0 then the equation becomes $bx + c = 0$, which is not of second degree

40. When one roots is 0 and the other is non zero, then sum of the roots is no-zero and product is zero

$$\Rightarrow -\frac{b}{a} \neq 0 \text{ and } \frac{c}{a} = 0$$
$$\Rightarrow b \neq 0 \text{ and } c = 0$$

41.

$$ax^2 + bx + c = \left\{x^2 + \frac{b}{a}x + \frac{c}{a}\right\}$$
$$= a\left\{\left(x + \frac{b}{2a}\right)^2 + \frac{c}{a} - \frac{b^2}{4a^2}\right\}, a > 0$$
$$= a\left\{\left(x + \frac{b}{2a}\right)^2 + \frac{4ac - b^2}{4a^2}\right\} > 0$$

For all real x only if $\frac{4ac - b^2}{4a^2} > 0$

i.e. if $b^2 - 4ac < 0$

42. For equal roots disc = 0

$\Rightarrow (\sqrt{2}\,p)^2 - 4.2.p = 0 \Rightarrow 2p(p - 4) = 0$

43. since $g(x)$ and $h(x)$ are integrals of the same function, therefore, $g(x) - h(x)$ is constant.

44. Put $x\,e^x = t$.

45. As $\int f'(x)\,dx = f(x) + C$, therefore, one value of $\int f'(x)\,dx$ is $f(x)$.

46.

$$\int \frac{x}{\cos^2 x}\,dx = \int x \sec^2 x\,dx$$
$$= x \tan x - \int \tan x\,dx.$$

(Integrating by parts taking x as the first function)

47.

$\int \frac{1}{\sqrt{1 - x^2}}\,dx = \sin^{-1} x = \frac{\pi}{2} - \cos^{-1} x$ and also, $\int \frac{1}{\sqrt{1 - x^2}}\,dx = -\int \frac{1}{\sqrt{1 - x^2}}\,dx = -\cos^{-1} x$.

48. In this case $T_2 - T_1 = 1$, $T_3 - T_2 = 2$, $T_4 - T_3 = 3$ and $T_5 - T_4 = 4$. Hence by symmetry $T_6 - T_5 = 5$

$\Rightarrow T_6 = T_5 + 5 = 11 + 5 = 16$

49. The given sequence is 1×2, 2×3, 3×4, 4×5,.....Hence, the next term = $5 \times 6 = 30$

50. $\sqrt{3}$, $2\sqrt{3}$, $3\sqrt{3}$,.......

51.

The given series is $\left(1 + \frac{1}{2}\right) + \left(1 + \frac{1}{4}\right) + \left(1 + \frac{1}{8}\right) + \left(1 + \frac{1}{16}\right) + \ldots$
So, next term $= 1 + \frac{1}{32} = \frac{33}{32}$

52. Given $a_n = a_{n-1} - 1$, therefore,

$a_3 = a_2 - 1 = 2 - 1 = 1$;

$a_3 = a_3 - 1 = 1 - 1 = 0$ and

$a_5 = a_4 - 1 = 0 - 1 = -1$

53.

Given $4 = \frac{a+b}{2}$ and $2 = \sqrt{ab}$
$$\Rightarrow \frac{2ab}{a+b} = \frac{2 \times 4}{8} = 1$$
$\Rightarrow$ H.M. between a and b is
$\Rightarrow$ a, 1, b are in H.P.

54. $f(x) = x^2 \Rightarrow f'(x) = 2x \,\forall\, x \in R$. Since

$f'(x) = 2x > 0$ for $x > 0$ and

$f'(x) = 2x < 0$ for $x < 0$, therefore on R, f is neither increasing nor decreasing. In fact, f is strict increasing

on $[0, \infty)$ and strict decreasing on $(-\infty, 0]$

55. $f(x) = mx + c$ is strict decreasing in R if $f'(x) < 0$ i.e. if M < 0

56.

$$f'(x) = \frac{d}{dx}\left(\tan^{-1} x\right) = \frac{1}{1 + x^2} > 0 \,\forall\, x \in R$$

$\therefore$ f is strict increasing on R

57. Here, $f'(x) = x/|x|$, which does not exist at $x = 0 \in (-2, 2)$. So Rolle's theorem is not applicable

58. Here f' (x) = 3x^2 – 12x + 9

= 3 (x – 1) (x – 3) < 0 iff x ∈ (1, 3)

59. f(x) = x^x ⇒ f' (x) = (1 = log x) x^x ∀ x > 0

f' (x) = 0 ⇒ 1 = log x = 0 (x^x > 0 ∀ x > 0)

⇒ log x = – 1 ⇒ x = e^{-1}. Also, f' (x) changes sign from – ve to + ve as we move from left to right through x = 1/e. Hence f(x) has a local minima at x = 1/e.

60. f' (x) = 1 + sin x ≥ 0 for all x ∈ R

(– 1 ≤ sin x ≤ 1, ∴ 0 ≤ 1 + sin x ≤ 2)

61. Looking into the alphabets there are six such pairs namely ON, HONE, ST, TRAPHO, TRAPHON, RAP.

1. ON - NO

2. HONE - EFGH

3. ST - ST

4. TRAPHO - OPQRST

5. TRAPHON - NOPQRST

6. RAP - PQR

62. In the given alphabet, last but one letter of alphabet is Y.

10th letter to the left of Y is O

8th letter to the right of O is W

63. Meaningful words are ROSE, SORE and EROS.

Note the meaning of the words SORE and EROS with the help of dictionary.

64. First letters are common. Second letters are:b, c, c, c, c. One of the four words having c is the last word. Let us see the third letters now ,there are: t, c, q, h. Clearly t is the last. Hence Actuate is the last word.

65. The new letter sequence is EDRPSEISNO

The seventh letter from the right is P

66. A is the sister of B and B is the daughter of C.

So, A is the daughter of C. Also, D is the father of C.

So, A is the granddaughter of D.

67. Daughter of uncle's father — Uncle's sister — Mother;

Mother's son — Brother

68. Daughter of your father — Your sister. So, the person's mother is woman's sister or the woman is person's aunt.

69. P, Q, R are children of same parents. So. S who is R's mother and T, who is R's father will be mother and father of all three.

However, it is not mentioned whether Q is male or female So, D cannot be definitely true.

70. Girls's father's only son— Girl's brother. Daughter in law of girl's grandmother can be their mother, or maternal uncle's wife, i.e. aunt. So relation cannot be determined.

71. - There are 8 letters in the word.

- The coded word can be obtained by taking the immediately following letters of word, expect the first and the last letters of the given word but in the reverse order. That means, in the coded form the first and the last letters have been interchanged while the remaining letters are coded by taking their immediate next letters in the reverse order.

72. Justification:

In the first and second statements, the common code digit is '4' and the common word is 'good'.

So, '4' stands for 'good'.

In the second and third statements, the common code digit is '7' and the common word is 'pictures'.

So, '7' means 'pictures'.

Thus, in the second statements, '8' means 'see'.

73. The letter of the word are written in a reverse order and then each letter is moved one step backward to obtain the code.

74. The first, second, third, fourth, fifth and sixth letters of th word are respectively moved two, three, four, five, six and seven steps forward to obtain the corresponding letters of the code.

75. In the given code, A = 2, B = 4, C = 6,.... , Z = 52.

So, ACT = 2 + 6 + 40 = 48 and

BAT = 4 + 2 + 40 = 46

76. '59' means Injurious habit' and '157' means 'stop bad habit' (from I). Thus, the common code number '5' stands for common word 'habit'. So. '9' represents 'injurious'.Hence, I is sufficient.

Also, '59' means Injurious habit' and '839' means 'smoking is injurious'. Thus, the common code number '9' stands for common word 'injurious'. So, '5' represents 'habit'. Thus, II is also sufficient.

77. From I, we have : D > A , D> C,

From II, we have : E >B > D.

Combining the above two, we get : E > B> D> (A and C).

So, E is the tallest.

Clearly, both the statements are needed to answer the question

78. From I and II, we conclude that there are 16 students above Reyna in rank. Thus, Reenats rank is 17th in the class So, both the statements are necessary.

79. From both the given statements, we find that Rahul is (35 - 25) = 10 years older than his brother,

who was born in 1964, So. Rahul was horn in 1954

Thus, both the given statements are needed to answer the query.

80. Even both the statements together are not sufficient to answer the question.

81. Graphical pictures that represent an object like file, folder etc are Icons.

82. None of the above

83. In mathematics and digital electronics, a binary number is a number expressed in the base-2 numeral system or binary numeral system, which uses only two symbols: typically 0 (zero) and 1 (one). The base-2 numeral system is a positional notation with a radix of 2. Each digit is referred to as a bit.

84. DOS is a family of disk operating systems. DOS primarily consists of MS-DOS and a rebranded. Only one program at a time can use them and DOS itself has no functionality to allow more than one program to execute at a time.

85. Oracle database (Oracle DB) is a relational database management system (RDBMS) from the Oracle Corporation.

86. Linux is a family of free and open-source software operating systems built around the Linux kernel. Typically, Linux is packaged in a form known as a Linux distribution for both desktop and server use.

87. DOS (Disk Operating System) is an operating system that runs from a hard disk drive. The term can also refer to a particular family of disk operating systems, most commonly MS-DOS (Microsoft Disk Operating System).

88. All of above

89. Microsoft Word is a word processor developed by Microsoft. It was first released on October 25, 1983 under the name Multi-Tool Word for Xenix systems.

90. New Document

91. Finish

92. None of above

93. The cells selected are marked for cutting

94. SQRT

95. Edit >> Paste Special >> Transpose

96. Ctrl+M

97. A new slide is inserted as third slide in presentation

98. All of above

99. Slide Layout

100. From Insert Menu choose Duplicate Slid

101. Cacophony

102. Capricious

103. Centrifuge

104. Chauvinist

105. Compendium

106. He said that he could not help me at present because he was himself in difficulty.

107. He told her that he wanted to meet her father.

108. He says that he doesn't want to play any more.

109. The government has announced that taxes will be raised.

110. Mohan said that they should go to see the Taj in moonlit night.

111. spot

112. management

113. adored

114. adorned

115. administration

116. it is the meek and the humble

117. sweeter

118. Blocks of Residential flats

119. all the information you want

120. awaiting

Mathematics

Q.1 If R is a relation from a non-empty set A to a non-empty set B, then

A. $R = A \cap B$
B. $R = A \cup B$
C. $R = A \times B$
D. $R \subset A \times B$

Q.2 Let R be the relation on N defined as $x\,R\,y$ iff $x + 2y = 8$. The domain of R is

A. {2, 4, 8}
B. {2, 4, 6, 8}
C. {2, 4, 6}
D. {1, 2, 3, 4}

Q.3 Which of the following is not an equivalence relation on I, then set of integers; $x, y \in I$:

A. $x\,R\,y \Leftrightarrow x + y$ is an even integer
B. $x\,R\,y \Leftrightarrow x < y$
C. $x\,R\,y \Leftrightarrow x - y$ is an even integer
D. $x\,R\,y \Leftrightarrow x = y$

Q.4 Let A = {1, 2, 3} and R = {(1, 1), (2, 2), (1, 2), (2, 1), (2, 3)} be a relation on A, then R is

A. reflexive
B. symmetric
C. antisymmetric
D. none of these

Q.5 Let A = {1, 2, 3}. Which of the following is not an equivalence relation on A?

A. {(1, 1), (2, 2), (3, 3)}
B. {(1, 1), (2, 2), (3, 3), (1, 2), (2, 1)}
C. {(1, 1), (2, 2), (3, 3), (2, 3), (3, 2)}
D. none of these

Q.6 If A and B are non-empty sets and A x B = B x A, then

A. A is a proper subset of B
B. B is a proper subset of A
C. A = B
D. None of these

Q.7 The number of all possible matrices of order 3 × 3 with each entry 0 or 1 is

A. 18
B. 512
C. 81
D. none of these

Q.8 $k\,I_2$ is the matrix

A. $\begin{bmatrix} k & k \\ 0 & 0 \end{bmatrix}$
B. $\begin{bmatrix} k & k \\ k & k \end{bmatrix}$
C. $\begin{bmatrix} 0 & k \\ k & 0 \end{bmatrix}$
D. $\begin{bmatrix} k & 0 \\ 0 & k \end{bmatrix}$

Q.9 If A is a matrix of order 3 × 4, then each row of A has

A. 3 elements
B. 4 elements
C. 12 elements
D. 7 elements

Q.10 If P is of order 2×3 and Q is of order 3×2, then PQ is of order

A. 2×3
B. 3×2
C. 3×3
D. 2×2

Q.11 If A and B are invertible matrices of the same order, then $(AB)^{-1}$ is equal to

A. $A^{-1}B^{-1}$
B. $A^{-1}B$
C. AB^{-1}
D. $B^{-1}A^{-1}$

Q.12 If A ={{m7.PNG}}, then

A. $A^3 = O$
B. $A^2 = O$
C. $A^2 = I$
D. none of these

Q.13 The ratio in which the join of (1, −2, 3) and (4, 2, −1) is divided by the XOY plane is

A. 1 : 3
B. 3 : 1
C. −1 : 3
D. None of these

Q.14 The direction cosines of the ray from p (1, −2, 4) to Q (−1, 1, −2) are

A. $< -2, 3, -6 >$
B. $< 2, -3, 6 >$
C. $< \dfrac{2}{7}, -\dfrac{3}{7}, \dfrac{6}{7} >$
D. $< -\dfrac{2}{7}, \dfrac{3}{7}, -\dfrac{6}{7} >$

Q.15 The equation $|\,\vec{r}\,|^2 - (\vec{r} \cdot \vec{a}) + \lambda = 0$ represents a sphere if

A. $a^2 > \lambda$
B. $a^2 < \lambda$
C. $a^2 = \lambda$
D. None of these.

Q.16

The line $\dfrac{x}{1} = \dfrac{y}{2} = \dfrac{z}{3}$ and the plane $2x - 4y + 2z = 3$ meet in

A. Only one point
B. No point
C. Infinitely many points
D. None of these

Q.17 The radius of the sphere whose centre is the pointy $C\,(3\,\hat{i} + 6\,\hat{j} - 2\,\hat{k})$ and which touches the plane $\vec{r} \cdot (2\,\hat{i} - 2\,\hat{j} - \hat{k}) = 10$ is

A. 7
B. $\dfrac{14}{3}$
C. 14
D. None of these

Q.18

Equation of any plane containing the line $\dfrac{x - x_1}{a} = \dfrac{y - y_1}{b} = \dfrac{z - z_1}{c}$ is $A\,(x - x_1) + B\,(y - y_1) + C\,(z - z_1) = 0$, where

A. $\dfrac{A}{a} = \dfrac{B}{b} = \dfrac{C}{c}$
B. $Ax_1 + By_1 + Ca_1 = 0$
C. $Aa + Bb + Cc = 0$
D. $ax_1 + by_1 + cz_1 = 0$

Q.19 Let f(x) be differentiable in (0, 4) and f(2) = f(3) and S = { c : 2 < c < 3, f′(x) = 0} then

A. S = { }

B. S has exactly one point
C. S has atleast one point
D. none of these

Q.20 Every continuous function is
A. increasing   **B.** decreasing
C. not differentiable   **D.** differentiable

Q.21 If the graph of a differentiable function y = f (x) meets the lines y = − 1, then the graph
A. meets the line y = 0 at least once
B. meets the line y = 0 at least twice
C. meets the line y = 0 at least thrice
D. does not meet the line y = 0

Q.22 In case of strict decreasing functions, slope of tangent and hence derivative is
A. positive
B. negative
C. zero
D. either negative or zero

Q.23 The function f(x) = 2− 3 x is
A. decreasing
B. increasing
C. neither decreasing nor increasing
D. none of these

Q.24 The function f(x) = x²− 2x is increasing in the interval
A. x ≠ − 1   **B.** x ≥ − 1   **C.** x ≠ 1   **D.** x ≥ 1

Q.25 $\int 2^{2x}\, 2^x\, dx =$

A. $\dfrac{2^{2^x}}{(\log\ 2)^2} + C$ **B.** $\dfrac{2^{2^x}}{\log\ 2} + C$

C. $\dfrac{2^{2^x}}{\log_2 e} + C$ **D.** none of these

Q.26

$$\int_0^2 x\,[x]\,dx =$$

A. $\dfrac{1}{2}$ **B.** $\dfrac{3}{2}$

C. $\dfrac{5}{2}$ **D.** none of these

Q.27

$$\int_0^{2\pi} (\cos\ x)^{2001}\, dx =$$

A. 2001   **B.** 2000
C. 1001   **D.** none of these

Q.28 The differential equation of all non-vertical line in a plane is

A. $\dfrac{d^2 y}{dx^2} = 0$ **B.** $\dfrac{d^2 x}{dy^2} = 0$

C. $\dfrac{dy}{dx} = 0$ **D.** $\dfrac{dx}{dy} = 0$

Q.29 The order of the differential equation whose general solution is

y = A cos x + B sin x + Ce⁻ˣ ; A , B, C being arbitrary constants, is

A. 1   **B.** 2
C. 3   **D.** none of these

Q.30 The slope at any point of a curve y = f (x) is given by

$\dfrac{dy}{dx}$ = 3x² and it passes

through (− 1, 1). The equation of the curve is
A. y = x³ + 2   **B.** y = − x³ − 2
C. y = 3x³ + 4   **D.** y = − x³ + 2

Q.31 If $\vec{a}$ is a proper vector, then number of unit vectors collinear with $\vec{a}$ is
A. 1   **B.** 2
C. 3   **D.** infinitely many

Q.32 If $\vec{a}$ and $\vec{b}$ are non-collinear proper vectors, then number of unit vectors at right angles to both $\vec{a}$ and $\vec{b}$ is
A. 1   **B.** 2
C. 4   **D.** infinitely many

Q.33

The vectors $2\hat{i} + 3\hat{j} - 6\hat{k}$ and $a\hat{i} + b\hat{j} + c\hat{k}$ are perpendicular when
A. a = 1, b = 2, c = 3   **B.** a = 3, b = 2, c = 1
C. a = 6, b = 2, c = 3   **D.** none of these

Q.34 If θ is the angle between vectors $\vec{a}$ and $\vec{b}$ such that $\vec{a} . \vec{b}$ ≥ 0, then

A. $0 \le \theta \le \pi$ **B.** $\dfrac{\pi}{2} \le \theta \le \pi$

C. $0 \le \theta \le \dfrac{\pi}{2}$ **D.** $0 < \theta < \dfrac{\pi}{2}$

Q.35

The magnitude of the resultant of vectors $\vec{a} = 2\hat{i} - \hat{j} + \hat{k}$ and $\vec{b} = \hat{i} + 2\hat{j} + 3\hat{k}$ is

A. $\sqrt{6}$ **B.** $\sqrt{34}$

C. $\sqrt{14}$ **D.** none of these

Q.36

The unit vector in the direction of sum of the vectors $\hat{i} + \hat{j} + \hat{k}, 2\hat{i} - \hat{j} - \hat{k}$ and $2\hat{j} + 6\hat{k}$ is

A. $\dfrac{1}{7}\left(3\hat{i} + 2\hat{j} + 6\hat{k}\right)$

B. $-\frac{1}{7}\left(3\,\hat{i}+2\,\hat{j}+6\hat{k}\right)$

C. $\frac{1}{49}\left(3\hat{i}+2\hat{j}+6\hat{k}\right)$

D. none of these

Q.37 The range of $\tan^{-1} x$ is

A. R

B. $\left(\frac{-\pi}{2},\frac{\pi}{2}\right)$

C. $(-\pi, \pi)$

D. $\left(\frac{\pi}{2},\frac{-\pi}{2}\right)$

Q.38 If $\theta = \tan^{-1} x$ then $\sin 2\theta$ is equal to

A. $\frac{2x}{1+x^2}$

B. $\frac{2x}{1-x^2}$

C. $\frac{1-x^2}{1+x^2}$

D. none of these

Q.39

If $\sin^{-1} x = \frac{\pi}{5}$, then $\cos^{-1}x$ is equal to

A. $\frac{\pi}{10}$

B. $\frac{3\pi}{10}$

C. $\frac{5\pi}{4}$

D. $\sqrt{1+x^2}$

Q.40 $\cot^{-1} 21 + \cot^{-1} 13 + \cot^{-1}(-8)$ is equal to

A. 0

B. $\cot^{-1} 26$

C. π

D. none of these

Q.41 $\sin(\cot^{-1}x)$ is equal to

A. $\sqrt{1+x^2}$

B. $\frac{1}{\sqrt{1+x^2}}$

C. $\frac{x}{\sqrt{1+x^2}}$

D. none of these

Q.42

$\cos^{-1}\left(\cos\left(-\frac{\pi}{3}\right)\right)$ is equal to

A. $-\frac{\pi}{3}$

B. $\frac{\pi}{3}$

C. $\frac{2\pi}{3}$

D. none of these

Q.43 A coin is tossed again and again. if tail appears on first three tosses, then the chance that head appears on fourth toss is

A. $\frac{1}{16}$

B. $\frac{1}{2}$

C. $\frac{1}{8}$

D. None of these

Q.44 If E_1 and E_2 are mutually exclusive events, then

A. $P(E_1) + P(E_2) \le 1$

B. $P(E_1) + P(E_2) \ge 1$

C. $P(E_1) + P(E_2) = 1$

D. None of these

Q.45 A man speaks truth in 75% cases. He throws a dice and reports that it is a six. The probability that it is actually a six is

A. $\frac{3}{8}$

B. $\frac{1}{5}$

C. $\frac{3}{24}$

D. None of these

Q.46 The probability that when 10 balls are distributed among 3 boxes, the first will contain 2 balls is

A. $\frac{2^8}{3^{10}}$

B. $\frac{{}^{10}C_2\, 2^8}{3^{10}}$

C. $\frac{{}^{10}C_2}{3^{10}}$

D. None of these

Q.47 If A and are two mutually exclusive events, then $P(A+B)$ is equal to

A. $P(A)\,P(B)$

B. $P(A) + P(B)$

C. $P(A)\,P(B') + P(A')\,P(B)$

D. $P(A)\,P(B') - P(A')\,P(B)$

Q.48 If E_1 and E_2 are two independent events, then $P(E_1 \cap E_2)$ is equal to

A. $P(E_1 \cap E_2) + P(E_2)$

B. $P(E_1) + P(E_2) + P(E_1 \cup E_2)$

C. $P(E_1)\,P(E_2)$

D. None of these

Q.49 Solution set of the inequality $x \ge 0$ is

A. half plane on the left of Y-axis

B. half plane on the right of Y-axis excluding the points on Y-axis

C. half plane on the right of Y–axis including the point on Y-axis

D. None of these

Q.50 Solution set of the inequality $y \le 0$ is

A. half plane below the X-axis excluding the points on X-axis

B. half plane below the X-axis including the point on X – axis

C. half plane above the X-axis

D. None of these

Q.51 Region represented by the inequalities $x \ge 0, y \ge 0$ is

A. First quadrant

B. second quadrant

C. third quadrant

D. fourth quadrant

Q.52 Objective function of a L.P.P. is

A. a constant

B. a function to be optimized

C. a relation between the variables

D. None of these

Q.53 Which of the following sets is not convex?
A. $\{(x, y) : x + y \leq 1\}$
B. $\{(x, y) : x^2 + y^2 > 1\}$
C. $\{(x, y) : x^2 + y^2 \leq 1\}$
D. none of these

Q.54 Which of the following sets is convex?
A. $\{(x, y) : x^2 + y^2 \geq 1\}$
B. $\{(x, y) : 2x^2 + 3y^2 \leq 6\}$
C. $\{9x, y) : 4 \leq x^2 + y^2 \leq 9\}$
D. none of these

Q.55 Which of the following is a polynomial?
A. 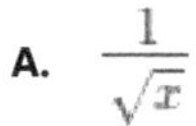 $\dfrac{1}{\sqrt{x}}$

B. $x^2 + x - -\sqrt{} + 3$

C. $ax^2 + bx + c$

D. none of these

Q.56 Roots of the equation $ax^2 + bx + c = 0$ are non-real if
A. $b^2 - 4ac < 0$
B. $b^2 - 4ac \leq 0$
C. $b^2 - 4ac \geq 0$
D. none of these

Q.57 The solution set of the equation
$$\sqrt{2y + 1} + \sqrt{y} = \text{is}$$
A. $\{\,\}$
B. $\{\,0\,\}$
C. $\{0, 4\}$
D. $\{\,4\,\}$

Q.58
If $x = \sqrt{2 + \sqrt{2 + \sqrt{2 + \ldots\ldots + to\ \infty}}}$ then x is equal to

A. $\sqrt{2}$
B. $\dfrac{1}{2}$

C. 2
D. none of these

Q.59 Sum of the roots of the equation $x^2 + |x| - 6 = 0$ is
A. 0
B. -1
C. 5
D. none of these

Q.60 The number of real solution of the equation $- 2 = x - x^2 = 2^x$ is
A. 2
B. 1
C. 0
D. none of these

Analytical Ability & Logical Reasoning

Q.61 Find the number of triangles in the given figure.

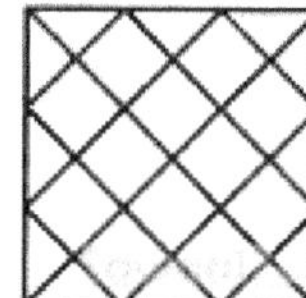

A. 28
B. 32
C. 36
D. 40

Q.62 Find the minimum number of straight lines required to make the given figure.

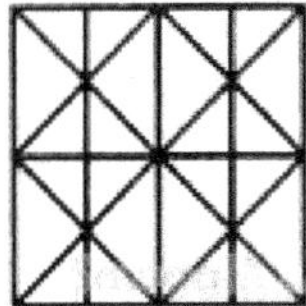

A. 11
B. 14
C. 16
D. 17

Q.63 What is the number of triangles that can be formed whose vertices are the vertices of an octagon but have only one side common with that of octagon?
A. 64
B. 32
C. 24
D. 16

Q.64 What is the number of straight lines and the number of triangles in the given figure.
{{n47.PNG}}
A. 10 straight lines and 34 triangles
B. 9 straight lines and 34 triangles
C. 9 straight lines and 36 triangles
D. 10 straight lines and 36 triangles

Q.65 Should a total ban be put on traping wild animals?
Arguments:
1. Yes. Trappers are making a lot of money
2. No. Bans on hunting and trapping are not effective
A. Only 1 is true
B. Only 2 is true
C. Either 1 or 2 is true
D. Neither 1 or 2 is true

Q.66 Should jobs be linked with academic degrees and diplomas?
Arguments:
1. No. A very large number of persons with meagre academic qualifications will apply
2. No. Importance of higher education will be diminished
A. Only 1 is true
B. Only 2 is true
C. Either 1 or 2 is true
D. Neither 1 nor 2 is true

Q.67 Should India become a permanent member of UN's Security Council?
Arguments:
I. Yes. India has emerged as a country which loves peace and amity.
II. No. Let us first solve problems of our own people like poverty, malnutrition.
A. Only argument I is strong
B. Only argument II is strong
C. Neither I nor II is strong
D. Both I and II are strong

Q.68 Should cutting of trees be banned altogether?
Arguments:
I. Yes. It is very much necessary to do so to restore ecological balance.
II. No. A total ban would harm timber based industries.
A. Only argument I is strong

B. Only argument II is strong
C. Neither I nor II is strong
D. Both I and II are strong

Q.69 Directions : For the Assertion (A) and Reason (R) below, choose the correct alternative
Assertion (A) : Pressure cookers are fitted with ebonite handles.
Reason (R) : Ebonite is strong.
A. Both A and R are true and R is the correct explanation of A.
B. Both A and R are true but R is NOT the correct explanation of A.
C. A is true but R is false.
D. A is false but R is true.

Q.70 Directions : For the Assertion (A) and Reason (R) below, choose the correct alternative
Assertion (A) : Pluto is the coldest planet
Reason (R) : It receives slanting rays of- the sun.
A. Both A and R are true and R is the correct explanation of A.
B. Both A and R are true but R is NOT the correct explanation of A.
C. A is true but R is false.
D. A is false but R is true.

Q.71 Directions : For the Assertion (A) and Reason (R) below, choose the correct alternative
Assertion (A) : Diamond is used for cutting glass.
Reason (R) : Diamond has a high refractive index.
A. Both A and R are true and R is the correct explanation of A.
B. Both A and R are true but R is NOT the correct explanation of A.
C. A is true but R is false.
D. A is false but R is true.

Q.72 Directions : For the Assertion (A) and Reason (R) below, choose the correct alternative
Assertion (A) : Eskimos reside in igloos.
Reason (R) : No other material except snow is available.
A. Both A and R are true and R is the correct explanation of A.
B. Both A and R are true but R is NOT the correct explanation of A.
C. A is true but R is false.
D. A is false but R is true.

Q.73 In a certain code language COMPUTER is written as RFUVQNPC. How will MEDICINE be written in that code language?
A. MFEDJJOE
B. EOJDEJFM
C. MFEJDJOE
D. EOJDJEFM

Q.74 In a certain code language,
'134' means 'good and tasty';
'478' means 'see good pictures' and
'729' means 'pictures are faint'.
Which of the following digits stands for 'see'?
A. 9
B. 2
C. 1
D. 8

Q.75 In a certain code, MONKEY is written as XDJMNL. How is TIGER written in that code ?

A. SHFDQ
B. HFDSQ
C. RSAFD
D. QDFHS

Q.76 If Z = 52 and ACT = 48, then BAT will be equal to
A. 39
B. 41
C. 44
D. 46

Q.77 Vaunt : Flaunt :: Disparate : ?
A. Similar
B. Homogenous
C. Contrast
D. Alike

Q.78 Seismography : Earthquake :: Taseometer : ?
A. Landslides
B. Strains
C. Resistances
D. Volcanoes

Q.79 Biped : Quadruped :: Ostrich : ?
A. Cat
B. Rabbit
C. Tortoise
D. Rat

Q.80 Fumble is to Finesse as Malign is to
A. Slander
B. Extol
C. Criticize
D. Assurance

Computer Awareness

Q.81 Window's settings are recorded in
A. WINDOWS.INI
B. WIN.INI
C. SYSTEM.INI
D. GROUP.INI

Q.82 Which network protocol is used to send Email?
A. FTP
B. SSH
C. POP3
D. SMTP

Q.83 When was the first e-mail sent?
A. 1963
B. 1969
C. 1971
D. 1974

Q.84 Operating System is the most common type of _______ software.
A. Communication
B. Application
C. System
D. Word Processing Software

Q.85 The memory which allocates space for DOS and application is called
A. Expanded memory
B. Cache memory
C. Virtual memory
D. Conventional memory

Q.86 The operating system creates _____ from the physical computer
A. Virtual space
B. Virtual computers
C. Virtual device
D. None

Q.87 Which menu bar selection would you access to open file?
A. Option
B. Help
C. View
D. None of above

Q.88 Which mode loads minimal set of drivers when starting Windows?
A. Safe Mode
B. Normal Mode
C. VGA Mode
D. Network Support Mode

Q.89 Short cut Ctrl + F is used to

A. Open Find and Replace Dialog box with activating Find Tab

B. Open Page Setup Dialog box with activating Layout Tab

C. Open Font Dialog Box with activating Font tab

D. Open File Save as Dialog box

Q.90 Short cut Ctrl + H is used to

A. Open Find and Replace Dialog box with activating Replace Tab

B. Open Format Dialog box activating Insert Hyper Link tab

C. Open Insert Dialog box activating Insert Hyper Link Tab

D. Open Insert Hyper Link Dialog box

Q.91 Short cut Ctrl + P used to

A. Open Paragraph Dialog Box

B. Open Page Format Dialog Box

C. Open Save Dialog Box

D. Open Print Dialog box

Q.92 Short cut Ctrl + T is used to

A. Hanging Indent

B. Left Indent

C. Open Tabs Dialog box

D. Terminate all opened Dialog box

Q.93 MS Excel provides the default value for step in Fill Series dialog box

A. 0   **B.** 1   **C.** 5   **D.** 10

Q.94 When a row of data is to be converted into columns

A. Copy the cells in row, select the same number of cells in row and paste

B. Copy the cells in column then choose Edit >> Paste Special, then click Transpose and OK

C. Copy the cells then go to Format >> Cells then on Alignment tab click Transpose check box and click OK

D. elect the cells then place the cell pointer on new cell and choose Edit >> Paste Special, mark Transpose check box and click OK

Q.95 Ctrl + D shortcut key in Excel will

A. Open the font dialog box

B. Apply double underline for the active cell

C. Fill down in the selection

D. None of above

Q.96 The short cut key Ctrl + R is used in Excel to

A. Right align the content of cell

B. Remove the cell contents of selected cells

C. Fill the selection with active cells to the right

D. None of above

Q.97 To insert a hyperlink in a slide

A. Choose Insert >> Hyperlink

B. Press Ctrl + K

C. Hyperlinks can't be inserted in slides

D. both a & b

Q.98 List Box and Text box

A. are some other than that in a list box the bullets are enabledv

B. are different. List boxes are used to present lists and can't be created with text boxes

C. Both of above

D. None of above

Q.99 Which of the following statement is true

A. You can insert text boxes from drawing toolbar in PowerPoint

B. You cannot insert text boxes from drawing toolbar in PowerPoint

C. Text boxes are provides when you choose a layout and can't be inserted afterwards

D. None of above

Q.100 When you delete a text box object from a slide in PowerPoint Presentation

A. The object is deleted but text box and the text inside is left on the slide

B. The text box is deleted and the text is pasted on the slide

C. The text box and text both are deleted

D. None of above

English

Q.101 Mr Alexgander / has purchased / new furnitures from Metro-Mall.

A. Mr Alexgander

B. has purchased

C. new furnitures from Metro-Mall

D. No Error

Q.102 Last year / many people / died from cholera epidemic.

A. Last year

B. many people

C. died from cholera epidemic

D. No Error

Q.103 Both the / girls helped / one another.

A. Both the   **B.** girls helped

C. one another   **D.** No Error

Q.104 Vijay is / very much / sorry about her misconduct.

A. Vijay is

B. very much

C. sorry about her misconduct

D. No Error

Q.105 She treated/ me as though / an old friend.

A. She treated   **B.** me as though

C. an old friend   **D.** No error

Q.106 This is a .... on his character.

A. Blot   **B.** Blur   **C.** Slur   **D.** Spot

Q.107 We didn't .... the programme to be such a huge success.

A. Accept   **B.** Except   **C.** Expect   **D.** Access

Q.108 I suffer from no .... about my capabilities.

A. illusion	B. doubts
C. hallucinations	D. imaginations

Q.109 The government, in a bid to make Bihar, a preferred investment destination, has _______ major schemes to create infrastructure at different stages.

A. launched   B. opposed   C. opened   D. pushed

Q.110 The student's aren't prepared ______ the examination

A. to give   B. to listen   C. to work   D. to take

Q.111 Select the pair which has the same relationship.

DIVA:OPERA

A. producer : theatre	B. director : drama
C. conductor : bus	D. thespian : play

Q.112 Select the pair which has the same relationship.

GRAIN : SALT

A. shard : pottery	B. shred : wood
C. blades : grass	D. chip : glass

Q.113 Select the pair which has the same relationship.

THRUST : SPEAR

A. mangle : iron	B. scabbard : sword
C. bow : arrow	D. fence : epee

Q.114 elect the pair which has the same relationship.

PAIN : SEDATIVE

A. comfort : stimulant	B. grief : consolation
C. trance : narcotic	D. ache : extraction

Q.115 Select the pair which has the same relationship.

LIGHT : BLIND

A. speech : dumb	B. language : deaf
C. tongue : sound	D. voice : vibration

Q.116 Our task had been completed before sunset.

A. We completed our task before sunset.

B. We have completed our task before sunset.

C. We complete our task before sunset.

D. We had completed our task before sunset.

Q.117 The boy laughed at the beggar.

A. The beggar was laughed by the boy.

B. The beggar was being laughed by the boy.

C. The beggar was being laughed at by the boy.

D. The beggar was laughed at by the boy.

Q.118 The boys were playing Cricket.

A. Cricket had been played by the boys.

B. Cricket has been played by the boys.

C. Cricket was played by the boys.

D. Cricket was being played by the boys.

Q.119 They drew a circle in the morning.

A. A circle was being drawn by them in the morning.

B. A circle was drawn by them in the morning.

C. In the morning a circle have been drawn by them.

D. A circle has been drawing since morning.

Q.120 They will demolish the entire block.

A. The entire block is being demolished.

B. The block may be demolished entirely.

C. The entire block will have to be demolished by the

D. The entire block will be demolished.

// Smart Answer Sheet //

Correct — Percentage of students who answered correctly. **Skipped** — Percentage of students who skipped.

Q.	Ans.	Correct / Skipped	Q.	Ans.	Correct / Skipped	Q.	Ans.	Correct / Skipped	Q.	Ans.	Correct / Skipped	Q.	Ans.	Correct / Skipped
1	D	87.04 % / 10.63 %	17	B	79.07 % / 16.13 %	33	C	85.82 % / 12.82 %	49	C	77.86 % / 13.62 %	65	D	76.58 % / 18.76 %
2	C	89.9 % / 10.09 %	18	D	88.33 % / 10.9 %	34	C	84.2 % / 10.5 %	50	B	78.05 % / 11.09 %	66	B	76.93 % / 22.73 %
3	B	77.68 % / 10.59 %	19	C	78.76 % / 10.7 %	35	B	86.93 % / 10.83 %	51	A	86.9 % / 11.47 %	67	A	87.77 % / 11.82 %
4	D	79.01 % / 13.96 %	20	C	85.98 % / 12.02 %	36	A	84.91 % / 14.21 %	52	B	82.45 % / 16.94 %	68	D	84.35 % / 10.72 %
5	D	86.4 % / 13.53 %	21	A	82.84 % / 10.01 %	37	B	89.16 % / 10.42 %	53	C	83.03 % / 10.52 %	69	C	85.99 % / 10.89 %
6	C	78.32 % / 13.87 %	22	D	77.47 % / 13.83 %	38	A	78.59 % / 11.34 %	54	B	78.48 % / 20.18 %	70	C	80.51 % / 14.3 %
7	B	79.02 % / 16.78 %	23	A	82.75 % / 13.09 %	39	B	84.39 % / 14.74 %	55	C	81.0 % / 17.44 %	71	B	87.55 % / 11.59 %
8	D	85.27 % / 10.59 %	24	D	82.13 % / 17.42 %	40	C	84.9 % / 14.36 %	56	D	81.44 % / 16.78 %	72	C	84.66 % / 11.27 %
9	B	89.81 % / 10.01 %	25	A	89.31 % / 10.35 %	41	B	86.44 % / 13.39 %	57	B	85.04 % / 12.04 %	73	D	85.42 % / 11.29 %
10	D	80.3 % / 11.19 %	26	B	78.9 % / 10.9 %	42	B	77.43 % / 10.87 %	58	C	77.95 % / 19.92 %	74	D	84.86 % / 12.07 %
11	D	86.95 % / 12.55 %	27	D	85.87 % / 12.51 %	43	B	81.69 % / 13.54 %	59	A	84.86 % / 13.26 %	75	D	88.43 % / 10.37 %
12	B	83.75 % / 12.15 %	28	A	82.76 % / 15.06 %	44	A	84.61 % / 15.01 %	60	C	78.63 % / 16.88 %	76	D	80.18 % / 16.25 %
13	B	87.32 % / 10.89 %	29	C	81.85 % / 16.46 %	45	A	88.71 % / 10.66 %	61	C	87.95 % / 11.88 %	77	C	78.3 % / 14.65 %
14	D	83.69 % / 14.2 %	30	A	78.56 % / 15.27 %	46	B	82.38 % / 13.13 %	62	B	87.04 % / 12.03 %	78	B	81.86 % / 15.28 %
15	A	80.08 % / 14.08 %	31	B	83.79 % / 15.41 %	47	B	86.01 % / 11.95 %	63	B	88.66 % / 11.08 %	79	A	81.74 % / 13.33 %
16	B	87.77 % / 10.81 %	32	B	89.25 % / 10.05 %	48	C	77.48 % / 13.26 %	64	C	81.9 % / 15.47 %	80	B	85.73 % / 13.6 %

Q.	Ans.	Correct / Skipped		Q.	Ans.	Correct / Skipped		Q.	Ans.	Correct / Skipped		Q.	Ans.	Correct / Skipped		Q.	Ans.	Correct / Skipped
81	B	83.79 % 13.72 %		89	A	76.01 % 16.29 %		97	D	77.84 % 14.51 %		105	B	76.32 % 22.56 %		113	D	79.64 % 18.84 %
82	D	81.19 % 11.02 %		90	A	82.69 % 17.31 %		98	A	79.93 % 15.69 %		106	C	84.17 % 15.33 %		114	B	88.52 % 10.07 %
83	C	77.21 % 10.89 %		91	D	88.33 % 10.71 %		99	A	82.84 % 13.05 %		107	C	77.84 % 20.39 %		115	A	86.06 % 12.24 %
84	C	83.2 % 12.8 %		92	A	83.31 % 10.7 %		100	C	89.4 % 10.05 %		108	A	79.84 % 20.07 %		116	D	78.78 % 15.27 %
85	D	86.17 % 13.3 %		93	B	80.19 % 11.81 %		101	C	78.68 % 19.93 %		109	A	79.9 % 14.81 %		117	D	79.1 % 12.34 %
86	B	80.63 % 11.36 %		94	D	88.0 % 10.82 %		102	D	88.06 % 10.09 %		110	D	87.77 % 10.72 %		118	D	79.98 % 16.06 %
87	D	77.48 % 14.95 %		95	C	77.41 % 10.84 %		103	C	89.44 % 10.29 %		111	D	78.55 % 11.46 %		119	B	80.65 % 15.89 %
88	A	89.73 % 10.24 %		96	C	78.35 % 10.13 %		104	B	80.68 % 16.69 %		112	D	85.59 % 11.71 %		120	D	86.48 % 11.13 %

//Hints and Solutions//

1. A relation from a non-empty set A to a non-empty set B is defined as a subset of A × B

2. Domain of R = {x ∈N : x R y for some y ∈ N}| = {2, 4, 6}

$$\begin{cases} 6 \ when \ y = 1 \\ 4 \ when \ y = 2 \\ 2 \ when \ y = 3 \end{cases}$$

∵ x = 8 − 2y, y ∈ N =
Note that in this case
R = {(2, 3), (4, 2), (6, 1)}

3. Since x , y does not imply y < x, therefore, x R y does not imply y R x. So the relation R is notsymmetric in this case

4. As (3, 3) ∉R , therefore, R is not reflexlive
As(2, 3) ∈ R but (3, 2) ∉ R, therefore, R is not symmetric
As both (1, 2) and (2, 1) are contained in R, therefore, R is not antisymmetric
(A relation R is antisymmetriciff x R y and y R x ⇒ x = y)

5. All the subsets of A× A, given in (a), (b) and (c) are equivalence relation on A, as they are reflexive, symmetric and transitive

6. Let x ∈ A, y ∴ B be arbitrary, then (x, y) ∈ A × B
⇒ (x, y) ∈ B × A (∵ A × B = B × A)
⇒x∈ B and y ∈ A
Hence A ⊂ B and B ⊂ A ⇒A = B

7. There are in total 9 entries and each entry can be selected in exactly 2 ways. Hence, the total
number of all possible matrices of the said type is 2^9.

8.

$$\begin{bmatrix} 1 & 0 \\ 0 & 1 \end{bmatrix}$$

9. Each row of A contains 4 elements.

10. PQ is of order 2 × 2

11. $(AB)^{-1} = B^{-1} A^{-1}$

12. $A^2 = AA$

$$\begin{bmatrix} 0 & 0 & 0 & 0 \\ 0 & 0 & 0 & 0 \\ 1 & 0 & 0 & 0 \\ 0 & 1 & 0 & 0 \end{bmatrix} \begin{bmatrix} 0 & 0 & 0 & 0 \\ 0 & 0 & 0 & 0 \\ 1 & 0 & 0 & 0 \\ 0 & 1 & 0 & 0 \end{bmatrix} = \begin{bmatrix} 0 & 0 & 0 & 0 \\ 0 & 0 & 0 & 0 \\ 0 & 0 & 0 & 0 \\ 0 & 1 & 0 & 0 \end{bmatrix}$$

13. Let A (1, −2, 3) and B(4, 2, −1). Let the plane XOY meet the line AB in the point C such that C divides [AB] in the ratio k : 1, then

$$C = \left(\frac{4k+1}{k+1}, \frac{2k-2}{k+1}, \frac{-k+3}{k+1} \right).$$

Since C lies on the plane XOY i.e. the plane
z = 0, therefore, $\frac{-k+3}{k+1} = 0 \Rightarrow k = 3$

14.

Now $\overrightarrow{PQ}$= P.V. of Q - P.V. of P
$= (-\hat{i} + \hat{j} - 2\hat{k}) - (\hat{i} - 2\hat{j} - 4\hat{k})$
$= -2\,\hat{i} + 3\,\hat{j} - 6\hat{k}$

Hence $|\overrightarrow{PQ}| = \sqrt{(-2)^2 + 3^2 + (-6)^2} = 7.$

So,the unit in the direction of $\overrightarrow{PQ}$ is

$\frac{1}{7}\overrightarrow{PQ} = \frac{1}{7}(2\hat{i} + 3\hat{j} - 6\hat{k}) = -\frac{2}{7}\hat{i} + \frac{3}{7}\hat{j} - \frac{6}{7}\hat{k}$

15.

The given equation is $|\hat{r}|^2 - 2(\hat{r} \bullet \hat{a}) + \lambda = 0 \Leftrightarrow |\vec{r}|^2 - 2(\vec{r} \bullet \vec{a}) + |\vec{a}|^2 + \lambda - |\vec{a}|^2 = 0$⇔(
$\vec{r} - \vec{a})^2 = |\vec{a}|^2 - \lambda$
$|\vec{r} - \vec{a}|^2 = a^2 - \lambda.$
This represents a sphere only if $a^2 \cdot \lambda > 0$.
i.e. if $a^2 \lambda$.

16. Any point on the given line is (t,2t,3 t). if lies in the given pane
if 2(t) − 4 (2 t) +2 (3t)
i.g. if 0 t = 3, which is not true for any t ∈R. Hence, the given line and the given plane do not meet any point.

17.

Since the sphere in reference touches the given plane $\vec{r} \bullet (2\hat{i} - 2\hat{j} - \hat{k}) = 10$
i.e. the plane 2x- 2y -z -10 =0, therefore, radius = length of perpendicular from the centre C (3,6, -2) upon the tangent plane
$$= \frac{|2 \times 3 - 2 \times 6 - (-2) - 10|}{\sqrt{2^2 + (-2)^2 + 1^2}} = \frac{14}{3}.$$

18. When a line lies in a plane, then it is at right angles to the normal to the plane. Here, d.n, of the line are < a,b,c,> and attitude numbers fof the plane are being taken as . So, we must have aA +bB + cC = 0.

19. Condition of Rolle's theorem are satisfied by f(x) in [2, 3].
Hence there exists atleast one real c in (2, 3) st. t f' (c) = 0
∴ the set S contains atleast one element

20. Every continuous function is not differentiable.

21. Since the graph cuts the lines y = − 1 and y = 1, therefore, it must cut y = 0 atleast once as the graph is a continuous curve in this case

22. In case of strict decreasing function, slope of tangent and hence derivative is either negative or zero. (For example, consider the function f(x) = − x³)

23. f(x) = 2 − 3x ⇒ f' (x) = − 3 < 0 ∀ x ∈ R.
So, f is a strict decreasing function

24. f(x) = x² − 2x
⇒ f' (x) = 2x − 2 = 2 (x − 1)
So f(x) in increasing if 2(x − 1) ≥ 0 i.e. of x ≥ 1

25.

Substitute $2^x = t$

$2^x \log 2 = \frac{dt}{dx} \Rightarrow 2^x \log 2\ dx = dt$

$\int 2^{2^x} 2^x dx = \int 2^t \frac{dt}{\log 2}$

$= \frac{1}{\log 2} \int 2^t dt = \frac{1}{\log 2} \cdot \frac{2^t}{\log 2} + C$

$= \frac{2^{2^x}}{(\log 2)^2} + C$

26.

For $0 \leq x < 1$, $[x] = 0$

and for $1 \leq x < 2$, $[x] = 1$

Hence $\int\limits_{0}^{2} x[x]\,dx = \int\limits_{0}^{1} x[x]\,dx + \int\limits_{1}^{2} x[x]\,dx$

27.

Let $I = \int\limits_{0}^{2\pi} (\cos x)^{2001}\,dx$

$= 2\int\limits_{0}^{\pi} (\cos x)^{2001}\,dx$

$(\because (\cos x)^{2001} = \cos^{2001}(2\pi - x))$

$= 0 \; (\because \cos^{2001}(\pi - x) = -\cos^{2001} x)$

We have used the results $\int\limits_{0}^{2a} f(x)\,dx$

$= \begin{cases} 2\int\limits_{0}^{a} f(x)\,dx & if\; f(2a - x) = f(x) \\ 0 & if\; (2a - x) = -f(x) \end{cases}$

28. Equation of any non-vertical line in a given plane is of the form y = mx + c, where m, c are

arbitrary constants. Differentiating twice w.r.t. x (to eliminate c,

m), we get $\dfrac{d^2 y}{dx^2} = 0$

29. since the general solution contains three arbitrary constants, therefore, the differential equation in reference must be of order 3.

30. {{o7.PNG}}

31.

As $\vec{a}$ is a non-zero vector $\hat{a} = \dfrac{\vec{a}}{|\vec{a}|}$ and $-\hat{a}$ are two unit vectors collinear with $\vec{a}$.

32. Since $\vec{a}$ and $\vec{b}$ are non –zero collinear vectors, therefore, $\vec{a} \times \vec{b}$ is a non zero vector at right angles to both $\vec{a}$ and $\vec{b}$. Hence

$\dfrac{\vec{a} \times \vec{b}}{|\vec{a} \times \vec{b}|}$ and $-\dfrac{\vec{a} \times \vec{b}}{|\vec{a} \times \vec{b}|}$ are the two unit vectors perpendicular to both $\vec{a}$ and $\vec{b}$

33.

Vectors $\left(2\hat{i} + 3\hat{j} - 6\hat{k}\right) \cdot \left(a\hat{i} + \hat{b} + \hat{c}\right) = 0$

if $2a + 3b - 6c = 0$

34.

$\vec{a} \bullet \vec{b} \geq 0 \Rightarrow ab\cos\theta \geq 0$

$\Rightarrow \cos\theta \geq 0 \Rightarrow 0 \leq \dfrac{\pi}{2}$

35.

Resultant of $\vec{a}$ and $\vec{b}$ means $\vec{a} + \vec{b}$.

Here $\vec{a} + \vec{b} = \left(2\hat{i} + \hat{j} + \hat{k}\right) + \left(\hat{i} + 2\hat{j} + 3\hat{k}\right)$

$= 3\hat{i} + 3\hat{j} + 4\hat{k}$

$\therefore |\vec{a} + \vec{b}| = \sqrt{3^2 + 3^2 + 4^2} = \sqrt{9 + 9 + 16}$

$= \sqrt{34}$

36.

Sum of the given vectors

$= \left(\hat{i} + \hat{j} + \hat{k}\right) + \left(2\hat{i} - \hat{j} - \hat{k}\right) + \left(2\hat{j} + 6\hat{k}\right)$

$= 3\hat{i} + 2\hat{j} + 6\hat{k}$

$\therefore$ The unit vector in the direction of the sum of the given vectors

$= \dfrac{3\hat{i} + 2\hat{j} + 6\hat{k}}{|3\hat{i} + 2\hat{j} + 6\hat{k}|} = \dfrac{3\hat{i} + 2\hat{j} + 6\hat{k}}{\sqrt{3^2 + 2^2 + 6^2}}$

$= \dfrac{1}{7}\left(3\hat{i} + 2\hat{j} + 6\hat{k}\right)$

37. Range of $\tan^{-1} x$ is

$\left(\dfrac{-\pi}{2}, \dfrac{\pi}{2}\right)$

38.

Given $\theta = \tan^{-1} x$, therefore,

$\sin 2\theta = \dfrac{2\tan\theta}{1 + \tan^2\theta} = \dfrac{2x}{1 + x^2}$

39.

$\cos^{-1} x = \dfrac{\pi}{2} - \sin^{-1} x = \dfrac{\pi}{2} - \dfrac{\pi}{5} = \dfrac{3\pi}{10}$

40.

Given $\dfrac{dy}{dx} = 3x^2 \Rightarrow y = x^3 + C$

since (– 1, 1) lies on the curve, therefore,

$1 = (-1)^3 + C \Rightarrow C = 2$

41.

$\sin(\cot^{-1} x) = \sin\theta$, where $\theta = \cot^{-1} x$

i.e. $x = \cot\theta$, $0 < \theta < \pi$

$\Rightarrow \sin(\cot^{-1} x) = \dfrac{1}{cosec\,\theta}$

$= \dfrac{1}{\sqrt{1 + \cot^2\theta}} = \dfrac{1}{\sqrt{1 + x^2}}$

42.

$\cos^{-1}\left(\cos\left(-\dfrac{\pi}{3}\right)\right) = \cos^{-1}\left(\cos\dfrac{\pi}{3}\right) = \dfrac{\pi}{3}$

43. Since the outcomes of successive throws of a coin are independent, therefore, the chance of occurrence or non-occurrence of head o fourth toss does not depend on the outcomes of first three tosses. Hence, the required probability=

$\dfrac{1}{2}$

44.

As E_1 and e_2 are mutually exclusive, therefore,

$E_1 \cap e_2 = \emptyset \Rightarrow E_1 \subset E_2^c$ and $E_2 \subset E_1^c$

$P(E_1) \leq P(E_2^c)$

$P(E_1) \leq P 1 - P(E_2)$

$P(E_1) + P(E_2) \leq 1.$

45. {{n22.PNG}}

46.

Each ball can be put in any one of the three boxes, therefore, the total number of ways in which all the balls can be put into three boxes is 3^{10}.
Tow balls can by chosen out of 10 in $^{10}C_2$ ways. When these balls are put into the first box, the remaining 8 balls can be put into the remaining two boxes in 2^8 ways. Hence, the number of ways in which the first box contains 2 balls = $^{10}C_2 \, 2^8$.
$\therefore$ Required probability = $\frac{^{10}C_2 \cdot 2^8}{3^{10}}$.

47. Given $A \cap B = \emptyset \Rightarrow P(A \cap B) = 0$

$P(A \cup B) = P(A) + P(B) - P(A \cap B)$

$= P(A) + P(B).$

48. E_1 and E_2 are independent

$P(E_1 \cap E_2) = P(E_1) P(E_2)$. (By definition)

49. Solution set of the given inequality is $\{(x, y) : x \geq 0\}$ i.e. the set of all points whose abscissae are
non – negative. All these points lie either on Y – axis or on the right of Y – axis.

50. Solution set of the given inequality is $\{(x, y): y \leq 0\}$ i.e. the set of all points whose ordinates are
non – positive. All these points lie either on X – axis or below X – axis.

51. Solution set of the given inequalities is

$\{(x, y) : x \geq 0\} \cap \{(x, y) : y \geq 0\} = \{(x, y) : x \geq 0, y \geq 0\}$ i.e. the set of all those points whose both coordinates are non – negative. All these points lei in the first quadrant (including points on +ve X – axis, + ve Y – axis and the origin).

52. Objective function is a linear function (of the variables involved) whose maximum or minimum value is to be found.

53. The set $\{(x, y) : 1 \leq x^2 + y^2 \leq 3\}$ is not convex as is clear from the adjoining figure. The segment A B is not contained in the set through the points A and B are contained in the set.

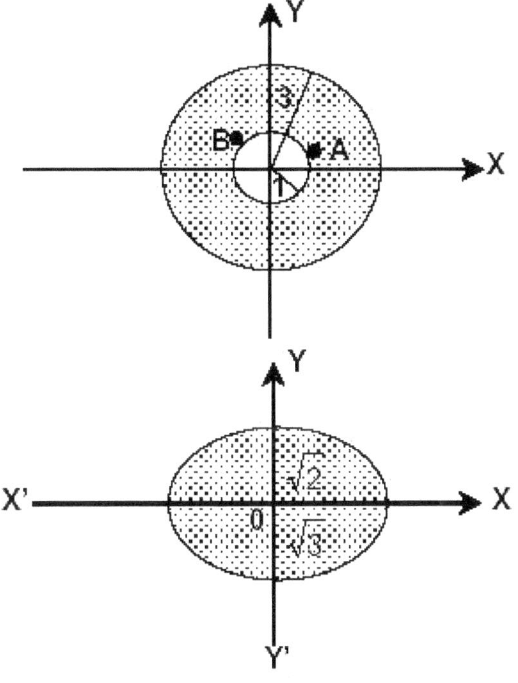

54.

The set $\{(x, y) : 2x^2 + 3y^2 \leq 6\} = \{(x, y): \frac{x^2}{3} + \frac{y^2}{2} \leq 1\}$ is the set of all points on and inside the ellipse

$\frac{x^2}{3} + \frac{y^2}{2} = 1$

55. A polynomial is of the form $a_0 + a_1x + a_2x^2 + \ldots + a_nx^n$, where n is a non-negative integer; $a_0, a_1,$
$a_2, \ldots, a_n$ are number real or complex. So $ax^2 + bx + c$ is a polynomial.

56. Roots are non-real if $b^2 - 4ac < 0$ and a, b, c are real numbers. Here, nothing is known about the
nature of coefficients, therefore, the criterion for non-real roots can be fixed. For example, for the equation
$ix^2 - 3ix - 4i = 0$, $b^2 - 4ac = (-3i)^2 - 4i(-4i) = -9 - 16 < 0$, but the roots are real.

57. {{n34.PNG}}

58.

$x = \sqrt{2 + \sqrt{2 + \sqrt{2 + \ldots\ldots + to \infty}}}$

$\Rightarrow x = \sqrt{2 + x},\ x > 0$

$\Rightarrow x^2 = 2 + x,\ x > 0$

$\Rightarrow x^2 - x - 2 = 0,\ x > 0$

$\Rightarrow (x - 2)(x + 1) = 0,\ x > 0 \Rightarrow x = 2$

59. Given equation is

$x^2 + |x| - 6 = 0$

$\Rightarrow |x^2| + |x| - 6 = 0$

$\Rightarrow (|x| + 3)(|x| - 2) = 0$

$\Rightarrow |x| = -3$ or 2 but $|x| \geq 0$

$\therefore |x| = 2 \Rightarrow x = -2$ or 2

Hence, the sum of the roots = $-2 + 2 = 0$

60.

Now, $-2 \cdot x - x^2 = -2 - (x^2 - x)$

$= -2 - \left(x^2 - x + \frac{1}{4}\right) + \frac{1}{4}$

$= -\frac{7}{4} - \left(x - \frac{1}{2}\right)^2 \leqslant -\frac{7}{4}$

for all $x \in R$ and $2^x \geq 0$ for all $x \in R$.

Hence, the given equation has no real solution

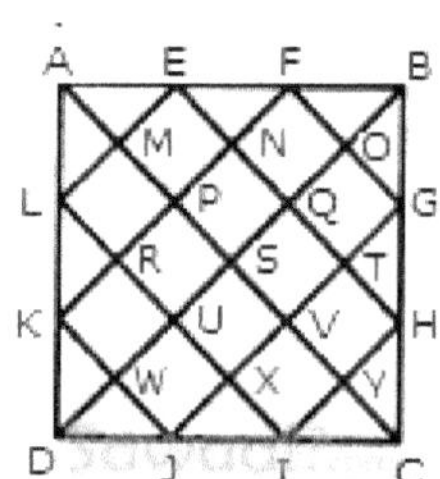

61.

The simplest triangles are AML, LRK, KWD, DWJ, JXI, IYC, CYH, HTG, GOB, BOF, FNE and EMA i.e. 12 in number.

The triangles composed of two components each are AEL, KDJ, HIC and FBG i.e. 4 in number.

The triangles composed of three components each are APF, EQB, BQH, GVC, CVJ, IUD, DUL and KPA i.e. 8 in number.

The triangles composed of six components each are ASB, BSG, CSD, DSA, AKF, EBH, GGJ and IDL i.e. 8 in number.

The triangles composed of twelve components each are ADB, ABC, BCD and CDA i.e. 4 in number.

Total number of triangles in the figure = 12 + 4 + 8 + 8 + 4 = 36.

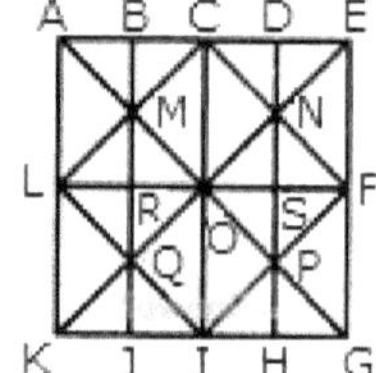

62.

The horizontal lines are AK, BJ, CI, DH and EG i.e. 5 in number.
The vertical lines are AE, LF and KG i.e. 3 in number.
The slanting lines are LC, CF, FI, LI, EK and AG i.e. 6 in number.
Thus, there are 5 + 3 + 6 = 14 straight lines in the figure.

63.

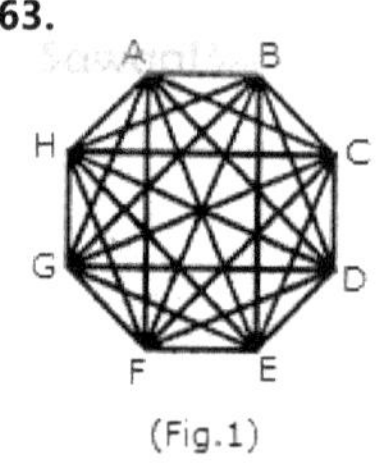

(Fig.1)

When the triangles are drawn in an octagon with vertices same as those of the octagon and having one side common to that of the octagon, the figure will appear as shown in (Fig. 1).

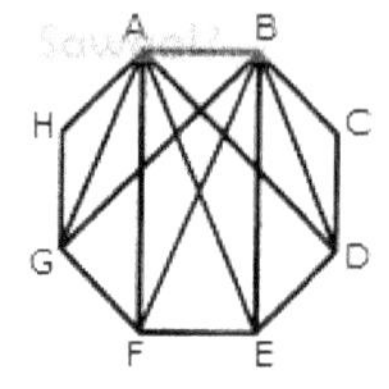

(Fig. 2)

Now, we shall first consider the triangles having only one side AB common with octagon ABCDEFGH and having vertices common with the octagon (See Fig. 2).Such triangles are ABD, ABE, ABF and ABG i.e. 4 in number.

Now, we shall first consider the triangles having only one side AB common with octagon ABCDEFGH and having vertices common with the octagon (See Fig. 2).Such triangles are ABD, ABE, ABF and ABG i.e. 4 in number.

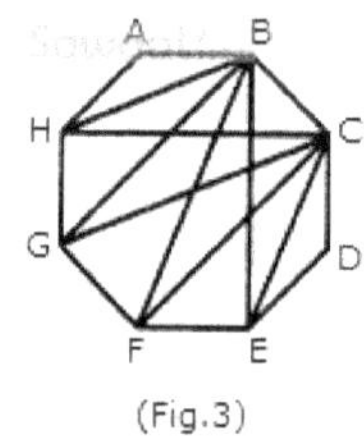

(Fig.3)

Similarly, the triangles having only one side BC common with the octagon and also having vertices common with the octagon are BCE, BCF, BCG and BCH (as shown in Fig. 3). i.e. There are 4 such triangles.

This way, we have 4 triangles for each side of the octagon. Thus, there are 8 x 4 = 32 such triangles.

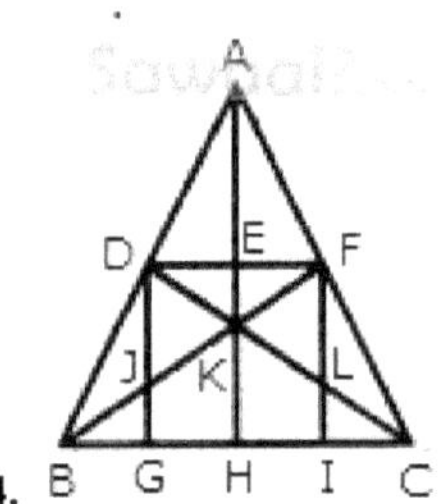

64.

The Horizontal lines are DF and BC i.e. 2 in number.
The Vertical lines are DG, AH and FI i.e. 3 in number.
The Slanting lines are AB, AC, BF and DC i.e. 4 in number.
Thus, there are 2 + 3 + 4 = 9 straight lines in the figure.

Now, we shall count the number of triangles in the figure.

The simplest triangles are ADE, AEF, DEK, EFK, DJK, FLK, DJB, FLC, BJG and LIC i.e. 10 in number.

The triangles composed of two components each are ADF, AFK, DFK, ADK, DKB, FCK, BKH, KHC, DGB and FIC i.e. 10 in number.

The triangles composed of three components each are DFJ and DFL i.e. 2 in number.

The triangles composed of four components each are ABK, ACK, BFI, CDG, DFB, DFC and BKC i.e. 7 in number.

The triangles composed of six components each are ABH, ACH, ABF, ACD, BFC and CDB i.e. 6 in number.

There is only one triangle i.e. ABC composed of twelve components.

There are 10 + 10 + 2 + 7 + 6+ 1 = 36 triangles in the figure.

65. Ban is necessary to protect our natural envoirnment .So none of the argument is strong enough

66. Delinking jobs with degrees will diminish the need for higher education as amny of them persue such education for jobs.So, only arg 2 is strong

67. (a) Only argument I is strong

68. (d) Both I and II are strong

69. The handles of pressure cookers are made of ebonite because it being a bad conductor of heat, does not heat up.

70. Pluto, being farthest from the sun, hardly gets the sun's rays. So, Pluto is the coldest planet.

71. Diamond is very hard due to its rigid three dimensional structure and so, it is used for cutting glass. Refractive index of diamond is high and gives it the greater transparency and brilliance.

72. Eskimos live in snow houses called igloos because snow, being a bad conductor of heat, these houses are warm inside.

73. - There are 8 letters in the word.
- The coded word can be obtained by taking the immediately following letters of word, expect the first and the last letters of the given word but in the reverse order. That means, in the coded form the first and the last letters have been interchanged while the remaining letters are coded by taking their immediate next letters in the reverse order.

74. Justification:
In the first and second statements, the common code digit is '4' and the common word is 'good'.
So, '4' stands for 'good'.
In the second and third statements, the common code digit is '7' and the common word is 'pictures'.
So, '7' means 'pictures'.
Thus, in the second statements, '8' means 'see'.

75. The letter of the word are written in a reverse order and then each letter is moved one step backward to obtain the code.

76. In the given code, A = 2, B = 4, C = 6,.... , Z = 52.
So, ACT = 2 + 6 + 40 = 48 and
BAT = 4 + 2 + 40 = 46

77. Vaunt - Vaunt means to boast or to praise about something excessively.
Flaunt - Flaunt also means to boast about something or to praise something.
Flaunt is the synonym of the word Vaunt.
Disparate - Disparate means essentially different in its kind or unlike or not able to be compared.

Then the required word is the synonym of Disparate.
Here in the given options, **Contrast** is the only word which is similar in meaning of Disparate.
 Hence, **Vaunt : Flaunt :: Disparate : Contrast.**

78. Seismography is an instrument to measure the intensity of an earthquake.
Similarly, taseometer is an instrument to measure strains.

79. A biped is an animal that uses two legs for walking and the quadrupeds are animals that use four legs for walking.
From the Given options, Cat only have 4 legs.
So **Biped : Quadruped :: Ostrich : Cat.**

80. Fumble means grope, mishandle, drop, mistake, blunder, bungle.
Finesse means skill, grace, elegance, assurance, diplomacy, discretion.
So, they are opposites.
Similarly,
Malign means slander or criticize.
Extol means being kind or good-natured. A person without finesse often fumbles. A person without extol in his heart often maligns.
Extol means praise or exalt, benevolence

81. The win.ini file is a Windows system file used with Microsoft Windows 3.x and 9x initialization that loads from the C:Windows directory and loads settings each time Windows boots. For example, the communication drivers, wallpaper, screen saver, languages and fonts are loaded each time the win.ini initializes. If this file becomes corrupt or bad, Windows will either not load, or have several errors as it loads.

82. SMTP (Simple Mail Transfer Protocol) is a TCP/IP protocol used in sending and receiving e-mail.

83. Sent by computer engineer **Ray Tomlinson** in **1971**, the email was simply a test message to himself. The email was sent from one computer to another computer sitting right beside it in Cambridge, Massachusetts, but it traveled via ARPANET, a network of computers that was the precursor to the Internet.

84. An operating system (OS) is system software that manages computer hardware and software resources and provides common services for computer programs.

After being initially loaded into the computer by a boot program, manages all the other programs in a computer. The other programs are called applications or application programs. The application programs make use of the operating system by making requests for services through a defined application program interface (API).

85. In DOS memory management, conventional memory, also called base memory, is the first 640 kilobytes (640 × 1024 bytes) of the memory on IBM PC or compatible systems. It is the read-write memory directly addressable by the processor for use by the operating system and application programs.

86. In computing, a virtual machine is an emulation of a computer system. Virtual machines are based on computer architectures and provide the functionality of a physical computer.

87. (d) None of above

88. Safe mode is a diagnostic mode of a computer operating system (OS). It can also refer to a mode of operation by application software. In Windows, safe mode only allows essential system programs and services to start up at boot. Safe mode is intended to help fix most, if not all problems within an operating system. It is also widely used for removing rogue security software.

89. (d) Open File Save as Dialog box

90. (a) Open Insert Hyper Link Dialog box

91. (d) Open Print Dialog box

92. If you like to use the keyboard to do your formatting, you may be interested in knowing how to format a paragraph to use a hanging indent just by using a keyboard shortcut. You do this in Word by pressing Ctrl+T.

93. (b) 1

94. (d) Select the cells then place the cell pointer on new cell and choose Edit >> Paste Special, mark Transpose check box and click OK

95. (c) Fill down in the selection

96. (c) Fill the selection with active cells to the right

97. (d) both a & b

98. (a) are some other than that in a list box the bullets are enabledv

99. (a) You can insert text boxes from drawing toolbar in PowerPoint

100. (c) The text box and text both are deleted

101. Change, Furnitures → Furniture

102. Sentence is correct.

103. Change, one another → each other

104. Very is used without **much** before adjectives and adverbs in the positive degree.
Here, Sorry is an adjective which has been used in the sense of sad. So, Correct Sentence is,
Vijay is very sorry about her misconduct.

105. Change, me as though → me like.

Do not use a noun phrase, immediately after as if and as though.

106. The correct option is **Slur**.
Speak (words) indistinctly so that the sounds run into one another.
Other uses of slur:
He was slurring his words like a drunk.
His speech was beginning to slur

107. We didn't expect the programme to be such a huge success.

108. I suffer from no **illusion** about my capabilities.

109. The government, in a bid to make Bihar, a preferred investment destination, has **launched** major schemes to create infrastructure at different stages.

110. The student's aren't prepared **to take** the examination

111. Diva (woman singer) plays a leading role in an opera(musical play). Similarly, thespian(actor) plays a leading role in a play.

112. Salt consists of grains and glass is made up of chips.

113. First is the action performed with the second. Spear is used to thrust(push suddenly or violently), similarly, Epee is used for fencing.

114. Sedative(type of drug) provides relief from Pain. Similarly, Consolation provides relief from grief.

115. Absence of Light will make Blind and absence of Speech will make Dumb.

116. We had completed our task before sunset.

The given sentence is in passive voice and it is in Past Perfect Tense.

To convert it into active voice, we just remove **been** from the given sentence and object (our)will be change into subject (We).

Rule :

Subject + had + V^3 + Other agents.

117. The beggar was laughed at by the boy.

Given sentence is in Past indefinite (Past simple) tense and it is in the active voice. To change it into Passive voice Object (the boy) will become subject and subject (The beggar) will be object. We also use helping verb of past simple tense was with V3 form of the main verb. Keep it in mind that the preposition **at** must be retained with the verb.

Rule :

Subject + (was /were) + V^3 + Other Agents.

118. Cricket was being played by the boys.

The given sentence is in Past Continuous Tense and it is in active voice. We need to change it into Passive voice.

Rule :

Subject + (was /were) + being + V^3 + Optional Agents.

119. A circle was drawn by them in the morning.

Given sentence is in Past simple tense and it is in active voice, we need to change it into passive voice.

Rule :

Subject + (was / were) + V^3 + Optional Agents.

120. The entire block will be demolished.

The given sentence contains one of Model verb **(Model Verb = will, shall, can, may, might, could, might, must, would)**. It is in active voice.

Rule :

Subject + Model verb + be + V3 + Optional Objects.

Mathematics

Q.1 Three identical dice are rolled. The probability that the same number will appear on each of them is

A. 1/6 **B.** 1/36 **C.** 1/18 **D.** 3/28

Q.2 A digit is selected at random form either of the two sets {1, 2, 3, 4, 5, 6, 7, 8, 9} and {1, 2, 3, 4,5,6, 7, 8, 9}.
What is the chance that the sum of the digits selected is 10?

A. 1/9 **B.** 10/81
C. 10/18 **D.** None of these.

Q.3 A coin with tail on both sides is tossed twice. The probability of getting 'a head' is

A. 1/2 **B.** 1 **C.** 0 **D.** 3/4

Q.4 The chance that an event E 'occurs' or does not occur' is

A. 0 **B.** 1
C. 2 **D.** None of these.

Q.5 Mean number of 'sixes' in for throws of a fair dice is

A. 6/4 **B.** 1/4 **C.** 1 **D.** 4/6

Q.6 From a deck of 52 cards, the probability of drawing a court card is

A. 4/13 **B.** 3/13 **C.** 1/13 **D.** 1/4

Q.7 If x > 1, the least value pf $2 \log_{10} x - \log_x (.01)$ is

A. 2 **B.** 4
C. 1 **D.** none of these

Q.8 If x > 0, x ≠ 1, then least value of $2 \log_{10} x - \log_x(.01)$ is

A. 2 **B.** 4
C. 1 **D.** None of these

Q.9 If a, b, c are positive real numbers, then minimum value of (b+c)/a+(c+a)/b+(a+b)/c is

A. 3 **B.** 2 **C.** 1 **D.** 6

Q.10 If A, B, C are the angles of a triangle, then minimum values of $\tan^2(A/2)+\tan^2(B/2)+\tan^2(C/2)$ is

A. 3√3 **B.** 1
C. √3 **D.** none of these

Q.11 If a, b, c are positive real numbers, then the minimum value of (a+b+c)(1/a)+(1/b)+(1/c)is

A. 8 **B.** 3 **C.** 10/3 **D.** 9

Q.12 If the product of n positive real numbers is unity, then their sum cannot be

A. greater then n **B.** less than n
C. equal to n **D.** none of these

Q.13
The vectors $\vec{a} = 2\hat{i} - 3\hat{j}$ and $\vec{b} = -4\hat{i} + 6\hat{j}$ are

A. coincident
B. parallel
C. perpendicular
D. neither parallel nor perpendicular

Q.14
The three vectors $7\hat{i} - 11\hat{j} + \hat{k}$, $5\hat{i} + 3\hat{j} - 2\hat{k}$ and $12\hat{i} - 8\hat{j} - \hat{k}$ form

A. an isosceles triangle
B. a right angled triangle
C. an equilateral triangle
D. collinear vectors

Q.15
If $\vec{a} \cdot \vec{a} = 0$, then $\vec{a}$ is a

A. free vector **B.** localized vector
C. null vector **D.** none of these

Q.16
If ABCDEF is a regular hexagon and $\vec{AB} = \vec{a}$, $\vec{BC} = \vec{b}$ and $\vec{AD}$ is equal to

A. $\vec{a} + \vec{b}$ **B.** $\vec{b} - \vec{a}$

C. $2\vec{b}$ **D.** none of these

Q.17 In a triangle ABC, D is the mid-point of side [BC] ; $\vec{AD}$ is equal to

A. $\vec{AB} + \vec{AC}$

B. $\frac{1}{2}(\vec{AB} + \vec{AC})$

C. $\vec{AB} - \vec{AC}$

D. none of these

Q.18 Direction cosines of the vector $\hat{i}$ are

A. < 1, 0, 0 > **B.** < 0, 1, 1 >
C. < 1, 0, 1 > **D.** none of these

Q.19 The differential equation satisfied by y=(A/x)+B is (A, B are parameters)

A. $x^2 y_1 = y$ **B.** $xy_1 + 2y_2 = 0$
C. $xy_2 = 2y_1 = 0$ **D.** none of these

Q.20 The family of curves represented by

$$\frac{dy}{dx} = \frac{x^2+x+1}{y^2+y+1}$$

and the family represented by

$$\frac{dy}{dx} + \frac{y^2+y+1}{x^2+x+1} = 0$$

A. touch each other
B. are orthogonal
C. are identical
D. none of these

Q.21 The solution of

$$\frac{dy}{dx} = \frac{ax+b}{cy+d}$$

represents a parabola when

A. $a=0,\ c=0$
B. $a=1,\ c=2$
C. $a=2,\ c=1$
D. $a=0,\ c\neq0$ or $c=0,\ a\neq0$

Q.22 The differential equation of all parabolas whose axes are along x-axis is

A. $y_2^2 + y_1 = 0$
B. $y_1^2 = y_2 = 0$
C. $y_1^2 + y_1 y_2 = 0$
D. $y_1^2 + yy_2 = 0$

Q.23 The differential equation of all parabolas whose axes are parallel to y-axis is

A. $\dfrac{d^3y}{dx^3} = 0$

B. $\dfrac{d^2y}{dx^2} = 0$

C. $\dfrac{d^2y}{dx^2} + \dfrac{dy}{dx} = 0$

D. none of these

Q.24 A particle, initially at origin, moves along x-axis according to the rule dx/dt= x + 4.

The time taken by the particle to traverse a distance of 96 units is

A. $\log_5 e$
B. $2 \log_e 5$
C. $2 \log_5 e$
D. $1/2\ (\log_5 e)$

Q.25 Rank of a non-zero matrix is always

A. 0
B. equal to 1
C. greater than 1
D. ≥ 1

Q.26 If A and B are two matrices such that A + B and AB are both defined, then

A. A and B can be any matrices
B. A, B are square matrices not necessarily of same order
C. A, B are square matrices of same order
D. number of columns of A = number of rows of B

Q.27 If A and B are symmetric matrices of order n (A ≠ B), then

A. A + B is skew symmetric
B. A + B is symmetric
C. A + B is a diagonal matrix
D. A + B is a zero matrix

Q.28

If $A = \begin{bmatrix} 1 & 0 \\ 0 & 1 \end{bmatrix}$, then $A^4 =$

A. $\begin{bmatrix} 1 & 0 \\ 0 & 1 \end{bmatrix}$
B. $\begin{bmatrix} 1 & 1 \\ 0 & 0 \end{bmatrix}$
C. $\begin{bmatrix} 0 & 0 \\ 1 & 1 \end{bmatrix}$
D. $\begin{bmatrix} 0 & 1 \\ 1 & 0 \end{bmatrix}$

Q.29

If $A + B = \begin{bmatrix} 1 & 0 \\ 1 & 1 \end{bmatrix}$ and $A - 2B = \begin{bmatrix} -1 & 1 \\ 0 & -1 \end{bmatrix}$, then $A =$

A. $\dfrac{1}{3} \begin{bmatrix} 1 & 1 \\ 2 & 1 \end{bmatrix}$

B. $\dfrac{1}{3} \begin{bmatrix} 2 & 1 \\ 1 & 2 \end{bmatrix}$

C. $\begin{bmatrix} 1 & 1 \\ 2 & 1 \end{bmatrix}$

D. none of these

Q.30 If a matrix A is symmetric as well as skew symmetric then A is a

A. diagonal matrix
B. null matrix
C. unit matrix
D. none of these

Q.31 A plane meets the co-ordinate axes at A, B and C such that the centroid of the triangle is (3, 3, 3). The equation of the plane is

A. $x + y + z = 3$
B. $x + y + x = 9$
C. $3x + 3y + 3z = 1$
D. $9x + 9y + 9z = 1$

Q.32

The distance of the plane

$$\vec{r} \cdot \left(\frac{2}{7}\hat{i} + \frac{3}{7}\hat{j} - \frac{6}{7}\hat{k} \right) = 1 \text{ from the origin is}$$

A. 1　　　　　　　　　　B. 7
C. 1/7　　　　　　　　　D. None of these

Q.33 The radius of the sphere through the points (4,3,0), (0,4,3), (0,5,0) and (4,0,3) is
A. 7　　　　　　　　　　B. 5
C. 7/5　　　　　　　　　D. None of these

Q.34 The points (4, 7,8), (−1, −2,1) and (1,2,5) are the vertices of a
A. Parallelogram　　　　B. Rhombus
C. Rectangle　　　　　　D. Square

Q.35 The equation xy = 0 in three dimensional space represents
A.　a pair of straight lines
B.　a plane
C.　a pair of planes at right angles
D.　a pair of parallel planes

Q.36

The distance of the planes.

$$\vec{r} \cdot \left(3\hat{i} + 4\hat{j} + 12\hat{k} \right) = 65 \text{ from the origin is}$$

A. 65　　　　　　　　　　B. 5
C. -5　　　　　　　　　　D. None of these

Q.37 if the roots of the equation $ax^2 + bx + c = 0$ are negative of each other, then
A. c = 0　　　　　　　　B. b = n = 0
C. b = 0　　　　　　　　D. b = 0, c ≠0

Q.38 If α, β are the roots of the equation $3x^2 + 4x + 7 = 0$, then the value of 1/α+1/β is
A. − 3/7　　B. −4/7　　C. −4/3　　D. −7/4

Q.39 The roots of the equation $4^x - 3.2^{x+2} = 32 = 0$ are
A. 1, 2　　　　　　　　B. 1, 3
C. 2, 3　　　　　　　　D. none of these

Q.40 If α, β are the roots of $x^2 + mx + m^2 = p = 0$, then the value of α+ αβ + β² + p is
A. m　　　　B. -m　　　　C. 0　　　　D. p

Q.41

If $x = 2 + 2 + \cfrac{1}{2 + \cfrac{1}{2 + \cfrac{1}{2 + \ldots}}}$ then the value of

A. √2−1　　　　　　　　B. √2+1
C. 3　　　　　　　　　　D. none of these

Q.42 The function $x \rightarrow ax^2 + 2x + 1$ has one double root if
A. a = 0　　　B. a = − 1　　C. a = 1　　D. a = 2

Q.43 If ABCD is a cyclic quadrilateral then cos A + cos B is equal to
A. 0　　　　　　　　　　B. cos C + cos D
C. -(cos C + cos D)　　　D. none of these

Q.44 If 5 sin θ = 3, then (secθ+tanθ)/(secθ−tanθ) is equal to
A. 1/4　　　　　　　　　B. 4
C. 2　　　　　　　　　　D. none of these

Q.45 cos 2θ is not equal to
A. $2\cos^2 θ - 1$　　　　　　B. $1 - 2\sin^2 θ$
C. $(1+\tan^2θ)/(1-\tan^2θ)$　　D. $(1-\tan2θ)/(1+\tan2θ)$

Q.46 If x = a cos θ + b sin θ and y = a sin θ − b cos θ then a² + b² is equal to
A. $x^2 - y^2$　　　　　　　B. $x^2 + y^2$
C. $(x + y)^2$　　　　　　　D. none of these

Q.47 The minimum value of $\sec^2 θ + \cos^2 θ$ is
A. 1　　　　　　　　　　B. 0
C. 2　　　　　　　　　　D. none of these

Q.48 tan x is periodic with period
A. π/2　　　B. π　　　C. 3π/2　　　D. 2π

Q.49 The area bounded by the curve y = f(x) x-axis the ordinates x = 1 and x = b is (b − 1) sin (3b + 4). then f(x) is
A.　(x − 1) cos (3x + 4)
B.　sin (3x + 4)
C.　sin (3x + 4) + 3 (x − 1) cos (3x + 4)
D.　cos (3x + 4)

Q.50

If $f(x) = A \sin \frac{\pi x}{2} + B$, $f'\left(\frac{1}{2}\right) = \sqrt{2}$ and $\int_0^1 f(x)\, dx = \frac{2A}{\pi}$ then A and B are

A. π/2 and π/2　　　　　　B. 4/π and 0
C. 0 and 4/π　　　　　　　D. none of these

Q.51

The values of the integral $\int_0^{1.5} \left[x^2\right] dx$ is equal to

A. 1.125　　　　　　　　B. 0.5
C. 2√2　　　　　　　　　D. none of these

Q.52 The area bounded by the curve y = x², the X-axis, and the line x = 2^{1/3} is divided into two equal areas by the lines x = k. The value of k is
A. $2^{1/3} - 1$　　B. 1　　C. $2^{-2/3}$　　D. $2^{-1/3}$

Q.53 If g′′(x) is continuous for all x, g(0) = f′(1) = 1 and if

$$\int_0^1 xg''(x)\, dx$$

vanishes , then the values of

g(1) is

A. 2　　　B. -2　　　C. 3　　　D. $4\frac{1}{2}$

Q.54

$$\int \frac{x^{\frac{1}{4}}}{1+x^{\frac{1}{2}}}\, dx \text{ is equal to}$$

A. $4\left(\dfrac{x^{\frac{3}{4}}}{3} - x^{\frac{1}{4}} + tan^{-1}\left(x^{\frac{1}{4}}\right)\right)$

B. $4\left(\dfrac{x^{\frac{3}{4}}}{3} - x^{\frac{1}{4}}\, tan^{-1}\left(x^{\frac{1}{4}}\right)\right)$

C. $4\left(\dfrac{x^{\frac{3}{4}}}{3} - x^{\frac{1}{4}} - tan^{-1}\left(x^{\frac{1}{4}}\right)\right)$

D. none of these

Q.55 The range of the function f(x) = x – [x] is

A. (a) [0, 1)　　　　**B.** [0, 1]
C. (0, 1)　　　　**D.** none of these

Q.56 Which of the following is an even function ?

A. √x　　　　**B.** $x^2 + \sin^2 x$
C. $\sin^3 x$　　　　**D.** none of these

Q.57 Let f(x) = |x–1| , then

A. $f(x) = \sqrt{\left(f(x)\right)^2}$

B. f(x +y) = f(x) + f (y)
C. f (|x|) = |f(x)|
D. f(x) = (f(x))²

Q.58 If f(x) = [x] and g(x) = x –[x], then which of the following functions is the zero function

A. (f + g) (x)　　　　**B.** (f g) (x)
C. (f - g) (x)　　　　**D.** (fog)

Q.59 Let f(x) = x, g (x) = 1/x and h(x) = f(x) g(x), then h(x) = 1 iff

A. x is a real number
B. x is a rational number
C. x is an irrational number
D. x is a real number ≠ 0

Q.60 If (1/4)ˣ= x, then x =

A. 0　　　　**B.** 1　　　　**C.** 1/2　　　　**D.** 2

Analytical Ability & Logical Reasoning

Q.61 Direction : Each of the following question consists of a statement followed by 2 arguments I and II.
Give answer
a)if only argument I is strong
b)if only argument II is strong
c)if either I or II is strong
d)if neither I or II are strong
e)if both I and II follow
Statement : In Italy, trains are more convenient and economical than cabs.
Argument :
I. Italy is an expensive city.
II. Train services are reasonably good in Italy.
A.　If only I is implicit
B.　If only II is implicit.
C.　If either I or II is implicit.
D.　If neither I nor II is implicit.

Q.62 Direction : Each of the following question consists of a statement followed by 2 arguments I and II. Give answer
a)if only argument I is strong
b)if only argument II is strong
c)if either I or II is strong
d)if neither I or II are strong
e)if both I and II follow
Statement : The survey for this year reports that the number of people living below poverty line has increased in urban areas.
Argument :
I. People living in rural areas are not below the poverty line.
II. A similar survey was conducted last year.
A.　If only I is implicit.
B.　If only II is implicit.
C.　If either I or II is implicit.
D.　If neither I nor II is implicit.

Q.63 Direction : Each of the following question consists of a statement followed by 2 arguments I and II. Give answer
a)if only argument I is strong
b)if only argument II is strong
c)if either I or II is strong
d)if neither I or II are strong
e)if both I and II follow
Statement : An advertisement by ABC clinic says that their medicine is very effective for fighting the problem of obesity.
Argument :
I. Other such type of medicines available in the market are not that effective.
II. Obesity cannot be controlled without medicines.
A.　If only I is implicit.
B.　If only II is implicit.
C.　If either I or II is implicit.
D.　If neither I nor II is implicit.

Q.64 Direction : Each of the following question consists of a statement followed by 2 arguments I and II.

Give answer

a)if only argument I is strong

b)if only argument II is strong

c)if either I or II is strong

d)if neither I or II are strong

e)if both I and II follow

Statement : A notice board on ABC mobile company says that if anybody has any kind of problem with his handset, he is free to contact their helpdesk immediately.

Argument :

I. Help desk will solve their all handset problems.

II. The problem will not be solved if complaint is not made immediately.

A. If only I is implicit.

B. If only II is implicit.

C. If either I or II is implicit.

D. If neither I or II is implicit.

Q.65 Direction : Each of the following question consists of a statement followed by 2 arguments I and II.

Give answer

a)if only argument I is strong

b)if only argument II is strong

c)if either I or II is strong

d)if neither I or II are strong

e)if both I and II follow

Statement : A paper advertisement by a ABC bank says that there education loan rates are lower than any other banks.

Argument :

I. Some other banks also provide education loans.

II. Different banks charge different interest rates on education loans.

A. If only I is implicit.

B. If only II is implicit.

C. If either I or II is implicit.

D. If both I and II are implicit.

Q.66 Leopard : cub :: Mule : ?

A. foal   **B.** cub   **C.** chick   **D.** poult

Q.67 Mole : pup :: Chicken : ?

A. cub   **B.** chick   **C.** cygnet   **D.** joey

Q.68 Crocodile : hatchling :: Leopard : ?

A. pup / calf   **B.** cub

C. foal   **D.** kid / billy

Q.69 Rabbit : bunny :: Anteater : ?

A. hatchling   **B.** caterpillar

C. pup   **D.** owlet

Q.70 Gull : chick :: Hummingbird : ?

A. infant   **B.** eyas   **C.** chick   **D.** antling

Q.71 P and Q are brothers of R. Q is son of S and T. S is the daughter of U. A is the father-in-law of T. B is son of U. What is the relationship of Q to B?

A. Nephew   **B.** Neice

C. Maternal Uncle   **D.** Paternal Aunt

Q.72 P and Q are brothers of R. Q is son of S and T. S is the daughter of U. A is the father-in-law of T. B is son of U. What is the relationship of P to B?

A. Nephew   **B.** Paternal Uncle

C. Neice   **D.** Paternal Aunt

Q.73 P and Q are brothers of R. Q is son of S and T. S is the daughter of U. A is the father-in-law of T. B is son of U. What is the relationship of P to A ?

A. Grandson   **B.** Son

C. Daughter   **D.** Father

Q.74 A is the sister of B. B is married to C. C is the son of D. A is the mother of E. F is the father of G. F has only 1 son and 1 daughter. G is the daughter of A. H is the son of B.

How is H related to C ?

A. Son   **B.** Daughter

C. Sister   **D.** Brother

Q.75 A is the sister of B. B is married to C. C is the son of D. A is the mother of E. F is the father of G. F has only 1 son and 1 daughter. G is the daughter of A. H is the son of B.

Find how is G related to D ?

A. Maternal Uncle   **B.** Paternal Uncle

C. Nephew   **D.** Granddaughter

Q.76 In a certain code

'facing problem with money' is coded as 'st np cg rt',

'money problem very serious' is coded as 'nt st np vw',

'serious with every person' is coded as 'rt nt pr ab',

'facing person each day' is coded as 'cg ab no cd'.

Based on the above data, answer the following questions.

Find the code word for 'Serious' ?

A. cd   **B.** vw   **C.** pr   **D.** nt

Q.77 In a certain code

'facing problem with money' is coded as 'st np cg rt',

'money problem very serious' is coded as 'nt st np vw',

'serious with every person' is coded as 'rt nt pr ab',

'facing person each day' is coded as 'cg ab no cd'.

Based on the above data, answer the following questions.

Find the code word for "**With**"?

A. cg   **B.** rt   **C.** nt   **D.** ab

Q.78 In a certain code

'facing problem with money' is coded as 'st np cg rt',

'money problem very serious' is coded as 'nt st np vw',

'serious with every person' is coded as 'rt nt pr ab',

'facing person each day' is coded as 'cg ab no cd'.

Based on the above data, answer the following questions.

Find the code word for "Facing"?

A. cg   **B.** rt   **C.** nt   **D.** ab

Q.79 Study the information below and answer the following question :

In a certain code language,

'committee to protect journalists' is written as 'es fr re pt',

'protect people in city' is written as 'ch ba mo fr'

'people to follow on' is written as 're dv ch gi'

'follow tips to protect' is written as 're gi fr yu'

How is the word "people" coded ?

A. pt   **B.** re   **C.** fr   **D.** ch

Q.80 Study the information below and answer the following question :

In a certain code language,

'committee to protect journalists' is written as 'es fr re pt',

'protect people in city' is written as 'ch ba mo fr'

'people to follow on' is written as 're dv ch gi'

'follow tips to protect' is written as 're gi fr yu'

How is the word "protect" coded ?

A. fr   **B.** re   **C.** ch   **D.** yu

Computer Awareness

Q.81 The data blocks of a very large file in the Unix file system are allocated using

A. contiguous allocation

B. linked allocation

C. indexed allocation

D. an extension of indexed allocation

Q.82 Consider a set of n tasks with known runtimes r1, r2, ... rn to be run on a uniprocessor machine. Which of the following processor scheduling algorithms will result in the maximum throughput ?

A. round robin

B. shortest job first

C. highest response ratio next

D. first come first serve

Q.83 Using a larger block size in a fixed block size file system leads to

A. better disk throughput but poorer disk space utilization

B. better disk throughput and better disk space utilization

C. poor disk throughput but better disk space utilization

D. poor disk throughput and poor disk space utilization

Q.84 A system uses FIFO policy for page replacement. It has 4 pages frames with no pages loaded to begin with. The system first access 100 distinct pages in some order and then access the same 100 pages but now in reverse order. How many page faults will occur ?

A. 197   **B.** 192   **C.** 196   **D.** 195

Q.85 Consider an OS capable of loading and executing a single sequential user process at a time. The disk head scheduling algorithm used is FCFS. If FCFS is replaced by shortest seek time first (SSTF), claimed by the vendor to give 50% better benchmark results, what is the expected improvement in the IN/OUT performance of user programs ?

A. 50%   **B.** 40%   **C.** 25%   **D.** 0%

Q.86 Acceptance testing is also known as

A. Grey box testing   **B.** White box testing

C. Alpha Testing   **D.** Beta testing

Q.87 The testing in which code is checked

A. Black box testing   **B.** White box testing

C. Red box testing   **D.** Green box testing

Q.88 Maintenance testing is performed using which methodology?

A. Retesting

B. Sanity testing

C. Breadth test and depth test

D. Confirmation testing

Q.89 Lower and upper limits are present in which chart ?

A. Run chart

B. Bar chart

C. Control chart

D. All of the mentioned

Q.90 What is Cyclomatic complexity?

A. Black box testing   **B.** White box testing

C. Yellow box testing   **D.** Green box testing

Q.91 GIF is the extension of which file

A. Image source format

B. bitmap image format

C. Cursor image file

D. Both b & c

Q.92 .ilb is the extension of which file

A. Intermediate StarOffice interface definition file.Initialization file.

B. Include file.

C. Initialization file.

D. Installation configuration file.

Q.93 What is the correct option of Extended Markup Language extension

A. .xl   **B.** .xml   **C.** .css   **D.** .eml

Q.94 What is the correct option of Compiled java source code file.

A. .class   **B.** .java   **C.** .CPP   **D.** .cxx

Q.95 .unx is the extension of which file

A. UNIX-update file

B. UNIX-create file

C. UNIX-specific makefile

D. UNIX-source file

Q.96 In how many generations a computer can be classified ?

A. 3   **B.** 4   **C.** 5   **D.** 6

Q.97 In order to tell Excel that we are entering a formula in cell, we must begin with an operator such as

A. $ **B.** @   **C.** +   **D.** =

Q.98 The basic architecture of computer was developed by

A. John Von Neumann **B.** Charles Babbage

C. Blaise Pascal **D.** Garden Moore

Q.99 Which protocol provides e-mail facility among different hosts ?

A. FTP **B.** SMTP

C. TELNET **D.** SNMP

Q.100 Fifth generation computers are based on

A. Artificial Intelligence

B. Programming Intelligence

C. System Knowledge

D. VVLSI

English

Q.101 To make clean breast of

A. To praise oneself

B. To gain prominence

C. To confess without of reserve

D. To destroy before it blooms

Q.102 To keeps one's temper

A. To become hungry

B. To be in good mood

C. To preserve ones energy

D. To be aloof from

Q.103 Choose the antonym of "**Foremost**"

A. Hindmost **B.** Unimportant

C. Mature **D.** Disposed

Q.104 Choose the antonym of "**Beautiful**"

A. Wonderful **B.** Graceful

C. Ugly **D.** Handsome

Q.105 Choose the antonym of "**Protects**"

A. Defends **B.** Deprives **C.** Deserts **D.** Devises

Q.106 Choose the Synonym of "FOSTERING"

A. Safeguarding **B.** Neglecting

C. Ignoring **D.** Nurturing

Q.107 Choose the Synonym of "PROPEL"

A. Drive **B.** Burst

C. Acclimatize **D.** Modify

Q.108 Choose the Synonym of "MASSIVE"

A. Strong **B.** Little **C.** Gaping **D.** Huge

Q.109 Find the correctly spelt word.

A. Adulation **B.** Adlation

C. Aduletion **D.** Addulation

Q.110 Find correct spelt word.

A. Connillatory **B.** Concilletry

C. Conciliatory **D.** Concilletry

Q.111 Find the correct spelt word.

A. Desiccate **B.** Desicate

C. Descicate **D.** Deccicate

Q.112 Find common error :

Ram was / senior to / Sam in college.

A. Ram was **B.** senior to

C. Sam in college. **D.** No error

Q.113 Find common error :

It was him / who came / running / into the classroom.

A. It was him **B.** who came

C. running **D.** into the classroom.

Q.114 Find common error :

The capital of Yemen / is situating / 2190 meters above / the sea level.

A. The capital of Yemen

B. is situating

C. 2190 meters above

D. the sea level.

Q.115 One Word Substitution :

A person who renounces the world and practices self-discipline in order to attain salvation

A. Sceptic **B.** Ascetic

C. Devotee **D.** Antiquarian

Q.116 Find One word-Substitution :

One who abandons his religious faith

A. Apostate **B.** Prostate **C.** Profane **D.** Agnostic

Q.117 Find One word-substitution :

A hater of knowledge and learning

A. Bibliophile **B.** Philologist

C. Misogynist **D.** Misologist

Q.118 Find out whether there is any grammatical error in below sentence.

We discussed about the problem so thoroughly / on the eve of the examination / that I found it very easy to work it out.

A. We discussed about the problem so thoroughly

B. on the eve of the examination

C. that I found it very easy to work it out.

D. No error

Q.119 Find out whether there is any grammatical error in below sentence.

If I had known / this yesterday / I will have helped him

A. If I had known

B. this yesterday

C. I will have helped him

D. No error

Q.120 I saw a ...... of cows in the field.

A. group **B.** herd **C.** swarm **D.** flock

// Smart Answer Sheet //

Correct — Percentage of students who answered correctly.   **Skipped** — Percentage of students who skipped.

Q.	Ans.	Correct / Skipped	Q.	Ans.	Correct / Skipped	Q.	Ans.	Correct / Skipped	Q.	Ans.	Correct / Skipped	Q.	Ans.	Correct / Skipped
1	B	84.13 % / 12.15 %	17	C	84.26 % / 10.03 %	33	B	88.73 % / 11.27 %	49	C	81.35 % / 14.64 %	65	D	77.93 % / 16.19 %
2	A	84.34 % / 10.65 %	18	A	87.21 % / 10.77 %	34	A	83.38 % / 15.12 %	50	B	87.34 % / 12.07 %	66	A	86.98 % / 13.0 %
3	C	77.47 % / 22.03 %	19	C	86.93 % / 11.83 %	35	C	83.07 % / 15.98 %	51	C	83.83 % / 11.75 %	67	B	86.96 % / 12.9 %
4	B	85.43 % / 11.41 %	20	B	76.18 % / 17.44 %	36	B	84.64 % / 11.1 %	52	B	87.54 % / 11.22 %	68	B	79.22 % / 11.16 %
5	D	77.99 % / 14.01 %	21	D	85.84 % / 13.04 %	37	C	80.05 % / 12.2 %	53	A	87.26 % / 10.36 %	69	C	79.3 % / 11.13 %
6	B	89.55 % / 10.25 %	22	D	85.15 % / 12.35 %	38	B	77.93 % / 15.83 %	54	A	78.2 % / 20.09 %	70	C	83.66 % / 14.97 %
7	B	77.09 % / 18.72 %	23	A	89.9 % / 10.05 %	39	C	76.17 % / 22.67 %	55	A	89.73 % / 10.06 %	71	A	89.61 % / 10.2 %
8	D	78.58 % / 13.47 %	24	B	83.9 % / 10.73 %	40	C	86.7 % / 12.39 %	56	B	84.6 % / 10.39 %	72	A	78.08 % / 10.51 %
9	D	76.02 % / 11.94 %	25	D	76.76 % / 22.22 %	41	B	78.43 % / 14.73 %	57	A	86.45 % / 11.85 %	73	A	83.6 % / 13.95 %
10	B	89.16 % / 10.5 %	26	C	88.05 % / 10.95 %	42	C	81.82 % / 12.42 %	58	D	80.61 % / 11.75 %	74	A	84.93 % / 13.03 %
11	D	89.2 % / 10.05 %	27	B	77.76 % / 21.24 %	43	C	82.2 % / 14.96 %	59	D	88.23 % / 10.41 %	75	D	82.38 % / 10.0 %
12	B	83.44 % / 13.24 %	28	A	88.0 % / 10.59 %	44	B	77.49 % / 18.08 %	60	B	80.33 % / 17.38 %	76	D	84.6 % / 13.61 %
13	B	87.96 % / 11.07 %	29	A	85.34 % / 10.15 %	45	C	79.19 % / 12.12 %	61	B	89.89 % / 10.01 %	77	B	76.87 % / 20.52 %
14	B	83.37 % / 13.81 %	30	B	89.0 % / 10.13 %	46	B	80.09 % / 13.9 %	62	B	88.02 % / 11.81 %	78	A	89.17 % / 10.15 %
15	C	84.65 % / 12.3 %	31	B	84.68 % / 12.9 %	47	C	87.49 % / 10.28 %	63	D	80.06 % / 15.27 %	79	D	77.96 % / 16.44 %
16	C	84.69 % / 13.59 %	32	A	76.23 % / 19.22 %	48	B	79.85 % / 17.83 %	64	A	86.79 % / 10.09 %	80	A	80.57 % / 15.5 %

Q.	Ans.	Correct / Skipped	Q.	Ans.	Correct / Skipped	Q.	Ans.	Correct / Skipped	Q.	Ans.	Correct / Skipped	Q.	Ans.	Correct / Skipped
81	D	85.3 % / 14.46 %	89	A	85.41 % / 14.44 %	97	D	85.3 % / 11.99 %	105	C	85.63 % / 11.26 %	113	A	86.17 % / 12.25 %
82	B	80.55 % / 17.13 %	90	B	88.67 % / 10.45 %	98	A	77.56 % / 14.93 %	106	D	83.18 % / 15.86 %	114	B	81.08 % / 11.57 %
83	D	89.46 % / 10.23 %	91	A	88.78 % / 10.08 %	99	B	76.93 % / 22.72 %	107	A	89.67 % / 10.28 %	115	B	88.7 % / 10.05 %
84	C	88.99 % / 10.51 %	92	A	88.75 % / 10.46 %	100	A	86.45 % / 12.08 %	108	D	88.54 % / 10.34 %	116	A	77.76 % / 18.65 %
85	D	77.19 % / 12.71 %	93	B	81.34 % / 13.76 %	101	C	77.81 % / 21.65 %	109	A	84.6 % / 10.61 %	117	D	87.27 % / 11.8 %
86	D	86.49 % / 11.61 %	94	A	84.97 % / 10.62 %	102	B	84.57 % / 10.79 %	110	C	86.15 % / 12.64 %	118	A	83.76 % / 15.0 %
87	B	86.81 % / 12.87 %	95	C	80.21 % / 11.69 %	103	B	84.57 % / 12.82 %	111	A	83.93 % / 11.91 %	119	C	82.41 % / 16.63 %
88	C	76.38 % / 19.92 %	96	C	81.76 % / 16.89 %	104	C	83.8 % / 10.71 %	112	D	76.34 % / 20.04 %	120	B	76.31 % / 11.46 %

//Hints and Solutions//

1. As (1,1,1), (2,2,2), (3,3,3), (4,4,4), (5,5,5), (6,6,6) are only favourable outcomes,

∴ Required probability = 6/216.

Hence, the required probability = 1/36

2. Two digits, one form each set can be selected in 99 = 81 ways.

Favourable outcomes are(1,9), (2,8), (3,7), (4,6), (5,5), (6,4), (7,3), (8,2) and (9,1).

3. Since the coin has tail on both the sides, therefore, the event 'a head' appears on any throw is impossible.

4. Let e be an event then P (E or not E) = P(E∪BE') = P (E) + P (E') = 1.

5. It is a case of Bernoullian trials where success is 'a six', p = 1/6 and n = 4.

So mean number of successes = np = 4*1/6.

6. Out of a total of 52 cards, number of court cards is 12.

7. As x > 1, therefore, $\log_{10} x > 0$.

Now, $2 \log_{10} x - \log_x (.01) = 2 \log_{10} x - \log_x (10^{-2}) = 2 (\log_{10}x + \log_x 10) = 2 (y+1/y)$

where $y = \log_{10}x > 0$

$= 2 \{(\sqrt{y}-1\sqrt{y})^2+2\} \ge 4$.

∴ Minimum value of given function is 4. Note that the value is 4 for x = 10.

(∵ $2 \log_{10} 10 \log_{10} (.01) 2 \times 1 - (-2) = 4$)

8.
For $0 < x < 1$, $\log_{10} x < 0$ and for $x > 1$, $\log_{10} x > 0$. When $x > 1$ the value of $2\log_{10}x - \log_x .01$ is greater than or equal to 4. However, for $0 < x < 1$,
$2 \log_{10} x - \log_x (.01) = 2 \log_{10} x - \log_x (10^{-2})$
$= 2 \log_{10} x + 2\log_x 10$
$= 2 \left(y + \frac{1}{y}\right)$ where $y = \log_{10} x < 0 \le -4$
(when $x < 0$, $x + \frac{1}{x} \ge -2$)
So, least value of the given function does not exist.

9.
Since a, b, c are positive real numbers, therefore,
$$\frac{\frac{a}{b} + \frac{b}{a}}{2} \ge \sqrt{\frac{a}{b} \frac{b}{a}} \quad (A.M. \ge G.M.)$$
$$\Rightarrow \frac{a}{b} + \frac{b}{a} \ge 2$$
Similarly, $\frac{b}{c} + \frac{c}{b} \ge 2$ and $\frac{a}{c} + \frac{c}{a} \ge 2$.
Adding these inequalities, we get
$$\frac{a}{b} + \frac{b}{a} + \frac{b}{c} + \frac{c}{b} + \frac{a}{c} + \frac{c}{a} \ge 6$$
$$\Rightarrow \frac{a+c}{b} + \frac{b+c}{a} + \frac{c+a}{b} \ge 6$$
Note that the value of given expression is 6 when a = b = c.

10.
If α, β, γ are any thee numbers then
$\alpha^2 + \beta^2 + \gamma^2 - \alpha\beta - \beta\gamma - \gamma\alpha$
$= \frac{1}{2}\left\{(\alpha - \beta)^2 + (\beta - \gamma)^2 + (\gamma - \alpha)^2\right\} \ge 0$
$\Rightarrow \alpha^2 + \beta^2 + \gamma^2 \ge \alpha\beta + \beta\gamma + \gamma\alpha$
$\Rightarrow \tan^2\left(\frac{A}{2}\right) + \tan^2\left(\frac{B}{2}\right) + \tan^2\left(\frac{C}{2}\right) \ge$
$\tan\frac{A}{2}\tan\frac{B}{2} + \tan\frac{C}{2} + \tan\frac{C}{2}\tan\frac{A}{2}$
$\Rightarrow \tan^2\left(\frac{A}{2}\right) + \tan^2\left(\frac{B}{2}\right) + \tan^2\left(\frac{C}{2}\right) \ge 1$
$\left(\because In\, a\, \Delta ABC,\, \tan\frac{A}{2}\tan\frac{B}{2} + \tan\frac{B}{2}\tan\frac{C}{2} + \tan\frac{C}{2}\tan\frac{A}{2} = 1\right)$
Note that the value of the given expression is 1 when
A = B = C = 60°.

11.
Since the arithmetic mean of any number of positive numbers is greater than or equal to their harmonic mean, therefore,
$\frac{a+b+c}{3} \ge \frac{3}{\frac{1}{a}+\frac{1}{b}+\frac{1}{c}}$
$\Rightarrow (a + b + c)\left(\frac{1}{a} + \frac{1}{b} + \frac{1}{c}\right) \ge 9$
Note that the value of the given expression is 9 when
a = b = c

12.
Let the numbers be $x_1, x_2, x_3, ...x_n$, then we are given that $x_1 x_2 x_3 ... x_n = 1$.
Also, $\frac{x_1 + x_2 + x_3 + ... + x_n}{n} \ge (x_1 x_2 x_3 ... x_n)^{\frac{1}{n}}$ $(A.M. \ge G.M.)$
$\Rightarrow x_1 + x_2 + x_3 + ... + x_n \ge n$
$(x_1 x_2 x_3 ... x_n = 1)$
Note that equality holds when
$x_1 = x_2 = x_3 = ... = x_n = 1$.

13.

$$\text{In this case } \vec{b} = -2\,\vec{a}$$

14.
If the given vectors are $\vec{a}$, $\vec{b}$ and $\vec{c}$, then $\vec{c} = \vec{a} + \vec{b}$ and also $\vec{a} \cdot \vec{b} = 0$, therefore, the given vectors form a right angled triangle.

15.

$$\vec{a} \bullet \vec{a} = 0 \Rightarrow \left|\vec{a}\right|^2 = 0 \Rightarrow \left|\vec{a}\right| = 0$$

16.
Each of the triangles AOB, BOC and COD is an equilateral triangle, O being the centre of the hexagon, therefore, ∠ AOD = 180° and $\vec{AD} = \vec{AO} + \vec{OD}$
$= \vec{BC} + \vec{BC} = 2\vec{BC} = 2\vec{b}$.
(ABCO and BCDO are parallelograms)

17.

$$\vec{AB} + \vec{AC} = \vec{AD} + \vec{DB} + \vec{AD} + \vec{DC}$$
$$= 2\vec{AD} + \left(\vec{DB} + \vec{DC}\right) = 2\vec{AD} + \vec{0}$$
$$= 2\vec{AD}$$

18. Vector

$\hat{i}$

makes angles 0°, 90° and 90° respectively with +ve directions of x-axis, y-axis and z-axis.

Hence direction cosines of i are < cos 0°, cos 90°, cos 90° .

i.e. < 1, 0, 0 >.

19. Given relation is $y = A/x + B$ ....(1)

Differentiating w.r.t. x, we get $y_1 = -A/x^2$ or $x^2 y_1 = -A$

Again differentiating w.r.t. x, we get

$x^2 y_2 + y_1 2x = 0$ or $xy_2 + 2y_1 = 0$

20.

Since $\frac{dy}{dx}$ is equal to the slope by the tangent and if we denote the two families by C_1 and C_2, then

$$\left(\frac{dy}{dx}\right)_{C_1} = \frac{x^2 + x + 1}{y^2 + y + 1},\ \left(\frac{dy}{dx}\right)_{C_2} = -\left(\frac{y^2 + y + 1}{x^2 + x + 1}\right)$$

$$\Rightarrow \left(\frac{dy}{dx}\right)_{C_1} \times \left(\frac{dy}{dx}\right)_{C_2} = -1$$

Hence, the two families are orthogonal.

21.

Given differential equation is $\frac{dy}{dx} = \frac{ax + b}{cy + d}$

$(cy + d)\, dy = (ax + b)\, dx$

$\frac{cy^2}{2} + dy = \frac{ax^2}{2} + bx + k,\ k \in R$

This will represents a parabola if exactly one term of second degree occurs i.e. if either $c = 0, a \neq 0$ or $c \neq 0, a = 0$.

22.

Equation of a parabola whose axis is along X-axis is
$y^2 = Ax + B$ ......(1)
If A and B are allowed to vary, then (1) is the equation of the said family (note that $A \neq 0$).
Differentiating (1) w.r.t x, we get
$2 yy_1 = A$.
Again differentiating w.r.t. x, we obtain
$2 (yy_2 + y_1 y_1) = 0$ or $yy_2 + y_1^2 = 0$

23.

Equation of any parabola whose axis is parallel to y-axis is of the form
$(x - h)^2 = \lambda (y - k), \lambda \neq 0$
Hence, the equation of the family of parabolas with axes parallel to y-axis can be written as $y = ax^2 + bx + c$, where a, b, c are arbitrary constants (note that $a \neq 0$). Differentiating thrice w.r.t. x, we get
$\frac{d^3 y}{dx^3} = 0$, which is the required differential equation.

24.

Given equation is $\frac{dx}{dt} = x + 4$

$$\Rightarrow \frac{dx}{x+4} = dt \Rightarrow \int \frac{dx}{x+4} = \int dt + C$$

$\Rightarrow \log_e (x + 4) = t + C$ ....(1)

When $t = 0$, $x = 0 \Rightarrow \log_e 4 = C$ ....(2)

From (1) and (2),

$$\log_e (x + 4) = t + \log_e 4 \Rightarrow t = \log_e \left(\frac{x+4}{4}\right)$$

when $x = 96$, $t = \log_e \left(\frac{96+4}{4}\right)$

$= \log_e 25 = 2 \log_e 5$

25. Rank of a non-zero matrix is always greater than or equal to 1.

26. A + B is defined $\Rightarrow$ A and B are of same order and AB is defined $\Rightarrow$ number of columns in

A equal the number of rows in B.

27. For x = 0, the determinant of L.H.S. becomes a determinant of skew symmetric matrix of oddorder (third) and hence its value is 0.

So, x = 0 is a root of the given equation.

28.

Now, $A^2 = AA = \begin{bmatrix} 1 & 0 \\ 0 & 1 \end{bmatrix} \begin{bmatrix} 1 & 0 \\ 0 & 1 \end{bmatrix} = \begin{bmatrix} 1 & 0 \\ 0 & 1 \end{bmatrix}$

$\Rightarrow A^4 = (A^2)^2 = (A^2)(A^2) = II = I$

29.

Given $A + B = \begin{bmatrix} 1 & 0 \\ 1 & 1 \end{bmatrix}$ ....(1)

and $A - 2B = \begin{bmatrix} -1 & 1 \\ 0 & -1 \end{bmatrix}$ ....(2)

Multiplying (1) by 2 and adding it to (2), we get
$(2A + 2B) + (A - 2B)$

$= 2 \begin{bmatrix} 1 & 0 \\ 1 & 1 \end{bmatrix} + \begin{bmatrix} -1 & 1 \\ 0 & -1 \end{bmatrix}$

$\Rightarrow 3A = \begin{bmatrix} 1 & 1 \\ 2 & 1 \end{bmatrix} \Rightarrow A = \frac{1}{3} \begin{bmatrix} 1 & 1 \\ 2 & 1 \end{bmatrix}$

30. Let A be both symmetric and skew symmetric,

then $A^t = A$ and also $A^t = -A$

$\Rightarrow A = -A \Rightarrow 2A = O.$

31. If OA = a, OB = b, and OC = c, then centroid of $\triangle$ ABC is $(a/3, b/3, c/3) = (3,3,3)$

a = b = c = 9 and hence, the equation of the palne is

x/a + y/b + z/c = 1

i.e. x/9 + y/9 + z/9 = 1

32.

The given equation is the form $\vec{r} \bullet \hat{n} = p$

where $\hat{n}$ is a unit vector and p > 0 i.e. in the normal form.

33. Each of the four point is at a fixed distance = 5 from the origin. So, radius of the sphere is 5 and centre at (0,0,0).

34. if the points (in order) are A, B, C and D, then [AC] and [BD] bisect each other $|AC| \neq |BD|$, $|AB| \neq BC$.

35. $xy = 0 \Leftrightarrow x = 0$ or $y = 0$. Hence locus of $xy = 0$ is the union of all points which lie in equation $xy = 0$ represents a pair of perpendicular planes.

36.

The given equation is

$\vec{r} \bullet (3\hat{i} + 4\hat{j} + 12\hat{k}) = 65$

or $\vec{r} \bullet \left(\frac{3}{13}\hat{i} + \frac{4}{13}\hat{j} + \frac{12}{13}\hat{k}\right) = 5$, $which$ is the form $\vec{r} \bullet \hat{n} = p$.

37. In this case, the sum of the roots is zero

$\Rightarrow -b/a = 0 \Rightarrow b = 0$

38. $1/\alpha + 1/\beta = (\alpha + \beta)/\alpha\beta = -(4/3)/(7/3) = -4/7$

39. The given equation can be written as $(2^x)^2 - 3.2^x . 2^2 + 32 = 0$

i.e. $t^2 - 12t + 32 = 0$, where $t = 2^x$

$\Rightarrow t = 8, 4$

$\Rightarrow 2^x = 2^3, 2^2$

$\Rightarrow x = 3$ or 2

40. here, $\alpha + \beta = -m/1 = -m$ and $\alpha\beta = m^2 + p$

Hence $\alpha^2 + \alpha\beta + \beta^2 + p$

$= (\alpha + \beta)^2 - \alpha\beta + p$

$= (-m^2) - (m^2 + p) + p = 0$

41.

Given $x = 2 + \frac{1}{x} \Rightarrow x^2 - 2x - 1 = 0$

$\Rightarrow \frac{2 \pm \sqrt{4+4}}{2} = 1 \pm \sqrt{2}$, but $x > 2$, therefore, $x = \sqrt{2} + 1$

42. Let $f(x) = ax^2 + 2x + 1$, then $f(x) = 0$ has a double root means that $f(x) = 0$ has equal roots

Hence $2^2 - 4a = 0$ (disc. = 0)

43. $A + C = 180°$ and $B + D = 180°$,

therefore, $\cos A + \cos B = \cos (180° - C) + \cos (180° - D) = -(\cos C + \cos D)$.

44.
$(\sec\theta + \tan\theta)/(\sec\theta - \tan\theta) = (1+\sin\theta)/(1-\sin\theta) = (1+3/5)/(1-3/5) = 4$

45. $\cos 2\theta = 2\cos^2\theta - 1$

$= 1 - 2\sin 2\theta = (1 - \tan 2\theta)/(1 + \tan 2\theta)$

46. Given $x = a\cos\theta + b\sin\theta$ .....(1)

and $y = a\sin\theta - b\cos\theta$ .....(2)

squaring (1) and (2) and adding, we obtain

$x^2 + y^2 = a^2 + b^2$

47. $\sec^2\theta + \cos^2\theta = (1/\cos^2\theta) + \cos^2\theta$

$= (\cos\theta - 1/\cos\theta)^2 + 2 \geq 2$

48. As $\tan(\pi + x) \tan x$ for all x, therefore, $\tan x$ is periodic with period π as π is the smallest positive number to satisfy the property.

49. From the given result, it is observed that an intergral of $f(x)$ is $(x - 1)\sin(3x + 4)$ which vanishes

at $x = 1$ and at b its value is $(b - 1)\sin(3b + 4)$

$\therefore f(x) = d/dx\{(x-1)\}\sin(3x + 4)\}$

$= 3(x-1)\cos(3x + 4) + \sin(3x + 4)$

50.

Given $f(x) = A \sin \frac{\pi x}{2} + B$

$\Rightarrow f'(x) = \frac{\pi A}{2} \cos \frac{\pi x}{2}$

$\Rightarrow f'\left(\frac{1}{2}\right) = \frac{\pi A}{2} \cos \frac{\pi}{4}$

$\Rightarrow \sqrt{2} = \frac{\pi A}{2} \cdot \frac{1}{\sqrt{2}} \Rightarrow A = \frac{4}{\pi}$

also, $\int f(x) \, dx = \int_0^1 \left(A \sin \frac{\pi x}{2} + B\right)$

$= \left[-\frac{2A}{\pi} \cos \frac{\pi x}{2} + Bx\right]_0^1$

$\Rightarrow \frac{2A}{\pi} = B - \left(\frac{-2A}{\pi}\right) \Rightarrow B = 0$

51.

$\int_0^{1.5} [x^2] \, dx = \int_0^1 [x^2] \, dx + \int_1^{\sqrt{2}} [x^2] \, dx + \int_{\sqrt{2}}^{1.5} [x^2] \, dx$

$= 0 + \int_1^{\sqrt{2}} 1 \, dx + \int_{\sqrt{2}}^{1.5} 2 \, dx$

52.

$\int_0^k x^2 dx = \int_k^{2^{\frac{1}{3}}} x^2 dx \Rightarrow \frac{k^3}{3} = \frac{2}{3} - \frac{k^3}{3}$

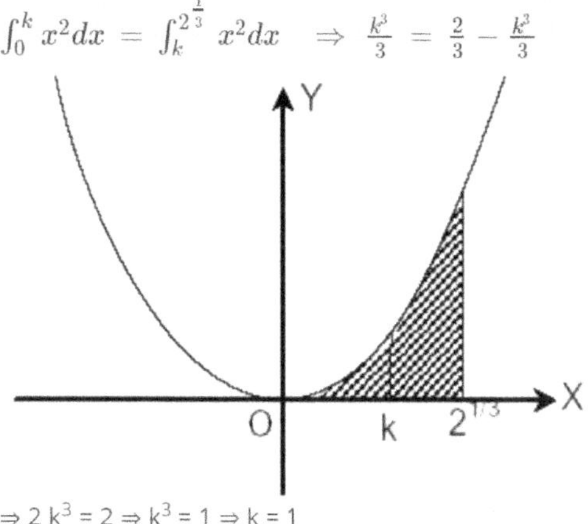

$\Rightarrow 2k^3 = 2 \Rightarrow k^3 = 1 \Rightarrow k = 1$

53.

Given $\int_0^1 x \, g''(x) \, dx = 0$, integrating L.H.S

by parts $= [xg'(x)]_0^1 - \int_0^1 g'(x) \, dx = 0$

$\Rightarrow g'(1) - (g(1) - g(0)) = 0$

$\Rightarrow g(1) = g'(1) + g(0) = 1 + 1 = 2$

54.

Substituting $x^{1/4} = t$ i.e. $x = t^4$

$\Rightarrow dx = 4t^3 \, dt$, we get

$\int \frac{x^{\frac{1}{4}}}{1 + x^{\frac{1}{2}}} dx = \int \frac{t \, 4t^3}{1 + t^2} dt = 4 \int \left(t^2 - 1 + \frac{1}{1+t^2}\right) dt$

55. Since $[x] \leq x < [x] + 1$,

therefore $[x] - [x] \leq x - [x] < [x] + 1 - [x]$

$\Rightarrow 0 \leq x - [x] < 1$

56. Let $f(x) = x^2 + \sin^2 x$, then $f(-x) = f(x)$, therefore, $f(x) = x^2 + \sin^2 x$ is an even function

57.

$$f(x) = |x - 1| = \sqrt{(x - 1)^2}$$
$$= \sqrt{|x - 1|^2} = \sqrt{(f(x))^2}$$

58. (fog)(x) = f(g(x)) = [x – [x]] = 0

($\because$ x – [x] lies in [0, 1) $\forall$ x $\in$ R)

59. h(x) = f(x) g(x) = x(1/x)=1

only if x $\neq$ 0

60. $\log_{1/4} x = x \Rightarrow x = (1/4)^x \Rightarrow x=1/2^{2x}$

$\Rightarrow x.2^{2x} = 1$, on inspection, we find that x = 1/2 satisfies if

Note that y = a^x, 0 < a < 1 and y = x meet in a unique point

61. Trains services are good that's why these are convenient

62. The survey compares the previous year data, so similar survey was taken last year also.

63. The statement does not say that other medicines are available for controlling obesity, and neither it says that only meds can control obesity.

64. Help desk is there to listen to problems and solve, so it will solve all the problems. And it is not necessary that the complaint is to me made immediately, the statement only says that whenever u have any problem, u can walk to help desk immediately too.

65. The rate is less than other banks mean that other banks also give loan. It is less than other banks so there are different rates.

66. By Analyzing the given analogy, we can infer that in the left side an adult name and its baby name is given i.e. cub is baby of Leopard

By Applying the same logic to the right side we can conclude that foal is the baby of Mule.

67. By Analyzing the given analogy, we can infer that in the left side an adult name and its baby name is given i.e. pup is baby of Mole

By Applying the same logic to the right side we can conclude that chick is the baby of Chicken.

68. By Analyzing the given analogy, we can infer that in the left side an adult name and its baby name is given i.e. hatchling is baby of Crocodile

By Applying the same logic to the right side we can conclude that cub is the baby of Leopard.

69. By Analyzing the given analogy, we can infer that in the left side an adult name and its baby name is given i.e. bunny is baby of Rabbit.

By Applying the same logic to the right side we can conclude that pup is the baby of Anteater.

70. By Analyzing the given analogy, we can infer that in the left side an adult name and its baby name is given i.e. chick is baby of Gull

By Applying the same logic to the right side we can conclude that chick is the baby of Hummingbird.

71.

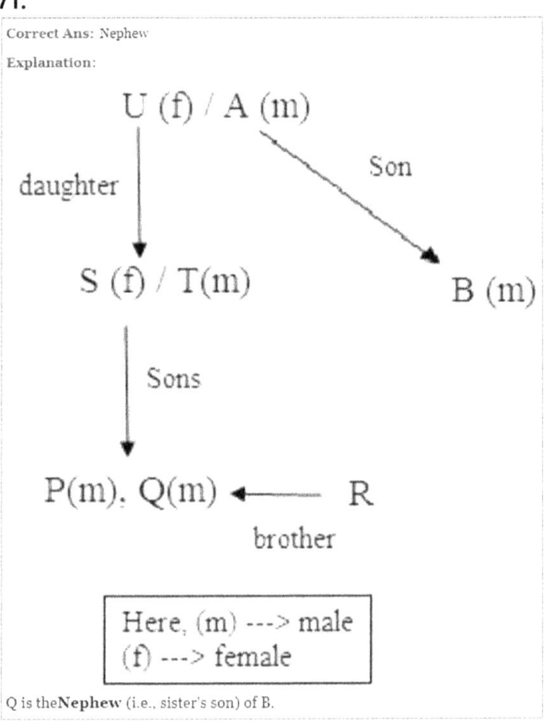

72.

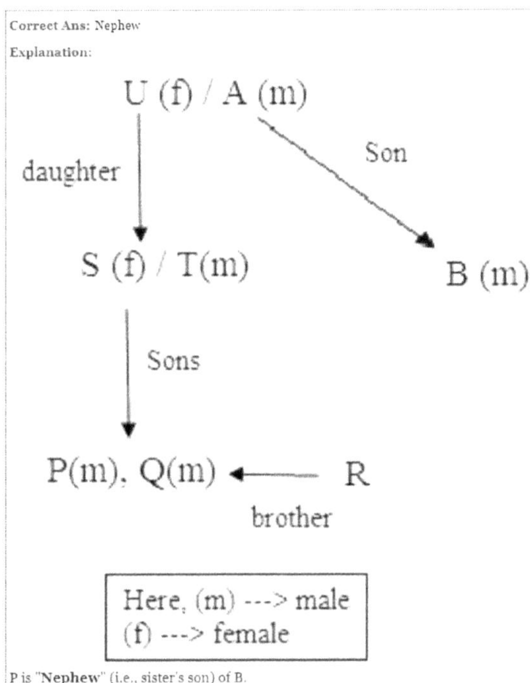

73.

Correct Ans: Grandson

Explanation:

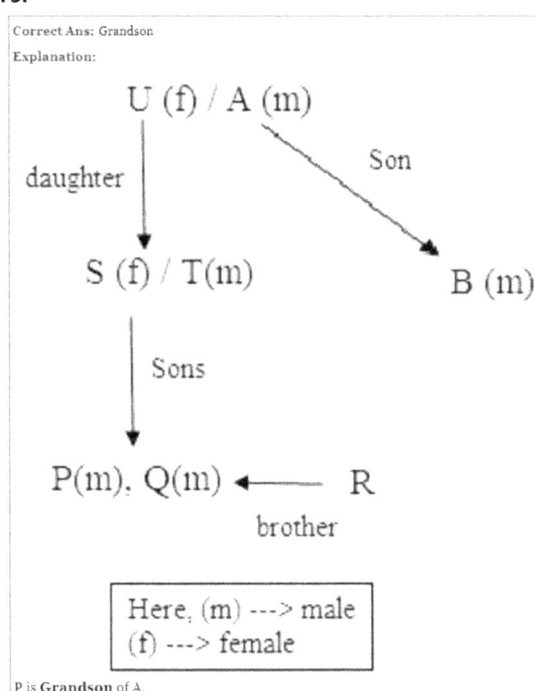

P is **Grandson** of A.

74.

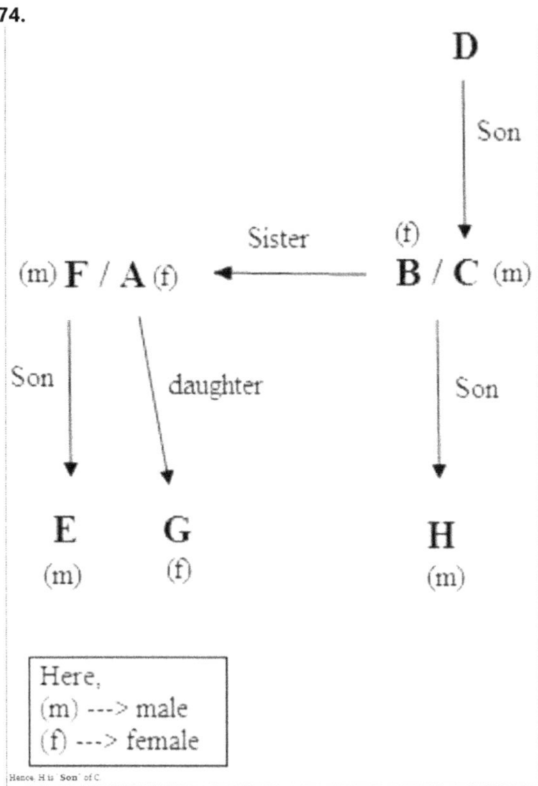

Hence, H is **Son** of C.

75.

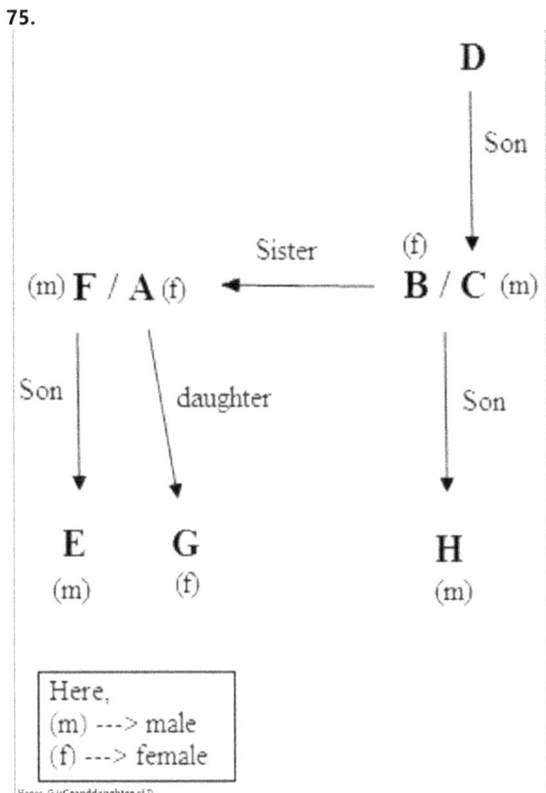

Hence, G is **Granddaughter** of D.

76.

Correct Ans: nt

Explanation:

Given,
I) 'facing problem with money' --- 'st np cg rt',
II) 'money problem very serious' --- 'nt st np vw',
III) 'serious with every person' --- 'rt nt pr ab',
IV) 'facing person each day' --- 'cg ab no cd'.

	Common Word	Common Code
From I and IV	facing	cg
From I, III	with	rt
From II, III	serious	nt
From III, IV	person	ab

Thus, the remaining words and their corresponding codes are:
"**problem / money**" --- "st / np"
"**very**" --- "vw"
"**every**" -- "pr"
"**each / day**" -- "no / cd"

77.

Correct Ans: rt

Explanation:

Given,
I) 'facing problem with money' --- 'st np cg rt',
II) 'money problem very serious' --- 'nt st np vw',
III) 'serious with every person' --- 'rt nt pr ab',
IV) 'facing person each day' --- 'cg ab no cd'.

	Common Word	Common Code
From I and IV	facing	cg
From I, III	with	rt
From II, III	serious	nt
From III, IV	person	ab

Thus, the remaining words and their corresponding codes are:
"**problem / money**" --- "st / np"
"**very**" --- "vw"
"**every**" -- "pr"
"**each / day**" -- "no / cd"

78.

Correct Ans: cg

Explanation:

Given,
I) 'facing problem with money' --- 'st np cg rt',
II) 'money problem very serious' --- 'nt st np vw',
III) 'serious with every person' --- 'rt nt pr ab',
IV) 'facing person each day' --- 'cg ab no cd'.

	Common Word	Common Code
From I and IV	facing	cg
From I, III	with	rt
From II, III	serious	nt
From III, IV	person	ab

Thus, the remaining words and their corresponding codes are:
"**problem / money**" --- "st / np"
"**very**" --- "vw"
"**every**" -- "pr"
"**each / day**" -- "no / cd"

79.

Correct Ans: ch

Explanation:

Given,
I) 'committee to protect journalists' --- '**es fr re pt**',
II) 'protectpeople in city' --- '**ch ba mo fr**'
III) 'peopletofollowon' --- '**re dv ch gi**'
IV) 'followtips toprotect' --- '**re gi fr yu**'

	Common Word	Common Code
From I, III and IV	to	re
From I, II and IV	protect	fr
From II, III	people	ch
From III, IV	follow	gi

Thus, the remaining words and their corresponding codes are:
"**committee / journalists**" --- "es / pt"
"in / city" --- "ba / mo"
"on" -- "dv"
"tips" -- "yu"

80.

Correct Ans: fr

Explanation:

Given,
I) 'committee to protect journalists' --- '**es fr re pt**',
II) 'protectpeople in city' --- '**ch ba mo fr**'
III) 'peopletofollowon' --- '**re dv ch gi**'
IV) 'followtips toprotect' --- '**re gi fr yu**'

	Common Word	Common Code
From I, III and IV	to	re
From I, II and IV	protect	fr
From II, III	people	ch
From III, IV	follow	gi

Thus, the remaining words and their corresponding codes are:
"**committee / journalists**" --- "es / pt"
"in / city" --- "ba / mo"
"on" -- "dv"
"tips" -- "yu"

81. Indexed allocation is used for the efficient direct access good use of disk space. However, it cannon t allocated very large files . Thus, the data blocks of very large file in unix system are allocated using an extension of indexed allocation or EXT2 file system

82. If the number of processors are increased then amount of work done is increased and time is decreased. In case of uniprocessor first come first serve gives the maximum throughput but when the case of known run time is considered shortest job first gives best performance

83. Throughput is the measure of total number of process completed per unit time. CPU utilization is referred to a process to keep CPU busy. Thus in case of large block size in fixed block size file system, CPU utilization is poorer and throughput is also decreased

84. 100 pages are accessed in some order 1->100 , this will result in 100 page faults.When accessed in reverse order there won't be any fault for page number 100,99,98,97. Therefore for the remaining 96 access, 96 faults would occur. Total 196 page faults

85. SSTF is optimal scheduling scheme for the access of file only. Therefore, the IN/OUT performance of the user program is determined by disk. So when FCFS is replaced by SSTF it improves only disk performance. This does not improve the entire IN/OUT performance . This implies improvement performance of user program is 0%

86. Acceptance testing is a test conducted to determine if the requirements of a specification or contract are met and is done by users.

87. White-box testing is a method of testing software that tests internal structures or workings of an application, as opposed to its functionality.

88. Maintenance Testing is done on the already deployed software. The deployed software needs to be enhanced, changed or migrated to other hardware. The Testing done during this enhancement, change and migration cycle is known as maintenance testing.

89. A run chart is used to monitor the behavior of a variable over time for a process or system. Run charts graphically display cycles, trends, shifts, or non-random patterns in behavior over time. It contains lower and upper limits.

90. Cyclomatic complexity measures the amount of decision logic in the program module. Cyclomatic complexity gives the minimum number of paths that can generate all possible paths through the module.

91. GIF is the extension of Image source format

92. .ilb is the extension of Intermediate StarOffice interface definition file.

93. .xml is the extension of Extended Markup Language

94. .class is Compiled java source code file.

95. .unx is the extension of UNIX-specific makefile.

96. There is 5 generation of computer available till now.

1st Generation of Computer = The period of first generation: 1946-1959. Vacuum tube based.

2nd Generation of Computer = The period of second generation: 1959-1965. Transistor based.

3rd Generation of Computer = The period of third generation: 1965-1971. Integrated Circuit based.

4th Generation of Computer = The period of fourth generation: 1971-1980. VLSI microprocessor based.

5th Generation of Computer = The period of fifth generation: 1980-onwards. ULSI microprocessor based.

97. In MS Excel, formulas are equations that perform various calculations in your worksheets. Though Microsoft has introduced a handful of new functions over the years, the concept of Excel spreadsheet formulas is the same in all versions of Excel 2016, Excel 2013, Excel 2010, Excel 2007 and lower.

All Excel formulas begin with an equal sign (=).

98. In 1945, Professor J. von Neumann, who was then working at the Moore School of Engineering in Philadelphia, where the E.N.I.A.C. had been built, issued on behalf of a group of his co-workers, a report on the logical design of digital computers.

99. SMTP (Simple Mail Transfer Protocol) is a TCP/IP protocol used in sending and receiving e-mail. However, since it is limited in its ability to queue messages at the receiving end, it is usually used with one of two other protocols, POP3 or IMAP that let the user save messages in a server mailbox and download them periodically from the server. SMTP usually is implemented to operate over Internet port 25.

Many mail servers now support Extended Simple Mail Transfer Protocol (ESMTP), which allows multimedia files to be delivered as e-mail.

100. Fifth generation computing devices, based on artificial intelligence, are still in development, though there are some applications, such as voice recognition, that are being used today. The use of parallel processing and superconductors is helping to make artificial intelligence a reality. Quantum computation and molecular and nanotechnology will radically change the face of computers in years to come. The goal of fifth-generation computing is to develop devices that respond to natural language input and are capable of learning and self-organization.

101. To make clean breast of : to disclose something openly.

102. To keeps one's temper : to maintain control of one's composure despite being angry or upset.

103. Hindmost : furthest back, latest or ultramodern.

Disposed : inclined or willing.

Mature : fully developed physically, full-grown.

Premature : occurring or done before the usual or proper time, too early.

Unimportant : lacking in importance or significance.

Foremost : most prominent in rank, importance, or position.

So, antonym is Unimportant.

104. Wonderful, Graceful, Handsome and Marvelous are more or less synonyms of Beautiful.

Ugly posses opposite meaning of Beautiful.

105. Defends: protect from harm or danger.

Deprives: prevent (a person or place) from having or using something

Devises: plan or invent (a complex procedure, system, or mechanism) by careful thought

Secures: fix or attach (something) firmly so that it cannot be moved or lost

Deserts: to abandon that is to stop supporting or looking after

Protects : keep safe from harm

So the correct answer is Deserts.

106. Safeguarding : a measure taken to protect someone or something or to prevent something undesirable.

Neglecting : fail to care for properly.

Ignoring : refuse to take notice of or acknowledge; disregard intentionally.

Nurturing : care for and protect (someone or something) while they are growing.

Fostering : encourage the development of (something, especially something desirable).

Synonym of Fostering is Nurturing.

107. Burst : break open or apart suddenly and violently, especially as a result of an impact or internal pressure.

Acclimatize : become accustomed to a new climate or new conditions, adjust

Modify : make partial or minor changes to (something).

Drive : propel or carry along by force in a specified direction.

Propel : carry along by force in a specified direction.

Synonym of Propel is Drive.

108. Strong : having the power to move heavy weights or perform other physically demanding tasks.

Little : small in size, amount, or degree.

Gaping : wide open.

Huge : extremely large; enormous.

Massive : exceptionally large.

Synonym of Massive is Huge.

109. Adulation

110. Conciliatory

111. Desiccate

112. The adjectives inferior, superior, senior, junior, prior etc. take the preposition to, not than. E.g.

She always felt inferior to her younger sister.

This material is superior to that.

113. Change, It was him into It was he

As complement of the Copulative verb is Nominative case.

114. Change, is situating → is situated

115. One word substitution is Ascetic.

Sceptic: a person inclined to question or doubt accepted opinions.

Ascetic: characterized by severe self-discipline and abstention from all forms of indulgence, typically for religious reasons.

Devotee: a person who is very interested in and enthusiastic about someone or something.

Antiquarian: relating to or dealing in antiques or rare books.

116. One word-Substitution is Apostate.

Prostate: a gland surrounding the neck of the bladder in male mammals and releasing a fluid component of semen.

Profane: (of a person or their behaviour) not respectful of religious practice; irreverent.

Agnostic: a person who believes that nothing is known or can be known of the existence or nature of God.

Apostate: a person who renounces or abandons a religious or political belief or principle.

117. One word-substitution is Misologist

Bibliophile: a person who collects or has a great love for books.

Philologist: learner of language, or linguist.

Misogynist: a person who hates women.

Misologist: A hater of knowledge and and learning.

118. We discussed the problem so thoroughly.

119. I would have helped him

120. A herd usually refers to a group of animals with hooves, like cows or sheep

Mock Test 09

Mathematics

Q.1 If A, B, C are the angles of a triangle, with C being an obtuse angle, then

A. tan A tan B < 1   **B.** tan A tan B > 1

C. tan A tan B = 1   **D.** none of these

Q.2 If integral values of x which satisfies $(5x - 1) < (x = 1)^2 < (7x - 3)$ is

A. 2   **B.** 3

C. 4   **D.** none of these

Q.3 cos (cos θ) > 0 for

A. $0 < \theta < \dfrac{\pi}{2}$ **B.** $0 < \theta < \pi$

C. $-\pi < \theta < \pi$ **D.** all real θ

Q.4 Minimum values of sin x + cos x is

A. 0   **B.** -1

C. -2√   **D.** none of these

Q.5 If a, b, c are positive real numbers, then the minimum value of

$$(a + b + c) \left(\tfrac{1}{a} + \tfrac{1}{b} + \tfrac{1}{c} \right) \text{ is}$$

A. 8   **B.** 3   **C.** $\dfrac{10}{3}$ **D.** 9

Q.6 If the product of n positive real numbers is unity, then their sum cannot be

A. greater then n   **B.** less than n

C. equal to n   **D.** none of these

Q.7 The probability of the having atleast one tail in 4 throws with a coin is

A. $\dfrac{15}{16}$ **B.** $\dfrac{1}{16}$ **C.** $\dfrac{1}{4}$ **D.** 1

Q.8 From each of the four married couples, one of the parteners is selected at random. The probability that those selected are of the same sex is

A. $\dfrac{1}{2}$ **B.** $\dfrac{1}{4}$ **C.** $\dfrac{1}{8}$ **D.** $\dfrac{1}{16}$

Q.9 Five letters are sent to different persons and addresses on the five envelopes are written at random. The probability that all the letters reach correct destiny is

A. $\dfrac{44}{120}$ **B.** $\dfrac{1}{120}$

C. $\dfrac{1}{5}$ **D.** None of these.

Q.10 A coin is tossed 6 times. The probability of getting a head three times is

A. $\dfrac{1}{2}$ **B.** $\dfrac{3}{64}$ **C.** $\dfrac{1}{8}$ **D.** $\dfrac{5}{16}$

Q.11 Three letters are written to different persons and addresses on the envelops are also written
Without looking at the addresses, the letters are put into the envelops ; the probability that letters go into
Right envelopes is

A. $\dfrac{1}{27}$ **B.** $\dfrac{1}{6}$ **C.** $\dfrac{1}{9}$ **D.** $\dfrac{1}{8}$

Q.12 From a deck of 52 cards, the probability of drawing a court card is

A. $\dfrac{4}{13}$ **B.** $\dfrac{3}{13}$ **C.** $\dfrac{1}{13}$ **D.** $\dfrac{1}{4}$

Q.13 $\cos^{-1}\left(\tfrac{1}{2}\right) + 2\sin^{-1}\left(\tfrac{1}{2}\right)$ is equal to

A. $\dfrac{\pi}{4}$ **B.** $\dfrac{\pi}{3}$ **C.** $\dfrac{\pi}{6}$ **D.** $\dfrac{2\pi}{3}$

Q.14 $\cot^{-1}\left(\tfrac{5}{3}\right) + \cos^{-1}\left(\tfrac{4}{5}\right) =$

A. 0

B. $\cos^{-1}\left(\dfrac{27}{2\sqrt{38}}\right)$

C. $\cot^{-1}\left(\dfrac{27}{11}\right)$

D. $\tan^{-1}\left(\dfrac{27}{11}\right)$

Q.15 The value of $\cos^{-1}(-1) - \sin^{-1}(1)$ is

A. $\dfrac{3\pi}{2}$ **B.** $-\dfrac{3\pi}{2}$ **C.** π   **D.** $\dfrac{\pi}{2}$

Q.16 $\tan^{-1} 3 - \tan^{-1} 2 =$

A. $\tan^{-1}\left(\dfrac{3}{2}\right)$ **B.** $\tan^{-1}\left(\dfrac{2}{3}\right)$

C. $\tan^{-1}\left(\dfrac{1}{7}\right)$ **D.** $\tan^{-1}\left(\dfrac{1}{5}\right)$

Q.17

If $\tan^{-1} x + \tan^{-1}\dfrac{1}{7} = \dfrac{\pi}{4}$, then x =

A. $\dfrac{3}{4}$ **B.** $\dfrac{6}{7}$ **C.** $\dfrac{4}{3}$ **D.** $\dfrac{7}{6}$

Q.18
If $\cos^{-1} x + \sin^{-1}\left(\dfrac{x}{2}\right) = \dfrac{\pi}{6}$, then x =

A. 0   **B.** $\dfrac{1}{\sqrt{2}}$ **C.** 1   **D.** $\pm\sqrt{3}$

Q.19 In a triangle ABC, D is the mid-point of side [BC] ;

$\overrightarrow{AD}$ is equal to

A. $\overrightarrow{AB} + \overrightarrow{AC}$

B. $\dfrac{1}{2}\left(\overrightarrow{AB} + \overrightarrow{AC}\right)$

C. $\overrightarrow{AB} - \overrightarrow{AC}$

D. none of these

Q.20

Direction cosines of the vector $\hat{i}$ are

A. < 1, 0, 0 >   **B.** < 0, 1, 1 >
C. < 1, 0, 1 >   **D.** none of these

Q.21 Direction cosines of the vector

$$\vec{v} = 2\hat{i} + 3\hat{j} - 6\hat{k} \text{ are}$$

A. < 2, 3, – 6>

B. $\left< \dfrac{2}{7}, \dfrac{3}{7}, -\dfrac{6}{7} \right>$

C. $\left< -\dfrac{2}{7}, -\dfrac{3}{7}, \dfrac{6}{7} \right>$

D. none of these

Q.22

Direction cosines of the vector

$$\vec{v} = a_1\hat{i} + a_2\hat{j} + a_3\hat{k} \text{ are}$$

A. < a_1 , a_2 , a_3 >
B. < – a_1 , – a_2 , – a_3 >

C. $\left< \dfrac{a_1}{|\vec{v}|}, \dfrac{a_2}{|\vec{v}|}, \dfrac{a_3}{|\vec{v}|} \right>$

D. none of these

Q.23 A vector with magnitude zero is called a
A. free vector   **B.** localized vector
C. position vector   **D.** null vector

Q.24 $\vec{a}$, $\vec{b}$ and $\vec{c}$ are the vectors with components (– 1, 2), (3, – 2) and (0, 5) respectively, then $\vec{a} + \vec{b} - 2\vec{c}$ is

A. $2\hat{i} + 10\hat{j}$ **B.** $-2\hat{i} + 10\hat{j}$

C. $2\hat{i} - 10\hat{j}$ **D.** $3\hat{i} + 2\hat{j}$

Q.25 The differential equation of all parabolas whose axes are parallel to y-axis is

A. $\dfrac{d^3 y}{dx^3} = 0$

B. $\dfrac{d^2 y}{dx^2} = 0$

C. $\dfrac{d^2 y}{dx^2} + \dfrac{dy}{dx} = 0$

D. none of these

Q.26
A particle, initially at origin, moves along x-axis according to the rule $\frac{dx}{dt} = x + 4$. The time taken by the particle to traverse a distance of 96 units is

A. $\log_5 e$ **B.** $2\log_e 5$

C. $2\log_5 e$ **D.** $\dfrac{1}{2}\log_5 e$

Q.27

The differential equation

$y\dfrac{dy}{dx} = a - x$ (a∈ R) represents

A. a family of circles with centres on y-axis
B. a family of circles with centres at origin
C. a family of circles with a given radius
D. a family of circles with centres on x-axis

Q.28 The area bounded by the curve $y^2 = 9x$ and the line x = 1, x = 4 and y = 0 in the first quadrants is
A. 7   **B.** 14   **C.** 28   **D.** 14/3

Q.29
The integrating factor of the differential equation $\frac{dy}{dx}$ (x log x) + y = 2 log x is given by
A. e^x **B.** log x

C. log (log x)   **D.** x

Q.30 The general solution of the differential equation
$$\frac{dy}{dx} = \frac{y}{x}$$

A. $y = \dfrac{k}{x}$, constant   **B.** y = k log x

C. log y = k x   **D.** y = k x

Q.31 Let f(x) = (x² − 4)^{1/3}, then f has a
A. local maxima at x = 0
B. local minima at x = 0
C. point of inflection at x = 0
D. none of these

Q.32 The normal to the curve 2y = 3− x² at (1, 1) is
A. x + y = 0   **B.** x + y + 1 = 0
C. x − y + 1 + 0   **D.** x− y = 0

Q.33 The equation of the tangent to the curve y² = 4ax at the point (at², 2at) is
A. t y = x + a t²   **B.** t y = x − a t ²
C. t x + y = a t³   **D.** none of these

Q.34 The function f(x) = x³ has a
A. local minima at x = 0
B. local maxima at x = 0
C. point of inflection at x = 0
D. none of these

Q.35 Let f(x) = x³ − 6x² = 9x + 18, then f(x) is strict deceasing in
A. (− ∞ , 1]   **B.** [3, ∞)
C. (− ∞ , -1]   **D.** [1, 3]

Q.36 The minimum value of f(x) = sin x cos x is

A. $\dfrac{1}{2}$ **B.** $-\dfrac{1}{2}$

C. 0   **D.** none of these

Q.37 The equation xy = 0 in three dimensional space represents
A. a pair of straight lines
B. a plane
C. a pair of planes at right angles
D. a pair of parallel planes.

Q.38 The distance of the planes.
$$\vec{r} \bullet \left(3\hat{i} + 4\hat{j} + 12\hat{k}\right) = 65 \text{ from the origin is}$$

A. 65   **B.** 5
C. -5   **D.** None of these.

Q.39

The planes $\vec{r} \bullet (2\hat{i} + 3\hat{j} - 6\hat{k} = 7$ and $\vec{r} \bullet \left(-\frac{2}{7}\hat{i} - \frac{3}{7}\hat{j} + \frac{6}{7}\hat{k}\right) = 0$ are

A. At right angles
B. Parallel
C. Equidistant from the origin

D. None of these

Q.40

The lines $\vec{r} = \left(\hat{i} + \hat{j} + \hat{k}\right) t + 3\hat{k}$ and $\vec{r} = \left(\hat{i} - 2\hat{j} + \hat{k}\right) s + 3\hat{k}$

A. Are skew
B. Are parallel
C. Intersect at right angles
D. None of these

Q.41

The equation $(\vec{r} - (\hat{i} + \hat{j})) \bullet (\vec{r} - (\hat{j} + \hat{k})) = 0$ represents

A. A pair of lines   **B.** A pair of planes
C. A sphere   **D.** None of these.

Q.42 The graph of the equation x² + y² = 0 in the three dimensional space is
A. X-axis   **B.** Y-axis
C. Z-axis   **D.** XY-plane

Q.43

If A + B = $\begin{bmatrix} 1 & 0 \\ 1 & 1 \end{bmatrix}$ and A −2B = $\begin{bmatrix} -1 & 1 \\ 0 & -1 \end{bmatrix}$, then A =

A. $\dfrac{1}{3}\begin{bmatrix} 1 & 1 \\ 2 & 1 \end{bmatrix}$ **B.** $\dfrac{1}{3}\begin{bmatrix} 1 & 1 \\ 2 & 1 \end{bmatrix}$

C. $\begin{bmatrix} 1 & 1 \\ 2 & 1 \end{bmatrix}$ **D.** none of these

Q.44 If a matrix A is symmetric as well as skew symmetric then A is a
A. diagonal matrix   **B.** null matrix
C. unit matrix   **D.** none of these

Q.45

If f(x) = x² + 4x −5 and A = $\begin{bmatrix} 1 & 2 \\ 4 & -3 \end{bmatrix}$ then f(A) =

A. $\begin{bmatrix} & -4 \\ 8 & 8 \end{bmatrix}$ **B.** $\begin{bmatrix} 2 & 1 \\ 2 & 0 \end{bmatrix}$

C. $\begin{bmatrix} 1 & 1 \\ 1 & 0 \end{bmatrix}$ **D.** $\begin{bmatrix} 8 & 4 \\ 8 & 0 \end{bmatrix}$

Q.46

If A = $\begin{bmatrix} 0 & 5 \\ 0 & 0 \end{bmatrix}$ and f(x) = 1 + x + x² + ...+ x¹⁶, then f(A) =

A. O   **B.** $\begin{bmatrix} 1 & 5 \\ 0 & 1 \end{bmatrix}$

C. $\begin{bmatrix} 1 & 5 \\ 0 & 0 \end{bmatrix}$ **D.** $\begin{bmatrix} 0 & 5 \\ 1 & 1 \end{bmatrix}$

Q.47

If $A = \begin{bmatrix} 1 & 0 \\ 2 & 0 \end{bmatrix}$ and $B = \begin{bmatrix} 0 & 0 \\ 1 & 12 \end{bmatrix}$, then

A. AB = O, BA = O
B. AB = O BA ≠ O
C. AB ≠ O, BA = O
D. AB ≠ O, BA ≠ O

Q.48 If the matrix AB = O, then
A. A = O or B = O
B. A = O and B = O
C. It is not necessary that either A = O or B = O
D. A ≠ O, B ≠ O

Q.49
Let $f(x) = x$, $g(x) = \frac{1}{x}$ and $h(x) = f(x) g(x)$, then $h(x) = 1$ iff

A. x is a real number
B. x is a rational number
C. x is an irrational number
D. x is a real number ≠ 0

Q.50

If $\left(\frac{1}{4}\right)^x = x$, then x =

A. 0   **B.** 1   **C.** $\frac{1}{2}$ **D.** 2

Q.51 If $\log (2x + 3) + \log (x-2) = 1$, then
A. $2x^2 - x - 7 = 0$
B. $2x^2 - x - 5 = 0$
C. $2x + 2^{-x} - 6 - e = 0$
D. $2x^2 - x - 6 + e = 0$

Q.52
If $y = \frac{1}{x-2}$, $x \neq 2$ for what value, if any, of x is $y^2 = -2y^3$?

A. −4   **B.** $-\frac{1}{2}$ **C.** 0   **D.** no value

Q.53 The domain of the function
$f(x) = \sqrt{|x| - x}$ is

A. [0, ∞)
B. (−∞, 0]
C. R
D. none of these

Q.54

If $f(x) = \frac{|x|}{x}$; $x \neq 0$; then
$|f(x) - f(-x)|$ is equal to

A. 0   **B.** 2
C. 1   **D.** none of these

Q.55
If $x = 2 + 2 + \cfrac{1}{2 + \cfrac{1}{2 + \cfrac{1}{2 + \dots}}}$ then the value of x is

A. $\sqrt{2} - 1$ **B.** $\sqrt{2} + 1$
C. 3   **D.** none of these

Q.56 The function $x \to ax^2 + 2x + 1$ has one double root if
A. a = 0   **B.** a = − 1   **C.** a = 1   **D.** a = 2

Q.57 The solution set of the equation $4^x - 3.2^{x+3} + 128 = 0$ is
A. {1, 2}   **B.** {2, 3}   **C.** {3, 4}   **D.** {4, 5}

Q.58 The number of real roots of the equation $2^{2x2-7x+5} = 1$ is
A. 0   **B.** 1   **C.** 2   **D.** 4

Q.59 If one roots of the equation $(x - 1)(7 - x) = \lambda$ is three times the other, then $\lambda =$
A. 0   **B.** -5
C. 5   **D.** none of these

Q.60
if $x = \sqrt{3 + \sqrt{3 + \sqrt{3 + \dots \, to \, \infty}}}$ then x is equal to

A. a rational number
B. an irrational number lying between 2 and 3
C. an integral number
D. none of these

Analytical Ability & Logical Reasoning

Q.61 Turkey : poult :: Reindeer : ?
A. chick
B. hatchling, chick
C. calf
D. cub

Q.62 Gorilla : infant :: Rabbit : ?
A. hatchling
B. calf
C. cub
D. bunny

Q.63 Reindeer : calf :: Bee : ?
A. squab / squeaker
B. hatchling
C. kid, billy
D. larva

Q.64 Turkey : poult :: Fox : ?
A. chick
B. kit/cub/pup
C. duckling
D. joey

Q.65 Ant : antling :: Hummingbird : ?
A. chick
B. lamb
C. gosling
D. stot / calf

Q.66 How is the word "knife" coded?
A. 3
B. 4
C. 5
D. None of the above

Q.67 How is the word "wrong" coded?
A. 4   **B.** 5   **C.** 6   **D.** 7

Q.68 How is the word "very" coded?

A. 3   **B.** 4   **C.** 2   **D.** 1

Q.69 How is the word "is" is coded ?
A. 6   **B.** 8   **C.** 7   **D.** 5

Q.70 How is the word "Wrong Knife" coded?
A. 47   **B.** 45   **C.** 75   **D.** 85

Q.71 Seven villages A, B, C, D, E, F and G are situated as follows:
E is 2 km to the west of B.
F is 2 km to the north of A.
C is 1 km to the west of A.
D is 2 km to the south of G.
G is 2 km to the east of C.
D is exactly in the middle of B and E.
How far is E from D (in km)?
A. 1 km   **B.** sqrt(20) km
C. 5 km   **D.** sqrt (26) km

Q.72 Seven villages A, B, C, D, E, F and G are situated as follows:
E is 2 km to the west of B.
F is 2 km to the north of A.
C is 1 km to the west of A.
D is 2 km to the south of G.
G is 2 km to the east of C.
D is exactly in the middle of B and E.
Which two villages are west of G?
A. D and C   **B.** F and E   **C.** C and A   **D.** G and E

Q.73 Seven villages A, B, C, D, E, F and G are situated as follows:
E is 2 km to the west of B.
F is 2 km to the north of A.
C is 1 km to the west of A.
D is 2 km to the south of G.
G is 2 km to the east of C.
D is exactly in the middle of B and E.
 A is in the middle of
A. C and F   **B.** C and G   **C.** B and D   **D.** C and B

Q.74 Seven villages A, B, C, D, E, F and G are situated as follows:
E is 2 km to the west of B.
F is 2 km to the north of A.
C is 1 km to the west of A.
D is 2 km to the south of G.
G is 2 km to the east of C.
D is exactly in the middle of B and E.
How far is E from F (in km) as the crow flies?
A. 5 km   **B.** 6 km   **C.** 4.5 km   **D.** 4 km

Q.75 Statement:
All heros are Zeros
All Zeros are villains
Some heroes are jokers
Conclusion:
I) Some Jokers are heroes
II) Some Zeros are jokers
III) Some villains are Zeros
A. All I ,II, III follows   **B.** Only I, II follow
C. Only II, III follow   **D.** Only I,III follows

Q.76 Statements:
Some Potatoes are onions
All onions are peanuts
All peanuts are samosas
Conclusion:
I) Some potatoes are peanuts
II) Some peanuts are potatoes
III) All onions are samosas
A. All follow   **B.** Only I, III follow
C. Only II, III, follow   **D.** Only I, II follows

Q.77 Statement:
I) All cocks are frogs
II) All cakes are jugs
III) Some cakes are cocks
Conclusion:
I) Some jugs are cocks
II) Some frogs are jugs
III) Some cocks are jugs
A. Only I, II follow   **B.** All I, II, III follows
C. Only I, III follows   **D.** Only II, III follows

Q.78 Statement :
I) All houses are windows.
II) All roads are windows
III) All toys are windows
Conclusions
I) Some toys are houses
II) Some roads are houses
III) Some roads are toys
A. None follows   **B.** Only I follows
C. Only II follows   **D.** Only III follows

Q.79 Statement:
I) Some rings are bangles
II) Some Bangles are beads
III) Some beads are flowers
Conclusions:
I) Some flowers are rings.
II) Some flowers are bangles
III) No ring is a flower.
A. None follows
B. Only I follows
C. Only II follows
D. Only either I or III follows

Q.80 Statements :
All desks are rooms
Some rooms are halls.
All halls are leaves.
Conclusions:
I)Some leaves are desks
II)Some halls are desks
III)Some leaves are rooms.
A. None follows   **B.** Only I follows
C. Only II follows   **D.** Only III follows

Computer Awareness

Q.81 The decoded instruction is stored in ______

A. IR   **B.** PC
C. Registers   **D.** MDR

Q.82 The instruction -> Add LOCA, R0 does ______

A. Adds the value of LOCA to R0 and stores in the temp register
B. Adds the value of R0 to the address of LOCA
C. Adds the values of both LOCA and R0 and stores it in R0
D. Adds the value of LOCA with a value in accumulator and stores it in R0

Q.83 Which registers can interact with the secondary storage?
A. MAR   **B.** PC   **C.** IR   **D.** R0

Q.84 During the execution of a program which gets initialized first?
A. MDR   **B.** IR   **C.** PC   **D.** MAR

Q.85 Which of the register/s of the processor is/are connected to Memory Bus?
A. PC   **B.** MAR
C. IR   **D.** Both PC and MAR

Q.86 ISP stands for _______
A. Instruction Set Processor
B. Information Standard Processing
C. Interchange Standard Protocol
D. Interrupt Service Procedure

Q.87 The internal Components of the processor are connected by ______
A. Processor intra-connectivity circuitry
B. Processor bus
C. Memory bus
D. Rambus

Q.88 ______ is used to choose between incrementing the PC or performing ALU operations.
A. Conditional codes
B. Multiplexer
C. Control unit
D. None of the mentioned

Q.89 The registers, ALU and the interconnection between them are collectively called as ____
A. process route   **B.** information trail
C. information path   **D.** data path

Q.90 ______ is used to store data in registers.
A. D flip flop
B. JK flip flop
C. RS flip flop
D. None of the mentioned

Q.91 The main virtue for using single Bus structure is ________
A. Fast data transfers
B. Cost effective connectivity and speed
C. Cost effective connectivity and ease of attaching peripheral devices

D. None of the mentioned

Q.92 ______ are used to overcome the difference in data transfer speeds of various devices.
A. Speed enhancing circuitory
B. b) Bridge circuits
C. Multiple Buses
D. Buffer registers

Q.93 To extend the connectivity of the processor bus we use ______
A. PCI bus   **B.** SCSI bus
C. Controllers   **D.** Multiple bus

Q.94 IBM developed a bus standard for their line of computers 'PC AT' called ____
A. IB bus
B. M-bus
C. ISA
D. None of the mentioned

Q.95 The bus used to connect the monitor to the CPU is ____
A. PCI bus   **B.** SCSI bus
C. Memory bus   **D.** Rambus

Q.96 ANSI stands for ________
A. American National Standards Institute
B. American National Standard Interface
C. American Network Standard Interfacing
D. American Network Security Interrupt

Q.97 ____ register Connected to the Processor bus is a single-way transfer capable.
A. PC   **B.** IR   **C.** Temp   **D.** Z

Q.98 In multiple Bus organisation, the registers are collectively placed and referred as ____
A. Set registers   **B.** Register file
C. Register Block   **D.** Map registers

Q.99 The main advantage of multiple bus organisation over a single bus is ____
A. Reduction in the number of cycles for execution
B. Increase in size of the registers
C. Better Connectivity
D. None of the mentioned

Q.100 The ISA standard Buses are used to connect ________
A. RAM and processor
B. GPU and processor
C. Harddisk and Processor
D. CD/DVD drives and Processor

English

Q.101 (solve as per the direction given above)
A. it is difficult   **B.** for anyone
C. to past time thus   **D.** no error

Q.102 Direction: Select the segment of the sentence that contains the grammatical error. If there is no error, mark 'No error' as your answer.

Sometimes politics (A)/ are a dirty business (B)/ to deal with. (C)/ No error (D)/

A. A   **B.** B   **C.** C   **D.** D

Q.103 (solve as per the direction given above)

A. i was there   **B.** many a time
C. in the past   **D.** no error

Q.104 (solve as per the direction given above)

A. my wife has got   **B.** a new job
C. a month ago   **D.** no error

Q.105 solve as per the direction given above

A. he was in such hurry
B. that he did not
C. wait for me
D. no error

Q.106 That rule is applicable ...... every one.

A. to   **B.** for   **C.** about   **D.** with

Q.107 Farida sings very well and ...... does salim.

A. even   **B.** too   **C.** also   **D.** so

Q.108 The waiter hasn't brought the coffee ...... I've been here an hour already.

A. till   **B.** up   **C.** yet   **D.** still

Q.109 You haven't had your lunch yet, ... you?

A. are   **B.** are not   **C.** have   **D.** have not

Q.110 Brothers must live in harmony. They must never fall ......

A. off   **B.** out   **C.** apart   **D.** away

Q.111 The prosecution failed in establish in every case today.

A. to   **B.** on   **C.** aas   **D.** upon

Q.112 The train will leave at 8.30 pm, we have been ready by 7.30pm so that, we can reach the station in time.

A. were   **B.** must be
C. are   **D.** should be

Q.113 Later he became unpopular because he tried to lord it on his followers.

A. to lord it for   **B.** to lord over
C. to lord it over   **D.** to lord it over on

Q.114 He dislikes the word dislike, isn't he

A. did not be   **B.** does not he
C. has not he   **D.** does he

Q.115 Anand has the guts to rise from the occasion and come out successfully.

A. in rising from   **B.** to raise with
C. to rise to   **D.** to raise against

Q.116 Laws of nature are not commands but statements of acts. The use of the word "law" in this context is rather unfortunate. It would be better to speak of uniformities in nature. This would do away with the elementary fallacy that a law implies a law giver. If a piece of matter does not obey a law of nature it is punished. On the contrary, we say that the law has been incorrectly started.

If a piece of matter violates nature's law, it is not punished because

A. it is not binding to obey it
B. there is no superior being to enforce the law of nature
C. it cannot be punished
D. it simply means that the facts have not been correctly stated by law

Q.117 Harold a professional man who had worked in an office for many years had a fearful dream. In it, he found himself in a land where small slug-like animals with slimy tentacles lived on people's bodies. The people tolerated the loathsome creatures because after many years they grew into elephants which then became the nation's system of transport, carrying everyone wherever he wanted to go. Harold suddenly realised that he himself was covered with these things, and he woke up screaming. In a vivid sequence of pictures this dream dramatised for Harold what he had never been able to put in to words; he saw himself as letting society feed on his body in his early years so that it would carry him when he retired. He later threw off the "security bug" and took up freelance work.

In his dream Harold found the loathsome creatures

A. in his village   **B.** in his own house
C. in a different land   **D.** in his office

Q.118 But I did not want to shoot the elephant. I watched him beating his bunch of grass against his knees, with the preoccupied grandmotherly air that elephants have. It seemed to me that it would be murder to shoot him. I had never shot an elephant and never wanted to. (Somehow it always seems worse to kill large animal.) Besides, there was the beast's owner to be considered. But I had got to act quickly. I turned to some experienced-looking Burmans who had been there when we arrived, and asked them how the elephants had been behaving. They all said the same thing; he took no notice of you if you left him alone, but he might charge if you went too close to him.

The phrase 'Preoccupied grandmotherly air' signifies

A. being totally unconcerned
B. pretending to be very busy
C. a very superior attitude
D. calm, dignified and affectionate disposition

Q.119 I felt the wall of the tunnel shiver. The master alarm squealed through my earphones. Almost simultaneously, Jack yelled down to me that there was a warning light on. Fleeting but spectacular sights snapped into ans out of view, the snow, the shower of debris, the moon, looming close and big, the dazzling sunshine for once unfiltered by layers of air. The last twelve hours before re-entry were particular bone-chilling. During this period, I had to go up in to command module. Even after the fiery re-entry splashing down in 81o water in south pacific, we could still see our frosty breath inside the command module.

The word 'Command Module' used twice in the given passage indicates perhaps that it deals with

A. an alarming journey
B. a commanding situation
C. a journey into outer space
D. a frightful battle.

Q.120 Laws of nature are not commands but statements of acts. The use of the word "law" in this context is rather unfortunate. It would be better to speak of uniformities in nature. This would do away with the elementary fallacy that a law implies a law giver. If a piece of matter does not obey a law of nature it is punished. On the contrary, we say that the law has been incorrectly started.

The author is not happy with word 'law' because

A. it connotes rigidity and harshness
B. it implies an agency which has made them
C. it does not convey the sense of nature's uniformity
D. it gives rise to false beliefs

// Smart Answer Sheet //

Correct Percentage of students who answered correctly. **Skipped** Percentage of students who skipped.

Q.	Ans.	Correct / Skipped	Q.	Ans.	Correct / Skipped	Q.	Ans.	Correct / Skipped	Q.	Ans.	Correct / Skipped	Q.	Ans.	Correct / Skipped
1	A	88.16 % / 11.33 %	17	A	81.98 % / 13.77 %	33	A	77.76 % / 17.32 %	49	D	85.06 % / 14.64 %	65	A	80.24 % / 13.94 %
2	B	84.59 % / 15.35 %	18	C	85.06 % / 13.71 %	34	C	88.02 % / 10.99 %	50	C	89.95 % / 10.04 %	66	C	82.25 % / 14.76 %
3	D	86.94 % / 11.79 %	19	B	81.41 % / 16.15 %	35	D	82.27 % / 15.93 %	51	C	82.88 % / 15.89 %	67	D	84.11 % / 11.99 %
4	C	89.36 % / 10.2 %	20	A	80.73 % / 13.75 %	36	B	83.97 % / 11.22 %	52	C	83.9 % / 12.92 %	68	C	86.87 % / 13.0 %
5	D	82.92 % / 12.97 %	21	B	80.45 % / 13.47 %	37	C	78.57 % / 13.05 %	53	C	77.82 % / 18.49 %	69	B	82.32 % / 14.04 %
6	B	86.17 % / 13.23 %	22	C	81.55 % / 11.34 %	38	B	82.65 % / 16.58 %	54	B	85.46 % / 14.06 %	70	C	84.4 % / 12.18 %
7	A	80.19 % / 12.74 %	23	D	79.13 % / 13.71 %	39	B	86.61 % / 12.93 %	55	C	76.32 % / 12.2 %	71	A	87.56 % / 10.15 %
8	C	81.77 % / 14.06 %	24	C	80.72 % / 17.3 %	40	C	81.29 % / 12.24 %	56	C	81.53 % / 12.84 %	72	C	80.89 % / 10.56 %
9	B	77.53 % / 11.12 %	25	A	88.67 % / 10.72 %	41	C	78.59 % / 14.02 %	57	C	80.36 % / 13.59 %	73	B	84.66 % / 10.65 %
10	D	86.17 % / 12.74 %	26	B	80.14 % / 10.31 %	42	C	88.24 % / 11.29 %	58	C	87.13 % / 12.06 %	74	D	87.9 % / 12.05 %
11	D	78.61 % / 14.56 %	27	D	88.98 % / 10.07 %	43	A	82.52 % / 10.73 %	59	C	83.26 % / 13.2 %	75	A	76.71 % / 17.17 %
12	B	88.97 % / 10.38 %	28	B	85.62 % / 11.26 %	44	B	83.63 % / 10.51 %	60	B	78.79 % / 10.91 %	76	A	87.61 % / 10.76 %
13	D	88.54 % / 11.39 %	29	B	79.07 % / 12.71 %	45	D	83.63 % / 15.03 %	61	C	83.59 % / 15.13 %	77	B	83.8 % / 11.05 %
14	D	76.7 % / 18.78 %	30	C	81.99 % / 10.64 %	46	B	82.19 % / 14.99 %	62	D	80.81 % / 11.14 %	78	A	77.63 % / 20.41 %
15	D	89.94 % / 10.04 %	31	B	85.75 % / 14.13 %	47	B	80.63 % / 19.03 %	63	D	76.67 % / 14.68 %	79	D	80.93 % / 13.73 %
16	C	78.99 % / 12.81 %	32	D	88.82 % / 10.21 %	48	C	85.19 % / 13.15 %	64	B	82.37 % / 10.21 %	80	D	84.16 % / 12.48 %

Q.	Ans.	Correct / Skipped		Q.	Ans.	Correct / Skipped		Q.	Ans.	Correct / Skipped		Q.	Ans.	Correct / Skipped		Q.	Ans.	Correct / Skipped
81	A	77.45 %	10.16 %	89	D	87.82 %	11.04 %	97	D	83.23 %	10.79 %	105	A	82.41 %	17.53 %	113	C	86.26 %	10.62 %
82	C	77.13 %	18.85 %	90	A	86.35 %	11.88 %	98	B	84.9 %	12.62 %	106	A	81.26 %	15.96 %	114	B	88.6 %	10.68 %
83	A	86.87 %	12.26 %	91	C	84.7 %	10.52 %	99	A	80.11 %	19.27 %	107	D	81.53 %	13.38 %	115	C	77.5 %	14.63 %
84	C	85.36 %	13.45 %	92	D	77.26 %	22.36 %	100	C	82.82 %	13.96 %	108	C	79.44 %	18.71 %	116	B	79.72 %	13.54 %
85	B	89.71 %	10.1 %	93	D	80.29 %	12.1 %	101	C	83.9 %	14.94 %	109	C	79.8 %	17.08 %	117	C	82.04 %	10.5 %
86	A	79.76 %	11.48 %	94	C	82.68 %	13.24 %	102	B	82.93 %	11.79 %	110	B	77.35 %	16.73 %	118	D	87.09 %	10.04 %
87	B	76.38 %	19.91 %	95	B	86.85 %	12.56 %	103	A	78.52 %	10.71 %	111	A	86.64 %	12.66 %	119	C	82.67 %	13.44 %
88	B	85.04 %	11.91 %	96	A	79.99 %	12.03 %	104	A	83.48 %	16.5 %	112	B	82.57 %	12.43 %	120	A	77.59 %	13.71 %

EDUGORILLA
PUBLICATION

//Hints and Solutions//

1.

Since C is obtuse, therefore,

$0 < A + B < 90° \Rightarrow A < 90° - B$

$\Rightarrow \tan A < \tan (90° - B)$

$(\because \tan x \text{ is strict increasing on } (0, \frac{\pi}{2}))$

$\Rightarrow \tan A < \cot B \Rightarrow \tan A < \frac{1}{\tan B}$

$\Rightarrow \tan A \tan B < 1.$

2. Given $5x - 1 < (x + 1)^2 < 7x - 3$

$\Rightarrow 5x - 1 < (x + 1)^2$

And $(x + 1)^2 < 7x - 3$

$x^2 - 3x + 2 > 0$

and $x^2 - 5x + 4 < 0$

$(x - 1)(x - 2) > 0$

And $(x - 1)(x - 4) < 0$

$(x < 1 \text{ or } x > 2)$

And $1 < x < 4 \Rightarrow 2 < x < 4$

The only integral value of x that lies in the interval (2, 4) is 3.
Hence x = 3 is the only solution.

3.

We know that $-1 \leq \cos\theta \leq 1$ for all θ and $\frac{\pi}{2} > 1$, therefore,

$-\frac{\pi}{2} < -1 \leq \cos\theta \leq 1 < \frac{\pi}{2}$ for all θ.

$\Rightarrow \cos\theta \in \left(-\frac{\pi}{2}, \frac{\pi}{2}\right)$ for all real θ.

$\Rightarrow \cos(\cos\theta) > 0$ for all $\theta \in R$.

$\left(\because \cos x > 0 \text{ for all } x \in \left(-\frac{\pi}{2}, \frac{\pi}{2}\right)\right)$

4.

Now, $\sin x + \cos x = \sqrt{2} \left(\frac{1}{\sqrt{2}}\sin x + \frac{1}{\sqrt{2}}\cos x\right)$

$= \sqrt{2} \sin\left(x + \frac{\pi}{4}\right)$

and $-1 \leq \sin\left(x + \frac{\pi}{4}\right) \leq 1$

$\Rightarrow -\sqrt{2} \leq \sqrt{2} \sin\left(x + \frac{\pi}{4}\right) \leq \sqrt{2}$

5.

Since the arithmetic mean of any number of positive numbers is greater than or equal to their harmonic mean, therefore,

$\frac{a+b+c}{3} \geq \frac{3}{\frac{1}{a}+\frac{1}{b}+\frac{1}{c}}$

$\Rightarrow (a + b + c)\left(\frac{1}{a} + \frac{1}{b} + \frac{1}{c}\right) \geq 9$

Note that the value of the given expression is 9 when
$a = b = c$

6.

Let the numbers be $x_1, x_2, x_3, ..., x_n$, then we are given that $x_1 x_2 x_3 ... x_n = 1$.

Also, $\frac{x_1+x_2+x_3+...+x_n}{n} \geq (x_1 x_2 x_3 ... x_n)^{\frac{1}{n}}$ $(A.M. \geq G.M.)$

$\Rightarrow x_1 + x_2 + x_3 + ... + x_n \geq n$

$(x_1 x_2 x_3 ... x_n = 1)$

Note that equality holds when
$x_1 = x_2 = x_3 = ... = x_n = 1$.

7. Required prob. = 1 – p (no tail)

$= 1 - {}^4C_0 \left(\frac{1}{2}\right)^4.$

8.

Required probability $= \frac{2}{2^4} = \frac{2}{16} = \frac{1}{8}.$

9. Five letters can be put into five addressed envelops in $^5P_5 = \cdot 5$ ways out of which only one is favourable to the event 'all the letters reach correct destiny'.

10.

Required probability $= \frac{{}^6C_3}{2^6} = \frac{20}{64} = \frac{5}{16}.$

11. There are three letters and three directed envelops, therefore, they can be put into the envelops in $^3P_3 = 3! = 6$ ways out of which only one is correct.

12. Out of a total of 52 cards, number of court cards is 12.

13.

$\cos^{-1}\left(\frac{1}{2}\right) + 2\sin^{-1}\left(\frac{1}{2}\right)$

$= \frac{\pi}{3} + 2\left(\frac{\pi}{6}\right) = \frac{2\pi}{3}$

14.

$\cot^{-1}\left(\frac{5}{3}\right) + \cos^{-1}\left(\frac{4}{5}\right)$

$= \tan^{-1}\left(\frac{3}{5}\right) + \tan^{-1}\left(\frac{\sqrt{1-\frac{16}{25}}}{4/5}\right)$

$\left(\because \cos^{-1} x = \tan^{-1}\left(\frac{\sqrt{1-x^2}}{x}\right) \text{ for } x > 0\right)$

15.

$\cos^{-1}(-1) - \sin^{-1}(1)$

$= \pi - \cos^{-1} 1 - \sin^{-1} 1 = \pi - 0 - \frac{\pi}{2} = \frac{\pi}{2}$

16.

$\tan^{-1} 3 - \tan^{-1} 2$

$= \tan^{-1}\left(\frac{3-2}{1+3\times 2}\right) = \tan^{-1}\left(\frac{1}{7}\right)$

17.

Given $\tan^{-1} x = \frac{\pi}{4} - \tan^{-1}\left(\frac{1}{7}\right)$,

taking tangents on the two sides, we get

$x = \frac{1-\frac{1}{7}}{1+\frac{1}{7}} = \frac{6}{8} = \frac{3}{4}$

18.

Clearly, x = 1 satisfies the given equation as

$\cos^{-1}(1) + \sin^{-1}\left(\frac{1}{2}\right) = 0 + \frac{\pi}{6} = \frac{\pi}{6}$

19.

$$\vec{AB} + \vec{AC} = \vec{AD} + \vec{DB} + \vec{AD} + \vec{DC}$$
$$= 2\,\vec{AD} + (\vec{DB} + \vec{DC}) = 2\,\vec{AD} + \vec{0}$$
$$= 2\,\vec{AD}$$

20.

Vector $\hat{i}$ makes angles 0°, 90° and 90° respectively with +ve directions of x-axis, y-axis and z-axis. Hence direction cosines of i are < cos 0°, cos 90°, cos 90° . i.e. < 1, 0, 0 >.

21.

$$\vec{v} = 2\,\hat{i} + 3\,\hat{j} - 6\,\hat{k}$$
$$|\vec{v}| = \sqrt{2^2 + 3^2 + 6^2} = 7$$

Hence $\hat{v} = \dfrac{1}{|\vec{v}|}(\vec{v}) = \dfrac{1}{7}(2\hat{i} + 3\hat{j} - 6\hat{k})$

$$= \tfrac{2}{7}\hat{i} + \tfrac{3}{7}\hat{j} - \tfrac{6}{7}\hat{k}$$

Hence d.c. of $\hat{v}$ are $<\tfrac{2}{7}, \tfrac{3}{7}, \tfrac{-6}{7}>$.

22.

Since

$$\hat{v} = \dfrac{\vec{v}}{|\vec{v}|} = \dfrac{a_1}{|\vec{v}|}\hat{i} + \dfrac{a_2}{|\vec{v}|}\hat{j} + \dfrac{a_3}{|\vec{v}|}\hat{k},$$

therefore, d.c. of $\hat{v}$ are

$$< \dfrac{a_1}{|\vec{v}|},\ \dfrac{a_2}{|\vec{v}|},\ \dfrac{a_3}{|\vec{v}|} >$$

23. A vector with magnitude zero is called a null vector.

24. $\vec{a} + \vec{b} - 2\vec{c} = (-1,2) + (3,-2) - 2(0,5)$
$= (-1 + 3 - 2.0,\ 2 - 2 - 2.5)$
$= (2, -10)$

25.

Equation of any parabola whose axis is parallel to y-axis is of the form
$(x - h)^2 = \lambda (y - k),\ \lambda \neq 0$
Hence, the equation of the family of parabolas with axes parallel to y-axis can be written as $y = ax^2 + bx +$

26.

Given equation is $\dfrac{dx}{dt} = x + 4$

$$\Rightarrow \dfrac{dx}{x+4} = dt \Rightarrow \int \dfrac{dx}{x+4} = \int dt + C$$

$$\Rightarrow \log_e (x + 4) = t + C \quad ....(1)$$

When t = 0, x = 0 $\Rightarrow \log_e 4 = C \quad ....(2)$

From (1) and (2),

$$\log_e (x + 4) = t + \log_e 4 \Rightarrow t = \log_e \left(\dfrac{x+4}{4}\right)$$

when x = 96, $t = \log_e \left(\dfrac{96+4}{4}\right)$

$$= \log_e 25 = 2\log_e = 5$$

27.

The given differential equation is
$y \dfrac{dy}{dx} = a - x \Rightarrow y\,dy = (a - x)\,dx$
$\Rightarrow \dfrac{y^2}{2} = \dfrac{(a-x)^2}{2(-1)} + C \Rightarrow (x - a)^2 + y^2 = 2C,$
which for different values of C (>0) represents a family of circles with centres on x-axis.

28.

$$\text{Required area} = \int_1^4 3\sqrt{x}\,dx = 3\left[\dfrac{x^{3/2}}{3/2}\right]_1^4$$

$$= 2(4^{3/2} - 1) = 2(8 - 1) = 14$$

29.

Given differential equation is
$$\dfrac{dy}{dx}(x \log x) + y = 2\log x$$

or $\dfrac{dy}{dx} + \dfrac{1}{x \log x}y = \dfrac{2}{x}$, linear in y,

an I.F. $= e^{\int \frac{1}{x \log x}\,dx} = e^{\log(\log x)} = \log x.$

30.

$$\dfrac{dy}{dx} = \dfrac{y}{x} \Rightarrow \dfrac{dx}{x} = \dfrac{dy}{y}$$

$$\log |x| = \log |y| + \log |c|,\ c \neq 0$$

$$|x| = |yc| \Rightarrow y = \pm\,\dfrac{1}{c}x = kx.$$

31.

$f(x) = \dfrac{2x}{3}(x^2 - 4)^{-\frac{2}{3}}$
$\Rightarrow f'(0) = 0.$ Also
for $x < 0$ (slightly), $f'(x) < 0$ and for $x > 0$ (slightly) $f'(x) > 0$. Hence f has a local minima at x = 0

32. (1, 1) lies only on the line $x - y = 0$, which ought to be the correct alternative.

33.

Given curve is $y^2 = 4zx \Rightarrow 2y\dfrac{dy}{dx} = 4a$

$$\Rightarrow \dfrac{dy}{dx} = \dfrac{2a}{y}$$

$\Rightarrow$ Slope of the tangent at $(at^2, 2at)$ is $\dfrac{2a}{2at} = \dfrac{1}{t}$

Hence, equation of tangent is
$y - 2at = \dfrac{1}{t}(x - at^2)$

34. $f'(0) = 0$, $f''(0) = 0$ and $f'''(0) = 6$. So, f has a point of inflexion at 0

35. $f'(x) = 3x^2 - 12x + 9$
$= 3(x - 1)(x - 3) < 0$
if $(x - 1)(x - 3) < 0$ i.e. $x \in (1, 3)$. Hence f is strict decreasing on [1, 3].

36.

$\sin x \cos x = \tfrac{1}{2}(\sin 2x)$ and minimum value of $\sin 2x$ is -1.

37. $xy = 0 \Leftrightarrow x = 0$ or $y = 0$. Hence locus of $xy = 0$ is the union of all points which lie in equation $xy = 0$ represents a pair of perpendicular planes.

38.

The given equation is

$$\vec{r} \bullet (3\hat{i} + 4\hat{j} + 12\hat{k}) = 65$$

or $\vec{r} \bullet (\frac{3}{13}\hat{i} + \frac{4}{1j} + \frac{12}{13}\hat{k}) = 5,$ *which* is the form $\vec{r} \bullet \hat{n} = p.$

39.

Direction numbers of the nomals to the two planes are < 2,3,− 6>. and < − $\frac{2}{7}$, $\frac{3}{7}$, $\frac{6}{7}$ >. which are proportional

40. Direction numbers of the two lines are < 1, 1,1 > and <1,− 2, 1> and both the lines pass through the point (0,03). Observe that 1.(1) + 1.(− 2) +1. (1) = 0. therefore, the lines intersect at right angles.

41. The given equation is of the form $(\vec{r} - \vec{a})\cdot(\vec{r} - \vec{b}) = 0$,which is the equation of a sphere in the diameter form.

42. $x^2 + y^2 = 0 \Leftrightarrow x = 0$ and $y = 0$
$\Leftrightarrow (x, y, z) = (0, 0, z) \Leftrightarrow (x, y, z)$ lies on Z-axis.

43.

$$= 2 \begin{bmatrix} 1 & 0 \\ 1 & 1 \end{bmatrix} + \begin{bmatrix} -1 & 1 \\ 0 & -1 \end{bmatrix}$$

$$\Rightarrow 3A = \begin{bmatrix} 1 & 1 \\ 2 & 1 \end{bmatrix} \Rightarrow A = \frac{1}{3} \begin{bmatrix} 1 & 1 \\ 2 & 1 \end{bmatrix}$$

$$\begin{bmatrix} 1 & 1 \\ 2 & 1 \end{bmatrix}$$

44. Let A be both symmetric and skew symmetric, then $A^t = A$ and also $A^t = -A$

$\Rightarrow A = -A \Rightarrow 2A = O.$

45.

$$f(A) = A^2 + 4A - 5 I$$

$$= \begin{bmatrix} 1 & 2 \\ 4 & -3 \end{bmatrix} \begin{bmatrix} 1 & 2 \\ 4 & -3 \end{bmatrix} + 4 \begin{bmatrix} 1 & 2 \\ 4 & -3 \end{bmatrix} - 5 \begin{bmatrix} 1 & 0 \\ 0 & 1 \end{bmatrix}$$

$$= \begin{bmatrix} 9 & -4 \\ -8 & 17 \end{bmatrix} + \begin{bmatrix} 4 & 8 \\ 16 & -12 \end{bmatrix} - \begin{bmatrix} 5 & 0 \\ 0 & 5 \end{bmatrix} = \begin{bmatrix} 8 & 4 \\ 8 & 0 \end{bmatrix}$$

46.

Here $A^2 = AA = \begin{bmatrix} 0 & 5 \\ 0 & 0 \end{bmatrix} \begin{bmatrix} 0 & 5 \\ 0 & 0 \end{bmatrix} = \begin{bmatrix} 0 & 0 \\ 0 & 0 \end{bmatrix} = O$

$\Rightarrow A^n = O$ for all $n \geq 2$

and $f (A) = I + A + A^2 + ... + A^{16} = I + A$

$$= \begin{bmatrix} 1 & 0 \\ 0 & 1 \end{bmatrix} + \begin{bmatrix} 0 & 5 \\ 0 & 0 \end{bmatrix} = \begin{bmatrix} 1 & 5 \\ 0 & 1 \end{bmatrix}$$

47.

Here, $AB = \begin{bmatrix} 1 & 0 \\ 2 & 0 \end{bmatrix} \begin{bmatrix} 0 & 0 \\ 1 & 12 \end{bmatrix} = \begin{bmatrix} 0 & 0 \\ 0 & 0 \end{bmatrix}$

and $BA = \begin{bmatrix} 0 & 0 \\ 1 & 12 \end{bmatrix} \begin{bmatrix} 1 & 0 \\ 2 & 0 \end{bmatrix} = \begin{bmatrix} 0 & 0 \\ 25 & 0 \end{bmatrix} \neq 0$

48.

$AB = O \Rightarrow |AB| = 0 \Rightarrow |A| . |B| = 0$
$\Rightarrow |A| = 0$ or $|B| = 0$
when AB = O, neither A nor B may be O.
For example if

$A = \begin{bmatrix} 1 & 0 \\ 0 & 0 \end{bmatrix}$ and $B = \begin{bmatrix} 0 & 0 \\ 1 & 0 \end{bmatrix}$, then

$AB = \begin{bmatrix} 1 & 0 \\ 0 & 0 \end{bmatrix} \begin{bmatrix} 0 & 0 \\ 1 & 0 \end{bmatrix} = \begin{bmatrix} 0 & 0 \\ 0 & 0 \end{bmatrix}.$

49.

$h(x) = f(x) g(x) = x\left(\frac{1}{x}\right) = 1$
only if $x \neq 0$

50.

$\log_{1/4} x = x \Rightarrow x = \left(\frac{1}{4}\right)^x \Rightarrow x = \frac{1}{2^{2x}}$
$\Rightarrow x.2^{2x} = 1$, on inspection, we find that
$x = \frac{1}{2}$ satisfies if
Note that $y = a^x, 0 < a < 1$ and $y = x$ meet in a unique point

51. $\log (2x + 3) + \log (x - 2) = 1$
$\Rightarrow \log_{(2x + 3) (x - 2)} = \log e$
$\Rightarrow (2x + 3) (x - 2) = e$
$\Rightarrow 2x^2 - x - 6 - e = 0$

52.

Note that $y = \frac{1}{x - 2} \neq 0$, therefore

$y^2 = - 2y^3 \Rightarrow 1 = - 2y \Rightarrow 1 = - \frac{2}{x - 2}$

$\Rightarrow x - 2 = - 2$

53. Since $|x| \geq x \forall x \in R$, therefore, $|x| - x \geq 0 \forall x \in R$. Hence $D_f = R$

54.

$$|f(x) - f(-x)| = \left| \frac{|x|}{x} - \frac{|-x|}{-x} \right|$$

$$= \left| \frac{|x|}{x} + \frac{|x|}{x} \right| = \left| \frac{2|x|}{x} \right|$$

$$= 2 \frac{|x|}{|x|} = 2, x \neq 0$$

55.

Given $x = 2 + \frac{1}{x} \Rightarrow x^2 - 2x - 1 = 0$

$\Rightarrow \frac{2 \pm \sqrt{4 + 4}}{2} = 1 \pm \sqrt{2}$, but x > 2, therefore, x = $\sqrt{2}$ ·

56. Let $f(x) = ax^2 + 2x + 1$, then $f(x) = 0$ has a double root means that $f(x) = 0$ has equal roots
Hence $2^2 - 4a = 0$ (disc. = 0)

57. The given equation is
$4^x - 3.2^{x+3} + 128 = 0$
$\Rightarrow 4^x - 3.2^{x+3} .2^3 + 128 = 0$
$\Rightarrow t^2 - 24t + 128 = 0$, where $t = 2^x$
$\Rightarrow t = 16, 8 \Rightarrow 2^x = 2^4, 2^3 \Rightarrow x = 3, 4$

58. Given equation is $2^{2x2-7x+5} = 1$

$\Rightarrow 2x^2 - 7x + 5 = 0$, which has both the roots real

$(\because$ disc. $= (-7)^2 - 4.2.5. = 9 > 0)$

59. Given equation is $(x - 1)(7 - x) = \lambda$

$\Rightarrow - x^2 = 8x - 7 = \lambda$

$\Rightarrow x^2 - 8x + 7 + \lambda = 0$

If the roots are α 3α, then

$4\alpha = 8$ and $3\alpha^2 = 7 + \lambda$

$\Rightarrow \lambda = 3(2)^2 - 7 = 5$

60.

Given $x = \sqrt{3 + \sqrt{3 - \sqrt{3 + \ldots}}}$

$\Rightarrow x = \sqrt{3 + x}, x > 0$

$\Rightarrow x^2 = x + 3$ and $x > 0$

$\Rightarrow x^2 - x - 3 = 0, x > 0$

$\Rightarrow x = \dfrac{1 \pm \sqrt{1 + 12}}{2}, x > 0$

$\Rightarrow x = \dfrac{1 + \sqrt{13}}{2}$, which is an irrational number lying between 2 and 3

61. By Analyzing the given analogy, we can infer that in the left side an adult name and its baby name is given i.e. poult is baby of Turkey

By Applying the same logic to the right side we can conclude that calf is the baby of Reindeer.

62. By Analyzing the given analogy, we can infer that in the left side an adult name and its baby name is given i.e. infant is baby of Gorilla

By Applying the same logic to the right side we can conclude that bunny is the baby of Rabbit.

63. By Analyzing the given analogy, we can infer that in the left side an adult name and its baby name is given i.e. calf is baby of Reindeer

By Applying the same logic to the right side we can conclude that larva is the baby of Bee.

64. By Analyzing the given analogy, we can infer that in the left side an adult name and its baby name is given i.e. poult is baby of Turkey

By Applying the same logic to the right side we can conclude that kit/cub/pup is the baby of Fox.

65. By Analyzing the given analogy, we can infer that in the left side an adult name and its baby name is given i.e. antling is baby of Ant

By Applying the same logic to the right side we can conclude that chick is the baby of Hummingbird.

66. Given,
I) 'light is very sharp' --- 8243,
II) 'right is very wrong' --- 2817,
III) 'knife is sharp' --- 548 and
IV) 'wrong and sharp' --- 476.

	Common Word	Common Code
From I, II and III	is	8
From I, III and IV	sharp	4
From I, II	very	2
From II, IV	wrong	7

Thus, the remaining words and their corresponding codes are:

light --- 3
right --- 1

67. Given
I) 'light is very sharp' --- 8243,
II) 'right is very wrong' --- 2817,
III) 'knife is sharp' --- 548 and
IV) 'wrong and sharp' --- 476.

	Common Word	Common Code
From I, II and III	is	8
From I, III and IV	sharp	4
From I, II	very	2
From II, IV	wrong	7

Thus, the remaining words and their corresponding codes are:

light --- 3
right --- 1
knife -- 5
and -- 6.

68. Given,
I) 'light is very sharp' --- 8243,
II) 'right is very wrong' --- 2817,
III) 'knife is sharp' --- 548 and
IV) 'wrong and sharp' --- 476.

	Common Word	Common Code
From I, II and III	is	8
From I, III and IV	sharp	4
From I, II	very	2
From II, IV	wrong	7

Thus, the remaining words and their corresponding codes are:

light --- 3
right --- 1
knife -- 5
and -- 6

69. (b) 8

70. Given,
I) 'light is very sharp' --- 8243,
II) 'right is very wrong' --- 2817,
III) 'knife is sharp' --- 548 and
IV) 'wrong and sharp' --- 476.

	Common Word	Common Code
From I, II and III	is	8
From I, III and IV	sharp	4
From I, II	very	2
From II, IV	wrong	7

Thus, the remaining words and their corresponding codes are:

light --- 3
right --- 1
knife -- 5
and -- 6

knife -- 5
and -- 6

71.

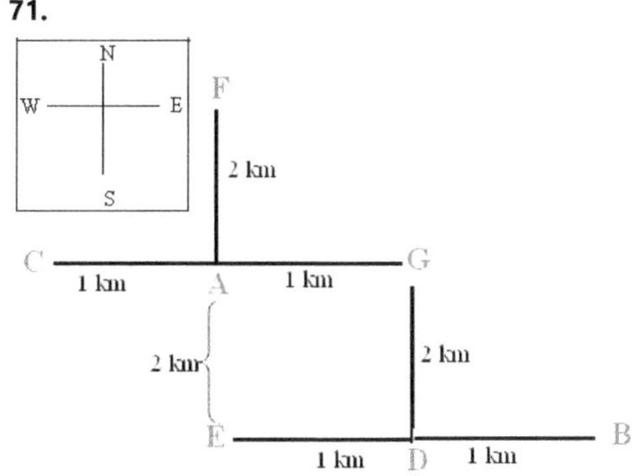

Clearly, E is at 1 km from D.

72.

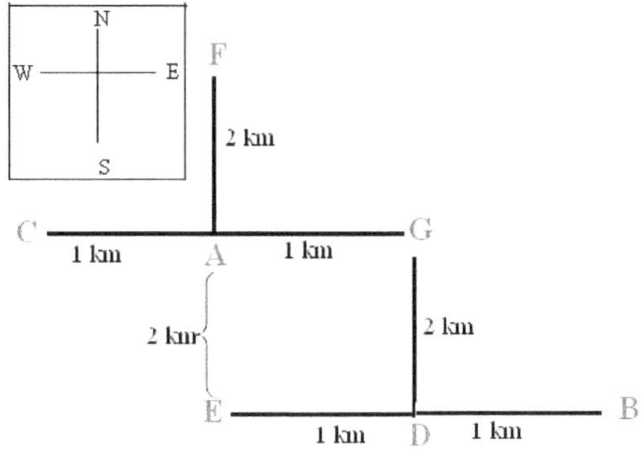

A and C are the two villages at the west of G

73.

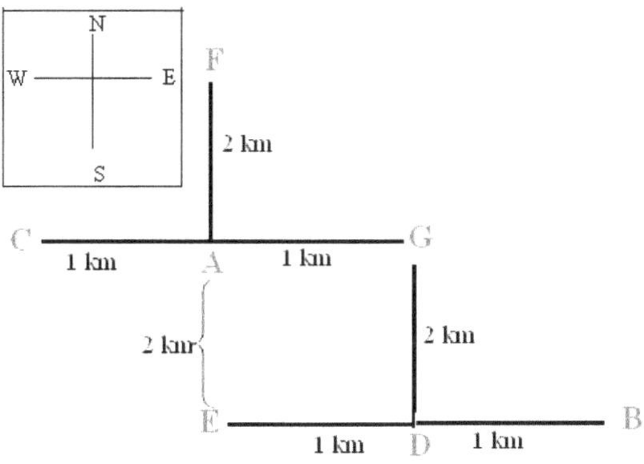

A is in the middle of "C and G"

74.

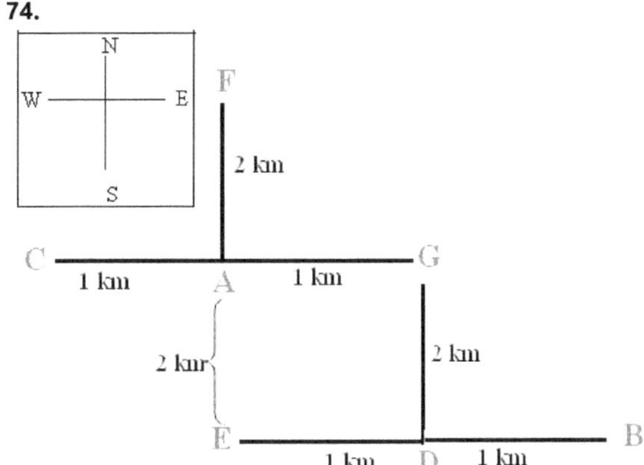

The distance of E from F is "4 km"

75. {{}}
According to the given statements:
Conclusion
I) Some Jokers are heroes ---> **True**
II) Some Zeros are jokers ---> **True**
III) Some villains are Zeros ---> **True**
Thus all the conclusions are True

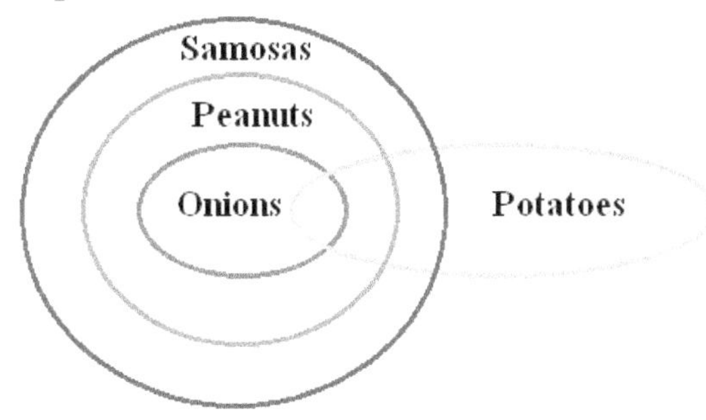

76.

According to the given statements:
Conclusion
I) Some potatoes are peanuts --> **True**
II) Some peanuts are potatoes --> **True**
III) All onions are samosas --> **True**
Thus all the conclusions are **True**

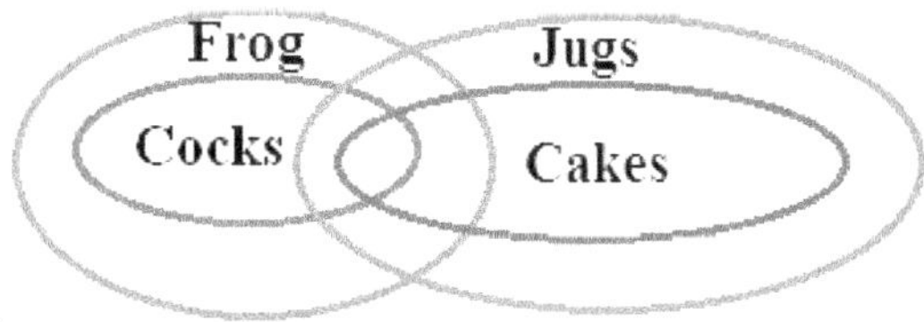

77.
According to the given statements:
Conclusion I) Some jugs are cocks ---- **True.**
Conclusion II) Some frogs are jugs ---- **True.**
Conclusion III) Some cocks are jugs ---- **True.**
Hence, all the three given conclusions follows the given statements.

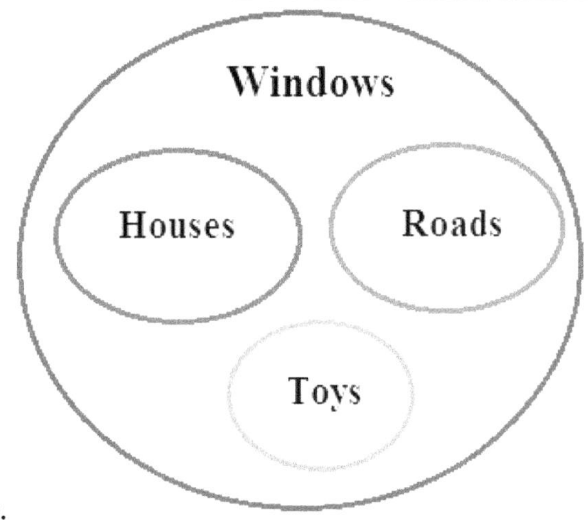

78.

According to the given statements,
Conclusions:
I) Some toys are houses ---> **False** (Because, direct relation between "Toys and Houses" is **not mentioned** in the given statements.)
II) Some roads are houses---> **False** (Because, direct relation between "Roads and Houses" is **not mentioned** in the given statements.)
III) Some roads are toys ---> **False**. (Because, direct relation between "Roads and Toys" is **not mentioned** in the given statements.)
Hence, None of the given conclusion follows.

79. According to the given statements,

Conclusions:
I) Some flowers are rings.--> **False** (Because, direct relation between "Flowers and Rings" is **not mentioned** in the given statements.)
II) Some flowers are bangles ---> **False** (Because, direct relation between "Flowers and Bangles" is **not mentioned** in the given statements.)
III) No ring is a flower---> **False** (Because, direct relation between "Flowers and Rings" is **not mentioned** in the given statements.)
Here **Some + No = Some notconclusion** is observed in the conclusions I and III.
So the answer will be Only **either I** or **III** follows.

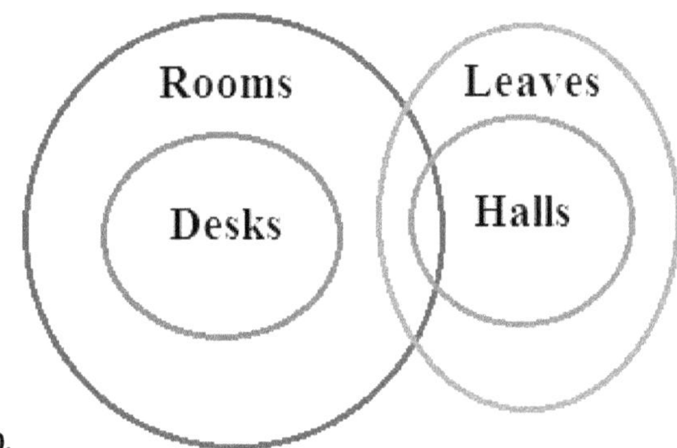

80.

Conclusion :
I) **False** ---> There is no direct relation between the leaves and desks in the given statements.

II) **False** ---> There is no direct relation between the halls and desks in the given statements.
III) **True** -----> According to the given second and third statements (i.e., "Some rooms are halls", "All halls are leaves"), **"Some leaves can be rooms"** So conclusion III follows the given statements.
So only Conclusion III follows.

81. Explanation: The instruction after obtained from the PC, is decoded and operands are fetched and stored in the IR.

82. (c) Adds the values of both LOCA and R0 and stores it in R0

83. MAR can interact with secondary storage in order to fetch data from it.

84. For the execution of a process first the instruction is placed in the PC.

85. MAR is connected to the memory BUS in order to access the memory

86. (a) Instruction Set Processor

87. The processor BUS is used to connect the various parts in order to provide a direct connection to the CPU.

88. The multiplexer circuit is used to choose between the two as it can give different results based on the input.

89. The Operational and processing part of the CPU are collectively called as a data path.

90. (a) D flip flop

91. By using a single BUS structure we can minimize the amount of hardware (wire) required and thereby reducing the cost.

92. By using Buffer registers, the processor sends the data to the I/O device at the processor speed and the data gets stored in the buffer. After that the data gets sent to or from the buffer to the devices at the device speed.

93. PCI BUS is used to connect other peripheral devices which require a direct connection with the processor.

94. (c) ISA

95. SCSI BUS is usually used to connect the video devices to the processor.

96. (a) American National Standards Institute

97. The Z register is a special register which can interact with the processor BUS only.

98. (b) Register file

99. (a) Reduction in the number of cycles for execution

100. (c) Harddisk and Processor

101. (c) to past time thus

102. The error lies in segment B.

Using 'is' in the place of 'are' to make the sentence correct.

In the Subject-Verb Agreement, subjects and verbs must agree with one another in number (singular or plural).

In the given sentence the subject is 'politics' which is singular and it will be followed by the singular verb, not by the plural verb.

The correct sentence: Sometimes politics is a dirty business to deal with.

Hence, the correct option is (B).

103. (a) i was there

'I have been there'

104. Explanation: The correct answer is

my wife got

105. The correct answer is He was in such a hurry

106. (a) to

107. (d) so

108. (c) yet

109. (c) have

110. (b) out

111. (a) to

112. (b) must be

113. (c) to lord it over

114. (b) does not he

115. (c) to rise to

116. (b) there is no superior being to enforce the law of nature

117. (c) in a different land

118. (d) calm, dignified and affectionate disposition

119. (c) a journey into outer space

120. (a) it connotes rigidity and harshness

Mathematics

Q.1

If $f(x) = \dfrac{1}{3x+1}$, then $f'(0)$

A. vanishes
B. is positive
C. is negative
D. does not exist

Q.2

If $y^2 = ax^2 + b$, then $\dfrac{d^2y}{dx^2}$ is equal to

A. ab/x^3
B. ab/y^3
C. ab/y^2
D. None of these

Q.3

If $x = at^2$, $y = 2at$, then $\dfrac{d^2y}{dx^2}$ is equal to

A. 0
B. $1/t^2$
C. $-\dfrac{1}{2at^3}$
D. none of these

Q.4 If $y = ae^{mx} + be^{-mx}$, then y2 is equal to

A. $-m^2 y$
B. $m^2 y$
C. my_1
D. none of these

Q.5 If $y = e^{mx}$, then y_n, $n \in N$, is

A. e^{mx}
B. $m\,n\,e^{mx}$
C. $m^n e^{mx}$
D. none of these

Q.6

If $y = \sqrt{x + \sqrt{x + \sqrt{x + \ldots\ldots + to\ \infty}}}$ then $\dfrac{dy}{dx} =$

A. $\dfrac{x}{y+1}$
B. $\sqrt{\dfrac{x}{y+1}}$
C. $\dfrac{1}{2y-1}$
D. $\dfrac{1}{2y+1}$

Q.7 A square matrix A is called idempotent if

A. $A^2 = I$
B. $A^2 = O$
C. $2A = I$
D. $A^2 = A$

Q.8 Rank of a non-zero matrix is always

A. 0
B. equal to 1
C. greater than 1
D. ≥ 1

Q.9 If a matrix A is symmetric as well as skew symmetric then A is a

A. diagonal matrix
B. null matrix
C. unit matrix
D. none of these

Q.10 If the matrix AB = O, then

A. A = O or B = O
B. A = O and B = O
C. It is not necessary that either A = O or B = O
D. A ≠ O, B ≠ O

Q.11

If $A = \begin{bmatrix} 0 & 0 & 0 & 0 \\ 0 & 0 & 0 & 0 \\ 1 & 0 & 0 & 0 \\ 0 & 1 & 0 & 0 \end{bmatrix}$, then

A. $A^3 = O$
B. $A^2 = O$
C. $A^2 = I$
D. none of these

Q.12 If A and B are two matrices such that A + B and AB are both defined, then

A. A and B can be any matrices
B. A, B are square matrices not necessarily of same order
C. A, B are square matrices of same order
D. number of columns of A = number of rows of B.

Q.13

The line $\dfrac{x-2}{3} = \dfrac{y+1}{2} = \dfrac{z-1}{-1}$ intersects the curve $x^2 + y^2 = r^2$, z = 0 if r =

A. 26
B. $\sqrt{26}$
C. 6
D. none of these

Q.14 The 0points A (4, −2,1), B (7,−4, 7), C (2,−5,10) and D (−1, −3,4) are the vertices of a

A. Tetrahedron
B. parallelogram
C. Rhombus
D. Square

Q.15 The direction cosines of X-axis are

A. < 0,0,1>
B. < 1,0,0>
C. < 0,1,0 >
D. < 0,1,1 >.

Q.16 A plane meets the co-ordinate axes at A, B and C such that the centroid of the triangle is (3, 3, 3). The equation of the plane is

A. x +y + z = 3
B. x + y + x = 9
C. 3x + 3y + 3z = 1
D. 9x + 9y + 9z = 1

Q.17

The distance of the planes.

$\vec{r} \bullet (3\hat{i} + 4\hat{j} + 12\hat{k}) = 65$ from the origin is

A. 65
B. 5
C. -5
D. none of these

Q.18 The graph of the equation $x^2 + y^2 = 0$ in the three dimensional space is

A. X-axis
B. Y-axis
C. Z-axis
D. XY-plane

Q.19 The order of the differential equation whose general solution is y = A cos x + B sin x + Ce^{-x} ; A , B, C being arbitrary constants, is

A. 1
B. 2
C. 3
D. none of these

Q.20 The general solution of the differential equation (1+y^2) dx + y (1 +x^2) dy = 0 is (C an arbitrary constant)

A. (1 + x^2) (1 + y^2) = 0
B. (1 +x^2) (1 +y^2) = C,
C. (1 + x^2) = C (1 + y^2)
D. (1 + y^4) = C (1 + x^2)

Q.21 The equation of the curve, whose slope at any point different from origin is y + y/x, is

A. y = x e^x + C, C ≠ 0
B. y = x e^x
C. x y = e^x
D. y + x e^x = C

Q.22 The differential equation satisfied by y = A/x+ B is (A, B are parameters)

A. $x^2 y_1 = y$
B. $xy_1 + 2y_2 = 0$
C. $xy_2 = 2y_1 = 0$
D. none of these

Q.23 A particle, initially at origin, moves along x-axis according to the rule dx/dt= x + 4. The time taken by the particle to traverse a distance of 96 units is

A. log$_5$ e
B. 2 log$_e$ 5
C. 2 log$_5$ e
D. 1/2 log$_5$ e

Q.24 The integrating factor of the differential equation dy/dx (x log x) + y = 2 log x is given by

A. e^x
B. log x
C. log (log x)
D. x

Q.25 Which of the following is not a vector quantity?

A. force
B. mass
C. weight
D. velocity

Q.26

If $\vec{a} = \hat{i} + 3\hat{j}$, $\vec{b} = -\hat{i} + \hat{j} + \hat{k}$, $\vec{c} = \hat{i} + \hat{j}$ and $\vec{a} + t\vec{b}$ is perpendicular to $\vec{c}$, then value of t is

A. 4
B. 2
C. -2
D. none of these

Q.27

If $\hat{a}$ and $\hat{b}$ are unit vectors such that $\hat{a} - 4\hat{b}$ is at right angles to $7\hat{a} - 2\hat{b}$, then the angle between $\hat{a}$ and $\hat{b}$ is

A. π/2
B. π/3
C. π/6
D. π/4

Q.28

If $\vec{a} \bullet \vec{a} = 0$, then $\vec{a}$ is a

A. free vector
B. localized vector
C. null vector
D. none of these

Q.29

Direction cosines of the vector $\hat{i}$ are

A. < 1, 0, 0 >
B. < 0, 1, 1 >
C. < 1, 0, 1 >
D. none of these

Q.30

The vectors $2\hat{i} + 3\hat{j} - 6\hat{k}$ and $a\hat{i} + b\hat{j} + c\hat{k}$ are perpendicular when

A. a = 1, b = 2, c = 3
B. a = 3, b = 2, c = 1
C. a = 6, b = 2, c = 3
D. none of these

Q.31 cot^{-1} 21 + cot^{-1} 13 + cot^{-1} (−8) is equal to

A. 0
B. cot^{-1} 26
C. π
D. none of these

Q.32

If cos (2 sin^{-1} x) = $\frac{1}{9}$ then x =

A. 2/3
B. -2/3
C. ± 2/3
D. none of these

Q.33 If cos (cos^{-1} x + sin^{-1} 1/2) = 0, then x =

A. 1
B. 0
C. 1/2
D. none of these

Q.34

If tan^{-1} x + tan^{-1} $\frac{1}{7}$ = $\frac{\pi}{4}$, then x =

A. 3/4
B. 6/7
C. 4/3
D. 7/6

Q.35

cos^{-1} $\left(\frac{1}{2}\right)$ + 2 sin^{-1} $\left(\frac{1}{2}\right)$ is equal to

A. π/4
B. π/3
C. π/6
D. 2π/3

Q.36 If x > 0, then tan^{-1} x + tan^{-1} (1/x) is equal to

A. 1
B. tan 1
C. π/2
D. none of these

Q.37 A man speaks truth in 75% cases. He throws a dice and reports that it is a six. The probability that it is actually a six is

A. 3/8
B. 1/5
C. 3/24
D. none of these

Q.38 The probability that a teacher will give an unannounced test during any class is 1/5.If a student is absent twice, then the probability that he misses atleast one test is

A. 2/5
B. 4/5
C. 7/25
D. 9/25

Q.39 An unbiased dice is rolled four times. The probability that the minimum number on any toss is not less than 3 is

A. 16/81
B. 1/81
C. 65/81
D. 80/81

Q.40 A coin with tail on both sides is tossed twice. The probability of getting 'a head' is

A. 1/2
B. 1
C. 0
D. 3/4

Q.41 Three letters are written to different persons and addresses on the envelops are also written Without looking at the addresses, the letters are put into the envelops ; the probability that letters go into Right envelopes is

A. 1/27
B. 1/6
C. 1/9
D. 1/8

Q.42 The probability of the having atleast one tail in 4 throws with a coin is

A. 15/16   **B.** 1/16   **C.** 1/4   **D.** 1

Q.43 Objective function of a L.P.P. is

A. a constant
B. a function to be optimized
C. a relation between the variables
D. None of these

Q.44 The optimal value of the objective function is attained at the points

A. On X –axis
B. On Y-axis
C. which are corner-points of the feasible region
D. none of these

Q.45 If $x \in R$, maximum value of $x - x^2$ is

A. 0   **B.** -1
C. 3   **D.** none of these

Q.46 The maximum value of $f = 4x + 3y$ subject to constraints $x \geq 0$, $y \geq 0$, $2x + 3y \leq 18$, $x + y \geq 10$ is

A. 35   **B.** 36
C. 34   **D.** none of these

Q.47 If the product of n positive real numbers is unity, then their sum cannot be

A. greater then n   **B.** less than n
C. equal to n   **D.** none of these

Q.48 If A, B, C are the angles of a triangle, with C being an obtuse angle, then

A. tan A tan B < 1   **B.** tan A tan B > 1
C. tan A tan B = 1   **D.** none of these

Q.49 Coefficient of x in the expansion of $(1 + 3x + 8x^2)^{10}$ is equal to

A. 10   **B.** 30
C. 80   **D.** none of these

Q.50 The number of terms which are free from fractional powers in the expansion of $(a^{1/5} + b^{2/3})^{45}$, $a \neq b$ is

A. 9   **B.** 15
C. 4   **D.** none of these

Q.51

The middle term in the expansion of $\left(x^2 + \dfrac{1}{x^2}\right)^{2n}$ is

A. $^{2n}C_n$ **B.** $^{2n}C_n \, x^{2n}$

C. $^{2n}C_n \, \dfrac{1}{x^{2n}}$ **D.** none of these

Q.52

In the expansion of $\left(x^3 - \dfrac{1}{x^2}\right)^{15}$, the term void of x is

A. $^{15}C_9$ **B.** 0
C. $^{15}C_6$ **D.** none of these

Q.53 Sum of coefficients in the expansion of $(1 + x - 3x^2)^{4163}$ is

A. 0   **B.** 1
C. -1   **D.** none of these

Q.54 Sum of coefficients in the expansion of $(1 + 2x - 4x2)^{1994}$ is

A. 2^{1994} **B.** 1
C. -1   **D.** none of these

Q.55 If A and B are non-empty sets and A x B = B x A, then

A. A is a proper subset of B
B. B is a proper subset of A
C. A = B
D. None of these

Q.56 A –B iff

A. $A \subset B$ **B.** $B \subset A$
C. $A = B$ **D.** $A \cap B = \phi$

Q.57 Number of relations that can be defined on the set A = {a, b, c, d} is

A. 24   **B.** 16   **C.** 4^4 **D.** 2^{16}

Q.58 Let $f(x) = x$, $g(x) = 1/x$ and $h(x) = f(x)\, g(x)$, then $h(x) = 1$ iff

A. x is a real number
B. x is a rational number
C. x is an irrational number
D. x is a real number $\neq 0$

Q.59

If $f(x) = \dfrac{|x|}{x}$; $x \neq 0$; then $|f(x) - f(-x)|$ is equal to

A. 0   **B.** 2
C. 1   **D.** none of these

Q.60 Which of the following is an even function?

A. $\sqrt{x}$ **B.** $x^2 + \sin^2 x$
C. $\sin^3 x$ **D.** none of these

Analytical Ability & Logical Reasoning

Q.61 In a certain code
'facing problem with money' is coded as 'st np cg rt',
'money problem very serious' is coded as 'nt st np vw',
'serious with every person' is coded as 'rt nt pr ab',
'facing person each day' is coded as 'cg ab no cd'.
Based on the above data, answer the following questions.
Find the code for the word "every"?

A. ab   **B.** nt   **C.** pr   **D.** vw

Q.62 In a certain code
'facing problem with money' is coded as 'st np cg rt',
'money problem very serious' is coded as 'nt st np vw',
'serious with every person' is coded as 'rt nt pr ab',
'facing person each day' is coded as 'cg ab no cd'.
Based on the above data, answer the following questions.

Find the code for the word "Person"?

A. ab   **B.** no   **C.** pr   **D.** nt

Q.63 In a certain code

'facing problem with money' is coded as 'st np cg rt',

'money problem very serious' is coded as 'nt st np vw',

'serious with every person' is coded as 'rt nt pr ab',

'facing person each day' is coded as 'cg ab no cd'.

Based on the above data, answer the following questions.

Find the code word for 'Serious'?

A. cd   **B.** vw   **C.** pr   **D.** nt

Q.64 In a certain code

'facing problem with money' is coded as 'st np cg rt',

'money problem very serious' is coded as 'nt st np vw',

'serious with every person' is coded as 'rt nt pr ab',

'facing person each day' is coded as 'cg ab no cd'.

Based on the above data, answer the following questions.

Find the code word for "With"?

A. cg   **B.** rt   **C.** nt   **D.** ab

Q.65 In a certain code

'facing problem with money' is coded as 'st np cg rt',

'money problem very serious' is coded as 'nt st np vw',

'serious with every person' is coded as 'rt nt pr ab',

'facing person each day' is coded as 'cg ab no cd'.

Based on the above data, answer the following questions.

Find the code word for "Facing"?

A. cg   **B.** rt   **C.** nt   **D.** ab

Q.66 P is 9 m to the south of K. K is 5 m to the east of H. H is 4 m to the north of B. L is 3 m west of B. D is 7 m south of L. G is 8 m east of D.

If point Z is 5 m to the west of point P, then what is the distance between B and Z?

A. 8 m   **B.** 9 m   **C.** 5 m   **D.** 2 m

Q.67 Bala walked 25 km towards west, took a left turn and walked 15 km. He again took a left turn and walked 30 km. He then took a right turn and stopped.

Instead of turning right at the end if he took left and walked 20km, what is the shortest distance to his starting point?

A. 3 sqrt(7) km   **B.** 2 sqrt(5) km

C. 7 sqrt(2) km   **D.** 5 sqrt(2) km

Q.68 Bala walked 25 km towards west, took a left turn and walked 15 km. He again took a left turn and walked 30 km. He then took a right turn and stopped.

Now he was facing which direction?

A. West   **B.** East   **C.** South   **D.** North

Q.69 There are 5 shops A, B, C, D and E. B is to the northeast of E. D is 2 km to the east of E, which is 6 km to the west of A. C is to the northwest of D and in the line of EB. D is 4km the south of B.

What is the shortest distance between between B and E?

A. 2 sqrt(7) km   **B.** 5 sqrt(2) km

C. 7 sqrt(2) km   **D.** 2 sqrt(5) km

Q.70 There are 5 shops A, B, C, D and E. B is to the northeast of E. D is 2 km to the east of E, which is 6 km to the west of A. C is to the northwest of D and in the line of EB. D is 4km the south of B.

What is the shortest distance between B and A

A. 5 sqrt(7) km   **B.** 4 sqrt(2) km

C. 6 sqrt(2) km   **D.** 3 sqrt(5) km

Q.71 Statements :

All desks are rooms

Some rooms are halls.

All halls are leaves.

Conclusions:

I)Some leaves are desks

II)Some halls are desks

III)Some leaves are rooms.

A. None follows   **B.** Only I follows

C. Only II follows   **D.** Only III follows

Q.72 Statements:

All stones are rivers .

All rivers are cars

Some cars are trains.

Conclusions

I) Some trains are stones

II Some cars are stones.

III)Some trains are rivers

A. None follows   **B.** Only I follows

C. Only II follows   **D.** Only III follows

Q.73 Statement :

Some glasses are spoons

Some jugs are spoons.

Conclusions:

I) All Jugs being glasses is a possibility .

II) Some spoons are Jugs

A. If only conclusion I follows

B. If only conclusion II follows

C. If either Conclusion I or Conclusion II follows

D. If both the conclusions follows

Q.74 Statement :

Some glasses are spoons

Some jugs are spoons.

Conclusions:

I) All Jugs being glasses is a possibility .

II) Some spoons are Jugs

A. If only conclusion I follows

B. If only conclusion II follows

C. If either Conclusion I or Conclusion II follows

D. If both the conclusions follows

Q.75 Statement :

I) Some bags are hots.

II) All hots are cakes.

Conclusion:

I) All cakes are bags

II) All bags are cakes.

A. If only conclusion I follows

B. If only conclusion II follows

C. If either Conclusion I or Conclusion II follows

D. If neither Conclusion I nor Conclusion II follows

Q.76 What is the two-digit number whose first digit is "a" and the second digit is "b"?. The number is greater than 9.

I. The number is multiple of 9.

II.The number is multiple of 3

A. I alone sufficient while II alone not sufficient to answer

B. II alone sufficient while I alone not sufficient to answer

C. Either I or II alone sufficient to answer

D. Both I and II are not sufficient to answer

Q.77 What is the two-digit number whose first digit is "a" and the second digit is "b"? The number is greater than 9.

I. The number is multiple of 52.

II. The sum of the digits "a" and "b" is 7.

A. I alone sufficient while II alone not sufficient to answer

B. II alone sufficient while I alone not sufficient to answer

C. Either I or II alone sufficient to answer

D. Both I and II are not sufficient to answer

Q.78 What is the two-digit number whose first digit is "a" and the second digit is "b"?. The number is greater than 9.

I. The number is multiple of 51.

II. The sum of the digits "a" and "b" is 6.

A. I alone sufficient while II alone not sufficient to answer

B. II alone sufficient while I alone not sufficient to answer

C. Either I or II alone sufficient to answer

D. Both I and II are not sufficient to answer

Q.79 What is the two-digit number ?

I. The difference between the two digits is 9.

II. The sum of the digits is equal to the difference between the two digits.

A. I alone sufficient while II alone not sufficient to answer

B. II alone sufficient while I alone not sufficient to answer

C. Either I or II alone sufficient to answer

D. Both I and II are necessary to answer

Q.80 What is the two-digit number ?

I. The difference between the two digits is 8.

II. The sum of the digits is equal to the difference between the two digits.

A. I alone sufficient while II alone not sufficient to answer

B. II alone sufficient while I alone not sufficient to answer

C. Either I or II alone sufficient to answer

D. Both I and II are necessary to answer

Computer Awareness

Q.81 What is the full form of WWW?

A. World Wide Web   **B.** World With Web

C. Work Wide Web   **D.** World Wide Wet

Q.82 Which of the following is not a search engine ?

A. Intel.com   **B.** Altavista.com

C. Excite.com   **D.** Infoseek.com

Q.83 The method for updating the main memory as soon as a word is removed from the Cache is called:

A. Write-through   **B.** Write-back

C. Protected write   **D.** Cache-write

Q.84 Address symbol table is generated by the____.

A. memory management software.

B. assembler

C. match logic of associative memory.

D. generated by operating system

Q.85 When a protocol specifies that address of the sender means the most recent sender and not the original source, what does this mean ?

A. Syntax   **B.** Timing

C. Semantics   **D.** Duplex

Q.86 Which of the following terms is just the connection of networks that can be joined together?

A. Internet

B. Virtual private network

C. Intranet

D. Extranet

Q.87 A computer checks the .... of user name and passwords for a match before granting access.

A. Website   **B.** Network

C. Backup file   **D.** Database

Q.88 Network components are connected to the same cable in the .... topology.

A. Star   **B.** Ring   **C.** Bus   **D.** Mesh

Q.89 What is backup ?

A. Adding more components to your network

B. Protecting data by copying it from the original source to a different destination

C. Filtering old data from the new data

D. None of the above

Q.90 WPA2 is used for security in ....

A. Ethernet   **B.** Bluetooth

C. Wi-Fi   **D.** None of these

Q.91 In Microsoft Excel, Ctrl+ down arrow key leads to __________ cell movement on spreadsheet.

A. One cell Left   **B.** End of row

C. End of column   **D.** One cell right

Q.92 Esc key in a windows keyboard is not used to _________.

A. Close a dialog-box

B. Run a selected command

C. Cancel a command

D. Close a selected drop-down list

Q.93 If you want to open "My Computer" on your computer, you will press _________.
A. Window + R   **B.** Window + E
C. Window + K   **D.** None of these

Q.94 "Ctrl + Up Arrow" is used to _________.
A. Moves the cursor one page up
B. Moves the cursor one line up
C. Moves the cursor one screen up
D. Moves the cursor one paragraph up

Q.95 Which of the following allow you to select more than one slide in a presentation.
A. Alt + Click each slide
B. Shift + Drag each slide
C. Shift + Click each slide
D. Ctrl + Click each side

Q.96 The expression can be described by which of the following gate?
A. AND   **B.** NOR   **C.** NAND   **D.** OR

Q.97 Identify the operation which is not a basic Boolean operation-
A. NOT   **B.** OR   **C.** FOR   **D.** AND

Q.98 Programmable logic arrays are made up of ___
A. AND gates and OR gates
B. AND gates
C. OR gates
D. NAND and NOR gates

Q.99 The word 'NOT' indicates in Boolean expression-
A. inversion   **B.** the same as
C. low   **D.** high

Q.100 Two- input NOR gate is equal to-
A. negative-NAND gate
B. negative-AND gate
C. negative-OR gate
D. All of the above

English

Q.101 In the following question, a sentence is divided into some parts. Find out which part of the sentence has an error. The number of that part is your answer. If there is no error, then choose (D) as your answer.
He is too much (A)/ worried about(B)/ his friend's reaction(C)/ to his statement. (D)/.
A. A   **B.** B   **C.** D   **D.** D

Q.102 In the following question, a sentence is divided into some parts. Find out which part of the sentence has an error. The number of that part is your answer. If there is no error, then choose (D) as your answer.
The Prince (A)/ came on the throne (B)/ at a very early age (C)/ No Error (D)
A. A   **B.** B   **C.** C   **D.** D

Q.103 In the following question, a sentence is divided into some parts. Find out which part of the sentence has an error. The number of that part is your answer. If there is no error, then choose (D) as your answer.
The earth we lived in (A)/ is enveloped (B)/ on all the sides by air (C)/ No Error (D)/.
A. A   **B.** B   **C.** C   **D.** D

Q.104 In the following question, a sentence is divided into some parts. Find out which part of the sentence has an error. The number of that part is your answer. If there is no error, then choose (D) as your answer.
The employers complained at (A)/the poor accommodation (B)/ they were given at the venue. (C)/ No Error (D)/.
A. A   **B.** B   **C.** C   **D.** D

Q.105 In the following question, a sentence is divided into some parts. Find out which part of the sentence has an error. The number of that part is your answer. If there is no error, then choose (D) as your answer.
Preetam is going (A)/directly to temple(B)/from the selection centre.(C)/No error(D).
A. A   **B.** B   **C.** C   **D.** D

Q.106 In the following questions , a sentence has been given in Direct/Indirect . Out of the four alternatives suggested, select the one which best expresses the same sentence in Indirect/ Direct .
The shopkeeper said, "Alas! There has been no sale today."
A. The shopkeeper exclaimed with sorrow that there had been no sale today.
B. The shopkeeper exclaimed that there was no sale that day.
C. The shopkeeper exclaimed with sorrow that there had been no sale that day.
D. The shopkeeper exclaimed that there had been no sale today.

Q.107 In the following questions , a sentence has been given in Direct/Indirect . Out of the four alternatives suggested, select the one which best expresses the same sentence in Indirect/ Direct .
The principal said, "Be quiet, girls."
A. The principal called the girls and ordered them to be quiet.
B. The principal commanded the girls that they be quiet.
C. The principal urged the girls to be quiet.
D. The principal said that the girls should be quiet.

Q.108 In the following questions , a sentence has been given in Direct/Indirect . Out of the four alternatives suggested, select the one which best expresses the same sentence in Indirect/ Direct .
Sheetal said to me, "How have you solved this problem?"
A. Sheetal asked me how I had solved that problem.
B. Sheetal asked me how I have solved that problem.
C. Sheetal asked me how I had solved this problem.
D. Sheetal asked me how I have solved this problem.

Q.109 In the following questions , a sentence has been given in Direct/Indirect . Out of the four alternatives suggested, select

the one which best expresses the same sentence in Indirect/ Direct .

The mother said, "My son is going to start his French classes from tomorrow."

A. The mother says that her son was going to start his French classes from the next day.

B. The mother told that her son was going to start his French classes from tomorrow.

C. The mother said that her son was going to start his French classes from the next day.

D. The mother said my son was going to start his classes from tomorrow

Q.110 In the following questions , a sentence has been given in Direct/Indirect . Out of the four alternatives suggested, select the one which best expresses the same sentence in Indirect/ Direct .

Mary said to Simon. "Sharon and Peter are getting engaged next month."

A. Mary told Simon that Sharon and Peter were getting engaged next month.

B. Mary told Simon that Sharon and Peter are getting engaged next month.

C. Mary told Simon that Sharon and Peter will be getting engaged next month.

D. Mary told Simon that Sharon and Peter was getting engaged next month.

Q.111 In the following question, sentence (s) is/are given with blank (s) to be filled in with an appropriate word (s) Some alternatives are suggested for the given question. Choose the correct alternative out of the given alternatives as your answer.

I will scold him when _____.

A. he will come   **B.** he comes

C. he would come   **D.** he had come.

Q.112 In the following question, sentence (s) is/are given with blank (s) to be filled in with an appropriate word (s) Some alternatives are suggested for the given question. Choose the correct alternative out of the given alternatives as your answer.

My sister's marriage passed _____ peacefully.

A. Away   **B.** By   **C.** Off   **D.** Out

Q.113 In the following question, sentence (s) is/are given with blank (s) to be filled in with an appropriate word (s) Some alternatives are suggested for the given question. Choose the correct alternative out of the given alternatives as your answer.

He _____ his camera on the table.

A. Laid   **B.** Lain   **C.** Lay   **D.** Lie

Q.114 In the following question, sentence (s) is/are given with blank (s) to be filled in with an appropriate word (s) Some alternatives are suggested for the given question. Choose the correct alternative out of the given alternatives as your answer.

It is mainly due to Peter's lethargy that the plan fell _____.

A. Off   **B.** Through   **C.** In   **D.** Out

Q.115 In the following question, sentence (s) is/are given with blank (s) to be filled in with an appropriate word (s) Some alternatives are suggested for the given question. Choose the correct alternative out of the given alternatives as your answer.

It was with this same .... fervor that Paul served Jesus in his ministry.

A. Enthusiastic   **B.** Mock

C. Zealous   **D.** Zeal

Q.116 In the following questions, a sentence has been given in Active Voice/ Passive Voice. Out of the four alternatives suggested, select the one which best expresses the same sentence in Passive/Active Voice.

The rebels attacked the workers in retaliation.

A. The workers were attacked by the rebels in retaliation.

B. The worker was attacked by the rebels in retaliation.

C. In retaliation, the rebels attacked the workers.

D. The workers have been attacked in retaliation by the rebels.

Q.117 In the following questions, a sentence has been given in Active Voice/ Passive Voice. Out of the four alternatives suggested, select the one which best expresses the same sentence in Passive/Active Voice.

I will write an essay.

A. An essay will have been written by me.

B. An essay will be written by me.

C. An essay has been written by me.

D. An essay had been written by me.

Q.118 In the following questions, a sentence has been given in Active Voice/ Passive Voice. Out of the four alternatives suggested, select the one which best expresses the same sentence in Passive/Active Voice.

The arrangements had been done by the time Mary reached.

A. By the time Mary reached, the arrangements had been finished.

B. The arrangements were finished by the time Mary reached.

C. Mary reached and the arrangements were done.

D. They had done the arrangements by the time Mary reached.

Q.119 In the following questions, a sentence has been given in Active Voice/ Passive Voice. Out of the four alternatives suggested, select the one which best expresses the same sentence in Passive/Active Voice.

He had completed the work.

A. The work has been completed by him.

B. The work was completed by him.

C. The work had been completed by him.

D. The work is completed by him.

Q.120 In the following questions, a sentence has been given in Active Voice/ Passive Voice. Out of the four alternatives suggested, select the one which best expresses the same sentence in Passive/Active Voice.

A great movie had been screened for all of us.

A. Someone had screened a great movie for us.

B. They had screened a great movie for all of us.

C. No one had screened a great movie for all of us.

D. It had screened a great movie for all of us.

// Smart Answer Sheet //

Correct Percentage of students who answered correctly.　　**Skipped** Percentage of students who skipped.

Q.	Ans.	Correct / Skipped	Q.	Ans.	Correct / Skipped	Q.	Ans.	Correct / Skipped	Q.	Ans.	Correct / Skipped	Q.	Ans.	Correct / Skipped
1	C	86.68 % / 12.87 %	17	B	85.44 % / 14.17 %	33	C	87.66 % / 11.31 %	49	A	82.29 % / 14.52 %	65	A	86.24 % / 10.59 %
2	B	82.37 % / 11.9 %	18	C	79.42 % / 16.68 %	34	A	88.42 % / 10.32 %	50	C	78.28 % / 20.1 %	66	C	83.08 % / 10.8 %
3	C	83.06 % / 15.83 %	19	C	78.03 % / 10.66 %	35	D	77.68 % / 16.27 %	51	A	80.32 % / 12.85 %	67	D	76.7 % / 13.34 %
4	B	80.49 % / 18.0 %	20	B	77.33 % / 15.63 %	36	C	77.02 % / 10.71 %	52	C	86.29 % / 13.03 %	68	C	83.07 % / 13.61 %
5	C	86.55 % / 11.29 %	21	B	77.23 % / 18.71 %	37	A	78.78 % / 17.39 %	53	C	86.97 % / 11.25 %	69	B	79.19 % / 18.55 %
6	C	87.79 % / 11.93 %	22	C	84.88 % / 11.55 %	38	D	88.93 % / 10.27 %	54	B	80.95 % / 11.55 %	70	B	76.08 % / 21.52 %
7	D	85.04 % / 11.42 %	23	B	79.56 % / 16.84 %	39	A	82.19 % / 13.75 %	55	C	85.2 % / 14.68 %	71	D	80.85 % / 14.21 %
8	D	80.88 % / 13.89 %	24	B	79.85 % / 12.14 %	40	C	82.06 % / 16.16 %	56	D	81.11 % / 11.44 %	72	C	85.97 % / 13.12 %
9	B	87.55 % / 12.39 %	25	B	79.21 % / 13.76 %	41	D	84.44 % / 10.21 %	57	D	83.0 % / 13.52 %	73	D	82.55 % / 17.23 %
10	C	80.21 % / 14.44 %	26	D	77.63 % / 19.39 %	42	A	76.95 % / 18.02 %	58	D	87.74 % / 11.91 %	74	D	88.61 % / 10.67 %
11	B	89.91 % / 10.05 %	27	B	89.44 % / 10.22 %	43	B	87.18 % / 10.48 %	59	B	82.91 % / 13.51 %	75	D	89.88 % / 10.05 %
12	C	81.59 % / 13.07 %	28	C	80.59 % / 14.56 %	44	C	83.19 % / 15.02 %	60	B	76.66 % / 14.29 %	76	D	77.24 % / 18.5 %
13	B	85.03 % / 11.59 %	29	A	84.63 % / 14.47 %	45	C	86.71 % / 12.03 %	61	C	85.79 % / 14.04 %	77	A	83.51 % / 12.83 %
14	B	87.41 % / 10.37 %	30	C	84.59 % / 12.49 %	46	D	77.74 % / 21.1 %	62	A	87.86 % / 11.64 %	78	A	88.62 % / 10.77 %
15	B	88.38 % / 11.33 %	31	C	86.31 % / 12.74 %	47	B	83.45 % / 12.55 %	63	D	78.41 % / 18.1 %	79	D	83.44 % / 13.04 %
16	B	87.33 % / 12.37 %	32	C	89.38 % / 10.29 %	48	A	88.93 % / 10.58 %	64	B	77.78 % / 12.38 %	80	D	77.89 % / 17.57 %

Q.	Ans.	Correct		Q.	Ans.	Correct		Q.	Ans.	Correct		Q.	Ans.	Correct		Q.	Ans.	Correct
		Skipped				Skipped				Skipped				Skipped				Skipped
81	A	80.37 %		89	B	79.02 %		97	C	81.45 %		105	B	86.58 %		113	A	85.3 %
		10.84 %				10.37 %				11.64 %				10.29 %				12.71 %
82	A	87.14 %		90	C	77.28 %		98	A	84.86 %		106	C	76.82 %		114	B	80.93 %
		10.58 %				11.97 %				14.28 %				18.04 %				15.37 %
83	B	84.98 %		91	C	88.7 %		99	A	80.9 %		107	C	84.04 %		115	C	89.85 %
		14.17 %				10.41 %				10.09 %				10.97 %				10.1 %
84	B	77.1 %		92	B	89.49 %		100	C	86.73 %		108	A	78.26 %		116	A	81.02 %
		11.77 %				10.16 %				10.75 %				13.82 %				10.89 %
85	C	78.38 %		93	B	76.55 %		101	D	80.91 %		109	C	79.6 %		117	B	77.06 %
		16.93 %				13.32 %				16.79 %				17.39 %				17.51 %
86	A	76.83 %		94	D	82.91 %		102	B	88.5 %		110	A	76.63 %		118	D	82.82 %
		16.93 %				14.28 %				10.8 %				12.36 %				11.99 %
87	D	89.17 %		95	C	85.72 %		103	A	79.57 %		111	B	82.24 %		119	C	82.51 %
		10.17 %				11.67 %				13.37 %				12.08 %				10.67 %
88	C	78.92 %		96	C	79.59 %		104	A	80.41 %		112	C	84.12 %		120	B	79.2 %
		12.41 %				13.77 %				10.17 %				11.47 %				11.29 %

//Hints and Solutions//

1.

$$f'(x) = \frac{-3}{(3x+1)^2} \Rightarrow f'(0) = \frac{-3}{1} = -3$$

2.

$$y^2 = ax^2 + b \quad \text{............ (1)}$$
$$\Rightarrow 2yy_1 = 2ax \Rightarrow y_1 = \frac{ax}{y} \quad \text{................. (2)}$$
$$\Rightarrow y_2 \frac{ya - ay_1}{y^2} = \frac{ay - a\left(\frac{a}{y}\right)}{y^2} = \frac{ab}{y^3} \ \text{(using (1))}$$

3.

$$\frac{dy}{dx} = \left(\frac{dy}{dt}\right) \Big/ \left(\frac{dx}{dt}\right) = \frac{2a}{2at} = \frac{1}{t} \ \text{..... (1)}$$
$$\text{and then } \frac{d^2y}{dx^2} = \frac{d}{dx}\left(\frac{1}{t}\right)$$
$$= -\frac{1}{t^2}\frac{dt}{dx} = -\frac{1}{t^2}\cdot\frac{1}{2at}$$
$$\frac{1}{t^2}\frac{dt}{dx} = -\frac{1}{t^2}\cdot\frac{1}{2at}$$

4. $y_1 = ae^{mx} m + be^{-mx}(-m)$

$\Rightarrow y_2 = ma\, e^{mx} m - mb\, e^{-mx}(-m)$

$\Rightarrow y_2 = m^2(ae^{mx} + be^{-mx}) = m^2 y$

5. For $y = e^{mx}$, $y_1 = e^{mx}\cdot m$, $y_2 = e^{mx} m^2$, ..., $y_n = e^{mx}m^n$

6.

$$\text{Given } y = \sqrt{x\ \sqrt{x + \sqrt{x + \ldots\ldots}}}\ to\ \infty$$
$$\Rightarrow y = \sqrt{x + y}$$
$$\Rightarrow y^2 = x + y \Rightarrow y^2 - y = x, \text{ dif. w.r.t.x,}$$
$$2y\frac{dy}{dx} - \frac{dy}{dx} = 1 \Rightarrow \frac{dy}{dx} = \frac{1}{2y - 1}$$

7. A square matrix A is idempotent; iff $A^2 = A$.

8. Rank of a non-zero matrix is always greater than or equal to 1.

9. Let A be both symmetric and skew symmetric, then $A^t = A$ and also $A^t = -A$

$\Rightarrow A = -A \Rightarrow 2A = O.$

10.

$AB = O \Rightarrow |AB| = 0 \Rightarrow |A| \cdot |B| = 0$

$\Rightarrow |A| = 0$ or $|B| = 0$

when AB = O, neither A nor B may be O.

For example if

$$A = \begin{bmatrix} 1 & 0 \\ 0 & 0 \end{bmatrix} \text{ and } B = \begin{bmatrix} 0 & 0 \\ 1 & 0 \end{bmatrix}, \text{ then}$$

$$AB = \begin{bmatrix} 1 & 0 \\ 0 & 0 \end{bmatrix} \begin{bmatrix} 0 & 0 \\ 1 & 0 \end{bmatrix} = \begin{bmatrix} 0 & 0 \\ 0 & 0 \end{bmatrix}.$$

11.

$A^2 = AA$

$$= \begin{bmatrix} 0 & 0 & 0 & 0 \\ 0 & 0 & 0 & 0 \\ 1 & 0 & 0 & 0 \\ 0 & 1 & 0 & 0 \end{bmatrix} \begin{bmatrix} 0 & 0 & 0 & 0 \\ 0 & 0 & 0 & 0 \\ 1 & 0 & 0 & 0 \\ 0 & 1 & 0 & 0 \end{bmatrix} = \begin{bmatrix} 0 & 0 & 0 & 0 \\ 0 & 0 & 0 & 0 \\ 0 & 0 & 0 & 0 \\ 0 & 1 & 0 & 0 \end{bmatrix}$$

12. A + B is defined $\Rightarrow$ A and B are of same order and AB is defined $\Rightarrow$ number of columns in A equal the number of rows in B.

13.

For the given curved z = 0, therefore, the line and the curve meet where $\frac{x-2}{3} = \frac{y+1}{2} = \frac{0-1}{1}$

i.e. where $\frac{x-2}{3} = 1$, $\frac{y+1}{2} = 1$

i.e. where x = 5, y = 1.

So, the given line and the given curve meet in the point (5, 1, 0). Since, this point lies on the curve also,

therefore, $5^1 + 1^2 = r^2$

$\Rightarrow r^2 = (26)^2$

$\Rightarrow r = \pm\sqrt{26}.$

14.

Here, the mid-point of [AC] is

$$\left(\frac{4+2}{2}, \frac{-2-5}{2}, \frac{1+10}{2}\right) = \left(3, -\frac{7}{2}, \frac{11}{2}\right)$$

And that of [BD] is

$$\left(\frac{7-1}{2}, \frac{-4-3}{2}, \frac{7+4}{2}\right) = \left(3, -\frac{7}{2}, \frac{11}{2}\right).$$

So, the diagonals [AC] and [BD] bisect each other.

$\Rightarrow$ ABCD is a parallelogram.

As $|AB| = \sqrt{3^2 + 2^2 + 6^2} = 7$ and

$|AD| = \sqrt{5^2 + 1^2 + 3^2} \neq |AB|$, therefore, ABCD is not a rhombus and naturally, it cannot be square.

15. The direction cosines of X-axis are < cos 0^0, cos 90° > i.e.< 1,00 >.

16.

If OA = a, OB = b, and OC = c, then centroid of $\triangle$ ABC is $\left(\frac{a}{3}, \frac{b}{3}, \frac{c}{3}\right) = (3, 3, 3)$

a = b = c = 9 and hence, the equation of the palne is

$\frac{x}{a} + \frac{y}{b} + \frac{z}{c} = 1$ i.e. $\frac{x}{9} + \frac{y}{9} + \frac{z}{9} = 1.$

17.

The given equation is

$$\vec{r} \bullet (3\hat{i} + 4\hat{j} + 12\hat{k}) = 65$$

$$\text{or } \vec{r} \bullet \left(\frac{3}{13}\hat{i} + \frac{4}{1j}\hat{i} + \frac{12}{13}\hat{k}\right) = 5, \text{ which is the form } \vec{r} \bullet \hat{n} = p.$$

18. $x^2 + y^2 = 0 \Leftrightarrow x = 0$ and $y = 0$

$\Leftrightarrow (x, y, z) = (0, 0, z) \Leftrightarrow (x, y, z)$ lies on Z-axis.

19. since the general solution contains three arbitrary constants, therefore, the differential equation in reference must be of order 3.

20.

Given differential equation is

$x(1 + y^2)\,dx + y(1 + x^2)\,dy = 0$

$\Rightarrow \dfrac{x}{1+x^2}\,dx + \dfrac{y}{1+y^2}\,dy = 0$

Integrating, we get

$\dfrac{1}{2}\log(1 + x^2) + \dfrac{1}{2}\log(1 = y^2) = k$

$\log(1 + x^2)(1 + y^2) = 2k$

$(1 + x^2)(1 + y^2)\,e^{2k} = C$

21.

Given $\dfrac{dy}{dx} = y + \dfrac{y}{x} \Rightarrow \dfrac{1}{y}\,dy\left(1 + \dfrac{1}{x}\right)dx$

$\log y = x + \log x + c \Rightarrow y = x\,e^{x+c}$

The curve in reference corresponds to c = 0.

22.

Given relation is $y = \dfrac{A}{x} + B$ ....(1)

Differentiating w.r.t. x, we get

$y_1 = -\dfrac{A}{x^2}$ or $x^2 y_1 = -A$

Again differentiating w.r.t. x, we get

$x^2 y_2 + y_1\,2x = 0$ or $xy_2 + 2y_1 = 0$

23.

Given equation is $\dfrac{dx}{dt} = x + 4$

$\Rightarrow \dfrac{dx}{x+4} = dt \Rightarrow \int \dfrac{dx}{x+4} = \int dt + C$

$\Rightarrow \log_e(x + 4) = t + C$ ....(1)

When t = 0, x = 0 $\Rightarrow \log_e 4 = C$ ....(2)

From (1) and (2),

$\log_e(x + 4) = t + \log_e 4 \Rightarrow t = \log_e\left(\dfrac{x+4}{4}\right)$

when x = 96, $t = \log_e\left(\dfrac{96+4}{4}\right)$

$= \log_e 25 = 2\log_e = 5$

24.

Given differential equation is

$\dfrac{dy}{dx}(x \log x) + y = 2 \log x$

or $\dfrac{dy}{dx} + \dfrac{1}{x \log x}\,y = \dfrac{2}{x}$, linear in y,

an I.F. $= e^{\int \frac{1}{x \log x}\,dx} = e^{\log(\log x)} = \log x.$

25. Mass is not a vector quantity.

26.

$(\vec{a} + t\,\vec{b})\cdot\vec{c} = 0$

$(1-t)\,\hat{i} + (3 + t)\,\hat{j} + t\,\hat{k}) \cdot (\hat{i} + \hat{j}) = 0$

$(1-t)\cdot 1 + (3 + t)\cdot 1 + t\cdot 0 = 0$

$4 = 0,$

which cannot be true for any $t \in R$

27.

Given $(\hat{a} - 4\hat{b})\cdot(7\hat{a} - 2\hat{b}) \perp (7\hat{a} - 2\hat{b})$

$\Rightarrow (\hat{a} - 4\hat{b})\cdot(7\hat{a} - 2\hat{b}) = 0$

$7\hat{a}\cdot\hat{a} - 2\hat{a}\cdot\hat{b} - 28\hat{b}\cdot\hat{a} + 8\hat{b}\cdot\hat{b} = 0$

$\hat{a}\cdot\hat{b} = \dfrac{15}{30} = \dfrac{1}{2}$

$\cos\theta = \dfrac{1}{2}$, θ being the angle between $\hat{a}$ and $\hat{b}$

$\theta = \dfrac{\pi}{3}$

28.

$$\vec{a}\cdot\vec{a} = 0 \Rightarrow |\vec{a}|^2 = 0 \Rightarrow |\vec{a}| = 0$$

29.

Vector $\hat{i}$ makes angles 0°, 90° and 90° respectively with +ve directions of x-axis, y-axis and z-axis. Hence direction cosines of i are < cos 0°, cos 90°, cos 90° . i.e. < 1, 0, 0 >.

30.

Vectors $(2\hat{i} + 3\hat{j} - 6\hat{k})\cdot(a\hat{i} + \hat{b} + \hat{c}) = 0$

if 2a + 3b – 6c = 0

31.

$\cot^{-1} 21 + \cot^{-1} 13 + \cot^{-1}(-8)$

$= \tan^{-1}\dfrac{1}{21} + \tan^{-1}\dfrac{1}{13} + \pi - \cot^{-1} 8$

$= \tan^{-1}\left(\dfrac{\frac{1}{21} + \frac{1}{13}}{1 - \frac{1}{21}\cdot\frac{1}{13}}\right) + \pi - \tan^{-1}\dfrac{1}{8} = \pi.$

32.

$\cos(2\sin^{-1}x) = \dfrac{1}{9}$

$\Rightarrow 1 - 2\sin^2(\sin^{-1}x) = \dfrac{1}{9}$

$\Rightarrow 1 - 2x^2 = \dfrac{1}{9}$

$\Rightarrow x = \pm\dfrac{2}{3}$

33.

$$\cos\left(\cos^{-1}x + \sin^{-1}\tfrac{1}{2}\right) = 0$$
$$\Rightarrow \cos^{-1}x + \sin^{-1}\tfrac{1}{2} = \tfrac{\pi}{2}, \tfrac{3\pi}{2}$$
$$\Rightarrow \cos^{-1}x + \tfrac{\pi}{6} = \tfrac{\pi}{2}$$
$$\text{or } \cos^{-1}x + \tfrac{\pi}{6} = \tfrac{3\pi}{2}$$
$$\Rightarrow \cos^{-1}x = \tfrac{\pi}{2} - \tfrac{\pi}{6}$$
$$\text{or } \cos^{-1}x = \tfrac{3\pi}{2} - \tfrac{\pi}{6}$$
$$\Rightarrow x = \cos\tfrac{\pi}{3} \text{ as } \cos^{-1}x \text{ cannot be greater than } \pi$$
$$\therefore x = \tfrac{1}{2}$$

34.

Given $\tan^{-1}x = \dfrac{\pi}{4} - \tan^{-1}\left(\dfrac{1}{7}\right)$,

taking tangents on the two sides, we get

$$x = \frac{1 - \frac{1}{7}}{1 + \frac{1}{7}} = \frac{6}{8} = \frac{3}{4}$$

35.

$$\cos^{-1}\left(\tfrac{1}{2}\right) + 2\sin^{-1}\left(\tfrac{1}{2}\right)$$
$$= \tfrac{\pi}{3} + 2\left(\tfrac{\pi}{6}\right) = \tfrac{2\pi}{3}$$

36.

$$\tan^{-1}x + \tan^{-1}\left(\tfrac{1}{x}\right)$$
$$= \tan^{-1}x + \cot^{-1}x = \tfrac{\pi}{2}$$

37.

Let E_1 : 'dice shows up a six' and E_2 : 'dice does not show up a six', then E_1 and E_2 are mutually exclusive and exhaustive. Also, $P(E_1) = \tfrac{1}{6}$ and $P(E_2) = \tfrac{5}{6}$.

Let E : 'the man reports that a six has come up then $P(E/E_1) = \tfrac{23}{4}$ and $P(E/E_2) = \tfrac{1}{4}$. By Bye's theorem

$$P(E_1/E) = \frac{P(E/E_1)\,P(E_1)}{P(E/E_1)\,P(E_1) + P(E/E_2)\,P(E_2)}$$
$$= \frac{\frac{3}{4} \times \frac{1}{6}}{\frac{3}{4} \times \frac{1}{6} + \frac{1}{4} \times \frac{5}{6}} = \frac{3}{3+5} = \frac{3}{8}.$$

38. required probability = 1 – p (student does not both test) = 1 – P (the teacher does not give test on both days)

$$1 - \left(1 - \tfrac{1}{5}\right)\left(1 - \tfrac{1}{5}\right) = 1 - \tfrac{16}{25} = \tfrac{9}{25}.$$

39. required probability = $(4/6)^4$.

($\because$ 3, 4, 5, 6 are favourable outcomes when a dice is rolled once)

40. Since the coin has tail on both the sides, therefore, the event 'a head' appears on any throw is impossible.

41. There are three letters and three directed envelops, therefore, they can be put into the envelops in $^3P_3 = 3! = 6$ ways out of which only one is correct.

42.

Required prob. = 1 – p (no tail)
$$= 1 - {}^4C_0 \left(\tfrac{1}{2}\right)^4.$$

43. Objective function is a linear function (of the variables involved) whose maximum or minimum value is to be found.

44. The optimal value of the objective function is attained at the corner points of the feasible region.

45.

Now, $x - x^2 = -(x^2 - x)$
$$= -\left(x^2 - x + \tfrac{1}{4}\right) + \tfrac{1}{4}$$
$$\Rightarrow x - x^2 = -\left(x - \tfrac{1}{2}\right)^2 + \tfrac{1}{4} \leqslant \tfrac{1}{4} \text{ for all } x \in R.$$
Note that $x - x^2 = \tfrac{1}{4}$ when $x = \tfrac{1}{2}$.

46. Observe the adjoining figure. Graph of the inequality $2x + 3y \leq 18$ together with $x \geq 0$, $y \geq 0$ is the region bounded by the figure triangle OAB (including the boundary points). Graph of the inequality $x + y \geq 10$ together with $x \geq 0$, $y \geq 0$ is the region of whole XOY plane except the points which lie within the triangle OCD. So feasible region is the empty set in this case.
No optimum is the empty set in this case. No optimum value of the objective function exists.

47.

Let the numbers be $x_1, x_2, x_3, \ldots, x_n$, then we are given that $x_1 x_2 x_3 \ldots x_n = 1$.
Also, $\dfrac{x_1 + x_2 + x_3 + \ldots + x_n}{n} \geqslant (x_1 x_2 x_3 \ldots x_n)^{\frac{1}{n}}$ $(A.M. \geqslant G.M.)$
$\Rightarrow x_1 + x_2 + x_3 + \ldots + x_n \geq n$
$(x_1 x_2 x_3 \ldots x_n = 1)$
Note that equality holds when
$x_1 = x_2 = x_3 = \ldots = x_n = 1$.

48.

Since C is obtuse, therefore,
$$0 < A + B < 90^\circ \Rightarrow A < 90^\circ - B$$
$$\Rightarrow \tan A < \tan(90^\circ - B)$$
$$\left(\because \tan x \text{ is strict increa} \sin g \text{ on } \left(0, \tfrac{\pi}{2}\right)\right)$$
$$\Rightarrow \tan A < \cot B \Rightarrow \tan A < \frac{1}{\tan B}$$
$$\Rightarrow \tan A \tan B < 1.$$

49. Now, $(1 + 3x + 8x^2)^{10} = \{1 + (3x + 8x^2)\}^{10} + {}^{10}C_0 + {}^{10}C_1 (3x + 8x^2) + {}^{10}C_2 (3x + 8x^2)^2 + \ldots + {}^{10}C10 (3x + 8x2)10$

$\therefore$ Coefficient of $x = {}^{10}C_1 . 3 = 10 \times 3 = 30$.

50. The general term in the expansion of $(a^{1/5} + b^{2/3})^{45}$ is $T_{r+1} = {}^{45}C_r (a^{1/5})^{45-r} (b^{2/3})^r = {}^{45}C_r\, a^{9-r/5}\, b^{2r/3}$. This will be free from fractional powers if both $r/5$ and $2r/3$ are whole numbers i.e. if $r = 0, 15, 30, 45$.

Hence, there are only four terms which are free from fractional powers.

51.

Here, the index is $2n$ an even number, therefore, there is only one middle term namely $\left(\frac{2n}{2}+1\right)$th i.e. $(n+1)$th term.

$\therefore$ Middle term $= {}^{2n}C_n (x^2)^{2n-n}\left(\frac{1}{x^2}\right)^n$

$= {}^{2n}C_n$

52.

Here, the general term

$$T_{r+1} = {}^{15}C_r(x^3)^{15-r}\left(-\frac{1}{x^2}\right)^r = {}^{15}C_r x^{45-5r}(-1)^r \dots (1)$$

This will not contain x if $45 - 5r = 0$ i.e. if $r = 9$.
Required term $= T_{9+1} = {}^{15}C_9 x^0(-1)^9 = -\,{}^{15}C_9 = -\,{}^{15}C_6.$

53. Let $(1 + x - 3x^2)^{4163} = a_0 + a_1x + a_2x^2 + \dots$

Put $x = 1$

$\Rightarrow (-1)^{4163} = a_0 + a_1 + a_2 + \dots$

$\Rightarrow$ Sum of coefficients $= (-1)^{4163} = -1$

54. Sum of coefficients is equal to the value of $(1 + 2x - 4x^2)^{1994}$ for $x = 1$ i.e. $(1 + 2 - 4)^{1994} = (-1)1994 = 1.$

55. Let $x \in A$, $y \therefore B$ be arbitrary, then $(x, y) \in A \times B$

$\Rightarrow (x, y) \in B \times A \ (\because A \times B = B \times A)$

$\Rightarrow x \in B$ and $y \in A$

Hence $A \subset B$ and $B \subset A \Rightarrow A = B$

56. $A - B = A$ iff A and B have no element in common

57. Since $n(A) = 4$, therefore, $n(A \times A) = 16$. Hence number of subsets of $A \times A = 2^{16}$. So, number of relations on $A = 2^{16}$.

58. $h(x) = f(x)\, g(x) = x(1/x) = 1$

only if $x \neq 0$

59.

$$\left| f(x) - f(-x) \right| = \left| \frac{|x|}{x} - \frac{|x|}{-x} \right|$$

$$= \left| \frac{|x|}{x} + \frac{|x|}{x} \right| = \left| \frac{2|x|}{x} \right|$$

$$= 2\,\frac{|x|}{|x|} = 2, \ x \neq 0$$

60. Let $f(x) = x^2 + \sin^2 x$, then $f(-x) = f(x)$, therefore, $f(x) = x^2 + \sin^2 x$ is an even function

61. Given,

I) 'facing problem with money' --- 'st np cg rt',

II) 'money problem very serious' --- 'nt st np vw',

III) 'serious with every person' --- 'rt nt pr ab',

IV) 'facing person each day' --- 'cg ab no cd'.

	Common Word	Common Code
From I and IV	facing	cg
From I, III	with	rt
From II, III	serious	nt
From III, IV	person	ab

Thus, the remaining words and their corresponding codes are:

"problem / money" --- "st / np"

"very" --- "vw"

"every" -- "pr"

"each / day" -- "no / cd"

62. Given,

I) 'facing problem with money' --- 'st np cg rt',

II) 'money problem very serious' --- 'nt st np vw',

III) 'serious with every person' --- 'rt nt pr ab',

IV) 'facing person each day' --- 'cg ab no cd'.

	Common Word	Common Code
From I and IV	facing	cg
From I, III	with	rt
From II, III	serious	nt
From III, IV	person	ab

Thus, the remaining words and their corresponding codes are:

"problem / money" --- "st / np"

"very" --- "vw"

"every" -- "pr"

"each / day" -- "no / cd"

63. Given,

I) 'facing problem with money' --- 'st np cg rt',

II) 'money problem very serious' --- 'nt st np vw',

III) 'serious with every person' --- 'rt nt pr ab',

IV) 'facing person each day' --- 'cg ab no cd'.

	Common Word	Common Code
From I and IV	facing	cg
From I, III	with	rt
From II, III	serious	nt
From III, IV	person	ab

Thus, the remaining words and their corresponding codes are:

"problem / money" --- "st / np"

"very" --- "vw"

"every" -- "pr"

"each / day" -- "no / cd"

64. Given,

I) 'facing problem with money' --- 'st np cg rt',

II) 'money problem very serious' --- 'nt st np vw',

III) 'serious with every person' --- 'rt nt pr ab',

IV) 'facing person each day' --- 'cg ab no cd'.

	Common Word	Common Code
From I and IV	facing	cg
From I, III	with	rt
From II, III	serious	nt
From III, IV	person	ab

Thus, the remaining words and their corresponding codes are:

"problem / money" --- "st / np"

"very" --- "vw"

"every" -- "pr"

"each / day" -- "no / cd"

65. Given,

I)'facing problem with money' --- 'st np cg rt',

II) 'money problem very serious' --- 'nt st np vw',

III) 'serious with every person' --- 'rt nt pr ab',

IV) 'facing person each day' --- 'cg ab no cd'.

	Common Word	Common Code
From I and IV	facing	cg
From I, III	with	rt
From II, III	serious	nt
From III, IV	person	ab

Thus, the remaining words and their corresponding codes are:

"problem / money" --- "st / np"

"very" --- "vw"

"every" -- "pr"

"each / day" -- "no / cd"

66.

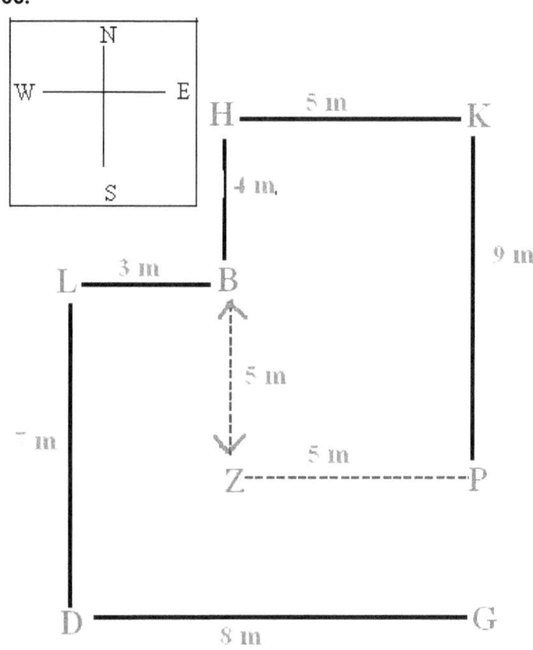

Given, the distance between K and P = 9 m

and the distance between H and B = 4 m

Thus the distance between B and Z = distance between (KP - HB)

= (9 - 4)

= 5 m

67.

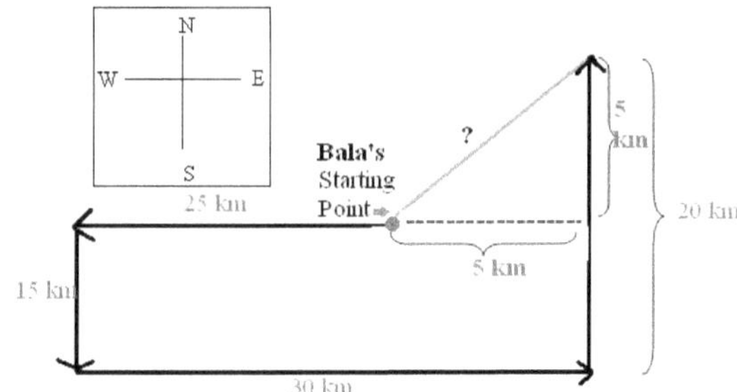

According to Pythagoras theorem,

Shortest distance to his starting point = sqrt (5^2 + 5^2)

= sqrt (25 + 25)

= sqrt (50)

= 5 sqrt(2) km

Therefore, Shortest distance to his starting point = 5 sqrt(2) km

68.

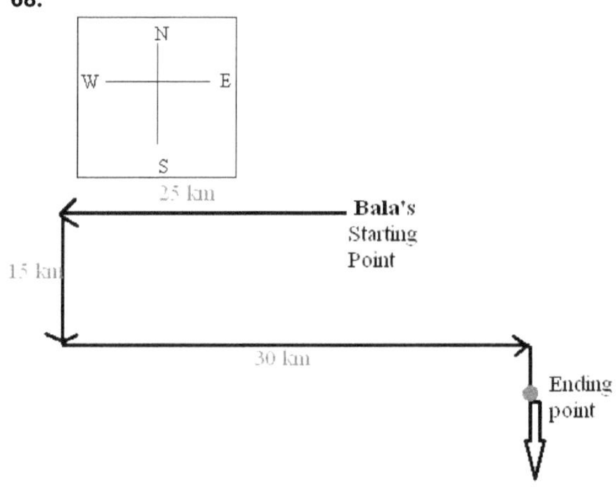

Now he was facing SOUTH direction

69.

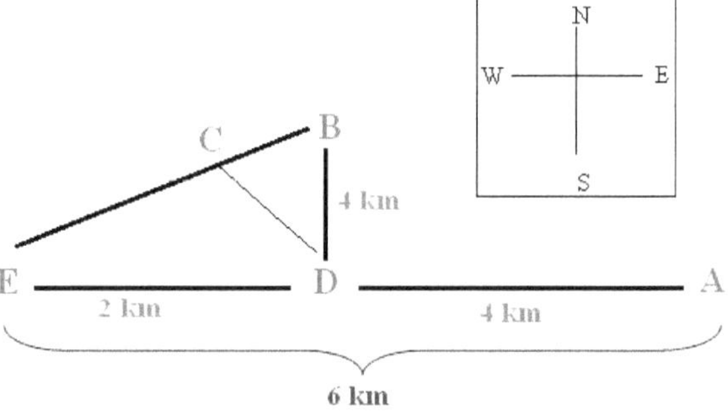

According to Pythagoras theorem,

Shortest distance between B and E = sqrt (BD^2 + DE^2)

= sqrt (4^2 + 2^2)

= sqrt (16 + 4)

= sqrt (20)

= 2 sqrt(5) km

Therefore, Shortest distance between B and E = 2 sqrt(5) km

70.

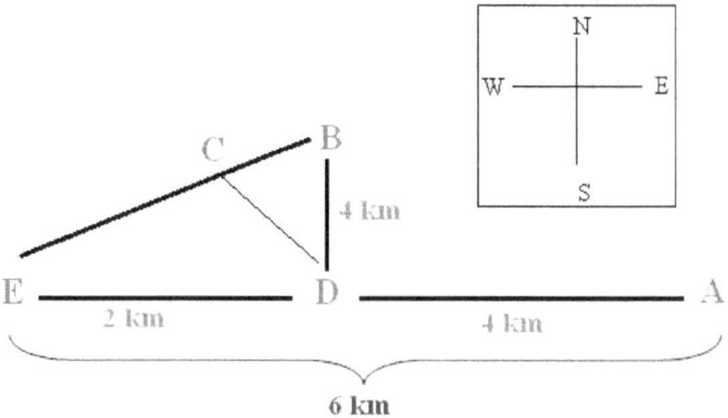

According to Pythagoras theorem,

Shortest distance between B and A = sqrt (BD^2 + DA^2)

= sqrt (4^2 + 4^2)

= sqrt (16 + 16)

= sqrt (32)

= 4 sqrt(2) km

Therefore, Shortest distance between B and A = 4 sqrt(2) km

71.

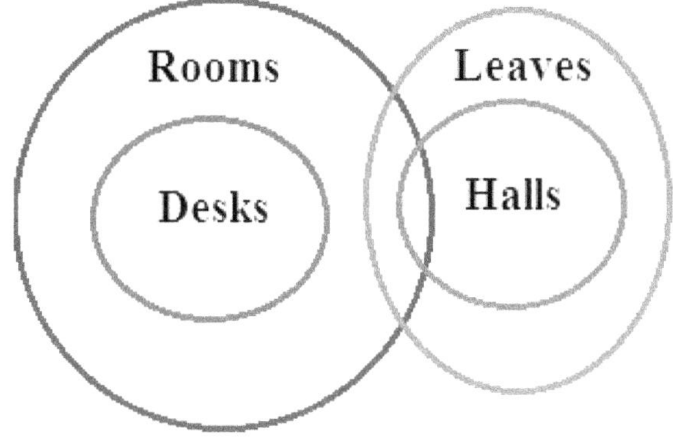

Conclusion :

I) False ---> There is no direct relation between the leaves and desks in the given statements.

II) False ---> There is no direct relation between the halls and desks in the given statements.

III) True -----> According to the given second and third statements (i.e., "Some rooms are halls", "All halls are leaves"), "Some leaves can be rooms" So conclusion III follows the given statements.

So only Conclusion III follows.

72.

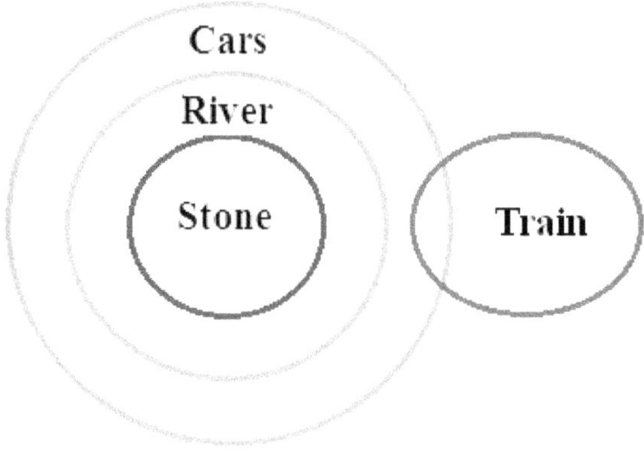

Conclusion

I) False ---> There is no direct relation between trains and stones in the given statements.

II) True ---> From first two statements, Some cars can be stones.

III) False ---> There is no direct relation between trains and rivers in the given statements.

Thus only Conclusion II follows.

73.

Conclusion I) According to the given statements, there is a possibility for "All Jugs being glasses". So, Conclusion I follows.

Conclusion II) According to given statements, "Some spoons are jugs". So, Conclusion II also follows.

So both the conclusions follows.

74.

Conclusion I) According to the given statements, there is a possibility for "All Jugs being glasses". So, Conclusion I follows.

Conclusion II) According to given statements, "Some spoons are jugs". So, Conclusion II also follows.

So both the conclusions follows.

75.

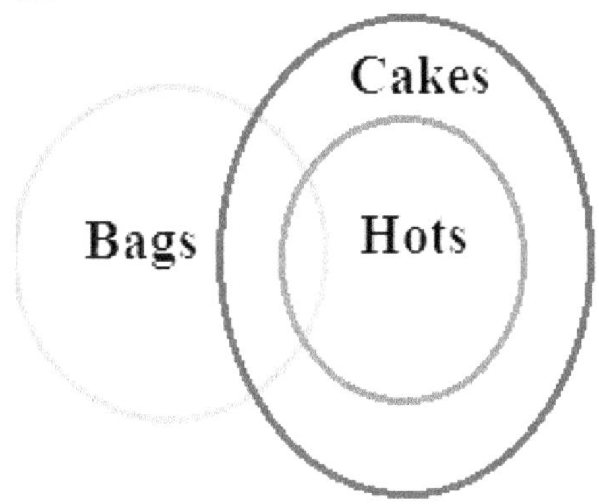

According to the given Statements, the possible conclusions relating to "Bags and Cakes" are:

1) Some bags are cakes.

2) Some cakes are bags.

So, "All cakes cannot be bags". Therefore conclusion I is False.

And also "All bags cannot be cakes". Therefore conclusion II is False.

Thus, neither Conclusion I nor Conclusion II follows.

76. What is the two-digit number whose first digit is "a" and the second digit is "b"?. The number is greater than 9.

I. The number is multiple of 9.

II.The number is multiple of 3

We cannot find out the number with the given course of action.

So,Both I and II are not sufficient to answer.

77. From statement I:

A two digit number, greater than 9 and multiple of 52 should be 52 itself.

Because, 2 x 52 = 104(3 digit number).

Therefore, I alone sufficient to answer.

From statement II:

A two digit number, greater than 9 and sum of the digit is 7.

It can be 16, 25, 34, 43, 52, 61.

So we cannot determine the required answer from the statement II alone.

Thus, I alone give the answer while II alone not sufficient to answer.

78. From statement I:

A two digit number, greater than 9 and multiple of 51 should be 51 itself.

Because, 2 x 51 = 102 (3 digit number).

Therefore, I alone sufficient to answer.

From statement II:

A two digit number, greater than 9 and sum of the digit is 6.

It can be 15, 24, 33, 42, 51, 60.

So we cannot determine the required answer from the statement II alone.

Thus, I alone give the answer while II alone not sufficient to answer.

79. Let the tens and unit digits be x and y respectively. Then,

From Statement I. $x - y = 9$.

From Statement II. $x + y = x - y$.

From I and II, we get $x - y = 9$ and $x + y = 9$.

On solving, we get $x = 9$ and $y = 0$.

Therefore, Required number is 90.

Thus, both Statements I and II are necessary to answer.

80. Given

Difference between two digits = 8

Sum of the digits = Difference between two digits

Let unit digit be b

Let tenth digit be a

Let difference between the digits be

$a - b = 8$ ---> 1)

Let Sum of the digits be

$a + b = 8$ ----> 2)

Solving 1 and 2

$2a = 16$

$a = 16 / 2$

$a = 8$.

Substuting a = 8 in eqn 2

$a + b = 8$

$8 + b = 8$

$b = 8 - 8$

$= 0$

Two digit number = 80.

Here both I & II are needed to solve the questions.

81. The World Wide Web (abbreviated as WWW or W3, commonly known as the Web) is a system of interlinked hypertext documents that are accessed via the Internet. With a web browser, one can view web pages that may contain text, images, videos, and other multimedia and navigate between them via hyperlinks.

82. Intel designs and builds the essential technologies that serve as the foundation for the world's computing devices.

83. In this method only cache location is updated during write operation.

84. During the first pass of assembler address symbol table is generated which contains the label used by the programmer and its actual address with reference to the stored program.

85. Protocol is a set of rules and regulations which manages the data communication system. Syntax refers to the structure or format of the data. Semantics means meaning of data. Here this issue is semantic issue.

86. The internet is a globally connected network system that uses TCP/IP to transmit data via various types of media. The internet is a network of global exchanges – including private, public, business, academic and government networks – connected by guided, wireless and fiber-optic technologies. It is connection of connections.

87. A database is an organized collection of data, generally stored and accessed electronically from a computer system. Where databases are more complex they are often developed using formal design and modeling techniques

88. A bus topology is a topology for a Local Area Network (LAN) in which all the nodes are connected to a single cable. The cable to which the nodes connect is called a "backbone". If the backbone is broken, the entire segment fails.

89. In information technology, a backup, or data backup, or the process of backing up, refers to the copying into an archive file of computer data so it may be used to restore the original after a data loss event.

90. WPA2 is a type of encryption used to secure the vast majority of Wi-Fi networks. A WPA2 network provides unique encryption keys for each wireless client that connects to it.

91. In Microsoft Excel, Ctrl+ down arrow key leads to End of column cell movement on spreadsheet.

92. Esc key in a windows keyboard is not used to Run a selected command. The key (frequently labeled Esc) found on most computer keyboards and used for any of various functions, as to interrupt or cancel the current process or running program, or to close a pop-up window.

93. In all versions of Windows, on pressing Windows key + E opens My Computer. Your computer's drives are listed under the "This PC" section on the left.

94. "Ctrl + Up Arrow" is used to moves the cursor one paragraph up. On the other hand, Ctrl + down Arrow key will take you to the last row of the spreadsheet or moves the cursor one paragraph down.

95. Shift + Click each slide allow you to select more than one slide in a presentation.

96. The given exression is the operation of NAND gate which is the combination of NOT gate and AND gate.

97. In Boolean expression there are such kind of operatios like OR, AND, NOT, NAND, NOR etc. but FOR is not any kind of Boolean expression.

98. A programmable logic array (PLA) is a kind of programmable logic device used to implement combinational logic circuits. The PLA has a set of programmable AND gate planes, which link to a set of programmable OR gate planes, which can then be conditionally complemented to produce an output.

99. The word 'NOT' is related to NOT gate which is an electronic circuit that produces an inverted version of the input at its output. It is also known as an inverter.

100. This is a NOT-OR gate which is equal to an OR gate followed by a NOT gate. The outputs of all NOR gates are low if any of the inputs are high.

101. If the quantity becomes too big, much is preceded by TOO: TOO MUCH + uncountable noun = an excessive quantity.

But in other cases 'MUCH' has the function of 'increasing', amplifying the adverb 'too'.

Too :

(1) Too means as well. For example:

Ex. - Your eye is swollen. Your lip is swollen too.

(2) Too conveys the idea of in excess. For example:

Ex. - Your cat is too fat.

102. The Prince came to the throne at a very early age.

came to- to come to be; develop or grow into

came across-To meet or find by chance

came upon-To discover or meet by accident.

came over-To change sides, as in a controversy.

103. The earth we live in is enveloped on all the sides by air.

The second part of the sentence is in present tense hence, First part should also be in the present tense. So, replace "lived" with "live".

104. "Complained about" is the correct phrase which means to voice one's annoyance or displeasure with someone or something.

Moreover "about" is a preposition used for 'on the subject of; concerning'.

105. Replace 'Directly' with 'direct'.

Direct (with commercial transportation/mass transit) - "without intermediate stops".

Directly - "immediately, with no further ado".

And as per the context of the sentence, he is going to his destination without stopping anywhere in route and journey

106. In reporting exclamations, the indirect speech is introduced by some verb expressing exclamation. 'Today' changes to 'that day'.

Structure of indirect speech in case of Exclamatory sentences are :

a. The reporting verb is changed into exclaim, cry, shout etc. according to the sense.

b. New words and phrases like. with joy/in joy, with sorrow/ in sorrow, in wonder etc. are used to express the meaning of exclamation. If the sense of exclamation is not clear, such phrases are not used.

c. That is used as a linking word.

d. The changed form becomes a statement form of the sentence.

Direct: The man said, "Alas! I am undone".

Indirect: The man cried out in sorrow that he was undone.

Direct: He said, "Hurrah! We have won the game".

Indirect: He exclaimed in joy that they had won the game.

Direct: He said to me, "What a funny boy you are!"

Indirect: He exclaimed in joy that I was a very funny boy.

Direct: He said, "What a fool I am!"

Indirect: He cried out with sorrow that he was a great fool.

[Note: 'great' is used before a noun]

Direct: He said, "What a long journey!"

Indirect: He exclaimed that it was a very long journey.

107. Correct answer: The principal urged the girls to be quiet.

The reported speech has an imperative sentence therefore 'to + present form of verb' is to be used.

Structure of indirect speech in case of imperative sentences:

a. Reporting verb is changed into tell, command or order, request - or beg or entreat or ask, forbid, according to the sense of the speech.

b. Reporting verb and Reported speech are joined by Infinitive 'to

Direct: He said to me, "Do it now"?

Indirect: He told me to do it then.

Direct: The captain said, "Soldiers, march on".

Indirect: The captain commanded the soldiers to march on.

108. Present perfect tense of reported speech will change into past perfect tense.

Structure of indirect speech in case of interrogative sentences :

(a) Reporting verb is changed into ask or enquire of.

(b) If or whether is used as a linking word.

(c) The auxiliary verb in the reported speech is used after the subject.

(d) If the sentence begins with who, which, what, how, when, where, why etc., these are not changed and if or whether is not used.

Note: The indirect speech becomes a statement and no question mark is used.

Direct: Nadim said to Nadia, "Are you reading now?"

Indirect: Nadim asked Nadia if she was reading then.

Direct: The man said to Sheila, "What is your name?"

Indirect: The man asked Sheila what her name was.

109. When the reporting verb is in the past tense, all present tenses inside the quotation marks will change to their corresponding past tenses.

The given sentence is in present continuous tense and it will change into the past continuous tense.

is/am/are + 1st form+ing → Change into Was/were + 1st form+ing

110. When the reporting verb is in the past tense, all present tenses inside the quotation marks will change to their corresponding past tenses.

The given sentence is in present continuous tense and it will change into the past continuous tense.

Is/am/are + 1st form+ing → Change into Was/were + 1st form+ing

111. If/when (conditional clauses) takes the present indefinite form of tense. The future real conditional (also called conditional 1) refers to a possible condition and its probable result. The structure is ...simple future ... if / when ... simple present ...

112. Pass off means to happen or to take place.

Example: The millennium passed off without any disasters.

113. 'Lay' refers to put (something) down gently or carefully.

'Lie' refers to (of a person or animal) be in or assume a horizontal or resting position on a supporting surface.

'Laid' is the past tense and past participle of 'lay' and 'Lain' is the past participle of 'lie'.

Contextually 'lay' and 'laid' is correct here but the subject 'He' is third-person singular pronoun thus it will take a third-person singular verb or past participle and 'lay' is a plural verb, thus 'laid' is an appropriate word to fill the blank.

114. phrasal verb "fall off" means to become fewer in number or less in amount.

"Fall through" means not happen as planned, be unsuccessful.

Ex – Our plans fell through at the last minute.

"Fall in" means collapse

"Fall out" means argue or quarrel with someone

115. 'zealous' means great energy or enthusiasm in pursuit of a cause or an objective.

 and 'Enthusiastic' refers to having or showing intense and eager enjoyment, interest, or approval.

There is only one difference between these two words that, 'Zealous' need an objective or a cause but in case of 'Enthusiastic' there is no need of an objective or a cause.

Moreover 'Fervor' is a noun and 'Zeal' is also a noun thus, 'Zeal' is inappropriate for the blank. Hence, we need an adjective to modify the noun 'Fervor'. So 'Zealous' is much appropriate answer.

'Mock' refers to not authentic or real, but without the intention to deceive, which is contextually wrong for the blank.

116. The given sentence is in past indefinite active voice and to change it into passive voice the rule is:-

S + V2 + O (active voice)

S + was/were + V3 + O (passive voice)

117. Modal + V1(present form) is changed to Modal+ be+ V3(past participle).

Will write --- will be written.

118. The given sentence is in passive voice of past perfect tense -

S + had + V3 + O (active voice)

O + had + been + V3 + S (passive voice)

119. Active: had + past participle

Passive: had + been + past participle

120. Where subject is not specifically provided, it is for us to supply one of the three subjects supplied, they is the most appropriate subject. Someone sounds mysterious and it makes no sense.

Given sentence is passive voice of past perfect tense and its rule of changing into active/passive voice is :

had+V3 (active voice)

had+been+V3 (passive voice)

// Notes //

// Notes //